CMMI®

Framework of Constellations for Building World-Class IT Organizations

Second Edition

CMMI®

Framework of Constellations for Building World-Class IT Organizations

Second Edition

Raghav S. Nandyal
CEO, SITARA Technologies
Bangalore

Tata McGraw Hill Education Private Limited
NEW DELHI

McGraw-Hill Offices

New Delhi New York St Louis San Francisco Auckland Bogotá Caracas
Kuala Lumpur Lisbon London Madrid Mexico City Milan Montreal
San Juan Santiago Singapore Sydney Tokyo Toronto

Tata McGraw Hill

Published by the Tata McGraw Hill Education Private Limited,
7 West Patel Nagar, New Delhi 110 008.

ISBN (13): 978-1-25-900213-7
ISBN (10): 1-25-900213-6

Vice-President & Managing Director—Asia Pacific: *Ajay Shukla*
Executive Publisher—Professional: *R Chandra Sekhar*
Assistant Sponsoring Editor—Science, Technology and Computing: *Simanta Borah*
Production Executive: *Rita Sarkar*
Manager—Sales and Marketing: *S Girish*
Deputy Marketing Manager—Science, Technology and Computing: *Rekha Dhyani*
Controller—Production: *Rajender P Ghansela*
Assistant General Manager—Production: *B L Dogra*

Typeset at Le Studio Graphique, Guru Shivir, 12, Sector 14, Gurgaon 122 001, and
printed at Rajkamal Electric Press, Plot No. 2, Phase IV, HSIIDC, Kundli, Sonepat, Haryana 131 028

Cover Design: Kapil Gupta, New Delhi

RXDAYCRXCDYZQA

The McGraw·Hill Companies

To

The three brightest stars in my constellation—

Shailaja, Sitara and Shreyas,

without whose loving support, patience and understanding,
this book would not have been possible

Foreword 1

This unique book is a thoughtful compilation of CMMI practice interpretations and software engineering principles, approaches and proven techniques that help the reader internalize all three CMMI models. Raghav accomplishes this by taking us on a tour of the 35 process areas, making a careful examination of their terminology, ideas, and practices and considering various proven management and technical approaches, methods, and techniques that help implement them; leaving us better equipped to make effective use of CMMI in process improvement.

I have had the pleasure of knowing Raghav for more than 10 years. Raghav has been a consultant with various CMMs for more than 17 years, including CMMI and the People CMM, with an emphasis on a holistic look at the needs of an organization and the careful integrated application of these models and related frameworks, such as those for Six Sigma. Raghav has been in the High Maturity field for as long as anyone, being part of the establishment of Motorola India Electronics Ltd. (MIEL) as one of the world's first official commercial maturity Level 5 organizations. Raghav is also the author of multiple books that contain many reflections and helpful observations from his many years in process improvement practice. Raghav is a true polymath and you will no doubt agree to this as you read this fascinating book (once I reached the section on business goals around page 39 or so, I could not stop reading it further).

I am amazed at the wealth of information contained in this book. Here, for the first time, is a systematic coverage of all three constellations of CMMI. Raghav has identified multiple techniques that have proven to add value across a range of organizational situations. Philosophically, Raghav is of the same mindset as Watts Humphrey and others, who hold to the idea that zero-defect software is a goal that the software engineering community should aspire to accomplish. However, because each organization has its own set of challenges and because behavioural change is difficult, each process improvement practitioner must guide the organization on a unique journey to become more effective at what it does. To do so, the process improvement practitioner must be well equipped and knowledgeable of multiple models, concepts, principles, and frameworks. In this book, Raghav has summarized his experience of almost 20 years in high maturity to provide the perspectives, insights, and knowledge that process improvement practitioner will need.

As I write this foreword, CMMI is being revised to Version 1.3. Among the most important changes are revisions to the high maturity practices (those situated at maturity Levels 4 and 5), primarily, to improve their clarity. Since Version 1.3 is still a work in progress, this book presents interpretations of those practices as they were written for Version 1.2. These interpretations are Raghav's carefully thought-through reflections, and given Raghav's background, they provide insightful and beneficial reading. I recommend you to consider his interpretations as those from a thoughtful and wise man and a careful thinker—one who has as much experience in this field as perhaps anyone else and whose writings are full of rich and nuanced perspective—but not as "legal opinions" on CMMI as a legal document.

This book is written by one of the most experienced practitioners of high maturity in the field (knows and has written about People CMM as well as CMMI), who has had time to reflect on a large variety of different engagements with different models to abstract unique interpretations. Raghav brings a broad perspective to approaching process improvement that allows him to direct attention to needs and concerns of different parties (for all three constellations, focusing on the whys of process improvements, at the same time acknowledging limitations to what we know). The book offers a unique tour of all 35 Version 1.2 process areas to help one with better hold the whole CMMI picture (i.e., a cognitive map), which is essential to obtaining best value for process improvement (sum is greater than the parts, not sub-optimizing, etc.). The quality and diversity of Raghav's reflections on the software engineering field, on its practice, on its measurement and analysis, and on lessons learned is extremely valuable.

Imagine holding a single volume that addresses all three constellations in some detail and from a wizened interpretation perspective. If you are curious about the other CMMI constellations, this book can help you decide whether to pursue them; and if you do decide to pursue them, it can help you with implementing your improvements in an integrated way!

For those who are mostly interested in CMMI for Development, you might want to jump directly to Chapter 2 for a review of software engineering methods that can be of benefit in implementing the engineering process areas. A caution from Raghav in this: 'you must acknowledge the best practice that is already performed by the organization's projects and make minimal interventions necessary to address gaps and the risks associated with those gaps'.

If you have already implemented CMMI for Development but are curious about the other two constellations, you should probably start with the review of all three models at the end of Chapter 1 and then jump to Chapter 3 for the systematic review of each process area. What I particularly like about Raghav's treatment is the emphasis on measurement and analysis—philosophically and technique-wise. Measurement by itself has no value—instead, it is an aid or lens to guide you in your work activities.

Finally, if you already know CMMI basics for one or more of the models, you might want to jump directly to the SITARA questionnaire extracts beginning on page 38, where much of the practical value of the book really begins. The earlier pages are more of a philosophical character, more thought provoking, and motivational than essential to deriving value from the rest of the book. I like the author's musings, sometimes provoking us to ask why something is or how to make better use of a concept.

This book is a unique companion for you on your process improvement journey, written by one of the world's most experienced and observant maturity Level 3–5 practitioners. This book will help you visualize the broader terrain available to you in process improvement and help you enrich your CMMI tool-kit to better address the opportunities and challenges that lie ahead. Raghav's voice is an independent one, one that does not necessarily align in every respect with anyone's conventional teaching, but is nevertheless, a beneficial, thought-provoking, and learned one, which is likely to be useful to you.

Dr. Michael Konrad
Senior Member of Technical Staff and CMMI Chief Architect
Software Engineering Institute, Carnegie Mellon University
Pittsburgh, USA

Foreword 2

I have known Raghav Nandyal since the time I came to teach one of the first Software CMM courses offered publically in India. Raghav was not only one of the most active participants in this three-day session, but he also came to the next offering. At first, I wondered whether I had failed him or he did not get it the first time. What I quickly learned was that he had a deep and earnest goal to learn the Software CMM in the best of possible ways, so that he could apply it and transfer practical knowledge to organizations he worked with. At that time, Raghav was working for a software house in India. Since then he has gone on to develop his own company, which provides consulting on CMMI and related subjects to numerous clients worldwide.

Not only did I teach Raghav Software CMM, but I was also invited to observe him in his candidacy to become a People CMM appraiser. Needless to say that he passed with flying colors. He has gone on to provide his services and interpretations of the various CMMI models provided by the SEI. One of the ways he has chosen to offer his learning, interpretations, and pragmatic approaches to using these models is through the various books he has written. He knows these models; he practices these models; and most importantly, he uses them in effective and practical ways—not in any bureaucratic manner, as is known to happen with quality/business models and standards. You will benefit by listening to him and heeding his advice.

In his new book—*CMMI®: Framework of Constellations for Building World-Class IT Organizations*—Raghav Nandyal is tackling bigger issues than merely providing an interpretation of the CMMI, although he provides one of the best and easiest-to-understand interpretations I have seen. More importantly, he is boldly asking questions of the SEI and the software community about the value and the best ways to achieve maximum payback through these models. We, as Lead Appraisers, have often been asked to clarify some of the fuzziness in the CMMI, which the SEI has left either unanswered or may not have a full answer yet. The SEI makes changes to the model slowly and deliberately. They cannot answer every discovered defect in the model as soon as it is discovered. We all need to wait for the next model version. While the new versions are evolved using experiences learned, the learning can take a long time for some aspects of the model.

Let me give an example: The initial CMM was developed by the SEI based on work done at IBM in the early 1980s, where we developed a "model" and "method" for IBM internal assessments. My group developed that model and method in 1983. We had little data as to what were best practices when we first began the work in IBM, but we had a foundation that was proven in instances. These instances were then generalized into an IBM approach and then became further generalized into SEI's CMM in the late 1980s. While I believe the generalization extended by the SEI added value to the software community, there still was very little data about what was a Level 4 and Level 5 organization when the

CMM was issued. Indeed, until the early 1990s, there was no organization of record that was a Level 4 or Level 5, even in the SEI's accounting. There was one project in IBM Houston for Space Shuttle, which was determined to be Level 5, but it was not yet at the organization level in IBM Houston.

Over the 1990s, various organizations used the model, learned from it, and were assessed at level 4 or Level 5. The data and learning from these assessments seemingly proved to SEI that the model was sufficiently correct for wide use. Let me digress to acknowledge that with the CMMI, SEI has a model that can only exist at a generic level, in an attempt to fit across the many diverse types of organizations to which it is being applied. This is necessary if it is to be applied across a wide population but brings inherent issues. Some of these are:

1. The CMMI model can only approximate giving a "how to do" approach. It can at best provide a "what to do" approach rather accurately, which even the SEI acknowledges. The SEI denies that they give any "how to dos", but even this is debated in the user community.
2. The model offers theory in some cases since there is still not sufficient evidence that the model feature is used, or should be used, in *all* organizations, as required by the SEI now—especially with the SEI's heavy emphasis on application of advanced statistical technique in all Levels 4 and 5 organizations.
3. The SEI continues to evolve their interpretation of what is a *must* and, thus, necessary to satisfy a level in the model. Some of this is acceptable since the software community is still learning how to use the best engineering practices correctly and consistently. However, this often leads to confusion as to what *must* be done by users, who then can overdo or not do enough.
4. While the SEI states that alternative practices are acceptable, they seem adamant about some very specific ways on "how to do" Levels 4 and 5 practices. If an organization does not show these specific ways with sufficient evidence, they could lose the appraisal rating when SEI audits the Levels 4 and 5s, all of whom are targeted for audits by SEI. This can be frustrating to organizations that are very successful meeting their business objectives, but do not use statistical techniques the way the SEI requires.

These issues do not mean that the CMMI is not useful. It is very useful and will continue to be useful, unless the SEI aggravates the user community, which would only make them seek out other models or standards to benchmark their capability or meet their business objectives. I do not want the CMMI to dissipate into non-existence and do not think it will, although some feel that is a likely outcome. It is a tool, and as with all tools, the user needs to understand—firstly, what problem they want to solve and secondly, which tool best meets that need.

This suggests that the CMMI may not be the most useful tool for all organizations. I believe and know this to be true based on over 45 years of work in the software community. Raghav raises the same questions and suggests that when the user understands these two points just noted, then the CMMI will be most useful to them.

At the same time, there are organizations that must and should be using the CMMI but, for some reason, are not. This is a true regret, since there is so much in this model that will particularly help many of these organizations when they know how to use it properly. None of us want to fail, none of us come to work to fail, but sometimes we cannot see our way out of the mire of a struggling organization. This is when a good understanding of how to use CMMI can be most helpful. Follow Raghav's suggestions and learning, and I expect your organization will benefit from this book.

Look particularly at his discussion on Cost of Quality (COQ). I have always been a believer that this one measure is prime in helping organizations best see how they run their software business. I am confused when I discuss the value of measuring COQ with organizations when I find they are not. How could they not be using it? But what a pleasure it is to see the eyes of the executives open wide when they realize that improvement in COQ goes right to the bottom line. Now they buy in, and buy in big time. With this comes continuous process improvement in the best of ways.

Read Raghav's discussions on CMMI requirements in Level 4, especially about Process Prediction Models, establishing Process Performance Baselines, Controlling sub-processes and ensuring Data Quality when doing analysis. These are not only well written but also show Raghav's deep understanding of what is required in a practical way for organizations to address continuous process improvement.

If you are reading this Foreword and have not yet bought the book, I advise to make the purchase, read it, contact Raghav should you have questions, and most importantly, use it to your best advantage.

Ronald Radice
Principal Partner, Software Technology Transition
rradice@stt.com
www.stt.com

Preface to the Second Edition

Since the writing of the previous edition on CMMI in 2004, the contours of the framework have changed and so have the interpretations, mainly for the better: there is more emphasis on a constellations approach to process improvement, which is better able to address the development, acquisition, and services scenarios, more integration of statistical thinking, which is so very essential for understanding high maturity concepts and to better understand the CMMI framework itself. The preface of the first edition of this book included some of these words which essentially remain true.

One of the most important necessary conditions for becoming a world-class organization is to have a system of practices for coordinated action among the different constituencies within an organization. In short, such a system of practices is called the process. It is even better if such a process aligns itself to the recommendations of a proven framework. Capability Maturity Model Integration project (CMMI®) is one such initiative sponsored by the U.S. Department of Defense to sort out problems using multiple Capability Maturity Models. The current version of the CMMI is version 1.3 and is a major improvement on the earlier CMMI version 1.1, but makes only modest changes to the previous version 1.2. It improves clarity on the expectations placed of practices in the high maturity process areas. Version 1.3 was released in November 2010, around the time this second edition of the book was in the final stages of production. Since version 1.3 was available just-in-time, we are able to offer the reader a comprehensive view of both the stable versions of the CMMI, namely version 1.2 and version 1.3. Changes which have occurred in version 1.3 appear in footnotes throughout the book and, in some cases, within the main text. *Note, however, that version 1.2, is the most widely institutionalized flavor of the CMMI currently in use in the industry.*

Interpretations in this book did not require any major rethinking since I was involved in the review of an interim draft release in December 2008 of the redline version of CMMI v1.2a and was privy to the types of changes that could occur. Version 1.2, in a sense, is more of a superset of version 1.3 with origins in version 1.1, understanding which will offer the reader a much better appreciation of the framework itself.

CMMI version 1.2 embodies the three source models of CMMI version 1.1—Capability Maturity Model for Software (SW-CMM) v2.0 draft C, Electronic Industries Alliance Interim Standard (EIA/IS) 731, and Integrated Product Development Capability Maturity Model (IPD-CMM) v0.98 along with supplier selection—into a single improvement framework to help in enterprise-wide process improvements.

CMMI in its current form is made up of three constellations: *development, acquisition,* and *services.* The practices of the development constellation of the CMMI lay out practices with which to address process improvements for the software and systems development process. Called the CMMI-DEV, this constellation includes hardware amplifications besides catering to the requirements of good team-based processes within what is termed as the Integrated Product and Process Development addition (*IPPD addition*)[1]. Addition, in CMMI, expands constellations to emphasize a particular aspect of its use. In this book, we will explore all three constellations of a framework, which can at best be described as a common-sense approach to the development and maintenance initiatives involving software and systems engineering. It would be my attempt to keep the interpretations of such a common-sense framework simple.

This major overhaul of the CMMI framework necessitated the publication of a comprehensive book that addresses the CMMI in its triumvirate *avatar* of CMMI-DEV (addressing the development aspects), CMMI-ACQ (addressing the acquisition aspects), and CMMI-SVC (addressing the services aspects). It now appears that the relevance of the triumvirate avatar of the CMMI holds good for all organizations. Even if an organization believes that the acquisition face of the CMMI does not apply to them since they do not acquire any products or services, they are bound to be a provider organization to someone. Such organizations would be much better able to comply with the acquisition organization's requirements if they are knowledgeable about the best practices and expectations of a typical acquisition organization. The same reasoning applies to the services face of the CMMI. Every organization is a service provider and a receiver of services during the course of executing their business. Understanding the expected best practices from a services dimension would be a much desirable process competency to build into the organizational process infrastructure.

To minimize the overhead of specifically culling out the version number of the CMMI throughout this book, we will be reviewing the three constellations in *the most widely institutionalized form*, version 1.2, while making references to version 1.3 where such changes are noticeable. While improvements to version 1.3 are possible and are being worked on constantly based on change requests submitted to the Software Engineering Institute (SEI), the fundamental process mind-set is not likely to change in future versions of the CMMI constellations. A preview of the changes based on version 1.3 release of the three constellations, presentations, and webinars delivered by the SEI of version 1.3 is presented in the Epilogue under the section: "What to Expect in Version 1.3 of the Three Constellations". Sixteen process areas within the CMMI model foundation (CMF) are common to all three incarnations of the CMMI.

The organization of the process areas in this book follows the staged representation of the three constellations based on the maturity level they *currently* belong into. Each process area will be interpreted in the context of the five capability levels[2] that they can possibly be institutionalized at from the continuous representation perspective. Each process area title is followed by a tagline which clearly identifies the constellation. It would also be more appropriate to offer interpretation of the 16 CMF process areas from this triumvirate perspective rather than interpreting them merely from one constellation—that is,

[1] Version 1.3 of CMMI-DEV no longer features IPPD addition. In doing so, it has brought in consistency across the three constellations. Note that both the constellations of CMMI-ACQ and CMMI-SVC did not feature IPPD in version 1.2.

[2] CMMI V1.3 no longer features five levels of capability; it will only have three levels. However, interpretations offered in this book for process areas which must improve institutionalization rigor described under capability levels 4 and 5 are extremely valuable to sustain high maturity measurement and analysis capability. The reader is advised to review these interpretations from such a perspective. Recall that V1.2 is more a superset of V1.3.

development, acquisition, or services. Those process areas categories which are constellation specific will be dealt with only from the perspective they are best addressed.

SITARA Technologies is one of the very early transition partners with the SEI on the CMMI, specializing in high-maturity/capability process institutionalization and appraisals. SITARA is currently designing the CMMI principles into the process frameworks of several world-class organizations as a CMMI implementation partner. This book synthesizes my current level of understanding of the two representations of the three CMMI constellations—staged and continuous models. Much of the information and data supporting this book is the result of my being a CMMI instructor authorized to teach the 'Introduction to CMMI' course and the two constellation supplements—CMMI-ACQ and CMMI-SVC—of the SEI. By virtue of being a certified high-maturity Standard CMMI Appraisal Method for Process Improvement (SCAMPI) lead appraiser on all three constellations of the CMMI framework using the SCAMPI method, I have validated that the CMMI practices indeed work to address efficiencies within a process if they are designed right. If there is anything like a framework that supports the notion of Design for Six Sigma for the software or systems development process, I would submit that it is the CMMI. I have reviewed the CMMI right from its 0.9 beta release stage around the second quarter of 2000 up to its current state at version 1.3. Results of SITARA's implementation experience with the CMMI and my interpretation of the CMMI are presented in this book. I am hopeful that the multiple perspectives of being a practitioner, an instructor, a coach, and a lead appraiser, while interpreting the CMMI, will provide the reader with the necessary information to make informed decisions.

Topics covered in this book put special emphasis on what the spirit and purpose behind a CMMI implementation ought to be. It will also help organizations that are currently pursuing the CMMI versions 1.1 and 1.2 and are interested to adopt and transition out to the constellation mode of the CMMI framework by suitably transforming the manifest process designs elegantly without adding overheads.

Why this book at this time?

This book is being written at a time when the CMMI version 1.2 has gained significant acceptance and has been institutionalized across the world since SEI announced the version change in August 2006. CMMI version 1.2 is made up of three constellations that are based on a core model framework. The current version is an evolution over versions 1.1 and 1.2, emphasizing a software and systems engineering discipline for product development. Version 1.1 transitioned from its earlier 1.02 version with the integration of supplier selection. Version 1.3 improves the clarity on high-maturity CMMI concepts and practices.

I was involved in the review of a draft release in December 2008 of the redline version of CMMI v1.2a, and have proposed over 50 change requests. As a practicing Six Sigma Black Belt, I have defined high-maturity concepts using the most rigorous and practical interpretations of the CMMI continuous representation. I am confident that this book will lay forth the expected changes and probably much more by way of how to interpret statistical analysis and use of probability models in the context of software/systems development. Barring a few configuration changes to the model, I did not anticipate any major rethinking involving the body of knowledge that was likely to result in the CMMI v1.3 (released in November 2010), which turned out to be true!

CMMI version 0.2 was publicly reviewed and used in initial pilot activities. Following the release of that version, improvement was guided by change requests from the public review, piloting organizations, and various focus group sessions. It is believed that the CMMI product team evaluated as many as 3,000 change requests to create CMMI version 1.0. Shortly thereafter, version 1.02 was released, which incorporated several minor improvements. Version 1.1 accommodates further improvements from early use as well as more than 1,500 change requests.

Both the CMMI model representations of the staged and the continuous are freely downloadable from the website of the SEI at Carnegie Mellon University (www.sei.cmu.edu) as technical reports with a reference of CMU/SEI-2010-TR-033 for CMMI-DEV, CMU/SEI-2010-TR-032 for CMMI-ACQ, and CMU/SEI-2010-TR-034 for CMMI-SVC. Therefore, my intention in this book is not to merely restate the practices, but to offer a synthesized understanding of how to interpret their intent into the process design of most software initiatives—*development, acquisition, services, maintenance, and systems integration*.

I would not say that this book will offer you all of the *how-to-do's*. My intention is only to offer you a range of possibilities and leave you to decide upon the best course of action. Many of the ideas and interpretations contained within this book have been designed into the manifest high-maturity processes of world-class multinationals and they have worked out well.

How to use this book?

Many times it is extremely useful to relate the CMMI concepts to non-software real-world examples—the day-to-day realities that meet the eye so very frequently. Such real-world equivalents offer clear, direct explanations to why it is worthwhile to consider institutionalizing best practices contained in models such as the CMMI constellations. Real-world equivalents bring meaning to the topics and establish their relevance and usefulness. I will offer as many such non-software examples as possible to illustrate the content in order to keep the explanations as humanistic as possible. Where it would be a lot better to relate to software or a systems example, I would offer such examples as well.

This book is intended to facilitate decision making right from the very beginning when you have to decide which model representation is best suited for you. It will greatly help organizations who have a working knowledge of process models and would like to transition to the CMMI. For the uninitiated, this book is designed to be a jewel box of implementation ideas and approaches. Since we deal with both aspects of the staged and the continuous models of all three constellations, discussion around each of the process areas is designed to help you decide what the most appropriate rigor behind the practices ought to be. Within the notion of the continuous representation, there is an explicit manner in which the process area itself can be transformed to achieve a high enough capability. This book will enable such an understanding.

At the very outset, I would submit that the continuous representation is ideally suited for organizations that have calibrated their processes at high maturity (level 4 or 5). After all is said and done, we will come to conclude that having the right systems and processes in place is only a necessary but not sufficient condition to operate at high maturity. Having a well-defined process that can demonstrate high capability means one *has* to internalize the customer requirements of quality constraints—the critical-to-quality factors known as the *voice-of-customer* (VOC). Each project within the same organization will have constraining factors that are unique to customer's perception of quality. The four most common constraining factors for any project are *cost, quality, scope,* and *time*. In order to accommodate these constraining factors, projects ought to devise and tailor practices that walk the talk for the practitioners. This means the tools employed could be different, the skills and knowledge employed could be different, and quite literally, the very process adopted itself may be different. A non-software example to highlight this would be in order.

Just because a person can drive a compact or a small car does not mean he can drive an E-class Mercedes Benz without the necessary preparation. The skills and techniques required to maneuver a small car are quite different from what are needed for driving a big car. Again, the skills, techniques, and supporting infrastructure that are required to drive on a bright sunny day are quite different from what are needed on a pitch-dark night during a snowstorm. The necessary preparation which projects have to apply to their respective development processes that differ in specific characteristics (the critical-to-X constraints) is what *process tailoring* is all about. To make this example even more relevant, I would add that the feedback (such as, from a measurement system) that an E-class Mercedes Benz offers a driver on the control panel is quite sophisticated and different from the capabilities of a small car with very little instrumentation and gauges to probe volatile driving conditions.

I would like the reader to mull over this thought: relevance of a metrics program and *enabling a nonintrusive mechanism* to establish software metrics that guide and inform those who deliver on project commitments are extremely critical. Establishing such a nonintrusive or a noninvasive metrics collection, analysis, and reporting process is the most difficult challenge for the development process involving software initiatives. Adding tasks to a human-intensive process only contributes to an increase in the cycle time from a development perspective. It is important to recognize and realize a fact that adding a step in a highly human-intensive process is definitely an overhead. But, does such an overhead offer a distinctive advantage which will otherwise be impossible to realize? If the answer is yes, then such overheads can be called as value adding and the imminent increase in cycle time is welcome.

A well-designed process that demonstrates high capability is one which has an appropriate response to accommodate customer preferences with respect to dealing with the four project constraints of cost, quality, time, and scope. Flexibility and applicability of the process has to deal with ensuring a suitable and appropriate process response to the circumstances surrounding project execution. A radical thought at this stage would be to highlight the importance of having a suite of process responses and not just a single process improvement paradigm to accommodate the widely varying project constraints. The answer to the question of '*Do we have the right process mind-set?*' is to have an affirmative response to '*Did we deliver as per customer expectations, on time and on budget?*' To me, anything else makes for a suboptimal process response.

Overview of the book

Chapter 1 deals with making the right executive decisions with respect to choice of the CMMI framework. Key concepts defining the staged and the continuous representations for all three constellations are presented. This chapter provides a good overview about the organization of the process areas into the four categories of process management, project management, support and engineering/acquisition/ service establishment, and delivery. A significant difference between the way staged and continuous representations look at process improvement is a view enabled by the continuous representation that offers for a single process area to improve its individual process capability up to an optimizing level.

For those of us who have a working knowledge of the earlier versions of CMMI or who have a background in the hugely successful Software CMM model, **Chapter 2**—'Process Perspectives and Overview of the CMMI'—offers an overview of the key differences between the current version of CMMI and its earlier makeup. Such a perspective is essential for understanding the potential payoffs and assessing the impact of transition, to protect existing investments which organizations might already have made in their CMMI v1.1 or v1.2 initiatives.

Chapter 3—'Software Engineering Perspectives'—offers the uninitiated a quick introduction to the fundamentals of software engineering. It describes the SITARA Synergy Approach, which is a life-cycle description combining the merits of the V-model and the spiral models. It also offers an object-modeling perspective with an example. Finally, SITARA's package selection and integration process is described to give a flavor for what is involved when commercial-off-the-shelf (COTS) integration is required for the successful deployment of a packaged solution. The reason why three different ideas are presented in this chapter is to highlight an important fact—process is not 'one size fits all!' Many processes might actually have to be designed and realized into practice depending upon the context.

Chapter 4 describes the seven Level 2 process areas of the CMMI-DEV. In addition, three new process areas of the CMMI-ACQ constellation and one new process area of the CMMI-SVC constellation will be discussed. In a sense these are the basic process areas serving as an effective foundation for process improvement. Focus of the Level 2 process areas is established to address practices in the engineering, acquisition, service establishment and development, support, and project management categories of the CMMI. Specific practices contained in the seven CMMI-DEV process areas of Requirements Management, Project Planning, Project Monitoring and Control, Supplier Agreement Management, Measurement and Analysis, Process and Product Quality Assurance, and Configuration Management are discussed. Following this, we will review the three CMMI-ACQ process areas of Agreement Management, Solicitation and Supplier Agreement Development and Acquisition Requirements Development and the one CMMI-SVC process area of Service Delivery.

Chapter 5 provides an interpretation for the 11 Level 3 process areas of CMMI-DEV. We will review three new process areas of the CMMI-ACQ and six new process areas of the CMMI-SVC constellation, of which two belong to project management and the remaining four to service establishment and delivery categories. Within the design of the CMMI-DEV structure, process management is enabled with three process areas along with engineering and high-maturity project management process areas. It is quite useful to note that a Level 3 process maturity within the CMMI-DEV addresses all the necessary engineering practices that are required for effectively managing both the software and systems engineering perspectives. Much of what the Level 3 process areas establish is to build a process improvement infrastructure that can be subjected to continuous improvement. Specific practices and the distinctions assumed by the generic practices as a result of making the transition into Level 3 maturity are described while interpreting Organizational Process Focus, Organizational Process Definition, Organizational Training, Requirements Development, product integration, Technical Solution, Verification, Validation, Risk Management, Integrated Project Management and Decision Analysis, and Resolution for CMMI-DEV. We shall subsequently explore Acquisition Technical Management, Acquisition Verification and Acquisition Validation of the CMMI-ACQ constellation, followed by Service Continuity, Capacity and

Availability Management, Service System Development, Service System Transition, Strategic Service Management, and Incident Resolution and Prevention of the CMMI-SVC. CMMI-DEV offers a basic engineering framework which supports the use of sound software engineering and systems engineering practices at the defined or Level 3 maturity with improvements that can be engineered. Having such an engineering framework is a prerequisite to addressing the Level 4 practices.

Chapter 6 describes the two Level 4 process areas of Quantitative Project Management and Organizational Process Performance. Design of the CMMI at Level 4 institutionalizes the practices behind the high-maturity project management and process management categories. Within the scope of the discussion of the specific practices of Quantitative Project Management, we will explore the possibility of rendering other lower-maturity process areas at a higher process capability. What such presupposition requires is that much of the enactment of the definitions for software engineering and systems engineering practices ought to have been complete and fully functional at Level 3. Such inferential understanding is possible with the way the CMMI practices are structured. Special emphasis is placed on the relevance of statistical process control for software. We will explore in depth what it means to establish process control, and whether it is possible to eliminate the special causes of variations altogether or to establish a stable process first before it can be rendered as a capable process with the Level 5 process areas.

Chapter 7 interprets the two Level 5 process areas of Organizational Innovation and Deployment and Causal Analysis and Resolution. As is apparent, much of the project management practices must be in place along with the necessary engineering framework before practices in these two process areas can be effectively rendered.

Writing style

I would like to acknowledge that I traditionally follow the time-tested Socratic method while relating to the subject matter. In one sense, a certain amount of repetition cannot be avoided because the undercurrents binding this very interesting but vast subject matter are highly intertwined and interlinked. In such situations, I find that instead of letting language become a limitation (by asking the reader to check several cross-references), I would rather state the obvious and bring in a fresh perspective. I have also found that a certain amount of repetition actually helps, since newer insights obtained can be based on a background of information already perused in the book, whereby serving as a good foundation to integrate the newer understanding with.

Typographical conventions

Names of process area and references to process areas of the three CMMI constellations appear with the first letter in capital letters. If the word is used in a general sense, then they are not capitalized. Example: when referring to Validation as a process area, then the first letter appears in capital, but when validation is referred to in the usual software engineering sense, then it is not.

RAGHAV S. NANDYAL

Preface to the First Edition

> *Everything should be made as simple as possible, but not simpler.*
>
> —Albert Einstein,
>
> *Source: The Art of Creative Thinking*—book by Robert Olson (1986).

One of the most important and 'necessary conditions' for becoming a world-class organization is to have a system of practices for coordinated action among the different constituencies within an organization. In short, such a system of practices is called the "process". Better still, if such a process aligns itself to the recommendations of a proven framework. And, Capability Maturity Model® Integration project (CMMI®) is one such initiative sponsored by the US Department of Defense to sort out problems using multiple Capability Maturity Models. The current version of the CMMI combines the three source models of—Capability Maturity Model for Software (SW-CMM) v2.0 draft C, Electronic Industries Alliance Interim Standard (EIA/IS) 731, Integrated Product Development Capability Maturity Model (IPD-CMM) v0.98 along with supplier selection—into a single improvement framework to help in enterprise-wide process improvements.

In this book, we will explore a framework which can at best be described as a 'common-sense' approach to the development and maintenance initiatives involving software and systems engineering. And, I will attempt to keep my interpretations of such a common-sense framework simple!

SITARA Technologies is one of the very early transition partners with the Software Engineering Institute on the CMMI. SITARA is currently designing the CMMI principles into the process frameworks of several world-class organizations as a CMMI implementation partner. This book synthesizes my current level of understanding of the two representations of the CMMI—staged and continuous models. Much of the information and data supporting this book comes as a result of my being a CMMI instructor authorized to teach the Introduction to CMMI course of the Software Engineering Institute. By virtue of being an authorized assessor on this framework using the SCAMPI method (Standard CMMI Appraisal Method for Process Improvement), I have validated that the CMMI practices indeed work to address efficiencies within a process, if they are designed right. If there is anything like a framework that supports the notion of being a Design for Six Sigma for the software or systems development process, I would submit that it is the CMMI! I have reviewed the CMMI right from its 0.9 beta release stage around the 2nd quarter of 2000 up to its current state at version 1.1. Results of SITARA's implementation experience with the CMMI and my interpretation of the CMMI are presented in this book. I am hopeful that, multiple perspectives of being a practitioner, an instructor, coach and a lead assessor, while interpreting the CMMI will provide you with the necessary information to make informed decisions.

Topics covered in this book lay special emphasis on what the spirit and purpose behind a CMMI implementation ought to be. It will also help organizations that are currently pursuing the Software CMM and are interested to adopt and transition out to the CMMI framework by suitably transforming the manifest process designs. Material addressing such Software CMM to CMMI transition is based on SITARA's very popular 'Learn CMMI as a Second Language' course designed for change agents and process champions to facilitate migration from the popular Software CMM into its integrated form as CMMI.

Why this book at this time?

This book is being written at a time when the SEI has announced the sun-setting of the Software CMM model by December 2003. CMMI will take its place. CMMI has stabilized as version 1.1 transitioning from its earlier 1.02 version with the integration of supplier selection.

CMMI version 0.2 was publicly reviewed and used in initial pilot activities. Following release of that version, improvement was guided by change requests from the public review, piloting organizations, and various focus group sessions. It is believed that the CMMI product team evaluated as many as 3,000 change requests to create CMMI version 1.0. Shortly thereafter, version 1.02 was released, which incorporated several minor improvements. Version 1.1 accommodates further improvements from early use as well as more than 1,500 change requests.

Both the CMMI model representations of continuous and the staged are freely downloadable off the website of the Software Engineering Institute at Carnegie Mellon University (www.sei.cmu.edu) as technical reports with a reference of CMU/SEI-2002-TR-011 and CMU/SEI-2002-TR-012. Therefore, my intention in this book is not to merely re-state the practices, but to offer what has been synthesized as an understanding of how to interpret their intent into the process design of most software initiatives—development, maintenance and systems integration.

I would not say that this book will offer you all the how to do's; my intention is only to offer you a range of possibilities and leave you to decide the best course of action. Many of the ideas and interpretations contained within this book have been designed into the manifest high maturity processes of world-class multinationals and it has worked out well.

How to use this book?

Francis Bacon said—'Age appears to be best in four things: old wood best to burn, old wine to drink, old friends to trust, and old authors to read'. Being my second book after I wrote on People CMM, it definitely makes me an older author. From my earlier experience, I have learnt the importance of keeping the message in the book as humanistic as possible without getting lost in the jargon of CMMI! Many times it is extremely useful to relate the CMMI concepts to nonsoftware examples—the day-to-day realities that meet the eye so very frequently. I will offer as many such non-software examples as possible to illustrate the content in order to keep the explanations as humanistic as possible. Where it would be a lot better to relate to software or a systems example, I would offer such examples as well.

This book is intended to facilitate decision making right from the very beginning when you have to decide which model representation is best suited for you. It will greatly help organizations who have a working knowledge of Software CMM and would like to transition to CMMI. For the uninitiated, this book is designed to be a jewel box of implementation ideas and approaches. Since we will deal with both aspects of the staged and the continuous models, discussion around each of the process areas is designed to help you decide what the most appropriate rigour behind the practices ought to be. Within the notion of the continuous representation, there is an explicit manner in which the process area itself can be transformed to achieve a high enough capability. This book will enable such an understanding.

At the very outset, I would submit that the continuous representation is ideally suited for organizations that have calibrated their processes at high maturity (level 4 or 5) on the Software CMM. After all is said and done, we will come to conclude that—having the right systems and processes in place is only a necessary condition, but not sufficient condition to operate at high maturity. And, having a well-defined process that can demonstrate high capability *has* to internalize the customer requirements of 'quality constraints'—the critical-to-quality factors via the voice-of-the-customer. Each project within the same organization will have constraining factors that are unique to customer's perception of quality. The four most common constraining factors for any project are: cost, quality, scope and time. In order to accommodate these constraining factors, projects ought to devise and tailor practices that 'walk-the-talk' for the practitioners. This means that, the tools employed could be different, skills and knowledge employed could be different and quite literally the very process adopted itself may be different. A non-software example to highlight this would be in order. "Just because a person can drive a compact or a small car in the B segment, does not mean he can drive an E-class Mercedes Benz without the necessary preparation. The skills and techniques required to maneuver a small car are quite different from what is needed for a big car. And again, the skills, techniques and supporting infrastructure that is required to drive on a bright sunny day are quite different from what is needed on a pitch-dark night during a snow storm." The '*necessary preparation*' which projects have to apply to their respective development processes that differ in specific characteristics (the critical-to-X constraints), is what process tailoring is all about. To make this example even more relevant, I would add that the feedback (such as, from a measurement system) that an E-class Mercedes Benz offers on the driver's control panel are quite sophisticated and different when compared to the capabilities of a small car with very little instrumentation and gauges to probe volatile driving conditions. Control panels of cars can be so sophisticated as to even indicate which of the 4 wheels of the car has a flat! Of course, it is a different matter that one would know it eventually!

What I would like to leave the reader with, at such an early stage in the book is this thought: relevance of a metrics program and *enabling a non-intrusive mechanism* to establish a metric that guides and informs those who deliver on project commitments is extremely critical. Establishing such a non-intrusive or a non-invasive metrics collection, analysis and reporting process is the most difficult challenge for the development process. And, adding tasks to a human intensive process only contributes to an increase in the cycle time from a development perspective. It is important to recognize and realize a fact that adding a step in a highly human intensive process is definitely an overhead. But, does such an overhead offer a distinctive advantage which will otherwise be impossible to realize? If the answer is yes, then I would call the overhead a 'value-adding component' and welcome the imminent increase in cycle time as a 'desirable' feature of the process. Again, a non-software example to illustrate the point: post September 11, 2001 the number of times and the variety of airline security screening procedures have increased by about 500 percent! There was nothing like physical frisking after an X-ray check; there was nothing like examining the contents of carry on baggage after they went through an X-ray machine; there was nothing like shoe-sniffers; there was nothing like a second level frisking at the time the boarding pass was sealed with security approval; there was nothing like a final third level frisking of those not so lucky passengers whose names are called out at random by the airline security staff just before one got into the aircraft. Note the relevance of this example to software development: all the above steps have to be carried out by human beings—they cannot be automated. Further, all these security steps are now part of a defined process that supposedly 'ensures and assures' the highest security of travel to passengers on board an aircraft. These steps most definitely delay the cycle time needed to make it into an aircraft. The same is true of a human intensive process such as software development and software verification. There is a very insignificant portion of these tasks that lends itself to process automation [Nandyal 1994]. I make the above statement based on a tool called *ISET: Integrated Software Engineering Toolkit,* which I developed based on a paper that was presented at the Motorola Software Engineering Symposium 1994, to demonstrate orders-of-magnitude reduction in cycle time just by automating some of the transitions in a development lifecycle. For example: from code to code standardization, use of a tool called ctab was shown to reduce cycle time by a factor of 1300X with about 99.9 percent increase to productivity for a 100-line code module, over a manual process. Obviously, this figure would grow dramatically as the size of the module grows. But such transition steps in a development process are very few—restricted to only those process transitions which are governed by well-defined logical propositions.

A well designed process that demonstrates high capability is one which has an appropriate response to accommodate customer preferences with respect to dealing with the four project constraints of cost, quality, time and scope. Flexibility and applicability of the process has to deal with ensuring a suitable and appropriate process response to the circumstances surrounding project execution. A radical thought at this stage would be to highlight the importance of having a suite of process responses and not just a single process improvement paradigm to accommodate the widely varying project constraints. Answer to the question of ***do we have the right process mindset?*** is to have an affirmative response to, ***did we deliver as per customer expectations, on-time and on-budget?*** To me, anything else makes for a sub-optimal process response.

Overview of the book

Chapter 1 deals with making the right executive decisions with respect to choice of the CMMI framework. Key concepts defining the staged and the continuous representations are presented. This chapter provides a good overview about the organization of the process areas into the four threads of—process management, project management, engineering and support. A significant difference between the way staged and the continuous representation look at process improvement is a view enabled by the continuous representation that offers for a single process area to improve its individual process capability up to an optimizing level.

For those of us who come from the Software CMM world, Chapter 2—'Look from the Software CMM World'—offers an overview of the key differences between Software CMM and the CMMI. Such a perspective is essential for understanding the potential pay-offs and for assessing the impact of transition to protect existing investments which organizations might already have made in their Software CMM initiatives.

Chapter 3—'Look from the Software Engineering World'—offers the uninitiated a quick introduction to the fundamentals of software engineering. It describes the SITARA Synergy Approach which is a lifecycle description combining the merits of the V-Model and spiral models. It also offers an object modeling perspective with an example. Finally, SITARA's package selection and integration process is described to give a flavor for what is involved when commercial-off-the-shelf (COTS) integration is required for a successful deployment of a packaged solution. The reason why three different ideas are presented in this chapter is to highlight an important fact—process is not 'one size fits all!' A process might actually have to be designed and realized into practice depending upon the context.

Chapter 4 describes the seven level 2 process areas. In a sense these are the basic process areas serving as an effective foundation for process improvement. Focus of the seven process areas is to address practices in the engineering, support and project management categories of the CMMI. Specific practices contained in the seven process areas of requirements management, project planning, project monitoring and control, supplier agreement management, measurement and analysis, process and product quality assurance and configuration management are discussed.

Chapter 5 provides an interpretation for the fourteen level 3 process areas. Within the design of the CMMI structure, process management is enabled with three process areas along with engineering and advanced project management process areas. It is quite useful to note that a level 3 process maturity within the CMMI addresses all the necessary engineering practices that are required for effectively managing both the software and systems engineering perspectives. Much of what the level 3 process areas establish is to build a process improvement infrastructure that can be subjected to continuous improvement. Specific practices and the distinctions assumed by the generic practices as a result of making the transition from level 2 maturity, are described while interpreting organizational process focus, organizational process definition, organizational training, requirements development, product integration, technical solution, verification, validation, risk management, integrated project management, integrated teaming, integrated supplier management, organizational environment for integration and decision analysis and resolution. What the CMMI offers at the Defined or level 3 maturity, is a basic engineering framework which supports the use of sound software engineering and systems engineering practices and improvements that can be rendered to them. Having such an engineering framework is a pre-requisite to addressing the level 4 practices.

Chapter 6 describes the two level 4 process areas of quantitative project management and organizational process performance. Within the scope of the discussion of the specific practices of quantitative project management, we will explore the possibility of rendering other lower maturity process areas at a higher capability. Design of the CMMI at level 4 enables practices behind the advanced project management and process management categories. What such a pre-supposition means is that much of the enactment of the definitions for software engineering and systems engineering practices ought to have been complete and fully functional at level 3. Such an inferential understanding is possible with the way the CMMI is structured. Special emphasis is placed on the relevance of statistical process control for software. We will explore in depth what it means to establish process control. Whether it is possible to eliminate special causes of variations altogether or to establish a stable process in the first place, before it can be rendered as a capable process with the level 5 process areas.

Chapter 7 interprets the two level 5 process areas of organizational innovation and deployment and causal analysis and resolution. As is apparent, much of the project management practices must be in place along with the necessary engineering framework before practices in these two process areas can be effectively rendered.

Chapter 8 offers a thorough understanding of what is involved in a SCAMPI appraisal or the standard CMMI appraisal method for process improvement. SCAMPI is an appraisal technique that is used with the CMMI framework.

I would like to acknowledge that I traditionally follow the time tested 'Socratic Method' while relating to the subject matter. In one sense, a certain amount of repetition cannot be avoided because the undercurrents binding this very interesting but vast subject matter are highly intertwined and interlinked. In such situations, I find that instead of letting language become a limitation (by asking the reader to check several cross-references) I would rather state the obvious and offer a different perspective along with a different explanation. I have also found that a certain amount of repetition actually helps, since newer insights obtained can be based on a background of information already perused in the book, whereby serving as a good foundation to integrate the newer understanding with.

RAGHAV S. NANDYAL

Acknowledgments

There is no substitute for knowledge gained from first-hand experience. Many of the implementation details contained in this book have their origins in the SITARA Process JewelBox™—a treasure trove of best practices resulting from research conducted at SITARA Technologies Pvt. Ltd. I would like to acknowledge and thank the sponsor of this work, SITARA Technologies, for generously supporting this initiative by enabling liberal use of SITARA Process JewelBox™ and to quote implementation aspects from it while interpreting the intent of the CMMI practices. I would like to acknowledge that the contents within this book with attributions to SITARA Process JewelBox™ are the intellectual property of SITARA Technologies Pvt. Ltd., whose copyright belongs to SITARA Technologies Pvt. Ltd.

I have had the good fortune to learn from the wisdom of several brilliant engineers, thought leaders and fellow professionals during my associations with world-class organizations such as Motorola, NYNEX Science & Technology, LG Group and Intelligroup. In the last ten years, I have been mostly delivering high-maturity process appraisals and process training on the CMMI constellations for customers of SITARA. Much of the material in these pages represents the intellectual output of the numerous fertile minds with whom I have had the good fortune to interact—directly and indirectly. I wish to express my appreciation for their contributions and upon the influence they had on synthesizing my own understanding about software engineering and management. Whatever the shortcomings of this book, they are mine; whatever its merits, I owe it entirely to this large brain trust. Knowledge in that sense is always acquired and there is nothing original about it. However, insights could be personal and I will leave you with these in good measure throughout the text in specific references contained in the 'Author's musing' sections.

I would like to express a deep sense of gratitude to Dr. Michael Konrad of the SEI for so very willingly accepting to write the foreword to this book, offering a triumvirate perspective of the CMMI framework. I have benefited immensely from presentations delivered by Mike concerning high-maturity thinking involving the CMMI framework during Software Engineering Process Group (SEPG) conferences and other SEI-sponsored events.

I would like to express my profound gratitude to Mr. Ronald Radice for readily accepting to rewrite the foreword for this edition. Professional interactions with Ron and the insights he offered on the Software CMM, when I took the 'Introduction to Software CMM' class several years ago, are still fresh in my memory. His interpretations transformed my understanding about Software CMM as more of a management paradigm for engineering and managing world-class organizations, rather than merely considering it as a new quality model!

I would like to make special mention of George Smith, who was then the managing director of Motorola India Electronics Ltd., under whose tutelage I had the privilege to grow my understanding about software engineering. I must say that if it had not been for the genius of George, the word CMM would not have existed in India. He brought CMM to India with the creation of the first commercial CMM Level 5 Company in the world for Motorola India in November 1993. I would like to acknowledge him as a mentor par excellence whose gentle persuasion initiated me into the world of technical paper publication. His sagacity and software engineering leadership are worthy of emulation. George in his characteristic mentoring style accepted to write a prologue for the first edition of this book, which is carried in this upgrade and I wish to express my heartfelt gratitude to him.

Professional interactions with SITARA's High Maturity CMMI implementation partner sites, notable among them being Motorola GSG India (MIEL), Motorola GSG Malaysia, Network Solutions Ltd, Intelligroup, the many divisions of Satyam Computer Services, ABB India Research Center, Software Development and Central Engineering division of MIMOS Berhad, and comments from over 1000 students taking SITARA's delivery of the SEI's popular 'Introduction to CMMI' training and SITARA's 'Learn CMMI As A Second Language' course, on which this material is based, were of remarkable value. To all these thought-provoking professionals and the large SITARA alumni who form my brain trust, a heartfelt 'thank-you'! This book offers a wealth of information and a number of practical examples of the application of high maturity practices, Six Sigma and other quantitative management strategies for CMMI. I would like to acknowledge the hard work of the many dedicated professionals of the Software Development and Central Engineering division of MIMOS Berhad who reported with great seriousness progress made using the monthly SITARA TQI for TQA^{sm} sessions (refer to interpretations for OID in chapter 7). Special thanks to the management of MIMOS Berhad for so very graciously permitting me to quote examples from their process capability baseline reports.

As always, the persistent encouragement and support of Shailaja Nandyal, my wife and co-founder of SITARA Technologies, made it easy for me to channel time and energy from my family and management responsibilities into creating this book. She diligently located books, magazines and newspaper articles for me–the day-to-day realities–with which to punctuate this book. My children Sitara and Shreyas have stood by me through this marathon exercise of revising and improving the content of the first edition by keeping track of the metrics they understand best—the number of pages and words that the book has grown to since they last saw it!

I would like to thank R. Chandra Sekhar, Saswata Mishra and the production team at McGraw Hill Education for believing in this project and for lending their support for an expeditious execution.

What I offer the reader in this book is my current level of understanding about software engineering and strategic management after significant reflection and internal dialogue. I believe the interpretations will offer the reader a bedrock understanding of what the CMMI is all about in its triumvirate avatar of CMMI-DEV, CMMI-ACQ and CMMI-SVC. I have enjoyed writing this book and I hope that you will enjoy reading it!

This book is a mechanism to establish a learning community with its readers. There is much to learn from your experiences and wisdom. Please share your success stories with me. Let me know how this book has helped you and what you have done differently as a result of reading this book. What tips and insights do you have that can be passed on to future readers? I am eager to hear from you!

Raghav S. Nandyal
CEO, SITARA Technologies Pvt. Ltd.
raghav_nandyal@SITARATECH.com
www.SITARATECH.com

Prologue

This book answers two very important questions. The first is "What is the difference between the CMM and the CMMI?", and the second is "How will the adoption of CMMI affect the organization?" The first question is of importance to those who have already adopted the CMM as a means of improving their software process. The second is of importance in managing the organization as it moves through successive stages of change that are produced from the adoption of the CMMI.

Both of these questions are important, but the second one is by far more important because it gives the management an insight into how the organization will change and therefore provides a way to measure the change on a daily basis, as well as manage it. Managing change in an organization is a difficult task. This book provides a guide to that change at an incremental level that is well thought out and based on the experience of many organizations.

It does not attempt to say how the activities of the CMMI should be implemented, for that is dependent on each organization's individual circumstances and business objectives. Rather, it provides a view of the organizational dynamics that will come into play as the organization changes in an individual area. It illustrates how an individual improvement in one area affects not only that area but other related areas as well.

It allows all concerned people to set their expectations from the start of adopting the CMMI as a process improvement paradigm whether they have already adopted the CMM or not. By setting the expectations it also allows all concerned to know if the activity that is evaluated at a certain level continues to be functioning at that level on a routine basis rather than having to wait for a formal evaluation. In the same way it allows people the ability to evaluate a change that has been implemented to see if the process and organizational dynamics have met the expectations laid out in this book. This is important because all implemented changes will not produce an actual improvement.

This book also allows the management to understand how the adoption of the CMMI and the resulting changes will change the way that the software process must be managed. One of the most difficult tasks for the management of any organization is to change how they manage. Just as the software process has evolved to a given state, so too has the management of the process evolved. Just as the existing software process has become ingrained in organizational behavior, so too has the management become ingrained in the organization. The CMMI may be an excellent approach to process improvement, but it gives no real indication of how management must change to get the most out of the ever evolving process that adopting the CMMI will produce. Here at last is a guide for managers as well as for technologists.

George Smith

Contents

Foreword 1 *vii*
Foreword 2 *ix*
Preface to the Second Edition *xiii*
Preface to the First Edition *xxi*
Acknowledgment *xxvii*
Prologue *xxxi*

1. Executive Decisions **1**

What every Sponsor should know about CMMI *1*
Evolution of the CMMI *8*
DFSS for a Software or Systems Development, Acquisition and Service Process *9*
The IDEAL[SM] Model *10*

2. Process Perspectives and Overview of the CMMI **31**

Introduction *31*
Principal Message of the Software CMM and the CMMI *32*
Overview of the CMMI-ACQ Constellation *43*
Overview of the CMMI-SVC Constellation *46*

3. Software Engineering Perspectives **50**

Introduction *50*
Branches of the Structured Analysis Family *51*
SITARA's Synergy Approach—Essay on Software Engineering *52*
SITARA's Package Selection and Integration Process—Essay on COTS (Commercial Off-the-Shelf) Software Integration *78*

4. Managed Level—Interpreting the Level 2 CMMI Process Areas **100**

Characteristics of a Level 1 (or Initial) Process *100*
Characteristics of a Level 2 Process (Managed Process) *102*
Requirements Management (REQM) CMMI-DEV, CMMI-ACQ and CMMI-SVC *103*

Project Planning (PP) CMMI-DEV, CMMI-ACQ and CMMI-SVC 115
Project Monitoring and Control (PMC) CMMI-DEV, CMMI-ACQ and CMMI-SVC 129
Configuration Management (CM) CMMI-DEV, CMMI-ACQ and CMMI-SVC 133
Measurement and Analysis (MA) CMMI-DEV, CMMI-ACQ and CMMI-SVC 136
Process and Product Quality Assurance (PPQA) CMMI-DEV, CMMI-ACQ and CMMI-SVC 143
Supplier Agreement Management (SAM) CMMI-DEV, CMMI-SVC 149
Agreement Management (AM) CMMI-ACQ 152
Solicitation and Supplier Agreement Development (SSAD) CMMI-ACQ 155
Acquisition Requirements Development (ARD) CMMI-ACQ 157
Service Delivery (SD) CMMI-SVC 160

5. Defined Level—Interpreting the Level 3 CMMI Process Areas 164

Characteristics of a Level 3 Process (Defined Process) 164
Requirements Development (RD) CMMI-DEV 167
Technical Solution (TS) CMMI-DEV 178
Product Integration (PI) CMMI-DEV 187
Verification (VER) CMMI-DEV 191
Validation (VAL) CMMI-DEV 200
Acquisition Technical Management (ATM) CMMI-ACQ 204
Acquisition Verification (AVER) CMMI-ACQ 207
Acquisition Validation (AVAL) CMMI-ACQ 208
Service Continuity (SCON) CMMI-SVC 208
Capacity and Availability Management (CAM) CMMI-SVC 212
Service System Development (SSD)-Addition CMMI-SVC 215
Service System Transition (SST) CMMI-SVC 218
Strategic Service Management (STSM) CMMI-SVC 220
Incident Resolution and Prevention (IRP) CMMI-SVC 222
Organizational Process Focus (OPF) CMMI-DEV, CMMI-ACQ and CMMI-SVC 225
Organizational Process Definition (OPD) CMMI-DEV (+IPPD), CMMI-ACQ and CMMI-SVC 230
Organizational Training CMMI-DEV, CMMI-ACQ and CMMI-SVC 234
Integrated Project Management (IPM) CMMI-DEV (+IPPD), CMMI-ACQ and CMMI-SVC 238
Risk Management (RSKM) CMMI-DEV, CMMI-ACQ and CMMI-SVC 244

Decision Analysis and Resolution (DAR) CMMI-DEV, CMMI-ACQ and CMMI-SVC *248*

6. Quantitatively Managed Level—Interpreting the Level 4 CMMI Process Areas **258**

Characteristics of a Level 4 Process (Quantitatively Managed Process) *258*
Organizational Process Performance (OPP) CMMI-DEV, CMMI-ACQ and CMMI-SVC *264*
Quantitative Project Management (QPM) CMMI-DEV, CMMI-ACQ and CMMI-SVC *272*

7. Optimizing Level—Interpreting the Level 5 CMMI Process Areas **278**

Characteristics of a Level 5 Process (Optimizing Process) *278*
Causal Analysis and Resolution (CAR) CMMI-DEV, CMMI-ACQ and CMMI-SVC *283*
Organizational Innovation and Deployment (OID) CMMI-DEV, CMMI-ACQ and CMMI-SVC *289*

Epilogue **299**
Appendix **311**
Glossary of Terms **315**
References **319**
Index **323**

1

Executive Decisions

AUTHOR'S MUSING

Uttisthata jagrata prapya varan nibodhata Ksurasya dhara nisita duratyaya Durgam pathas tat kavayo vadanti (Katha Upanishad 1.3.14)

Arise! Awake! Stop not till the goal is reached. The path to perfection is sharp as the razor's edge, hard to tread so declare the wise sages.

This profound and eternal truth, this wisdom from the Katha Upanishad, summarizes the real meaning of continuous process improvement. In the context of the CMMI constellations, goals address the implementation and institutionalization aspects of the disciplines addressed by them, perfection of which remains the quest within a process improvement program.

WHAT EVERY SPONSOR SHOULD KNOW ABOUT CMMI

The purpose of Capability Maturity Model® Integration (CMMI®) is to provide guidance for improving the organization's processes and its ability to manage the development, acquisition and maintenance of products and services. CMMI places proven practices into a structure that helps organizations to assess their maturity and process area capability, establish priorities for improvement and guide in the implementation of these improvements.

The principal philosophies communicated within the CMMI framework are all around us. We come across them in daily newspapers and magazines. We observe process orientation or lack of it in day-to-day circumstances that shape our destinies. Its lack, for instance, can manifest itself in a breakdown in public services. This lack of process orientation or of a methodical execution of activities invariably accounts for the innumerable number of problems within a system. Examples of systemic failures arising from a lack of process orientation abound, as in a report carried by Reuters in a newspaper not too long ago about a hospital in Seattle, Washington [Gale 2002]:

"Even the best surgeons occasionally, leave foot-long, metal instruments inside their patients, though it happens very rarely", officials at a Seattle hospital said. "Just days after announcing, they were paying a tumor patient $97,000 for leaving a retractor inside him after surgery, the medical center said similar accidents happen about once a year. ... Until now, the hospital has counted needles, sponges and other small surgical items, but not larger instruments, of which doctors might use as many as 600 in a single surgery."

And more recently on November 30th, 2009, newspapers across India reported the following:

"The Common Admission Test (CAT) for MBA, which for the first time has employed an online format, kick-started on a wrong note on Saturday with servers crashing across several test centres. Around 10,000 students had showed up across the country for the first day of the 10-day series of this online test. The test did not start at the designated time and when it did, a large number of students encountered technical glitches. Each had their own account to share. While for some, the problem began with the system rejecting their password, others reported the screen going blank. Some others had to contend with screens where words appeared but pictures went missing. This was not all. Some students suffered a setback while proceeding with the test, which ended abruptly after they answered three/four questions."

Commonplace incidents such as the above are reported day in and day out. Applying a process to day-to-day management and decision-making is no longer *a nice thing to have*; in most organizations process orientation serves well as a core competency. It would be extremely useful and instructive to relate such day-to-day events that one reads, to the practices advocated in the CMMI. Doing so highlights the fact that the practices contained in the CMMI are a set of well-organized best practices prescribing a management philosophy and offers a structured framework for developing software and systems effectively.

A question that is often raised during executive sessions with the sponsor is, '*What are the minimal steps we need to execute in order to get a CMMI level 5?*' This is a profound question, the answer to which would vary depending upon who is asking it. For a high-maturity organization transitioning from a legacy framework such as the CMMI version 1.1, this question has to deal with issues concerning 'process optimization', a minimalist approach to rendering cost-effective, efficient and agile methods. For a level 1 organization or a low-maturity process, this question is symbolic of a defeatist approach. One of the most useful points to note is that in order to differentiate effectively, one needs to be different from the competition. Quality in a product and service offering is a very good differentiator. Differentiation always comes with intrinsically relevant overheads such as testing, quality assurance and reviews or audits to ensure excellence in product or service quality with inspection practices. Quality cannot happen by chance; it has to be designed into the process. Process checks and controls while emphasizing adherence to a defined process help to maximize the benefits of implementing a program of process improvement, which are:

- Learning and knowing more about the circumstances that surround the current context of execution
- Ensuring a structured mechanism to minimize the impact of variation

Irrespective of the level of process maturity, if the essence behind the process improvement program does not translate into the above two fundamental philosophies, this same program will soon become an add-on activity carried out purely for its own sake. Practicing the discipline advocated by the CMMI framework can be both enjoyable and rewarding. The reader should reflect on this aspect while reading the book.

CMMI is a change management framework and the CMMI itself has undergone several major changes from its earlier version. CMMI in its current form is made up of three constellations: development, acquisition and services. The practices of the development constellation of the CMMI lay out practices with which to address process improvements for the software and systems development process. Called the CMMI-DEV, this constellation includes hardware amplifications besides catering to the requirements of good team-based processes within what is termed as **IPPD addition** or the Integrated Product and Process Development addition.[1] Addition, in CMMI, expands constellations to emphasize a particular aspect of its use. All three constellations of the CMMI contain two representations—staged and continuous.

The current version of the CMMI is version 1.3 and is a major improvement on the earlier CMMI version 1.1, but makes only modest changes to the previous version 1.2. It improves clarity on the expectations placed of practices in the high maturity process areas. Version 1.3 was released in November 2010, around the time this second edition of the book was in the final stages of production. Since version 1.3 was available just-in-time, a comprehensive view of both the stable versions of the CMMI, namely version 1.2 and version 1.3 *for all three constellations* is offered in this book. Such a comprehensive view of the incremental changes to all three constellations is not currently available in any book of this kind. It is bound to leave the reader better equipped to make informed decisions as regards impact of this change on investments to ongoing process improvements, and provide a careful assessment of the wisdom and return-on-investment in pursuing a multi-model strategy or a multi-disciplinary improvement initiative. Modest changes which have occurred in version 1.3 appear in footnotes throughout the book and in some cases, within the main text. *Note however that version 1.2, is the most widely institutionalized flavor of the CMMI currently in use in the industry.*

Staged Representation of CMMI Version 1.2

Staged CMMI is structured around five levels of process maturity. Each process maturity level is an evolutionary plateau resulting from institutionalization of well-defined practices contained within process areas.

- Level 1 (Initial maturity level) process maturity is the default level at which an organization would perform if there were no governing processes. Processes at this level can be characterized as being *ad hoc* and chaotic.
- At Level 2 (Managed maturity level), a sense of process repeatability is established through well-defined project management standards with an ingrained process discipline. In the CMMI-DEV constellation, there are a total of seven process areas within this level, which are internally cohesive and mutually exclusive. In the CMMI-ACQ, there are a total of nine process areas within this level, and in the CMMI-SVC, there are a total of eight process areas within this level.

[1] Version 1.3 no longer features IPPD addition. Nonetheless, good team-based processes are extremely important. Such an emphasis on teaming results in version 1.3 by including one IPPD related specific practice to OPD and IPM. Doing so has brought in consistency across the three constellations.

- Level 3 (Defined maturity level) is the next stage in process maturity, which results from instituting engineering management with a defined process. In the CMMI-DEV constellation, there are a total of 11 process areas within this level—a majority of them addressing engineering activities. In the CMMI-ACQ, there are a total of nine process areas within this level and in the CMMI-SVC, there are a total of 12 process areas within this level.
- When a process is under statistical process control (SPC) using quantitative management, a level 4 (Quantitatively managed maturity level) is established. A significant amount of professional interpretation is called for to apply SPC to software. There are two process areas within level 4 which are common to all the three constellations.

After significant research, SITARA's surmise is that level 4 is all about maintaining a good control on Cost of Poor Quality (COPQ), and thereby minimizing the impact of variation arising out of special causes. So, if there is one metric that a level 4 must consciously collect and minimize, it should be the COPQ.

Author's Musing

The focus of application of high maturity practices throughout the book is based on a new definition for special and common cause variation as relevant in 'software engineering'. This new definition is also required since the book goes to great lengths explaining why both common and special cause variations are 'assignable' causes and why it is impossible to eliminate them in software. Common cause has a source of variation assignable to something within the process control. Special cause has a source of variation assignable to something outside the process control.

- The highest level of software maturity, level 5 (Optimizing maturity level), is awarded to a process when the established process at level 4 is under continuous process improvement through good change management. There are two process areas within level 5, which are again common to all the three constellations.

SITARA's surmise is that level 5 is all about maintaining a good control on Cost of Quality or, more appropriately, Cost of Assuring Quality (COAQ), and thereby minimizing the impact of variation arising out of common causes. So, if there is one metric that a level 5 must consciously collect, it should be COAQ.

In several observations from sites employing high-maturity practices, Cost of Quality is known as the sum total of Cost of Poor Quality and Cost of Assuring Quality.

The biggest challenge in measuring the real cost of quality as well as that of poor quality lies in the fact that numerous quantifiable parameters and qualitative factors actually influence their true value. Besides, establishing a non-intrusive measurement system that can measure process parameters without hampering productivity and morale issues among engineers is difficult in software. Therefore, it is important to note that these measures are at best a good approximation of what is known. What is unknown will remain hidden from view. What is important though is that the process must make consistent use of the parameters of interest that are being adopted, for defining these measures.

There is today a significant emphasis attached to statistical and probabilistic modeling involving high-maturity CMMI practices. Just as all applications involving statistical and mathematical modeling of random unpredictable behavior are approximate, software engineering models of process performance are no different. The current emphasis of high-maturity CMMI practices on prediction-based statistical modeling using regression equations and the expectation of a high degree of accuracy using coefficient of determination (R^2 and R^2 adjusted) is in the author's opinion misplaced. An anecdote which appeared recently in *Discover Magazine* best sums up the dilemma of prediction.

> "Terrorist attacks are not only deadly but also frustrating because of their randomness and unpredictability. In a study in *Nature*, however, researches have put forth a mathematical model that shows terrorist attacks and insurgencies are not as scattershot as they seem. After compiling 50,000 acts of violence across nine historic and ongoing insurgencies including Iraq, Afghanistan and Northern Ireland, Neil Johnson and his team found a relationship between size of an attack and how often it occurs. By plotting the distribution of the frequency and size of events, a bunch of researchers found that insurgent wars follow an approximate power law, in which the frequency of attacks decreases with increasing attack size to the power of 2.5. Which means that, for any war, an attack with 10 causalities is 316 times more likely to occur than one with 100 causalities. Researchers have used power laws to try to find order in natural phenomena like a size versus frequency pattern in earthquakes or avalanches. Johnson and his colleagues argue that the pattern arises as insurgent wars lack a coherent command network and operate more as a soup of groups in which cells form and disband when they sense danger, then reform in different sizes and composition."
>
> Now the crux of the issue: "Other researchers doubt the reliability of the model. For one thing, terror cells battle one another and probably aren't as free to break up and re-form as the study suggests. And the number of insurgents in a fight might not stay close to constant. But Michael Spagat says: "We could never say with certainty that there were going to be 10 attacks on one day, for example. But, the model could predict whether a given day carried a lighter or heavier probability of a deadly attack." [Moseman 2009]

Such questions concerning reliability and a generic applicability of prediction models is the case even with process performance models involving software engineering activities. We will defer this topic to chapters 6 and 7, where high-maturity process areas of the CMMI will be interpreted.

Author's Musing

What is a statistical model? A statistical model is an equation based on a system of assumptions that can generate artificial data using a set of parameters that represent important aspects of it. Models establish a structure with which the two activities of *estimation* and *hypothesis testing* can be enabled.

A broad definition of an approximate measure of Cost of Poor Quality model is:

Cost of Poor Quality (of service or a product) =
Cost of Poor Quality In-process + Cost of Poor Quality Outside-process

(Contd)

Cost of Poor Quality In-process =
Cost of rework + Cost of process change + Cost of infrastructure change

Cost of Poor Quality Outside-process =
Cost of non-availability + Cost of lost opportunities + Cost of penalty

A broad definition of an approximate measure of Cost of Assuring Quality model is:

Cost of Assuring Quality (of service or a product) = Cost of Assuring Quality In-process + Cost of Assuring Quality Outside-process

Cost of Assuring Quality In-process = Cost of development + Cost of appraisal + Cost of prevention + Cost of training + Cost of testing + Cost of tools used – Savings resulting from reuse – Savings from cycle time reduction

Cost of Assuring Quality Outside-process = Cost of validation + Cost of sales + Cost of marketing – Savings resulting from repeat business

It would be a lot more reasonable and practical to establish a measure called Total Cost of Ownership which could be defined as:

Total Cost of Ownership = Cost of Poor Quality + Cost of Assuring Quality

I have seen organizations defining COQ as a percentage of the total effort more as a static number. COQ or what I would like to refer to as COAQ cannot be a 'static' number! It is always a 'dynamic number' based on the many parameters that define its details, and it is practical to define it as having a range of values operating in a band spread across the life cycle. And it is also better to know these values in terms of the total cost of ownership rather than as a percentage of the total effort. This is because effort spent has a direct correlation to the competence levels of those working on the problem.

Therefore, COAQ and Total Cost of Ownership are good candidate metrics for tracking, using a statistical process control chart.

Continuous Representation of CMMI Version 1.2

The notion of establishing process maturity in the continuous representation of CMMI is only incidental. Continuous CMMI is structured into four categories in all three constellations. Three of these categories, Process Management, Project Management and Support, are common to all three constellations. In the CMMI-DEV constellation, these categories are Engineering, Process Management, Project Management and Support. In the CMMI-ACQ constellation, these categories are Acquisition[2], Process Management, Project Management and Support. In the CMMI-SVC constellation, these categories are: Service Establishment and Delivery, Process Management, Project Management and Support. Process areas are the building blocks of the CMMI constellations that establish organizational process maturity. Practices contained in the process areas serve as the primary guiding principles for effective process design and fall under one of the four categories relevant to the three constellations.

- Engineering category of CMMI-DEV: Practices within the engineering category establish a structured framework for issues concerning development and maintenance activities for both

2 CMMI-ACQ version 1.3 renames this category as Acquisition Engineering.

software and systems engineering. Six process areas within this category contain practices which are highly interdependent and work effectively when considered as an ensemble.[3]

- Process Management category: These are practices that cut across projects and have relevance at an organizational level. Both basic and advanced practices within the process management category help to establish the organization's intent to define, quantitatively measure, improve and innovate a process-based response to the day-to-day execution of project requirements. The five process areas in this category are common to all three constellations spanning levels 3, 4 and 5 in the staged equivalent.
- Project Management category: These practices are mostly relevant at the project level. They address the critical-to-quality performance issues that are unique to the project. In the CMMI-DEV constellation, the six process areas in this category span levels 2, 3 and 4 in the staged equivalent. In the CMMI-SVC constellation, the nine process areas in this category span levels 2, 3 and 4 and the CMMI-ACQ constellation organizes six process areas in this category to span levels 2, 3 and 4 in the staged equivalent. It is important to note that the CMMI-SVC and CMMI-ACQ constellations identify Requirements Management, an engineering category process area of the CMMI-DEV, in the Project Management category. In order to bring in consistency across constellations, it is believed that the next version of the CMMI-DEV is likely to reshuffle Requirements Management into the Project Management category.
- Support category: Practices that establish a foundation for serving the needs of other process areas are aggregated into this category. These are mostly organizational practices which help to institutionalize the process intent. Five process areas belonging to the support category are common to all three constellations.
- Acquisition category of CMMI-ACQ: Practices within the acquisition category establish a structured framework for issues concerning acquisition of products and services. Practices in the CMMI-ACQ, constellation are designed to build a cohesive process to enable a network of competencies, wherein the acquiring organization leverages the capabilities of supplier organizations. Six process areas within this category contain practices which are distributed into levels 2 and 3 in the staged equivalent.
- Service Establishment and Delivery: Practices within the service establishment and delivery category address the institutionalization of best practices by organizations that must develop and improve processes related to delivering cost-effective services. Such delivery capability should also consider minimizing process overheads while juggling between development of solutions and delivery of services based on such solutions.

AUTHOR'S MUSING

What could be a simplistic definition of institutionalization? *Formalizing an informal process using professional judgment!*

[3] Version 1.3 moves Requirements Management process area into the Project Management Category. With this regrouping of process areas, the Engineering category of CMMI-DEV v1.3 will only have 5 process areas.

EVOLUTION OF THE CMMI

The CMMI models are organized as constellations of best practices. When first conceived, the CMMI was developed as a well-documented set of practices addressing the development of products and services covering the product life cycle from conceptualization through retirement. Based on the CMMI version 1.2 framework, the CMMI version 1.1 *mutated* into three constellations addressing specific aspects of development, acquisition and services. CMMI for Development (CMMI-DEV) version 1.2 provides a comprehensive integrated solution for the development and maintenance activities applied to products and services. CMMI-DEV version 1.2 released by the Software Engineering Institute (SEI) in August 2006 builds itself upon version 1.1. The version 1.1 of CMMI enabled the establishment and growth of the organizational process framework addressing the disciplines of software and systems engineering. Practices within the CMMI are a synthesis of best practices from its reference source models Capability Maturity Model for Software version 2.0 draft C; EIA Interim Standard 731 (Systems Engineering Capability Model); and Integrated Product Development Capability Model, draft version 0.98 (IPD-CMM). The primary design goals while arriving at the CMMI framework were to integrate these source models, eliminate inconsistencies and reduce duplication, and in so doing, to offer a common integrated vision of improvement for all the elements and process constituencies within an organization. Being sensitive to legacy effort on its reference source models, the CMMI-DEV comes in two flavors—staged and continuous representations—applicable to software engineering projects or systems engineering projects or to both. As the word 'staged' connotes, organization of the process areas into clusters of practices establishes a stable evolutionary plateau. And in the 'continuous' representation, the process areas are organized into four categories, viz. project management, process management, support and engineering.

Following the success of CMMI models for development organizations, the need was identified for a CMMI model addressing the acquisition environment and the service industry. While the CMMI-ACQ version 1.2 released by the SEI in November 2007 addressed the requirements for an acquisition environment, the CMMI-SVC version 1.2, released in February 2009, was designed to meet the requirements of the service industry. The CMMI-ACQ model collection includes acquisition best practices from government and industry. CMMI-ACQ integrates bodies of knowledge that are essential for an acquirer. The CMMI-SVC model is a collection of best practices that is generated from the CMMI v1.2 architecture and framework to provide guidance on developing and improving mature service practices. With the service industry assuming importance as a significant driver of worldwide economic growth, service practices are a key contributor to the performance, customer satisfaction and profitability of the economic community. CMMI-DEV may be treated as a reference for the *development of the service system*, which supports delivery of the service in a services context. In like manner, CMMI-DEV may be treated as a reference for *supplier-executed activities* for systems engineering, software development and hardware design work in an acquisition initiative.

Making the right executive decisions with respect to choosing the CMMI framework that is best suited to your needs, i.e., the staged or the continuous representation is half the battle won! Key concepts defining the staged and the continuous representations are therefore presented first.

DFSS FOR A SOFTWARE OR SYSTEMS DEVELOPMENT, ACQUISITION AND SERVICE PROCESS

Having used the CMMI constellations within a very robust Six Sigma program, an observation can be made at the outset that CMMI framework and architecture promote a Design for Six Sigma (DFSS) for the software or the systems development process in the development, acquisition and services context. An assertion such as this could easily pass off as an over-hyped position statement for a hot new idea if it is not explained. What would you call a process which is designed around a framework that promotes minimizing both common and special causes of variation by establishing a cognitive map (for up to 80 per cent of the CMMI can be committed to memory, and this book will provide mnemonics to enable this)? Better still, what would you call a process, if the very mechanism to build process capability is dictated by the framework itself? In this sense, the CMMI is to software or systems development process, what DFSS is to manufacturing.

Author's Musing

Establishing a cognitive map of the process is possible with CMMI. Just as you do not need to look up Kernighan and Ritchie when you know how to code in C language, you will not need to refer to an organizational standard software process (OSSP) or the CMMI framework descriptions when you can establish a cognitive map of the model. This helps to very effectively reduce or minimize common cause of variation.

The design and structure of the CMMI framework enables rendering process improvement in a self-sufficient manner. This view of the CMMI is best appreciated and gets highlighted in its continuous representation, wherein deploying the higher-maturity process areas belonging to the levels 4 and 5 naturally lead to an increase in capability levels, thereby improving the process capability baselines of other lower-maturity process areas operating at maturity levels 2 and 3. This aspect is elaborated upon later in this chapter when describing the characteristics of capability levels 4 and 5 for process areas. We will also explore this in greater detail in Chapters 6 and 7 while interpreting the level 4 and level 5 process areas.

A simple improvement cycle which fosters DFSS thinking includes the following steps:

- Get started
- Determine where you are
- Determine where you want to be
- Make a plan
- Execute the plan
- Learn lessons and do it all over again with the new understanding

The power of this simple improvement process is in repeating this cycle. The IDEAL^{SM} Model is one such framework that facilitates process improvement.

THE IDEAL^{SM} MODEL

The CMMI uses the approach of the IDEAL model (Figure 1.1) to define process improvements. IDEAL is an acronym using the first letters of the words Initiating–Diagnosing–Establishing–Acting–Learning. It can be considered as a model to effect process improvement. It is based on the Shewhart–Deming cycle of Plan–Do–Check–Act or the PDCA cycle.

The stimulus for change can be proactive, that is, when given an opportunity to improve, or it could be reactive, which is more as a result of the fear of negative consequences. As exercising individual autonomy is possible only when the stimulus for change comes as a proactive response, it is useful to stay in this mode without letting trepidation become the motive for process change. A proactive response will therefore involve evaluation of business objectives and aligning process improvements to such objectives.

Initiating Setting the context and establishing sponsorship involves clarifying the scope of changes involved, identifying all relevant stakeholders or groups that are likely to be affected as a result, and focusing on the overall management of the change initiative. Since most problems originate as management problems and not so much a technical problem, many a times, it is important for the management to change

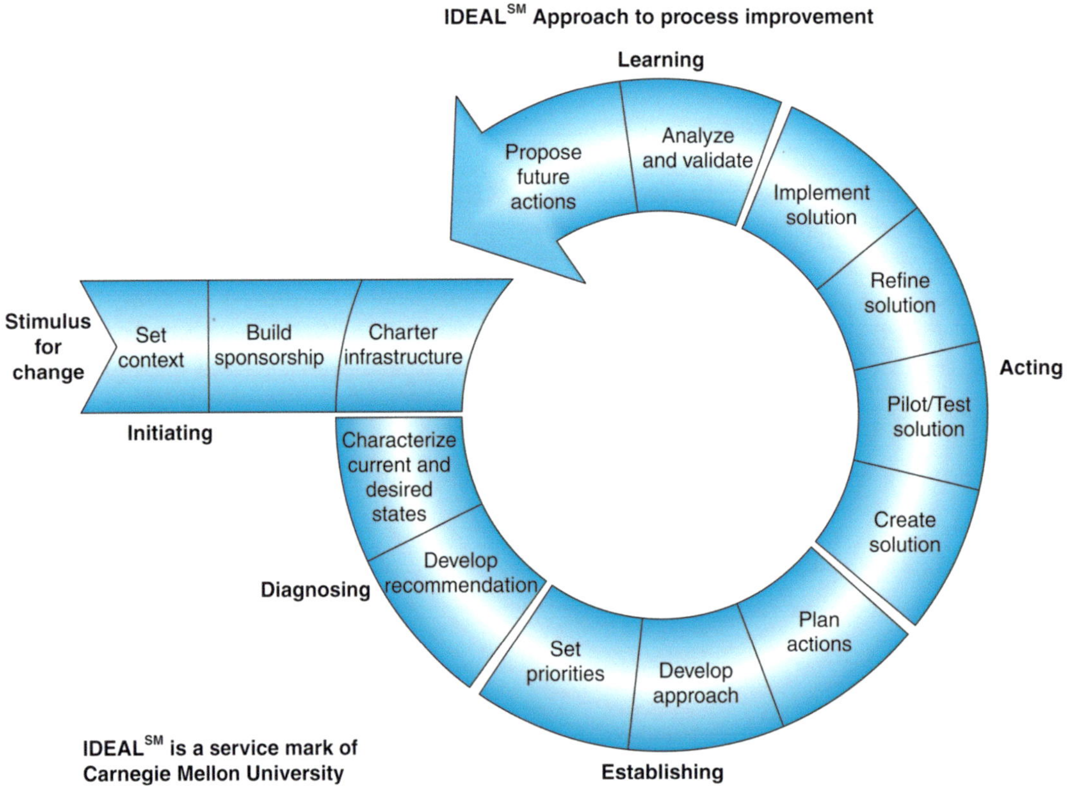

Fig. 1.1 The IDEAL^{SM} Model

Source: Adapted from People Capability Maturity Model Carnegie Mellon University [1995] with permission before the people in the trenches, do. In order to say we have complete sponsorship, it is important to get to an emphatic yes, to the change initiative from the last person in the lineup for process improvement. It would then be appropriate to put the basic infrastructure in place and take the necessary steps to *diagnose* the reasons demanding a change.

Diagnosing This phase of the process improvement paradigm focuses on characterizing the current state of practice by identifying the strengths and weaknesses of the process using a formal assessment process, which is a structured review of the organizational process and product assets as interpreted against the CMMI model. This cycle is repeated as and when significant improvements are perceived. The focus of this phase is on ensuring that strengths become stronger and weaknesses are addressed through appropriate improvements.

Development of findings and recommendations to rectify the weaknesses is based on an action plan for improving the state of practice. The findings from an assessment or an appraisal and recommendations establish the rationale for a follow-on improvement program. Strategy and sequence for implementing the recommendations should be prioritized and documented in the process improvement action plan. Not every recommendation needs to be worked on at once; some must be addressed earlier and some later. Going for the low-hanging fruits may solve most issues.

Establishing Setting up the right teams for process action must be based on assignment of each major recommendation to the relevant stakeholders. Team-building and team-based activities are critical for effective implementation. A senior executive of the organization must formally kick off the team launch and team-building exercises. Each of the established teams must plan their own activities and become responsible for ensuring successful implementation of the process changes into the process infrastructure. Integration of the team activities is best done by a group of senior executives or the process engineering group—an embodiment of process champions who work to accomplish the objectives established for the process program. Periodic reviews by a process engineering group along with a senior executive of the organization are important to reinforce a positive message about the intent of the process improvement program.

Acting For every process recommendation worked on, it is important for the respective process owner (or process action teams) to answer—*Is the change getting better or is it getting bitter?* A useful mechanism to help obtain clarity in this respect is with Standard CMMI Appraisal Method for Internal Process Improvement (SCAMPI) Class C and Class B appraisals, process audits or incremental appraisals [Nandyal 2007]. Every new procedure, standard or tool that gets developed for a solution must be put through a few iterations of piloting on selected projects. When pilot results prove useful, they can then be deployed over a larger organizational context to verify whether the growth is harmonious. The role played by the collection of measures or metrics that directly relate to measuring the efficacy of the change is emphasized. The goal-question-metric paradigm of Victor Basili is a very useful technique to address the effectiveness of the change program. The only way to keep the measurement and verification aspects of the change management program working in step and synchronously with changes to the process is to ensure that these activities are used to objectively evaluate the quality of the new processes.

Learning or Leverage After an objective evaluation of the process change, it is possible to hone the practices into skills by documenting lessons learnt, revising the scope of implementation and restructuring the process engineering group if business situations have changed. Many a time it might become necessary to revise the organizational approach for the next assessment. Since process maturity is a journey and not a goal, importance must be given to repeating the cycle of improvement and sustaining the momentum for right process alignment.

> **AUTHOR'S MUSING**
>
> The real leverage from using the IDEAL model comes after the L phase! It is the number of iterations you go through with the IDEAL process improvement that dictates how strong the process becomes over time.

What does Improvement Mean?

The word improvement means different things to different organizations based on business objectives and how progress is measured internally. What is important is to ensure that improvement is based on a long-term, strategic and core competency perspective. When such thinking is in place, having the right systems becomes only a necessary but not sufficient condition to operate at high process maturity. When such thinking exists, the questions that get asked are: *What is the expected impact of improvement on the bottom line? And how will we measure this impact?* A well-managed process improvement initiative ought to assure quality of services and products with an ability to measure such impact through a definite reduction to both the cost of poor quality (at level 4) and cost of quality (at level 5). Though not a silver bullet, having a process framework is still the only available option for structured development. Even though some practices might appear to be bizarre and dysfunctional today, it is important to recognize that they were at one time a successful response to the circumstances that once surrounded the organizational context. If circumstances have changed, process improvement has to address those changes which are necessary to ensure an organizational response that is both relevant and congruent in the changed context.

It would be useful to keep in mind that significant amount of tailoring and interpreting the CMMI constellations is necessary to get the best value from the CMMI framework and architecture. We will review all three constellations, in the staged and continuous representations in this book. Understanding the distinctions of both representations helps to make informed management decisions.

Which Representation to Choose? The Staged, or the Continuous or Both?

Central to both representations is the notion of a process area which is the basic building block made up of a collection of related practices. A group of process areas aggregated in a way that is set forth in the CMMI framework and architecture at each maturity level establishes organizational process maturity by building the necessary management and engineering practices into the process infrastructure. Both representations of the CMMI have two types of goals: specific and generic. Specific goals are used for determining the sufficiency of practices employed by practitioners, whereas generic goals help in leaving behind a lasting representation of the process. All three constellations of the CMMI are structured similarly.

In the staged representation, process improvements are rendered in progressive, evolutionary steps from the managed level (or level 2) reaching up to the optimizing level (or level 5). In doing so, practices within a group of process areas at each level are institutionalized. Practices which have the connotation of being an implementation feature are called specific practices; fulfilling these specific practices will enable the accomplishment of specific goals within the process infrastructure.

Like with any new technology, the CMMI constellations bring with them a whole glossary of definitions and terms which are unique and used in a manner that is best possible only in the context of the CMMI. We will explore this terminology in a systematic manner by improving our understanding of the CMMI one step at a time. As and when we come across something unique in the CMMI, we will gain all the knowledge that is necessary for us to develop a good understanding of the same. In a sense, topics are built upon concepts presented earlier and therefore a certain amount of repetition cannot be avoided if we need to synthesize our understanding. The reader is advised to read and understand the concepts as presented in the sequence in which they unfold in each chapter.

The distinctive features of the staged and continuous representations are summarized in the following table.

Staged Representation	***Continuous Representation***
Provides a proven sequence of improvements, beginning with basic management practices and progressing through a predefined and proven path of successive levels, each serving as a foundation for the next	Permits the selection and order of improvements that best meet the organizational business objectives and mitigates the organization's areas of risks
Permits comparisons across and among organizations through the use of maturity levels	Enable comparison across and among organizations on a process area by process area basis or by comparing results through the use of equivalent staging

The *staged representation* of the CMMI has five maturity levels: levels 1 to 5. Each maturity level is composed of process areas which define the necessary focus by prescribing the governing practices and the rigor which ought to exist within the manifest process framework. At level 2 for instance, the focus is on inculcating a process discipline in projects through appropriate levels of project management. At level 3, the focus is on the growth of project specific management practices by tailoring the organizational standard process. Tailoring addresses the changing project requirements around the engineering characteristics and constraints of operation through process definition. At level 4, process rendering is based on keeping the focus on quantitative aspects of the process by identifying the critical-to-X parameters (where X can be cost, quality, time and scope) and composing an appropriate process response by identifying the special causes of process variation and minimizing the overall cost of poor quality. At level 5, the focus is on reducing and minimizing the cost of quality with a view to insulate the impact of common causes of process variation. One of the positive aspects of the staged representation of the CMMI framework is that the model itself defines the rigor or richness behind the practices, required in order to qualify for the maturity level. This rigor is defined to be the capability level 3 (or defined capability) for each of the different process areas.

In the *continuous representation*, the notion of organizational maturity is only incidental. The true intention behind a continuous representation is to challenge the manifest rigor or richness of the practices to accommodate higher levels of process capabilities for each of the individual process areas. Hence, increasing the level of process area capability is the major reason why organizations would opt for the continuous representation. Therefore, organizations should choose the continuous representation only after they know enough about their organizational process maturity, say at least till after they have reached the level 3, and are now interested in adding richness to the practices by focusing on the rigor of institutionalization. When the practices are incomplete, a capability level of 0 is awarded to the individual process areas. At this level of rigor, the identification of even the essential practices governing the process area is incomplete and therefore its performance is not obvious. An example of an essential practice in Project Planning, for instance, is to *establish project estimates for time, cost and effort*. When the process area is at the performed or the capability level 1, the basic practices governing this process area, identified in the CMMI model as *specific practices*, ought to be established within the process framework.

Example: In Project Planning, three specific goals have to be fulfilled by supporting practices to establish a level 1 rigor:

1. Establish estimates
2. Develop a project plan
3. Obtain commitment to the plan

Each of these specific goals has a set of specific practices which needs to be fulfilled. For example, the goal 'Establish estimates' contains the following specific practices:

- Estimate the scope of the project
- Establish estimates of work product and task attributes
- Define project life cycle
- Determine estimates of effort and cost

Level 1 is called the initial process maturity, and the capability level of process areas at this level cannot be determined since practices supporting the intent of the process areas are incomplete. In other words, the capability level of a process area is said to operate at zero capability or the incomplete level. *Level 1 maturity is the natural lower limit into which practices within an organization tend to decay due to inherent process entropy, if adequate management oversight mechanisms and engineering controls are not in place.*

If capability level 1 can be sustained, the specific practices within the process area can now be transformed to take on the rigor of a managed level of capability by establishing another set of practices—called the generic practices belonging at the capability level 2—together with the specific practices. Metaphorically, think of these practices as those growing on top of a core set of practices, much like the peels of an onion.

At this stage, it is useful to highlight the naming conventions within the CMMI framework. Generic goals are abbreviated as GGs and are required to meet the objective of process institutionalization. There are five GGs corresponding to the five capability levels that can be defined for a process area. They are abbreviated as GG1 through GG5. GGs are achieved with the help of generic practices (GPs), or through effective alternative practices that meet the same objective—of fulfilling a GG. To build a capability level

2, GG2 needs to be fulfilled. And this is done through the ten GPs of GP2.1 through GP2.10. These 10 GPs are common across the three constellations and apply to all process areas of the CMMI. Hence, the goal is referred to as 'generic goal'.

Likewise, for GG3 to be fully institutionalized, two more GPs—GP3.1, Establish a defined process; and GP3.2, Collect improvement information—need to be rendered into the process design along with the ten practices that institutionalize GG2. For GG4, two additional GPs—GP4.1, Establish quality objectives; and GP4.2, Stabilize sub-process performance—need to be rendered over the GG3 capability. Finally, for GG5 to be fully institutionalized, GP5.1 (Ensure continuous process improvement) and GP5.2 (Correct root causes of problems) need to be rendered over the GG4 capability.

Author's Musing

Staged or continuous or maybe a combination approach, where you borrow a little of the staged ideas and a little from the continuous and derive benefits from both, should make for an optimal process improvement program.

Characteristics of a Capability Level 1 Process Area

When the specific goals of a process area alone are fulfilled, the process area is known to operate at a capability level 1 or at the *performed level*. At the performed level, the process is only capable of performing the specific practices required to fulfill the specific goals. We have seen that when the process area is incompletely rendered (or when a specific goal fails to meet the intended rigor of practice), the process capability of the process area is said to be incomplete or at level 0. The notion of individual process areas having a unique, *but flexible* capability level is a concept from the continuous representation.

A mere enabling of a capability level 1 or achievement of specific goals does not make for an enduring or a lasting process. However, practices contained at the level 1 establish the required understanding by bringing the process area into organizational focus. Therefore a capability level 1 process area brings the overall organizational maturity down by one level, at which it belongs in the staged representation. For example, if a process area categorized under maturity level 4 displays a level 1 capability, then the maximum organizational maturity that can be established is a level 3 provided the rest of the process areas adhere to the requirements of the CMMI. We will explore this further in subsequent chapters.

Author's Musing

A capability level 1 process area has fewer activities to perform, and therefore fewer virtues.

Characteristics of a Capability Level 2 Process Area

Once the process area has demonstrated specific practices with specific goal fulfillment, it now has an ability to grow the practices in rigor by employing the institutionalization or the generic practices. Process areas begin to grow in capability levels as the generic practices are institutionalized and get established into the process. After the attainment of capability level 1, the next logical evolutionary step for a process area is to render a capability level 2 into the process design. This is done using the ten generic practices as follows:

GP2.1 **Establish an Organizational Policy**

Establish and maintain an organizational policy for planning and performing the process.

GP2.2 **Plan the Process**

Establish and maintain the plan for performing the process.

GP2.3 **Provide Resources**

Provide adequate resources for performing the process, developing the work products, and providing the services of the process.

GP2.4 **Assign Responsibility**

Assign responsibility and authority for performing the process, developing the work products, and providing the services of the process.

GP2.5 **Train People**

Train the people performing or supporting the process as needed.

GP2.6 **Manage Configurations**

Place designated work products of the process under appropriate levels of control.

GP2.7 **Identify and Involve Relevant Stakeholders**

Identify and involve the relevant stakeholders of the process as planned.

GP2.8 **Monitor and Control the Process**

Monitor and control the process against the plan for performing the process and take appropriate corrective action.

GP2.9 **Objectively Evaluate Adherence**

Objectively evaluate adherence of the process against its process description, standards, and procedures, and address noncompliance.

GP2.10 **Review Status with Higher Level Management**

Review the activities, status, and results of the process with higher level management and resolve issues.

The most important design feature governing the CMMI model is that this generic practices template repeats itself across all three constellations for each process area. When these ten generic practices are incorporated into a single process area, it acquires a new capability level. The capability at which the process area begins to operate is called the *managed level* or *level 2*.

It is important to take note of what happens to the organizational maturity. In the continuous representation, as observed earlier, the notion of organizational maturity is only incidental and inferential:

it is not something that the model aims to achieve explicitly. The only reason for engaging in process improvement with the continuous representation is to enhance the capability of a process area. However, the equivalent organizational maturity based on the capability profile displayed by process areas operating at capability level 2 can be inferred as follows by reviewing the staged representation.

To achieve an organizational maturity level 2, the staged representation groups the following seven process areas of the CMMI-DEV into a cluster of process areas operating at capability level 2 resulting in an evolutionary plateau where the process begins to operate as a managed level. The seven process areas belonging to the level 2 maturity in the CMMI-DEV are as follows:

Requirements Management (REQM)
Project Planning (PP)
Project Monitoring and Control (PMC)
Supplier Agreement Management (SAM)
Measurement and Analysis (MA)
Process and Product Quality Assurance (PPQA)
Configuration Management (CM)

These process areas have to operate at capability level 2 by design in the staged representation. And in doing so, maturity level 2 is realized. The same idea is extended in the case of continuous representation in, what is called as, *equivalent staging*. In equivalent staging, when the above seven process areas in the continuous representation establish the ten generic practices GP2.1 through GP2.10, a new capability level at level 2 or the managed capability level for these individual process areas is rendered. As a cluster, they build an equivalent organizational maturity level for the organizational process at maturity level 2 or the managed level. The point to note is that there may be other process areas operating at different capability levels. For purposes of discussion at the moment, their capability levels are inconsequential. The only thing that matters is that the above seven process areas of the CMMI-DEV continuous representation need to establish a capability level 2 or the managed level. In the context of CMMI-ACQ, the nine process areas belonging to maturity level 2 need to operate at capability level 2. They are as follows:

Requirements Management (REQM)
Project Planning (PP)
Project Monitoring and Control (PMC)
Agreement Management (AM)
Solicitation and Supplier Agreement Development (SSAD)
Measurement and Analysis (MA)
Process and Product Quality Assurance (PPQA)
Configuration Management (CM)
Acquisition Requirements Development (ARD)

Similarly, in the context of CMMI-SVC, the eight process areas belonging to maturity level 2 need to operate at capability level 2. The eight process areas in the CMMI-SVC are as follows:

Requirements Management (REQM)
Project Planning (PP)[4]
Project Monitoring and Control (PMC)[5]
Supplier Agreement Management (SAM)
Service Delivery (SD)
Measurement and Analysis (MA)
Process and Product Quality Assurance (PPQA)
Configuration Management (CM)

From what has been discussed so far, one can take note of the following phrases and their definitions:

Definition: Organizational Maturity
The extent to which an organization has explicitly and consistently deployed processes that are documented, managed, measured, controlled and continually improved. Organizational maturity may be measured with appraisals.

Definition: Process Capability
The range of expected results that can be achieved by following a process.

Characteristics of a Capability Level 3 Process Area

By enabling a capability level 2 rigor for the process areas at the managed level of process maturity, the design of the CMMI framework and architecture ensures continuity of purpose, both among practices of the level 2 process areas and at the next level of maturity—called the defined process. Process definition addressing the intent of process areas contained in the three common categories of process management, project management and support are rendered together with engineering category while dealing with CMMI-DEV constellation; acquisition category while dealing with CMMI-ACQ constellation; and service establishment and delivery category process areas while dealing with CMMI-SVC constellation.

Within the continuous representation of all three CMMI constellations, process areas are organized into four categories. A significant difference between the ways, the staged and the continuous representations treat process improvement is a mechanism enabled by the continuous representation that permits a single process area to improve its individual process capability up to the optimizing level. The principal difference from a process improvement viewpoint is that within the continuous representation, such improvements can be rendered along two dimensions. At an organizational level, the purpose of process improvement is to establish overall process maturity. And as it applies to individual process areas, the purpose of process improvement is to establish process capability.

---

[4] Version 1.3 of the CMMI-SVC constellation renames this process area as "Work Planning".

[5] Version 1.3 of the CMMI-SVC constellation renames this process area as "Work Monitoring and Control".

After enabling a capability level 2 for the process areas belonging to maturity level 2, it is now possible to channel this capability toward a new dimension using two generic practices at capability level 3.

GP 3.1 Establish a Defined Process

Establish and maintain the description of a defined process.

GP 3.2 Collect Improvement Information

Collect work products, measures, measurement results, and improvement information derived from planning and performing the process to support the future use and improvement of the organization's processes and process assets.

These generic practices ensure that the constellation-specific process areas belonging to the maturity level 2 establish a definition for themselves along with an ability to continuously improve the characteristics of the practices. In doing so, the two generic practices GP3.1 and GP3.2 help in the *institutionalization of a defined process*, thus achieving generic goal 3—institutionalize a defined process.

The core of the CMMI-DEV practices with strong engineering and process orientation can be rendered through effective process management and support practices. For the organizational process to reach a new evolutionary plateau at the defined level, the following 11 process areas require to be defined into the process infrastructure with a defined or level 3 capability for each one of them:

Requirements Development (RD)
Technical Solution (TS)
Product Integration (PI)
Verification (VER)
Validation (VAL)
Organizational Process Focus (OPF)
Organizational Process Definition + IPPD (OPD+IPPD)
Organizational Training (OT)
Integrated Project Management + IPPD (IPM+IPPD)[6]
Risk Management (RSKM)
Decision Analysis and Resolution (DAR)

In the context of CMMI-ACQ, the nine process areas belonging to maturity level 3 need to operate at capability level 3. The nine process areas in the CMMI-ACQ are as follows:

Acquisition Technical Management (ATM)
Acquisition Verification (AVER)
Acquisition Validation (AVAL)
Organizational Process Focus (OPF)
Organizational Process Definition (OPD)

[6] Version 1.3 of the CMMI-SVC constellation renames this process area as "Integrated Work Management".

Organizational Training (OT)

Integrated Project Management (IPM)

Risk Management (RSKM)

Decision Analysis and Resolution (DAR)

Similarly, in the context of CMMI-SVC, the 12 process areas belonging to maturity level 3 need to operate at capability level 3. The 12 process areas in the CMMI-SVC are as follows:

Service System Development (SSD—An Addition)

Service System Transition (SST)

Strategic Service Management (STSM)

Incident Resolution and Prevention (IRP)

Organizational Process Focus (OPF)

Organizational Process Definition (OPD)

Organizational Training (OT)

Integrated Project Management (IPM)

Risk Management (RSKM)

Service Continuity (SCON)

Capacity and Availability Management (CAM)

Decision Analysis and Resolution (DAR)

When the above process areas are institutionalized at a capability level 3, together with the constellation-specific level 2 process areas, a *defined maturity* or *level* 3 process is established. Within the notion of the staged representation of the CMMI-DEV, the defined maturity results if and only if all of the 18 process areas of the CMMI-DEV constellation have a level 3 capability. In the CMMI-ACQ, the defined maturity results if and only if all the 18 process areas of this constellation have a level 3 capability, and in the CMMI-SVC if and only if the 20 process areas of this constellation have a level 3 capability.

The same holds true even in case of the continuous representation with an equivalent staging of the process area profile. However, the continuous representation permits the organization to focus only on these 18 process areas of the CMMI-DEV, for instance, and to increase the individual process capabilities of the process areas further up, to a level 4 or the *quantitatively managed* level of capability or even beyond, to the level 5 capability or the *optimizing level*. Increasing the individual process capabilities beyond the level 3, up to level 5, is not explicit in the way in which the staged representation is rendered. The same effect can be had, however, by enabling the level 4 and level 5 capabilities for process areas. We will explore these in the remainder of this chapter.

Early indications of the likely changes to the CMMI in version 1.3 are that capability levels 4 and 5 will be removed from the continuous representation. Nevertheless, the interpretations offered in this book under the descriptions for capability levels 4 and 5 are absolutely critical if an organization would like to sustain high process maturity. In order to align with the future version of the CMMI which is work-in-progress at the time of writing this book, it might be useful to understand capability levels 4 and 5 as one of the several ways for ensuring–**'how a process area would demonstrate a high maturity measurement and analysis capability'**. Interpretations offered under capability levels 4 and 5 must be viewed in context of high maturity considerations even though the CMMI continuous representation is likely to bring such practices within the scope of high maturity process areas. We shall now understand the characteristics of high capability process areas or, how to build a high maturity measurement and analysis capability for a process area.

AUTHOR'S MUSING

Even though version 1.3 of the CMMI constellations might eliminate the requirement for a process area to operate beyond capability level 3, interpretations found in this book describing such higher capability manifestations of a process area are extremely important to understand how the transition from a level 3 process maturity to the higher process maturity of Quantitative Management and Optimizing levels are made. This book retains capability level 4 and 5 interpretations and descriptions for process areas since the author believes that all high process maturity transition must translate into rendering process areas at their highest capability. Keeping this perspective in mind, the reader should review such material as essential for enabling high maturity measurement and analysis capability.

Characteristics of a Capability Level 4 Process Area[7]

In the continuous representation, enabling a level 4 process capability for a process area is both an engineering and management decision governed by good professional judgment. More than that, a strong customer emphasis driven by return-on-investment studies, dictated by what to measure and how to render the critical-to-X factors, where X could be quality, cost, scope and time, is important. In recent times, 'critical-to-value' and 'critical-to-performance' factors are also in vogue within the software services paradigm.

The two generic practices that help the defined process capability to grow and assume a 'quantitatively managed' capability for a process area are as follows:

GP4.1 **Establish Quantitative Objectives for the Process**

Establish and maintain quantitative objectives for the process that address quality and process performance based on customer needs and business objectives.

GP4.2 **Stabilize Sub-process Performance**

Stabilize the performance of one or more sub-processes to determine the ability of the process to achieve the established quantitative quality and process-performance objectives.

[7] CMMI V1.3 will no longer feature capability level 4; it will only have three levels in both the staged and continuous representations. However, interpretations offered in this book for process areas which must improve institutionalization rigor described under capability levels 4 and 5 are extremely valuable to sustain high maturity measurement and analysis capability. The reader is advised to review these interpretations from such a perspective.

It is instructive to note that it is not always necessary nor is it recommended to render every process area at a capability level 4. There have to be strong business justifications along with the need to control the basic behavior of a process based on a study of the outcomes from process execution. A good way to know if we are getting anywhere by enabling a level 4 capability is to gain an insight into what the overall cost-of-poor-quality is, through practicing a level 4 process. The cost-of-poor-quality metric helps to keep a tab on the cost of rework and the rework effort.

By institutionalizing quantitative management of the process, the two generic practices GP4.1 and GP4.2 enable the realization of generic goal 4 or *institutionalize a quantitatively managed process.*

It is here that the two representations of the staged and continuous tend to converge. Common to all three constellations of CMMI-DEV, CMMI-ACQ and CMMI-SVC, the same capability level 4 effects can be had if the two process areas belonging at the organizational maturity level 4 are enabled. They are as follows:

Organizational Process Performance (OPP)

Quantitative Project Management (QPM)

Specific practices of these two process areas, to a great degree, establish the basis for institutionalizing the generic practices GP4.1 and GP4.2. In a sense, the level 4 process areas of the staged representation can only be applied to the process area practices defining the level 2 and level 3 organizational maturity levels. A point worth noting is that the specific practices of both Organizational Process Performance and Quantitative Project Management cannot stand on their own in isolation. Specific practices of these process areas have to be applied to other lower-maturity process areas that offer the maximum possibility and applicability for establishing what is critical-to-X from the customer's point of view.

Once a solid foundation of quantitative understanding of the process characteristic is established, it is useful to explore the possibility of enhancing the process capability to an 'optimizing level' in the continuous representation.

Characteristics of a Capability Level 5 Process Area[8]

At the optimizing level of process capability, a stable metric for cost-of-poor-quality can be used to identify and estimate the extent to which special causes of variation have been minimized. Ideally, this cost should be zero. However, in reality, it can never be so, as long as you factor for rework effort. Customers almost always change their requirements contributing to rework effort.

Based on a sound understanding of what the process is capable of delivering, common causes of variation can be analyzed to identify potential opportunities within the process that can help reduce the overall cost-of-quality. Effective audits, peer reviews and process appraisals can help in the study of root causes of problems or process variations. A capability level 5 process knows enough about process

8 CMMI V1.3 will no longer feature capability level 5; it will only have three levels in both the staged and continuous representations. However, interpretations offered in this book for process areas which must improve institutionalization rigor described under capability levels 4 and 5 are extremely valuable to sustain high maturity measurement and analysis capability. The reader is advised to review these interpretations from such a perspective.

discontinuities even before they occur by establishing a well-compiled list of common causes of process variation.

It is needless to emphasize that the law of diminishing returns begins to apply to the investments made for process improvements. Meaning, the *voice-of-process (VOP)* (process rigor) becomes more capable than the *voice-of-customer (VOC)* (customer expectations or critical-to-quality parameters). There has to be a strong management thrust to study the potential payoffs for keeping the rigor of execution so tight when there are no customer mandates justifying or backing such decisions. Besides, such process rigor cannot be justified to apply across all projects in execution. This calls for obvious overheads with respect to data stratification and analysis based on project clustering or for specific process patterns. Process specialists must explore the benefits of collecting data and metrics specific to such projects while maintaining them separate from the rest of the projects.

The generic practices that help establish a level 5 capability for a process area are as follows:

GP5.1 Ensure Continuous Process Improvement

Ensure continuous improvement of the process in fulfilling the relevant business objectives of the organization.

GP5.2 Correct Root Causes of Problems

Identify and correct the root causes of defects and other problems in the process.

These generic practices are best institutionalized by using the specific practices of the level 5 process areas belonging to the staged representation. Common to the three constellations of CMMI-DEV, CMMI-ACQ and CMMI-SVC are the level 5 process areas:

Organizational Innovation and Deployment (OID)

Causal Analysis and Resolution (CAR)

It is very clear from the above discussion that process areas have a natural tendency to scale up (or down) their individual capability levels with every enablement (or a backward transition) to the overall organizational maturity.

Therefore the approach adopted in this book will explain the basic characteristics of the process area by offering an explanation as to what the specific practices mean and their interpretation along the five capability levels wherever such a rigor is possible to establish.

Author's Musing

A CL 5 or CL 4 process area does not necessarily mean that it is better institutionalized than a CL 3 process area. But most definitely, a CL 3 process area is better institutionalized than a CL 2 or a CL 1 process area.

The Road Ahead

This book addresses the needs of a broad audience: systems developers, software developers, managers and practitioners of the software engineering or systems engineering disciplines in development, acquisition and services environments. We will explore the conditions that must exist to motivate process improvement, and the role of the three CMMI constellations in this context.

Within the context of the CMMI, systems engineering refers to domain engineering. CMMI is a framework that addresses both the software and systems engineering aspects of development, with a specific focus on product development. The distinction between software and systems is very sketchy, with each discipline depending upon the other for optimal execution. Software development initiatives have had a chronic problem in dealing with cost overruns, schedule slippage and failure to achieve performance objectives, with every initiative asking for better quality, faster execution and cheaper costs. But, how does one get the better, faster, cheaper combination without understanding how this can be done?

Since a good portion of the CMMI can be committed to memory, there is a greater chance that executing a process using the CMMI framework becomes more of a *behavioral change* than a symptomatic treatment of the problem. It is useful to note that what can be committed to memory, and executed from off a cognitive map, tends to have a minimal variation. This feature of the CMMI, where one can commit about 80 to 90 per cent of the framework to memory, is a very important attribute of the framework itself, which helps in minimizing or reducing variation in execution outcomes. In this book, we will explore a few mnemonics that will help the reader to internalize the concepts of the CMMI. There is a greater probability that in doing so, process improvements will become more of a behavioral change in individuals who use the process to minimize variation.

Author's Musing

While processing logical information, the three entities that come into play are input, output and processing. Variation in output (which is what causes defects in software) can be minimized if and only if the input has acceptable degrees of variation within a tolerance that governs the input property.

Processing can then address how these controlled inputs are transformed consistently to get controlled outputs. In order to keep output variation within tolerable limits, rendering improvements to processing or the manner in which execution is rendered on controlled inputs becomes the focus. Process engineering involves establishing such an understanding, of how the process should be optimized and made efficient in order to ensure that given low variation to input parameters, output quality becomes predictable.

Within the CMMI, there are two approaches that *process improvements* can take: a staged approach or a continuous approach. The staged approach symbolizes the legacy that is attributed to the reference source model of Software CMM, which advocated methodical and evolutionary growth of process capability across five maturity levels.

We will digress for a moment here, and summarize the common-sense approach adopted by the CMMI to build process capability using the CMMI. In all three constellations of the CMMI, there are five maturity levels for the process and, across these levels, practices are organized into what is known as process areas. A process area is a collection of practices that help to institutionalize and implement a certain aspect of the process, for example, Project Planning or Configuration Management, and so on. Process areas help in managing a process by gradually creating a discipline for software development, acquisition or services. At the level 2, process areas help to establish a fundamental process discipline through effective project management. Practices that establish the focus for improvement at level 2 have a project management orientation. Mastering the practices at the level 2 process maturity ensures a foundation of management practices, wherein repeatability of the process ensures increasing the probability of success in execution.

At level 3, the CMMI constellations focus on enabling a process definition to manage the engineering, acquisition or service establishment and delivery of software. Practices belonging to Organization Process Focus and Organization Process Definition help to organize a basic approach for software development with the CMMI-DEV, for acquisition with CMMI-ACQ and for services with CMMI-SVC by defining a process life cycle. The process life cycle serves the purpose of establishing a standard development framework at the organizational level and projects are managed according to a tailored project life cycle based on this Organizational Process Definition to accommodate specific project characteristics and constraints of operation. Project Planning and project tracking practices at the level 2 helps manage the tailored process using Integrated Project Management process areas. Emphasis on minimizing variation in execution outcomes is rendered by building a common understanding and orientation for practitioners on both the process and the domains of engineering with Organizational Training. To ensure collaboration between engineering and management activities leading to the development of dependable software solutions and services, practices belonging to the engineering category (CMMI-DEV), acquisition category (CMMI-ACQ) and the service establishment and delivery category (CMMI-SVC) enable establishing a shared vision on project objectives. Practices belonging to Verification and Validation (CMMI-DEV) are used to ensure objectivity in assessing work product quality.

Now that a basic process definition has been rendered, improvements to it could be based on the practitioner's experiences gained from iterating and using the defined process. Quantitative management of the process is based on identifying the critical performance characteristics on the basis of both the process and product parameters. Practices of Organizational Process Performance help to manage the quality of the defined process, which directly correlates to product/service quality, and practices of Quantitative Project Management help in establishing process performance goals and process capability baselines. Organizational Process Performance builds on top of good Integrated Project Management, engineering, services and acquisition practices depending upon the constellation.

At this stage, the process is better able to control or address change management using a development framework which can be continually improved using continuous process improvement. The process areas of OID and CAR help to deal with the issues related to change management.

The question, *Should we always go one step at time in a staged progression or can we skip levels?*, gets answered with the continuous CMMI representation, which offers a flexible adoption of practices depending upon the process requirements. By organizing the process areas into four categories, the focus of process improvement shifts to address practices belonging to these constellation-specific categories. The sequence of process improvement is not specified. The basic philosophy of continuous representation is to improve the capability levels of individual process areas; organizational maturity is only incidental. The flexibility which continuous representation offers is with the degree of detail to which practices within a process area are developed. Process areas are therefore depicted as a profile of individual process area capabilities. The basic assumption that continuous representation makes is that process areas are independent and that they can move up or down their capability levels pretty much on their own. This, we know, is not quite the case with the staged representation. Process areas in the staged representation are interdependent upon each other and work as a group to establish organizational maturity.

To a large degree, at least till process areas reach a capability level of 3 or defined capability, this assumption of independence surrounding process area capability is theoretically correct, but not practically so. It is only reasonable to the extent that the fundamental objective of any worthwhile process improvement program is to have a minimum organizational maturity target of 3. At this level, a requirement as per the CMMI model is that the minimum capability level of the required process areas must be 3 or at the defined capability level. This qualifier is quite reasonable since at an organizational maturity of level 2, the constellation-specific process areas by themselves add very little value, if any. It is only when the process areas at the maturity level 3 are also institutionalized that the process program has any value. With this qualifier in place, it is now reasonable to explore the *independence* of process areas in the context of improving process area capability. Not every process area can establish quantitative management, nor is it required to.[9] Only those process areas which lend themselves well to quantitative understanding based on a valid reason to conduct a critical-to-X study—where X can be any of the known project constraints such as cost, quality, scope or time—need be defined for quantitative analysis. Therefore, the practicality of establishing process area capability independent of the rest of the process areas is possible only after a minimum capability of level 3, or the defined capability, is established.

The rendering of process area capability profile takes place along two dimensions. The degree of implementation detail which is represented along the Y-axis determines the capability level which addresses the question—*how well do we want a process area to perform?* Answering this question provides an explanation that demonstrates the richness or a higher capability level for a process area. The process areas are laid out along the X-axis as illustrated in Figure 1.2.[10]

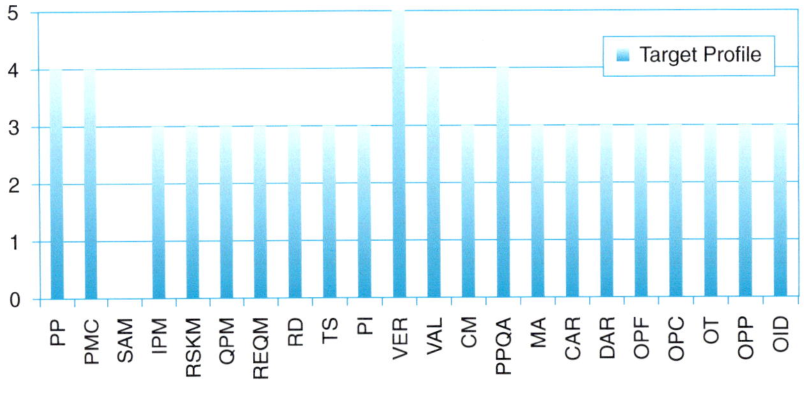

Fig. 1.2 An Example Target Profile which the Units Must Meet

Source: Adapted from SITARA Process JewelBox™ © SITARA Technologies Pvt. Ltd. 2002 with permission

[9] This could probably be one of the reasons why version 1.3 of the CMMI constellations has removed the requirements for capability levels 4 and 5 in the continuous representation.

[10] Since the continuous representation eliminates the requirements for higher capability process areas in version 1.3, a target profile featuring process areas manifesting a capability level beyond level 3 will not hold any relevance. In which case, the whole notion of a target profile and its relevance would become redundant.

Just as a higher-maturity level builds on top of a lower-maturity process, the capability levels for a process area also grow on top of the previous capability levels. Capability levels are defined in what is known as the generic goal. Capability level 1 is rendered when generic goal 1, stated as *Achieve Specific Goals*, is fulfilled. Generic goals themselves are achieved when the generic practices related to these goals are institutionalized. In the case of capability level 1, there is only one generic practice, called the GP1.1, perform specific practices, which needs to be fulfilled. Achieving specific goals of a process area would therefore establish a capability level 1 for a process area. In order to achieve a structural congruence within the CMMI, specific goals are rendered with the help of specific practices, which, as the name suggests, are specific to a process area and work the discipline advocated by the process area into the design of the process. The purpose behind the specific practices can be fulfilled equally well with the use of alternative practices which would meet the same intent in letter and spirit.

Along the lines of what will be described in later chapters when we deal with the CMMI process areas, it is recommended for the process program to conceive and come up with as many alternative ways of achieving the same intent behind the specific practices. The power behind both making a practice applicable to the organizational context (within known project constraints) and making the objectives behind process improvement meaningful to the organization is to ensure that alternative practices are conceived to fit the demands and challenges of customer needs with a well-serving organizational process. The role played by the process engineering group in ensuring that practices followed have a certain organizational relevance is very important. The purpose of having a process engineering group is also to ensure that both the best and the worst practices are brought to surface periodically and are evaluated for applicability across the organization. Process improvement must also take on a holistic view. Overemphasizing improvements to the software process alone or to the systems process alone, without commensurate changes to the way people interact with each other in the system, will make for a lopsided process improvement program.

With reference to Figure 1.3, if the key premise is to ensure that process improvement becomes a core competency, then the three interacting parts to this system—people, process and technology—as a triad must focus on a holistic improvement as a system. A well-managed change initiative ought to consider improvements to all three of the above system components, while taking note of the significance

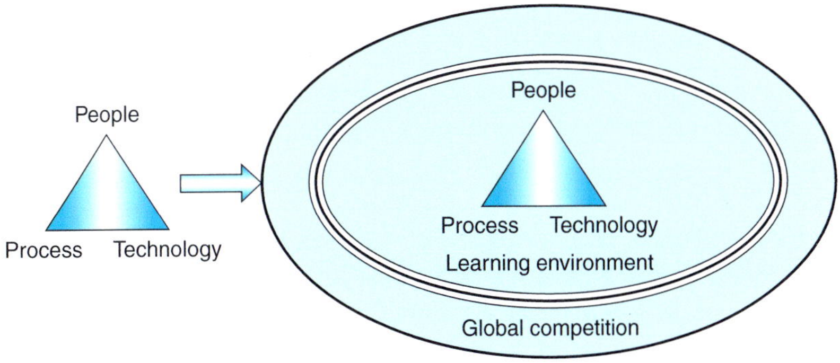

Fig. 1.3 People–Process–Technology Triad

Source: Adapted from People Capability Maturity Model Carnegie Mellon University [1995] with permission of creating a learning environment as the necessary compeller within global competition. Productivity improvement makes sense only when equal emphasis is placed on all three. Here again, an overemphasis on improvements to just any one of them without suitable adjustments to the other two will yield a lopsided change management program with poor gains or return on investment.

While improvements to the process is a high leverage option, a useful thought to bear in mind is that in this very dynamic systemic interplay, the only learning component is provided by the people who define and use the process. For an interested reader, the People, CMM is a framework that can be explored further to understand what it takes to build a nurturing environment where people are valued for the knowledge and skills they possess. An environment that is supportive and conducive to learning promotes competency development. Using the People, CMM practices together with the practices of the CMMI helps to build a much stronger process improvement program [Curtis 2002] [Nandyal 2003].

CMMI-DEV is a model which enables such a systemic view to render process improvements to both systems and software engineering while offering a strong humanistic touch through the specific practices of Integrated Product and Process Development. CMMI-ACQ is a model that integrates bodies of knowledge essential for an acquirer. CMMI-SVC model provides guidance for the application of CMMI best practices by the service provider organization.

We will digress here a bit to understand metaphorically, the basic motivation for process improvement, which is to reduce and minimize the impact of variation in execution outcomes—by using a defined process with a non-software example.

If I am told to park my car in a parking lot between two parking lines and to repeat this process a few times, the probability that I will be able to consistently park my car in the same manner and demonstrate this capability is very low if the number of iterations is not increased significantly. When the number of iterations is increased significantly, then the probability of my parking the car between the two parking lines comes closer to 1, limited only by my own intrinsic abilities to repeat this task—the common cause variation. Once my natural capability limits tend to stabilize and demonstrate a capability that is far superior to the parking limits established, there is a great possibility that I would be in a position to park my car even if the parking line limits are narrowed, thereby establishing a new capability with a much lower degree of variation in execution outcomes. If a completely new execution outcome is required, which is more aggressive than the established parking line limits, then the only known solution is to change *me*—the driver! This is because I have reached my maximum tolerance limits, based on my own intrinsic abilities.

Let us picture this one now: while I am parking my car, there is another car pulling in simultaneously from the opposite direction or from the side, without my knowing. Then, even though my natural capability to park my car between the parking lines is very high, this assignable cause or special cause brings about a variation in my ability to park (execution outcome) that exceeds the tolerance limits established by the parking lines. Under the influence of special causes of variation, I might park my car in a manner where I might be off limits from the parking lines to a very great extent. But then, if the parking lines themselves are not defined, then the whole notion of variation itself does not hold any meaning.

In the software development world, a basic definition of the software development process is a prerequisite before a study of variation is attempted. By defining a development process, we ensure that variation in execution outcomes is controlled, which is characterized as the *voice-of-process (VOP)*. *Repeated use* of the development process is the only known solution to ensure consistency, thereby minimizing variation. Once the process of execution attains a natural process capability, then the only way to establish a new zone of operation is by either changing the process or the technology that supports the process. In all three CMMI constellations, technology change management and process change management are addressed within two process areas called OID and CAR, which belong to the level 5 maturity.

In the chapters that follow, each process area will be interpreted and described with relevance to all three constellations of the CMMI, using the following template, wherever applicable. It is useful to note that the rigor required for establishing capability levels 4 and 5 is not justified for *all* process areas. Such process areas which may not have relevance beyond a capability level 3 rigor will not find an interpretation beyond level 3.

- How does a process area look when it operates at a capability level 1 (or the performed level)?
- How does a process area transform its capability when the transition to capability level 2 (or the managed level) is made?
- How does a process area transform its capability when the transition to capability level 3 (or the defined level) is made?
- How does a process area transform its capability when the transition to capability level 4 (or the quantitatively managed level) is made? Meaning: **How does a process area demonstrate a high maturity measurement and analysis capability?**
- How does a process area transform its capability when the transition to capability level 5 (or the optimizing level) is made? Meaning: **How does a process area demonstrate a high maturity measurement and analysis capability?**

The above template has been chosen to highlight the following facts:

- It is not possible to operate every project at a high capability because of the many influences including the law of diminishing returns, which shape the destiny of a project.
- It is very natural for a high-maturity process, such as a level 5 one, to have projects which are being executed in a level 1 mode. However, such instances would be an exception rather than the rule; the process improvement program would do *what is necessary* to put some controls on such projects and leave them alone as having a business reason for diktat. The obvious business reason is to stay in business long enough for it to be profitable! Besides, only a profitable company can afford to indulge in continuous process improvement and do it right.
- It is possible and is to be expected that a process area which is operating at capability level 5 today may, at the worst, slip to a capability level 3, the moment the innovation becomes *defined* into the organizational process, or if the causes of a variation have a *defined* process response that is now part of the organizational standard software process (OSSP). This ping-pong effect, which at SITARA, we term as *process harmonic*, where a capability level 5 process area that once demonstrated the institutionalization of capability level 5 generic practices, having gained control over minimizing the impact of special and common causes of variation through a process definition, transforms itself to a capability level 3, is an excellent recognition of the framework of the fact that continuous process improvement is *continuous* and that the only purpose it serves is *to learn and know more about things we did not know earlier*. Again, one need not be perturbed or feel a sense of remorse

because process area which operated at capability level 5 *slipped back* to a capability level 3. There is nothing like slipping back because as a result of this, the OSSP has only become rich. Adding richness and rigor to a development process ought to be perceived in the same manner as one might think about other competency development initiatives. Building robust process definitions at CL3 should help to sustain process capability.

Author's Musing

CMMI is not a magic wand! A discerning application of the framework should first explore whether an issue is a process issue, behavioral issue or a business issue and make use of the right tool to address the same. Business issues have to be resolved using a management process. Behavioral issues have to be addressed using an oversight process which ensures individual commitment.

2

Process Perspectives and Overview of the CMMI

AUTHOR'S MUSING

A positive return on investment (RoI) from a process improvement program is a 'given'; don't even bother about it. If you do not have a positive RoI, then something is wrong with the way you are engineering and managing your change initiative. What might be necessary for the sponsor to note is that even games meant for entertainment have rules and definitions on how to play them! Software initiatives are far too serious and hence some ground rules must be put in place in order to enable practitioners to establish a shared vision of the development context. Prescribing a process is nothing more than establishing such a shared vision.

INTRODUCTION

As programming complexities began to increase and program code size started to swell over the years, one could feel the need to establish a life cycle of some sort for a planned development of the product. This need for establishing a life cycle was felt as early as the 1960s. It has assumed a new terminology today—the *process model*, aptly coined to encompass its new role of being able to accommodate a continuously developing and market-driven approach to the product development effort. In the 1970s, recognition of synergy as the contributing factor for product development gave impetus to the idea of improving support systems as well as communication across product planning, requirements, design, integration and test phases. Then, in the 1980s information access and information sharing assumed greater importance with software development graduating from being a localized activity to being a *globally distributed* effort. Then in the 1990s with the release of Software CMM, the need for a structured development using a framework began to grab the attention of the industry. Since early 2000, such a model-based approach has grown to be widely accepted, with the Software CMM gaining recognition as the *de facto* industry reference for *excellence in software engineering*. The CMMI is a transformation of the Software CMM to include a process-driven system's engineering life cycle primarily for product development. For a practitioner who may not be well versed with the model-based approach to software and systems engineering, it would be useful to get a bird's-eye view of the principal messages contained in any good process model.

PRINCIPAL MESSAGE OF THE SOFTWARE CMM AND THE CMMI

Everything ought to start in chaos and degenerate into chaos if sufficient oversight and controls are not exercised. A process model must therefore break down complexity and organize practices as a cohesive set of internally congruent requirements with which to realize the goals of structured development. Since not every practice can be attempted at the same time, the model must introduce practices to streamline execution in an orderly manner. The fundamental place to start exercising control and oversight is on a project. A process model must contain practices with which project execution can be streamlined first. It is only after every project in execution has a consistent set of practices, with which successful execution can be demonstrated, should the model attempt streamlining execution from an organizational perspective. Since a process is not a one-size-fits-all, at the organizational level, the process must be capable of adapting itself to the requirements of a project. Such tailoring options must be exercised with adequate confidence only after gaining sufficient experience from repeated usage of a defined process. The necessary focus to build competencies to minimize variation ought to be supported at the organizational level. Only after sufficient experience is gained with the usage of a process can one attempt to quantify and establish realistic goals for process outcomes. Measurement and analysis of process parameters assumes greater significance in discerning causes of variation as being either assignable or common cause. At this stage, process control uses quantitative and statistical rigor to ensure adequate understanding of the mechanisms that must be designed in the process to minimize causes of variation. It is more likely to address assignable or special causes of process variation since process management will involve either an engineering work-around or a project management strategy to deal with the uncertainty. Once this stage is reached, it is likely that process performance objectives are limited to the competencies of those behind the process. Breakthrough performance with controlled insertion of either technology or process changes after studying pilot results is possible only after sufficient knowledge about the process capability is obtained.

CMMI refers to the cohesive set of internally congruent collection of practices with which to realize the goals of structured development as process area. Practices prescribe the implementation and institutionalization aspects of the goals of the process area. A group of process areas form an evolutionary plateau to determine the organizational maturity. Organizational maturity can be gauged on the basis of a range of values from 1 to 5, with 1 being the lowest level of maturity.

Level 1 process is called the initial or *ad hoc* process and is the default level to which processes will naturally decay into if sufficient care is not exercised to prevent process dilution. By instilling a fundamental process discipline through the practice of effective project management, a level 1 process begins to move away from repeating the same mistakes by enabling well-defined roles and responsibilities for individuals who take ownership of the process. The quality assurance function is established to own the process and to ensure availability of process support for engineering solutions. Configuration management is used to ensure that integrity of intermediate work products, leading up to the final product, and is maintained through effective and progressive tracking of their evolution. Projects use effective planning and tracking mechanisms to ensure that they have a consistent mechanism to manage constraints of operation. When using external sources to assist in developmental activities, subcontracts and suppliers are managed through practices defined using subcontract or supplier management. When practices in these categories establish a process discipline to a degree that is necessary and sufficient to support intelligent decision making, the process can be considered to have established a fundamental capability to repeat its successes. However, since the process is dependent upon the heroics of a few individuals, should the project characteristics or the constraints of operation change, then there is a good probability that successful delivery and realization of project objectives may not be achieved.

It is only after establishing a level 2 process maturity that a level 3 process can be realized. That is the philosophy in a staged model. Establishing process maturity is an evolutionary mechanism which takes place in progressive stages, step by step. For instance, in the CMMI-DEV constellation, the transition from a repeatable, *managed process* at level 2 to a *defined process* at level 3 is made possible with the creation of a *software/systems development framework* through a process definition *to enable engineering management*. This development framework is supported by an effective internal process infrastructure by articulating standards, procedures, templates, guidelines and a mechanism to tailor them depending upon the project's constraints of operation—cost, quality, scope or time. One of the most significant changes that get institutionalized in a level 3 process is a mechanism available for studying effectiveness of processes and improving upon them. An embodiment of this is a process engineering group (PEG)—a prerequisite for institutionalizing a level 3 process. The PEG is a group of technical and process specialists who review the strengths and opportunities for improvement of the process and institutionalize such improvements using process action teams. These teams establish appropriate action plans to internalize the corrective actions from process audits and process retrospectives. A significant focus is also provided to engineer the software solution using tailored life cycles which are driven by a development life cycle.

Establishing the necessary process definitions is the first step toward minimizing the impact of variation. Execution results and outcomes of execution are that much more predictable and consistent if everyone uses a common framework for developing software solutions. With such a development infrastructure in place, it is now possible to study the influences of assignable causes of variation that inhibit the true realization of process capability (and therefore process maturity). A level 4, process begins to collect data that are relevant to the project's constraint of operations resulting from project execution and establishes a control mechanism to quantitatively define the goals or targets for the critical processes that are in use. When execution outcomes deviate significantly from the norm, causal analysis to identify the assignable or root causes of variation are explored. A level 4 process also minimizes the impact of such special causes of variation on project execution using process retrospectives which study and analyze the underlying reasons.

After insulating the process against the assignable causes of process variation, the next step is to ensure that impact due to common causes of variation is minimized through effective defect prevention and corrective actions. A mechanism for continuous process improvement is put in place for effective change management using process and technology change management practices designed to minimize defects. While defect identification and reasons for process variation are studied at level 4, effective prevention steps using a process or technology solution is rendered in a level 5 process. Therefore, when the CMMI-DEV is viewed as a staged model, improvements to the process to build capability take place in a progressive, evolutionary manner—*one maturity level at a time*. These maturity level transitions are described best in Figure 2.1.

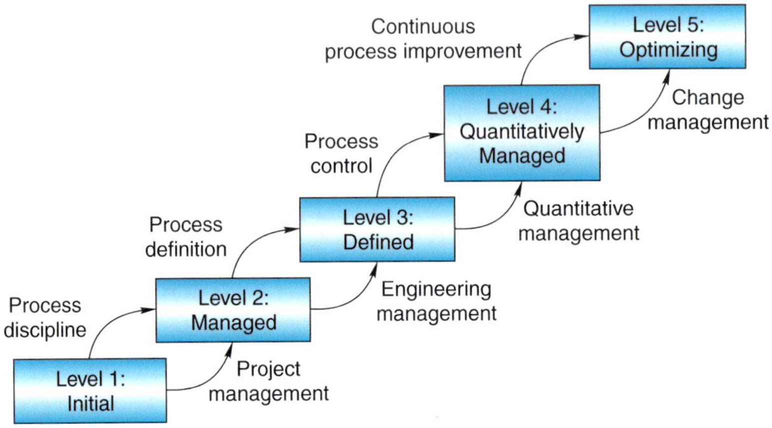

Fig. 2.1 Structure of the CMMI Version 1.2

Source: Adapted from Capability Maturity Model V1.1 Carnegie Mellon University [February 1993] with permission

We have understood thus far that in the staged representation of the CMMI maturity levels are transcended by fulfilling a group of mutually supportive process areas, and that in the continuous representation the emphasis is on improving categories such as process management, project management, support, engineering, acquisition and service establishment and delivery. Emphasizing improvements to the relevant categories and enhancing the capability of individual process areas is the fundamental governing characteristic in the continuous representation. We will now extend our understanding about the two CMMI representations, gained from Chapter 1, to the next level of detail. What follows is relevant to all the three constellations of CMMI.

The staged CMMI is organized into five maturity levels: *initial, managed, defined, quantitatively managed* and *optimizing*. Each maturity level is based on a group of process areas. These process areas have two types of goals: specific and generic. As the name suggests, specific goals are unique to a process area. Therefore the specific goals of, say the Requirements Management process area, are unique to this process area and do not repeat in, say the Project Planning process area or any other process area. Being specific to the process area, these goals govern the basic execution of the practices to support the intent or purpose behind the process area. The specific goals are fulfilled by meeting the intent of specific practices. Since specific practices are unique to a process area, they can also be looked upon as being the activities that must be performed to meet the purpose of a process area. In other words, specific practices help to fulfill the implementation objectives—represented in the specific goals (Figure 2.2).

Generic goals on the other hand are generic to all the process areas. Meaning, they repeat themselves, are common to every process area and help in institutionalizing the intent behind the process area across the organization. We have seen earlier that this intent is rendered through the institutionalization practices of what is called the 'generic practices'.

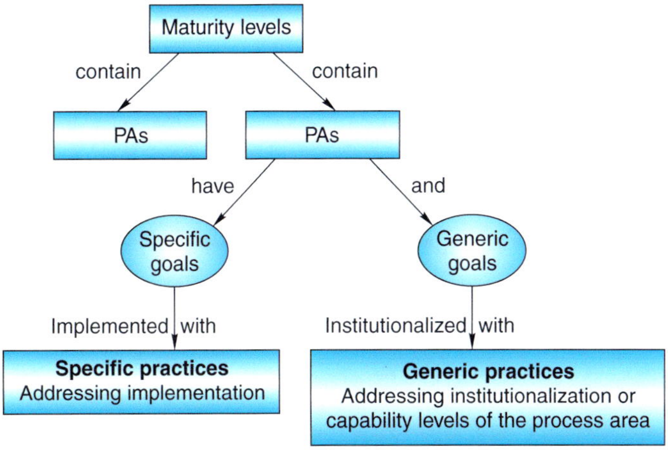

Fig. 2.2 Structure of the CMMI Staged Representation

Source: Adapted from Capability Maturity Model Integration V1.1 Carnegie Mellon University [March 2002] with permission

It is useful to point out a model feature here of the staged representation: the maximum expected capability of any process area in the *staged representation* is a defined level or capability level 3. Achieving a capability above a level 3 is neither expected nor is it a model requirement. This feature, wherein a process area attains a maximum capability of a level 3 *in its stable operating state*, is not an aberration as it might appear, and the reader might refer to the notion of *process harmonic* described in Chapter 1. The only generic goal that is applicable within the staged CMMI is GG2 for all process areas with a maturity level 2 scope and GG3 for all process areas beyond the maturity level 2 scope (levels 3–5). Each process area has only one generic goal for this reason, and theoretically, a process area is expected to operate either at a capability level 2 (for a maturity level 2) or at a capability level 3 (for all other maturity levels).

The continuous CMMI is also based on the same notions of organizing practices into process areas that have specific and generic goals, with specific goals addressing the unique characteristics of a process area and the generic goal addressing the institutionalization of the intent. The only distinction is that there are six potential dimensions in which an individual process area can operate. The default level is the capability level 0—or incomplete process capability. At this default level, practices of a process area are characterized as being chaotic and often *ad hoc* without adequate richness to demonstrate the satisfaction of even the specific goals, which are the most fundamental building blocks for any process area. The specific goals establish the basic purpose of a process area and are characterized by the minimal activities required to meet the intent of the process area. The specific practices of the process area help with the institutionalization of specific goals. In other words, they help in the structuring of the activities that have to be performed to support the intent and purpose behind the process area. Therefore, attainment of a capability level 1 is called *performed process capability*. Level 1 capability is rendered when generic goal 1 is fulfilled, meaning *all* the specific goals of a process area are fully supported with adequate practices. Think of these practices, which help to accomplish the intent of the specific goals, as *core practices*. These core practices are the base or foundation upon which the rest of the practices of a process area depend.

Metaphorically, envision the core practices as those resembling the *core of an onion*. Once the core practices are established, the institutionalization aspects of a process area can then become the focus. Enhancing the capability of the process area is akin to growing the *peels of an onion*. Attainment of a capability level 2 for a process area is possible only when the core of the process area is in place. Capability level 2 gets rendered when GG2 is institutionalized through the intent of the ten level 2 generic practices of GP2.1 through GP2.10, namely:

GP2.1 **Establish and maintain an organizational policy for planning and performing the process.**

GP2.2 **Establish and maintain the plan for performing the process.**

GP2.3 **Provide adequate resources for performing the process, developing the work products, and providing the services of the process.**

GP2.4 **Assign responsibility and authority for performing the process, developing the work products, and providing the services of the process.**

GP2.5 **Train the people performing or supporting the process as needed.**

GP2.6 **Place designated work products of the process under appropriate levels of control.**

GP2.7 **Identify and involve the relevant stakeholders of the process as planned.**

GP2.8 **Monitor and control the process against the plan for performing the process and take appropriate corrective action.**

GP2.9 **Objectively evaluate adherence of the process against its process description, standards, and procedures, and address noncompliance.**

GP2.10 **Review the activities, status and results of the process with higher level management and resolve issues.**

Institutionalization of the above ten generic practices is common to all process areas contained in the three constellations to result in a capability level 2 rigor.

After capability level 2 is established, a process area can grow in dimension to a capability level 3—*the defined capability level*—by fulfilling the intent behind the generic goal 3 by rendering generic practices GP3.1 and GP3.2. After a capability level 3 is established, a process area can potentially scale up to a capability level 4—*the quantitatively managed capability level*—by meeting the intent of generic practices GP4.1 and GP4.2, and further up to a capability level 5—*the optimizing capability level*—by meeting the intent of generic practices GP5.1 and GP5.2. It is not expected, nor is it justified, to place every process area at capability levels 4 or 5. It is not only expensive to do so but it is also harder to justify the reasons. Some process areas are greatly influenced by special causes or assignable causes of variation. Thus, minimizing the impact of such assignable or special causes of variation should be uppermost in mind when considering the scaling of the capability of a process area to level 4. Some examples of CMMI process areas that have this potential to reach a capability level 4 are as follows: Requirements Management, Requirements Development, Project Planning and Project Monitoring and Control. The other candidates are all of the example process areas that will be cited next for the capability level 5 (since capability level 5 can be grown only on top of an existing capability level 4).

Then, there are other process areas which are most influenced by common causes of variation, and insulating these influences through proper process design is something that should be explored in such cases. Some examples of process areas that have the potential for establishing a capability level 5 are as follows: Process and Product Quality Assurance, Verification, Validation, Technical Solution and product integration.

One of the most useful features of the CMMI is that a good 80–90 per cent of the CMMI framework can be committed to memory! This gives one the power to practice the CMMI almost naturally, without compromising on the CMMI requirements. It is useful to make a mention here that if an activity is executed almost as if it were second nature—from out of a cognitive map—*chances of having large degrees of variation in the execution outcome can be minimized.* It is only when such a degree of confidence is rendered within every practitioner that a process design can be termed as a true DFSS process.

From years of working with process design, it might be concluded that there are two essential requirements for any software process design to be called a DFSS software process. They are the following:

- The framework itself must support process improvement.
- The structure and the framework must fit in the memory as a cognitive map.

At SITARA, we call these requirements the sufficiency conditions for a process to qualify as a DFSS process. It is only when these two sufficiency conditions for a process design are met, can one guarantee minimal variation in its execution outcomes. The good news is that CMMI fulfills both these sufficiency conditions. We will explore mnemonics which will be helpful to build such a cognitive map of the CMMI framework in the mind, and it is almost a guarantee that one will be able to commit about 80–90 per cent of the CMMI framework to memory and execute process activities from this cognitive map.

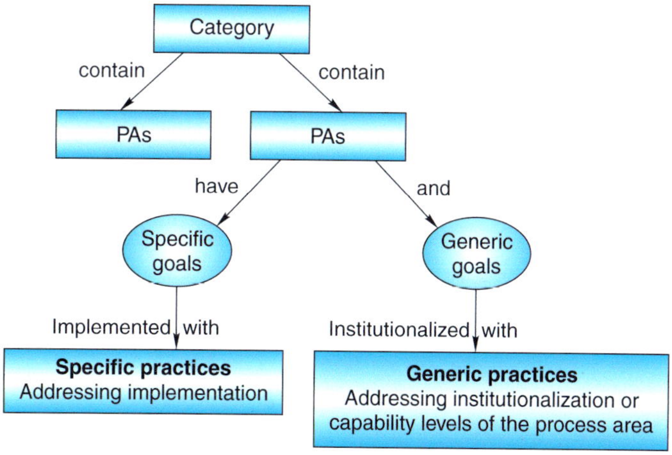

Fig. 2.3 Structure of the CMMI Continuous Representation

Source: Adapted from Capability Maturity Model Integration V1.1 Carnegie Mellon University [March 2002] with permission

Process area such as Requirements Management or Project Planning is said to be fulfilled when the goals supporting its purpose are satisfied. Goal satisfaction on a process area is rendered by ensuring that implementation and institutionalization are addressed in the process context. In the CMMI constellations, there are two types of goals—specific goal and generic goal. Specific goals address the implementation aspects of the CMMI and the generic goals address the institutionalization aspects of the process (Figure 2.3).

For example, let us consider Requirements Management of the CMMI-DEV constellation:

- The purpose of Requirements Management is to manage the requirements of the project's products and product components, and to identify inconsistencies between those requirements and the project's plans and work products.

This purpose is achieved with the following specific goal:

SG1: Manage Requirements

- Requirements are managed and inconsistencies with project plans and work products are identified.

The above specific goal is met if the intent behind the following practices is rendered in the process:

Specific Practices for Requirements Management

- Obtain an understanding of requirements
- Obtain commitment to requirements
- Manage requirement changes
- Maintain bidirectional traceability of requirements
- Identify inconsistencies between project work and requirements

Definition: Specific Goal
A specific goal applies to a process area and addresses the unique characteristics that describe what must be implemented to satisfy the process area.

Institutionalization aspects of a process area are the mechanisms that make the practice component a permanent feature of the process. There are five generic goals in the CMMI continuous representation—1 through 5—and each one of these serves a well-defined purpose to increase the capability levels for a process area. This is akin to enhancing the richness of practices of the process area based on improvement objectives. And we have seen what the five capability levels are, in Chapter 1.

Since improvement means different things to different organizations, it might help to answer the following questions:

- What are your business goals?
- How do you measure progress?

Since improvement must take on a long-term strategic view, it might help to answer the following questions:

- What is the expected impact on the bottom line?

- How will impact be measured?
- What is your current response to process improvement?

It would be worth your while to articulate responses to these questions before proceeding further. SITARA uses a standard questionnaire to evoke an organizational response to these critical questions which is released from the SITARA Process JewelBox™ in Appendix. Typically these are the answers (but not exhaustive) which we receive from the executive team consisting of the CEO and the leadership team during the executive planning session:

- What are your business goals?
- What is the expected impact on the bottom line?
  - To minimize the impact of rework and its effects on employee morale
  - To grow domain competencies and to be able to effectively manage customer expectations by proactively participating in problem definition and crafting of the solution
  - To ensure retention of the knowledge base within an infrastructure that helps to provide effective access to information, when needed by those who need it
  - To minimize impact of attrition to business risk by enabling shared understanding of the project among as many individuals using a medium of communication that is understood by all
  - To reduce the transition time and flatten the learning curve from one phase to another wherein project experiences of earlier phases are captured as lessons learnt or as best practices
  - With geographically separated teams: to offer a consistent, repeatable and uniform look and feel for the solutions irrespective of who does it or from which geographic location the service is provisioned—improve professionalism
  - We know that we have pockets of excellence. We would like to study the contributing factors to such excellence orientation and make it our general business response.
  - We would like to be better than the competition when it comes to ensuring speed of execution and quality of outputs
  - We would like to insulate, isolate, eliminate and minimize the impact of change on the basic business processes which form our core competency
  - To be excellence oriented at all times and improve our image in the customer's eye
  - To internalize external best practices without having to reinvent the wheel with maximum alignment to existing business practices in the organization
  - Where possible, we would like to do more for less with effective tool deployment and automation in order to reduce the boredom from executing monotonous tasks
  - To know how much of what is needed and ensure that we will be able to deliver on expectations
  - To be able to calibrate our process using acceptable process benchmarks such as the CMMI
  - To increase profitability by making conscious effort to improve return on investment by minimizing the cost of poor quality and cost of quality

- How do you measure progress?
- How will impact be measured?
    - We will conduct an initial assessment of our process, establish a road map for collective action and render the improvements after prioritizing the recommendations using our business goals
    - We know our current defect levels for our products; we should be able to set goals in order to minimize the defect density
    - Increase the importance of process compliance in the organization and ensure that there are near-zero process noncompliances; where necessary, we will study the number of waivers we have provided over a period of time
    - Conduct periodic audits of the process and ensure that audit reports are used in a healthy way—to tailor the process where it is genuinely felt
    - We must be able to see the growth of process assets and number of improvement suggestions being recommended over a period of time
    - Practitioners must feel that they are empowered to use the process framework to make the day-to-day changes that are so very crucial for our business success
    - We know we are making progress if the number of customer complaints come down; or the post-release defects is down by a significant percentage, which we can define based on our business constraints
    - We will track our process achievements using a target profile

The CMMI framework was created with the following design objectives:

- Integrate the source models, eliminate inconsistencies and reduce duplication
- Reduce the cost of implementing model-based process improvement
- Be sensitive to impact on legacy efforts

With the following perceived benefits:

- Efficient, effective assessment and improvement across multiple process disciplines
- Reduced training and assessment costs
- A common, integrated vision of improvement for all elements of an organization
- Integration of systems engineering and software environments for additional productivity and quality gains

We will formally capture the process areas of the three constellations of the CMMI both as a continuous and staged representation before we proceed with their interpretation.

The CMMI-DEV continuous representation is organized along four categories (Figurre 2.4):

- Process management
- Project management
- Engineering
- Support

CATEGORY	PROCESS AREAS
Process management	Organizational Process Focus Organizational Process Definition + IPPD Organizational Training Organizational Process Performance Organizational Innovation and Deployment
Project management	Project Planning Project Monitoring and Control Supplier Agreement Management Integrated Project Management + IPPD Risk Management Quantitative Project Management
Engineering	Requirements Management Requirements Development Technical Solution Product Integration Verification Validation
Support	Configuration Management Process and Product Quality Assurance Measurement and Analysis Decision Analysis and Resolution Causal Analysis and Resolution

Fig. 2.4 CMMI-DEV Continuous Representation

Source: Adapted from Capability Maturity Model Integration for Development V1.2 Carnegie Mellon University [August 2006] with permission

The CMMI-DEV staged representation is organized along five process maturity levels characterizing the process evolution (Figure 2.5):

- Level 1 or Initial Process Maturity
- Level 2 or Managed Process Maturity
- Level 3 or Defined Process Maturity
- Level 4 or Quantitatively Managed Process Maturity
- Level 5 or Optimizing Process Maturity

Level	Focus	Process areas	Quality, Predictability
5 Optimizing	***Continuous process improvement***	Organizational Innovation and Deployment Causal Analysis and Resolution	↑
4 Quantitatively Managed	***Quantitative management***	Organizational Process Performance Quantitative Project Management	
3 Defined	***Process standardization***	Requirements Development Technical Solution Product Integration Verification Validation Organizational Process Focus Organizational Process Definition +IPPD Organizational Training Integrated Project Management +IPPD Risk Management Decision Analysis and Resolution	
2 Managed	***Basic project management***	Requirements Management Project Planning Project Monitoring and Control Supplier Agreement Management Measurement and Analysis Process and Product Quality Assurance Configuration Management	
1 initial			Risk Rework

Fig. 2.5 CMMI-DEV Staged Representation

Source: Adapted from Capability Maturity Model Integration for Development V1.2 Carnegie Mellon University [August 2006] with permission

CMMI-DEV V1.2 Summary

CATEGORY	*L2*	*L3*	*L4*	*L5*	*Number of PAs*
Support	CM PPQA MA	DAR		CAR	(5 PAs)
Process Management		OPF OPD+IPPD OT	OPP	OID	(5 PAs)
Project Management	PP PMC	IPM+IPPD RSKM SAM	QPM		(6 PAs)

(Contd)

CATEGORY	*L2*	*L3*	*L4*	*L5*	*Number of PAs*
Engineering	REQM[1]	RD PI TS VER VAL			(6 PAs)

OVERVIEW OF THE CMMI-ACQ CONSTELLATION

Organizations must stick to their knitting if they have to sustain leadership in their designated core competencies.

In such situations, it is more likely that acquiring organizations should strike healthy relationships with suppliers who can augment their capabilities. Practices in the CMMI-ACQ constellation are designed to build a cohesive process to enable a network of competencies, wherein the acquiring organization leverages capabilities of supplier organizations. These practices are based on a common foundation of practices, called the CMMI Model Foundation (CMF), addressing process management, project management and support. The CMF is common to the three CMMI constellations of CMMI-DEV (development), CMMI-SVC (services) and CMMI-ACQ (acquisition). The 16 core process areas are the following: Organizational Process Focus, Organizational Process Definition, Organizational Training, Organizational Process Performance, Organizational Innovation and Deployment, Configuration Management, Measurement and Analysis, Process and Product Quality Assurance, Decision Analysis and Resolution, Causal Analysis and Resolution, Project Planning, Project Monitoring and Control, Requirements Management, Integrated Project Management, Risk Management and Quantitative Project Management.

CMMI-ACQ is a Constellation within the CMMI Framework

The practices contained in the process areas of the CMMI-ACQ constellation help to improve both the technical and business process reviews by building synergies between the acquiring organization and the supplying organization. Even though such synergistic relationships are expected to develop in both the acquiring and supplying organizations, from an appraisal perspective, institutionalization of the CMMI-ACQ practices applies to the 'acquisition organization' process and not to the 'supplier organization' process. So, when we deal with practices associated with say, Acquisition Verification or Acquisition Validation, the practices have to be interpreted in relationship to the acquiring organization and not to the supplying organization. However, building the necessary communication processes that help to establish good teamwork between the acquiring organization and the supplying organization holds the key to the successful implementation of the CMMI-ACQ constellation. With such mechanisms in place, it is possible to ensure that the synergies so developed between the acquiring organization and the supplying

[1] REQM is a project management category process area in version 1.3. Therefore, the number of process areas in the engineering category is 5 and the number of process areas in the project management category is 7 in version 1.3.

Category	Process areas
Process management	Organizational Process Focus (OPF) Organizational Process Definition (OPD) Organizational Training (OT) Organizational Process Performance (OPP) Organizational Innovation and Deployment (OID)
Project management	Project Planning (PP) Project Monitoring and Control (PMC) Integrated Project Management (IPM) Requirements Management (REQM) Risk Management (RSKM) Quantitative Project Management (QPM)
Acquisition	Acquisition Requirements Development (ARD) Acquisition Technical Management (ATM) Acquisition Verification (AVER) Acquisition Validation (AVAL) Agreement Management (AM) Solicitation and Supplier Agreement Development (SSAD)
Support	Configuration Management (CM) Process and Product Quality Assurance (PPQA) Measurement and Analysis (MA) Decision Analysis and Resolution (DAR) Causal Analysis and Resolution (CAR)

Fig. 2.6 CMMI-ACQ Continuous Representation

Source: Adapted from Capability Maturity Model Integration for Acquisition V1.2 Carnegie Mellon University [August 2007] with permission

organization is a positive and healthy insightful relationship, without it being an adversarial relationship based only on oversight. Under such circumstances, cooperation and coordination of activities leading to a predictable performance of the solution or product that is being developed for the end customer becomes possible by understanding the dependencies between the acquiring and supplying organizations.

The CMMI-ACQ constellation defines six areas where such cooperation and coordination is foreseen.

They are: Solicitation and Supplier Agreement Development, Agreement Management, Acquisition Requirements Development, Acquisition Technical Management, Acquisition Verification and Acquisition Validation. The most common acquirer process while dealing with suppliers must include mechanisms for sourcing suppliers, development and award of supplier agreements and managing the acquisition of capabilities. The six CMMI-ACQ process areas address the primary needs that enable a process-based solution to address such acquirer–supplier relationships. Such needs must include effective Requirements Management, Risk Management, Configuration Management, Verification and Validation, program integration and Project Planning. Requirements Management process area is assigned as a project management category process area of the CMMI-ACQ.

The CMMI-ACQ continuous representation is organized along four categories (Figure 2.6):

- Process Management
- Project Management

- Acquisition[2]
- Support

The CMMI-ACQ staged representation is organized along five process maturity levels characterizing the process evolution (Figure 2.7):

- Level 1 or Initial Process Maturity
- Level 2 or Managed Process Maturity
- Level 3 or Defined Process Maturity
- Level 4 or Quantitatively Managed Process Maturity
- Level 5 or Optimizing Process Maturity

Maturity level	Process areas
5 Optimizing	Causal Analysis and Resolution (CAR) Organizational Innovation and Deployment (OID)
4 Quantitatively Managed	Quantitative Project Management (QPM) Organizational Process Performance (OPP)
3 Defined	Organizational Process Focus (OPF) Organizational Process Definition (OPD) Organizational Training (OT) Integrated Project Management (IPM) Risk Management (RSKM) Acquisition Technical Management (ATM) Acquisition Verification (AVER) Acquisition Validation (AVAL) Decision Analysis and Resolution (DAR)
2 Managed	Acquisition Requirements Development (ARD) Agreement Management (AM) Project Planning (PP) Project Monitoring and Control (PMC) Requirements Management (REQM) Configuration Management (CM) Process and Product Quality Assurance (PPQA) Measurement and Analysis (MA) Solicitation and Supplier Agreement Development (SSAD)

Fig. 2.7 CMMI-ACQ Staged Representation

Source: Adapted from Capability Maturity Model Integration for Acquisition V1.2 Carnegie Mellon University [August 2007] with permission

[2] CMMI-ACQ Version 1.3 renames this category as Acquisition Engineering.

CMMI-ACQ V1.2 Summary

Category	***L2***	***L3***	***L4***	***L5***	***Number of PAs***
Support	CM PPQA MA	DAR		CAR	(5 PAs)
Process Management		OPF OPD OT	OPP	OID	(5 PAs)
Project Management	PP PMC **REQM**	IPM RSKM	QPM		(5 PAs) + REQM
Acquisition[3]	AM SSAD ARD	ATM AVER AVAL			(6 PAs)

OVERVIEW OF THE CMMI-SVC CONSTELLATION

CMMI-SVC has been written to cater to the needs of a diverse set of industry requirements. From small, through big, to enterprises across the oceans, all need to use the practices of the CMMI-SVC, making them appropriate to their needs and demands. Other initiatives involving Service Delivery and best practices such as IT Infrastructure Library (ITIL) might also need to be reused as appropriate to minimize overheads while institutionalizing CMMI-SVC practices. There is bound to be a clash of definitions and interpretations since both ITIL and CMMI-SVC are vying to dominate the service industry. But, both ITIL and CMMI-SVC provide best practices with which to promote a quality approach to *delivery services* and *achieving business effectiveness and efficiency*. Service is an intangible and non-storable product resulting from business execution.

Based on initial piloting results, even though the CMMI-SVC has emphasized its applicability to any service organization delivering services as varied as training, logistics, maintenance, refugee services, lawn care, book shelving, research, consulting, auditing, independent verification and validation, human resources, financial management, health care and IT services, *it might just be an exaggeration*. Only time will tell. Because, with a good portion of the CMMI-SVC based on 16 process areas of the CMMI Model Foundation (CMF), whose relevance and applicability were primarily intended for use with software and systems processes, broadening the scope of the seven CMMI-SVC process areas in a limitless manner is yet to be proven.

Like CMMI for Development (CMMI-DEV), the services constellation is a collection of best practices. Organizations must develop and improve processes related to delivering cost-effective services. Such delivery capability should also consider minimizing process overheads while juggling between

[3] CMMI-ACQ Version 1.3 renames this category as Acquisition Engineering. AM and SSAD are regrouped into the Project Management Category. The number of process areas in the Acquisition Engineering category are 4 and the Project Management Category has 8 process areas.

Maturity level	Process areas
Process management	Organizational Process Focus (OPF) Organizational Process Definition (OPD) Organizational Training (OT) Organizational Process Performance (OPP) Organizational Innovation and Deployment (OID)
Project management	Project Planning (PP) Project Monitoring and Control (PMC) Supplier Agreement Management (SAM) Requirements Management (REQM) Integrated Project Management (IPM) Risk Management (RSKM) Service Continuity (SCON) Capacity and Availability Management (CAM) Quantitative Project Management (QPM)
Service establishment and delivery	Service Delivery (SD) Service System Development (SSD) Service System Transition (SST) Strategic Service Management (STSM) Incident Resolution and Prevention (IRP)
Support	Configuration Management (CM) Process and Product Quality Assurance (PPQA) Measurement and Analysis (MA) Decision Analysis and Resolution (DAR) Causal Analysis and Resolution (CAR)

Fig. 2.8 CMMI-SVC Continuous Representation

Source: Adapted from Capability Maturity Model Integration for Services V1.2 Carnegie Mellon University [February 2009] with permission

development of solutions and delivery of services based on such solutions. CMMI-SVC embodies the best practices required of a service provider in 24 process areas–16 of which are common to all CMMI constellations, 7 are service-specific process areas and 1 of the process areas is an addition. *An addition in the CMMI parlance can be informative material, a specific practice, a specific goal or a process area that extends the scope of a model or emphasizes a particular aspect of its use.* Therefore institutionalizing additions in the process infrastructure is not entirely optional as one might imagine, from an appraisal perspective. It might be useful to consider institutionalization of additions using generic practices of the CMMI constellations. Just as with CMMI-ACQ, Requirements Management process area is assigned as a project management category process area of the CMMI-SVC. It is likely that Requirements Management will be reassigned to the project management category in the CMMI-DEV in the next version. Presently it is an engineering category process area in CMMI-DEV.

Like all CMMI constellations, the CMMI-SVC also allows for either an incremental improvement of a process area (with continuous representation) or improvement of an entire group of process areas required to be institutionalized at a maturity level (with staged representation). Since both representations essentially provide the same content, either of the representations can be chosen while ensuring the achievement of business objectives.

The CMMI-SVC continuous representation is organized along four categories (Figure 2.8):

- Process Management
- Project Management
- Service Establishment and Delivery
- Support

The CMMI-SVC staged representation is organized along five process maturity levels characterizing the process evolution:

- Level 1 or Initial Process Maturity
- Level 2 or Managed Process Maturity
- Level 3 or Defined Process Maturity
- Level 4 or Quantitatively Managed Process Maturity
- Level 5 or Optimizing Process Maturity

Maturity level	Process areas
5 Optimizing	Causal Analysis and Resolution (CAR) Organizational Innovation and Deployment (OID)
4 Quantitatively Managed	Quantitative Project Management (QPM) Organizational Process Performance (OPP)
3 Defined	Organizational Process Focus (OPF) Organizational Process Definition (OPD) Organizational Training (OT) Integrated Project Management (IPM) Risk Management (RSKM) Service System Development (SSD) Service System Transition (SST) Strategic Service Management (STSM) Incident Resolution and Prevention (IRP) Service Continuity Management (SCON) Capacity and Availability Management (CAM) Decision Analysis and Resolution (DAR)
2 Managed	Service Delivery (SD) Supplier Agreement Management (SAM) Project Planning (PP) Project Monitoring and Control (PMC) Requirements Management (REQM) Configuration Management (CM) Process and Product Quality Assurance (PPQA) Measurement and Analysis (MA)

Fig. 2.9 CMMI-SVC Staged Representation

Source: Adapted from Capability Maturity Model Integration for Services V1.2 Carnegie Mellon University [February 2009] with permission

CMMI-SVC V1.2 Summary

Category	***L2***	***L3***	***L4***	***L5***	***Number of PAs***
Support	CM PPQA MA	DAR		CAR	(5 PAs)
Process Management		OPF OPD OT	OPP	OID	(5 PAs)
Project Management	PP PMC SAM **REQM**	IPM RSKM **SCON** **CAM**	QPM		(8 PAs) + REQM
Service Establishment & Delivery	SD	SSD SST STSM IRP			(5 PAs)

Author's Musing

If you are considering an early adoption of conducting RoI studies for the process program, separating this research along the four categories of the constellation-specific engineering/acquisition/service establishment and delivery, process management, project management and support makes for a much more effective and controlled improvement program. Visibility into the areas with the largest payoffs in your 'organizational context' is a lot better than aggregating returns and understanding RoI as [(Savings) + (Profits)]/[(Cost) + (Losses)].

3

Software Engineering Perspectives

AUTHOR'S MUSING

There are no shortcuts to building maturity. Much like any 'process' involving the mysteries of Mother Nature, you just need to have seen enough to know enough! The best way to appreciate the process is to experience the process.

INTRODUCTION

This chapter has been written keeping in mind the requirements of a student fresh from school, who, on stepping into the corporate world, finds it difficult to connect what was taught with what is expected. One can empathize with the student, since the author was through this unsettling experience himself many years ago. What school prepares an engineer for is to be a hacker or, at best, an exceptional programmer, who takes pride in compiling code in the brain! What the corporate world expects of an engineer is a more staid professional whose work can be understood by peers.

Such preparation for the uninitiated is rarely available, except for a few lucky ones who work in large organizations where software engineering training is mandatory during employee induction and culture acclimatization. While this chapter is not a substitute for a lengthier treatise on software engineering which the software engineering classics have to offer, it nevertheless fills a great vacuum by providing a practical side to the discipline of software engineering while focusing on *what they don't teach you at school*. For students fresh from school or those who just want a quick Software Engineering 101 course, this chapter provides a perspective to software engineering using SITARA's Synergy Approach and Package Selection and Integration Process. At the heart of the CMMI lies such a vision; it enables the integration of a development process and of the commercial off-the-shelf software (COTS) solutions. While the CMMI is suggestive of what such a process should constitute, this chapter supplements this understanding with how to render the same making references to the CMMI process areas. We will first review the Synergy Approach and conclude with the Package Selection and Integration Process—both of which are technical reports released from the SITARA Process JewelBox™.

An ideal software development process exhibits virtues of being an optimizing process where the end of phase deliverables are correct, complete and consistent while accommodating the real-life requirements involving design for change. In order to make the process of developing software repetitively with consistent results, automation of the software development process should be addressed where possible. An important point which must not be forgotten while being process oriented is that the customer is not buying the process, but it is buying the product. The software solution is being developed with a customer in mind. So, without customer orientation, process improvement is meaningless. Process is only a means to an end but not the end in itself. Oftentimes, emphasis on the process is so much that the true spirit behind it, namely, the development of reliable software solutions with a customer focus, is forgotten.

BRANCHES OF THE STRUCTURED ANALYSIS FAMILY

Everything that goes on in a system can be classified into three categories:

- What is being done: *the process, operation* or *algorithm*
- To what is the process or algorithm being applied: *the data, material* or *information content of the system*
- When is the process or algorithm being applied: *this is commonly called control*

Functional Decomposition

The process-oriented branch was introduced by Ed Yourdon. For real-time analysis, the work is primarily due to Hatley and Pirbhai. The analyst starts out by thinking of the system as a single large process. S/he then divides this primary process into two or more sub-processes and describes the data connections between them (meaning, the problem is analyzed). This activity is repeated until a large number of simple, primitive processes have been defined. The next step centers on creating the control. The order of execution of the processes is then defined through state models. Organization of data comes about as a derivative of the processes and their need to link together. Relatively little is said on data organization in the methods based on functional decomposition. The characteristics of this branch are *process*, control and data, *in that order.* The advantages with this approach are that it is the most widely known method, it is intuitively appealing and therefore easy to comprehend and, in the non-real-time form, the model notation is simple. Disadvantages with this approach are that it drives the implementation toward more code and less data and the method is irreproducible, in that two analysts working the same problem often produce very different models.

Event Response

The control-oriented branch first appeared in *Essential System Analysis*, by Stephen McMenamin and John Palmer in 1984 [McMenamin and Palmer, 1984]. The analyst views the system as a black box that makes preplanned responses to external stimuli. The analyst first identifies discrete incidents that occur outside the system, known as *external event*. These external events can be readily derived from requirements; they act to describe the system boundary precisely. Members of this branch of system analysis look like *control*, process and data, *in that order of emphasis*. The advantages with this method are that it is fairly reproducible and the models produced by this method are easy to understand. Disadvantages are that it assumes requirements are complete and consistent, it is highly unstable if requirements change, it leads to code-heavy implementation and the real-time extensions use a complex notation.

Object-Oriented Analysis

The data-oriented branch was first developed in 1979 but appeared as a published material by Shlaer and Mellor in 1988. This approach starts by defining objects and attributes—that is, the data—derived from the real-world problem. Life cycles of the objects are then formalized in state models; this is based on operating policies and physics of the world. The hallmark of object-oriented branch is *data*, control and process, *with data being the rallying point*. The advantages with this approach are that reproducible design drives implementation toward minimal data-driven code, it is stable when requirements are likely to change and it uses simple, elegant notation. Disadvantages with this approach are that it is not always easy to see what happens when the system is presented with an external event. Because of the nontraditional look and feel, skepticism sometimes arises when the method is introduced: *it is not intuitively obvious whether the method will work*.

We shall first establish an understanding of what a software life cycle is and provide a flavor for the required mind-set while adopting the functional decomposition and the object-oriented approaches. Object Modeling Technique (OMT), popularized by James Rumbaugh, will be used to present the ideas relevant to the object-oriented approach. We will review the major steps involved with the help of an example of a real-time digital clock. This example is not intended to be a complete solution.

SITARA'S SYNERGY APPROACH—ESSAY ON SOFTWARE ENGINEERING

The purpose of this essay is to offer an orientation for composing a development life cycle necessary to integrate software and systems engineering. The Synergy Approach was crafted by the author in a process design exercise in early 1995, and his belief in it has only been reinforced after learning more about the CMMI. For a software development initiative to qualify as an institutionalized discipline, outcomes must be person independent but process dependent, after according due recognition for the importance to have competent people. Such a process would have a well-articulated set of activities that govern the development and subsequent maintenance of software. Teams not only document what they do but they also do what is documented as the system of practices: *the process*. Such a process is made up of manageable phases of execution, describing activities performed on well-defined inputs after verifying the entry criteria. Deliverables at the end of each phase are reviewed to isolate errors and a baseline is established which forms the input to the next phase. The development process found here is not intended to be a software life cycle of its own. Experiences with existing best practices, coupled with practical needs from many development projects that were undertaken by the author, have been the major inputs in defining an illustrative process.

To answer, *how the Synergy Approach is different from the waterfall model, the V model and the spiral model,* it would be necessary to review these models against the Synergy Approach. The waterfall approach advocates sequential execution of phases while falling through the life cycle of development. The Synergy Approach accommodates the real-life situation of continuous change which the waterfall model does address. By doing away with the separate development and verification and validation phases of the V model, it exploits the synergy of the team to build robust solutions. By getting the entire team, both from the development and testing sides, together to provide perspective-based reviews of each phase of the life cycle, it reduces the need to iterate among phases that is addressed by the spiral model—but when poorly managed, this can lead to the proverbial death spiral! The Synergy Approach improves the chances of building quality into the end of phase deliverables by emphasizing *doing the right thing right the first time using collaborative development and test teams.*

Author's Musing

The simplest way of getting to doing the right things right the first time, I have observed, is to make sure that a practitioner has enough clarity on what is expected, and to proceed with the definition of the solution only after eliciting enough information about the problem. Getting help in the form of training, from subject matter experts and domain specialists, is a definite common-sense approach.

The illustrative life cycle described is a common-sense approach to breaking down complexity. The governing idea behind the Synergy Approach is to build a quality product with the help of development and test teams motivated by the spirit of interdependence and teamwork. As the competition to excel as a world-class software company heats up, it becomes important to deliver a quality product (zero *known* defect software), delivered on time meeting the market window of the product meeting both the customer and end user expectations. To meet such demands, it is necessary to exploit the synergistic outcome of putting to use the very best available in each individual of the team while building competency communities. Such teams must be geared toward interdependence and teamwork while emphasizing automation of as many of the tasks as involved in achieving the goal of producing quality software products. These teams are responsible for creating repositories or reuse libraries of competency assets resulting within their groups. End-of-phase deliverables or configuration items must be well documented in a consistent fashion so as to be easily understood by peer reviewers. Reviews are quality checkpoints where errors are isolated. All configuration items should be reviewed until all *known* defects are removed. A defect is defined as errors that have escaped a phase into the next one; undetected error is a defect.

Keeping the psychologist George Miller's famous magic number of 7±2 linear simplification of a complex process, this approach is made up of six phases, culminating with the final customer approval. Customer involvement in as many of the end-of-phase reviews as possible is a very desirable step and should be scheduled in the project plan. A configuration item is a peer-reviewed work product that would be archived at the end of each phase. Changes to the configuration item as a result of changed customer requirements are made using a well-defined version control process that is under the control of the software configuration manager (SCM) in large teams or the project manager (PM) in small teams. The

SCM of a software development team can also be the technical lead of the project, also called the software systems engineer (SSE). Note that in the best-executed projects, these are role-plays and not titles that people carry. Phases of the life cycle in Figure 3.1 include the following:

- Requirements definition phase
- Requirements analysis and high-level design phase
- Detailed design phase
- Coding or implementation phase
- Code standardization and unit-testing phase
- System integration and system-testing phase
- Alpha and beta testing and customer approval phase

In both the waterfall and V models, two separate teams conduct the development and testing activities independently, an approach that does not augur well in practice. Oftentimes, with such independence governed by the principal motivating factor for the testing team—*a test case must break the system*—needless conflicts occur, with the production of near-zero defect software with emphasis on reduced cycle times. This is because the amount of quality and robustness that can be built into a product in the software system testing phase comes at a cost and is extremely difficult, if not impossible. Imagine the consequences of having to redo the design because of system test reports that get generated just before the product is to be shipped. The promotion of the concept of an independent product development and test team does not hold in a zero defect software development environment. It would be ideal if such teams work as integrated teams, a concept strongly advocated even in the CMMI.

Technical Pool Organization into Competency Communities

Some of the key areas in which the software development effort will require expertise are the following:

- Graphical user interfaces
- Configuration management and computer languages
- Software tool support and network administration
- System integration and system testing
- Software quality assurance and metric collection
- Databases
- Domain
- Vendor support information and in-house tool development
- Programming languages and unit testing

The idea behind the project organization structure depicted in Figure 3.2 is to build in-house subject matter experts (SMEs), who will work interdependently to provide software solutions. The CMMI recognizes such groups as home organization, which the People CMM refers to as competency communities [Nandyal 2003].

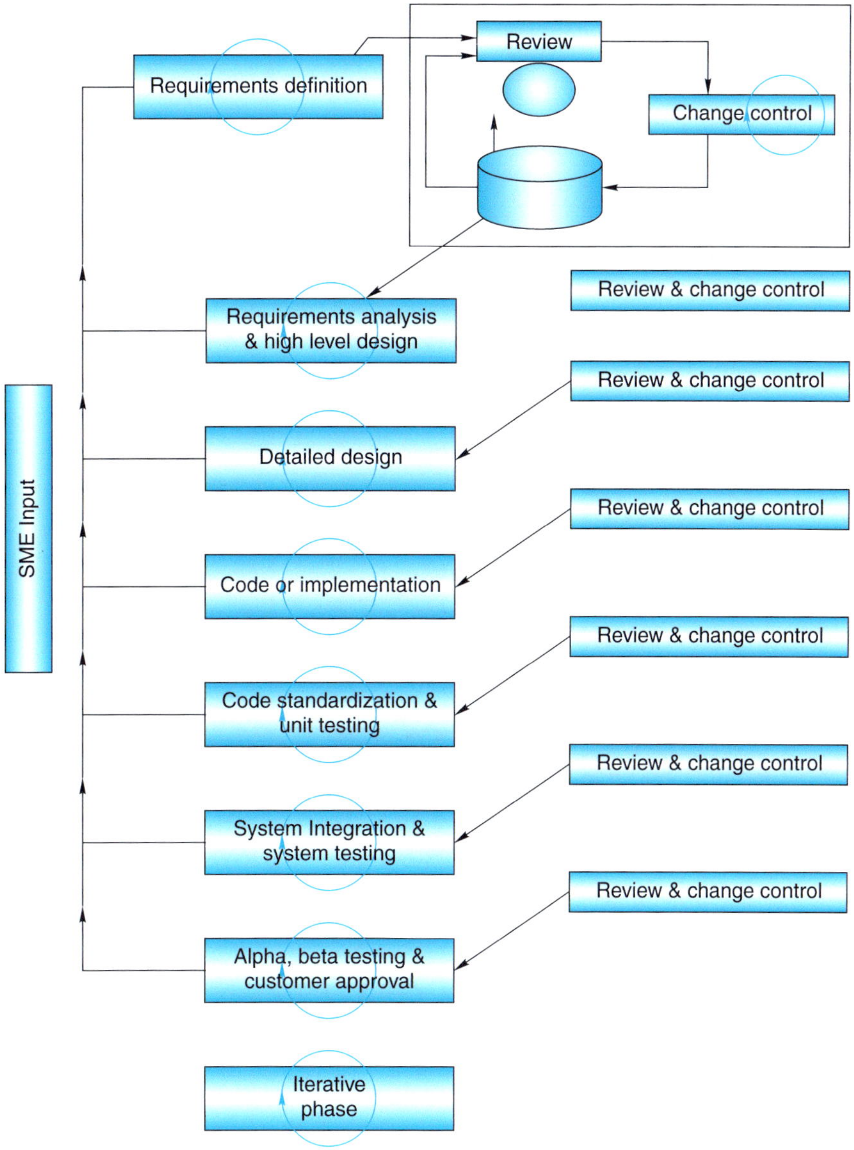

Fig. 3.1 SITARA Synergy Approach Lifecycle Description

Source: Adapted from SITARA Process JewelBox™ © SITARA Technologies Pvt. Ltd. 2002 with permission

Project Organization Structure

SME—subject matter expert

SSE—software systems engineer

PM—project manager or program manager

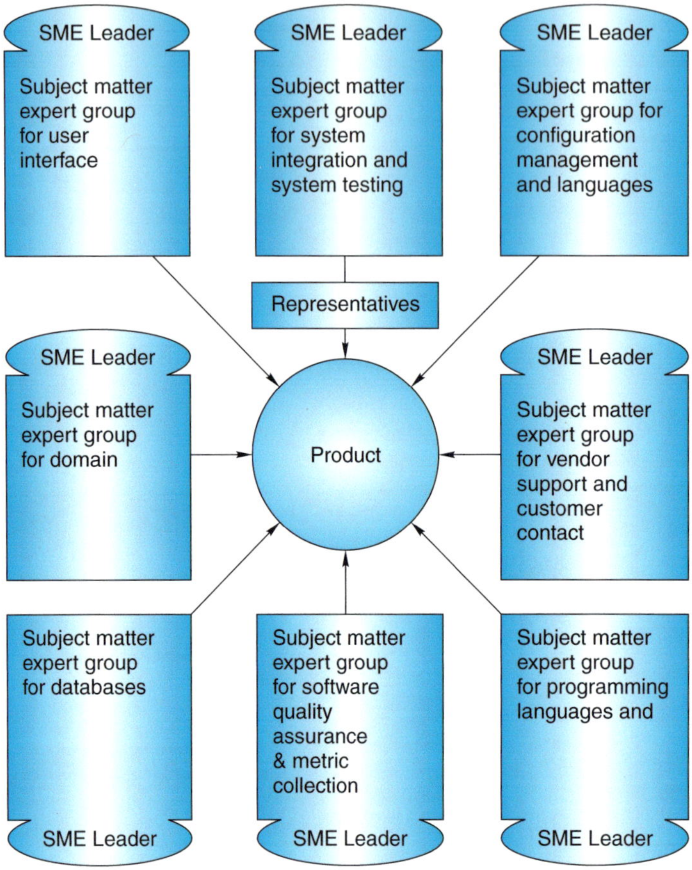

Fig. 3.2 Project Organization in SITARA Synergy Approach (Example of home organization—project organization structure for CMMI)

Source: Adapted from SITARA Process JewelBox™ © SITARA Technologies Pvt. Ltd. 2002 with permission

[SITARA Technical Reports: SITARA 2001b]

Requirements Definition Phase

The requirements definition phase management is assisted by representatives from the technical pool, who carry out a feasibility study to evaluate the customer's wish list. The nature of activities in this phase involves project staffing and establishing the project schedule. Identification of the right staff profile and evaluation of the additional training required for team members is ensured in this phase. Configuration items or the end-of-phase deliverables from this phase are established in a functional requirements specifications (FRS). The corresponding system acceptance specifications (SASs) establish inputs to the software system-testing activities. An FRS must emphasize *what* the system will do rather than *how* it is to be done. The FRS must also document *what the system will not do*. Oftentimes, failure to recognize these implicit requirements leads to rework in the design phase, causing an increase in the cycle time of system development.

AUTHOR'S MUSING

Members belonging to the organizational workforce who share knowledge, skills and process abilities of a particular domain or workforce competency constitute a competency community. Establishing competency communities or in-house subject matter experts who aggregate and complement each other's competencies is the only known option for growing organizational capability. Process outcomes become predictable in a quantitative sense only when competent individuals use a capable or mature process. One of the biggest issues, a competency community addresses is to minimize 'rework due to lack of domain understanding'—the hidden factor which is a common cause variation. And one of the greatest advantages of having a competency community is that a significant opportunity for leverage from 'reuse' of competency-based assets becomes possible with the creation of reuse repositories.

The focus of this phase is on functionality that is fundamental to achieving performance objectives under known constraints of operation based on data or information flow and content. An SSE collaborates with the SMEs assigned to the project to define the FRS, which is a logical and functional decomposition of the overall system behavior. These logical or functional units state the objectives that would be accomplished from each functional unit in as detailed a manner as possible. Logical units may be decomposed further into sub-requirements, which when put together accomplish the overall requirements of the unit. The product FRS can be established as the configuration item. Together with the FRS, a project management plan establishes project schedules in a system project management plan (SPMP). The SPMP will undergo modification in the requirements analysis phase to help draw up more realistic project deadlines. At the end of the requirements phase, the SPMP details the need for a phased delivery of the product or determines whether the project is doable within the time constraints. The SPMP will also make an assessment of whether the resources—manpower, money and tools—to execute the project are available. It is important to be able to distinguish between customer needs from the customer wants for better prioritization.

Example: *Problem Statement*: It is required to build a real-time clock featuring the display of time.

FRS: *Functional Requirements Specification*

R1. Develop a real-time clock that will display time using system clock as initial input.

R2. The display of time can either be in the 24-hour format or in the AM/PM format.

R3. The time can be set to any valid value after the system initializes itself to the system time.

  R3.1 Validation of user-selected time must be done in both the formats.

  R3.2 Invalid time must prompt the user to correct the mistake.

R4. The display shall update itself at the end of every minute.

R5. The display format shall be as HH:MM AM/PM in the AM/PM format.

R6. The display format shall be HH:MM in the 24-hour format.

The FRS will, in addition, have an architecture context diagram, which establishes the boundary between the system and the environment. The architecture context diagram in Figure 3.3 establishes the inputs, interfaces and outputs for the time display system. It offers insights into the hooks that would have to be designed to get the system time and also the formatting that would be necessary for the display. It also suggests that the necessary hooks to receive user inputs must be designed as well. The architecture context diagram defines the architecture flow diagram identifying the data flows, starting with a data context diagram. The data context diagram illustrated in Figure 3.4, partitions the architecture into two parts: the first part consists of information and processes within the scope of the system and the second is outside the scope of the system.

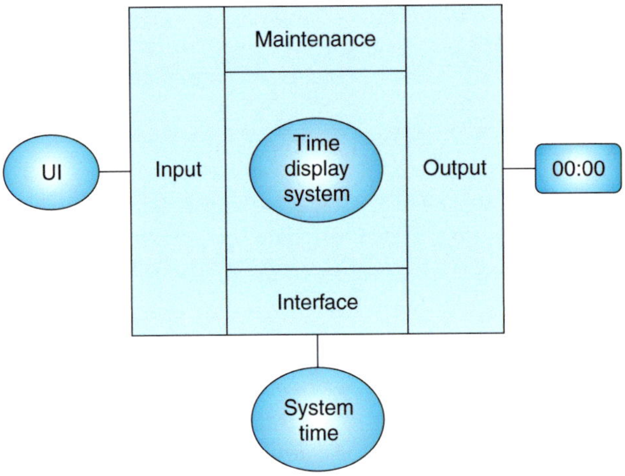

Time display system:	The software solution that has to be built
Interface:	The system interface to other processes
Maintenance:	The interface available for tuning the time display system
Input:	User access to the time display system
Output:	Interface will display the output to the user
UI:	User inputs to modify the time

Fig. 3.3 Architecture Context Diagram

Source: Adapted from SITARA Process JewelBox™ © SITARA Technologies Pvt. Ltd. 2002 with permission

[SITARA Technical Reports: SITARA 2001b]

Since deliverables are impacted by customer-imposed standards for software development, design standards, design representation, coding standards and testing standards, it is important for the requirements-gathering team to recognize them. When a feasibility study is undertaken, technical and nontechnical risks will be involved. Suitable abatement procedures must therefore be well thought out.

Requirements Analysis and High-Level Design Using Functional Decomposition Method

The input to this phase is primarily the FRS. Other inputs could be domain literature and user's manual. If customer-supplied software and customer-imposed tools for development have to be used, then tool-related documents such as the user's guide and reference guides, source code and integrating strategies form a very useful input to this phase. Two very important inputs to this phase are the Red Book and the White Book. The Red Book documents the mistakes committed in the past on similar projects and serves three essential purposes: *avoid repeating the same error, project a positive quality orientation at all times* and, finally, *do the right thing right the first time based on lessons learnt*. The White Book is domain specific in nature and documents the best practices from similar projects. These two books are typically developed in the code standardization and unit-testing phase, and will be updated right through to the customer approval phase.

The requirements analysis phase commits or allocates requirements into *processes* in a data flow diagram. A process is a function or a collection of functions that accomplish the functionality of the allocated requirements, and, when integrated as a whole, implement the solution. This method of evolution provides a top-down solution to a software problem. The very first process bubble, known as the context diagram (Figure 3.4), will be the time display system, which receives the system time at initialization. It could also receive user modifications subsequently and will send the time output for display. This bubble or process is called process 0 of DFD 0 (Data Flow Diagram 0).

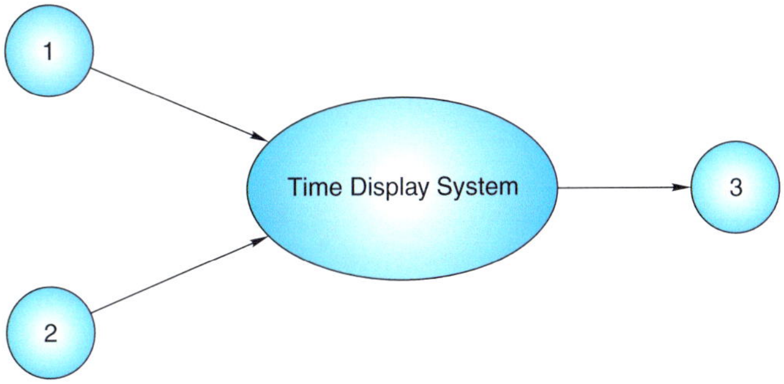

1: User input to the system for modification of time
2: System input providing the system time
3: Output from the time display system displaying the time

Fig. 3.4 Context Diagram

Source: Adapted from SITARA Process JewelBox™ © SITARA Technologies Pvt. Ltd. 2002 with permission [SITARA Technical Reports: SITARA 2001b]

We work our way down from this top-level bubble or process, which can be decomposed into the following: *validate time* process or bubble, *format time* process, *update time* process, *error handler* process and *display time* process. Other sub-processes may form a layer of support that could be either system/

tool dependent. Without getting into the details, the purpose here is to merely highlight the organization of the solution (Figure 3.5).

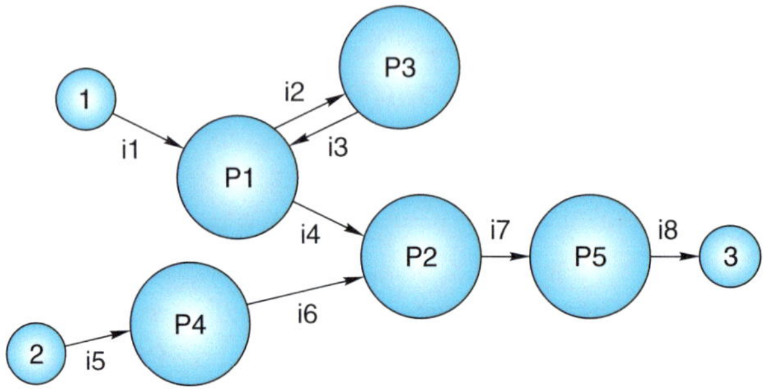

Time Display System

P1: Validate time process
P2: Update time
P3: Error handler process
P4: Get system time process
P5: Format time and display time processes
i1: User input
i2: User input string
i3: Validation status
i4: Validated string
i5: System time
i6: System time for update
i7: Updated time for display
i8: Formatted time string for display

Fig. 3.5 Data Flow Diagram for Time Display System

Source: Adapted from SITARA Process JewelBox™ © SITARA Technologies Pvt. Ltd. 2002 with permission [SITARA Technical Reports: SITARA 2001b]

Each of the above processes will have a corresponding process specification (PSpec) to describe the functionality that will be accomplished by the process, or the process will further undergo decomposition into sub-processes. What is important is the data balancing—meaning whatever data flows into the process bubble must be consumed in the process bubble itself. For composite data composed of many primitive elements, the definition should ensure full utilization of all the data primitives with no additions. For a thorough understanding, please refer to *Strategies for Real-Time System Specification* [Hatley and Pirbhai, 1988]. Corresponding to each one of these processes, traceability to the original requirements is established. So, a traceability matrix comprising the requirement that the process traces back to must be generated. The format in which the PSpec will have to be written must consist of the following:

TITLE:
INPUTS:
OUTPUTS:
PROCESSING:

A sample PSpec for *Validate time* process could be the following:

TITLE: Validate time
INPUTS: Time
OUTPUTS: Validated time status
PROCESSING:
Determine the input time format.
Check if the time is valid in the format in which it has to be displayed.
IF the time has a valid format, THEN return a VALID status. ELSE return an INVALID status.

It is important to note that the PSpec merely describes the processing without getting into details of *how* the processing needs to be done and *what* the variables/flags are, as well as the values they will be set to. The end-of-phase configuration items which are the inputs to the detailed design phase are as follows:

1. The data flow diagrams and control flow diagrams
2. Process specifications (PSpecs)
3. Interface specifications (ISpecs)
4. Data dictionary

Analysis using Object Modeling Technique

An analysis through OMT consists of developing three models—the object model, the dynamic model and the functional model. The resulting three models are inputs to the design phase. In Shlaer–Mellor's *Object Oriented Approach to Domain Analysis*, the corresponding equivalents to the three models are the Information Model (object model), State Model (dynamic model) and Process Model (functional model).

Object Model

The object model identifies the classes that could result from problem definition, their associations and the attributes of each class. An object model only addresses the static behavior of the system. The following steps will result in the object model:

1. Identify objects and classes
2. Identify associations
3. Identify attributes

Object An object is an abstraction of a set of real-world things. All the real-world things in the set, the instances, have the same characteristics; and all instances are subject to and conform to the same rules. *Object* in OOA represents a typical, but unspecified member of a class.

Attribute An attribute is the abstraction of a single characteristic possessed by all the instances that were themselves abstracted as an object.

Relationship A relationship is an abstraction of a systematic pattern of association between real-world things that were themselves abstracted as objects.

Types of Objects Perhaps the easiest objects to develop are those, based on abstraction of *tangible things*. They may also be abstracted for *roles* of things, rather than for the thing itself. Specifications or quality criteria provide another basis for abstraction. Objects may be useful aggregations of equipment. They can be defined to reflect steps in the process of manufacturing.

States Each state represents a condition of the object during which a defined set of rules, laws and policies apply.

Events Occurrences that signal when an instance of an object is moving from one stage of its life cycle to another.

Actions The processes, queries and transactions necessary to draw an object through its life cycle into actions in the object's state model.

Step 1: Identify Objects and Classes

Objects and classes can be recognized from the problem statement by identifying all the nouns and adjectives in it. The candidate classes identified from the knowledge of the problem statement are shown in Figure 3.6.

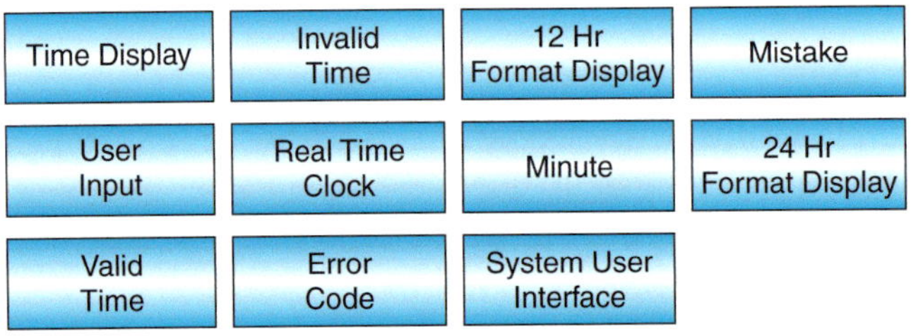

Fig. 3.6 Time Display System Classes Identified from the Knowledge of Problem Domain

Source: Adapted from SITARA Process JewelBox™ © SITARA Technologies Pvt. Ltd. 2002 with permission [SITARA Technical Reports: SITARA 2001b]

Having identified the classes from the problem statement, we will now discard classes that are redundant, irrelevant and vague, attributes of classes, operations, roles and implementation constructs. Since this is based purely on judgment, a good rule of thumb to decide this is to identify classes that have adjectives qualifying them, and if a class cannot stand by itself because of being trivial, then it can also be discarded (Figure 3.7). The following are the steps involved:

Step 1. Class Real-Time Clock represents the module we are going to design, and its scope is too vast to be considered as a class.

Step 2. Classes Error Code, Invalid Time, Mistake and Minute are vague; hence, they are discarded.

Step 3. Classes Time Display System and Real-Time Clock are redundant; hence, we discard one of them, say the Real-Time Clock.

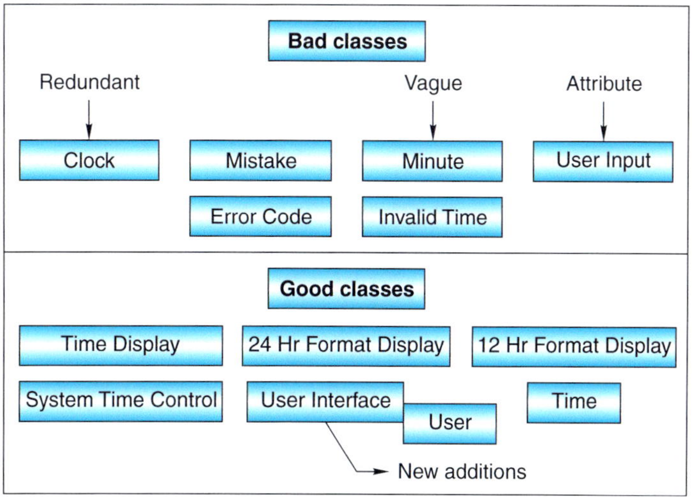

Fig. 3.7 Eliminate Unnecessary Classes and Add New Classes to the Time Display System Problem

Source: Adapted from SITARA Process JewelBox™ © SITARA Technologies Pvt. Ltd. 2002 with permission [SITARA Technical Reports: SITARA 2001b]

If adding a few classes based on the domain analysis of the problem helps to improve the overall structure of the system, then we add a few classes. Figure 3.7 segregates the bad classes from the good classes.

Step 2: Identify Associations

The following associations are identified for the time display system problem:

Verb Phrases

Real-Time Clock shall ***display*** the time

Time clock ***shall use*** the system clock

Time can be ***set*** to any valid values

Validation of user selected time must be done

Invalid time must ***prompt*** the user

Display shall ***update*** itself at the end of every minute

Figure 3.8 shows the initial object model and the associations among the objects.

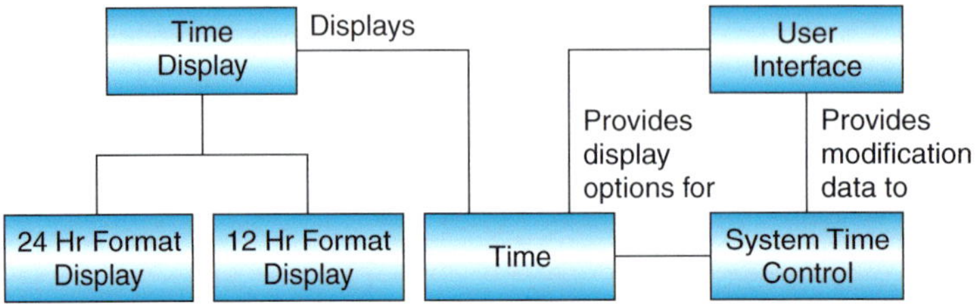

Fig. 3.8 Initial Object Model with Inheritance

Source: Adapted from SITARA Process JewelBox™ © SITARA Technologies Pvt. Ltd. 2002 with permission [SITARA Technical Reports: SITARA 2001b]

Step 3: Identify Attributes

Attributes are identified for each class as required for the design of the time display system. Table 3.1 gives the class names with their relative attributes.

Table 3.1 Class-Attribute description

Class	*Attributes*
Time	Display Option System Time
Time Display	Nil
24 Hr Format Display	24 Hours Format
12 Hr Format Display	12 Hours Format
System Time Control	Change Info. System Time
User Interface	New time display option

Until now we have identified the classes, their associations and their attributes. Now we can combine this information to form our object model for the time display system with attributes and inheritance. Figure 3.9 depicts this model.

Dynamic Model

The dynamic model identifies the dynamic behavior of the system. It tries to emulate the behavior of the system under normal and abnormal conditions. This model is used to formalize the life cycles or life histories of objects and relationships. In order to simplify the system of communication, state diagrams

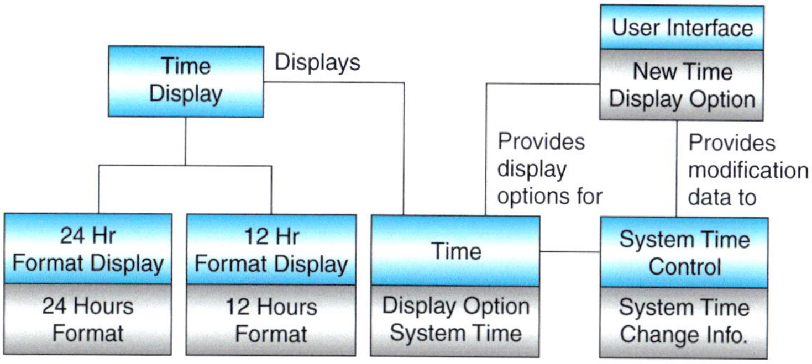

Fig. 3.9 Object Model with Inheritance and Attributes

Source: Adapted from SITARA Process JewelBox™ © SITARA Technologies Pvt. Ltd. 2002 with permission [SITARA Technical Reports: SITARA 2001b]

and transition tables communicate by means of events and are organized in layers. The following steps will result in the dynamic model:

1. Prepare scenarios
2. Identify event trace for each scenario
3. Build state diagrams

Step 1: Prepare Scenarios

Scenarios of typical interactions are prepared.

Scenario 1

The following is a scenario where the user needs to initialize the display option:

User provides the display option.

Display option is written to the display storage from where it is to be read at the beginning of every session.

Scenario 2

In the following scenario, the user changes the time successfully:

User provides the time.

User provided time is checked for validity.

Format of user-provided time is acceptable.

Time to display is modified according to the information provided by the user.

Scenario 3

In the following scenario, the user fails to change the time successfully:

User provides the time.

User-provided time is checked for validity.

Format of user-provided time is not acceptable.

User is prompted to provide correct format.

Scenario 4

In the following scenario, the user needs to display time:

User requests for time display.
System time is obtained from OS.
Display option is obtained from display storage.
Time is displayed depending upon the display option.
Time is updated after every 1min, to show the latest system time
Display continues until user discontinues the display.

Step 2: Identify Event Trace for Each Scenario

Event traces are identified for some of the scenarios. Figures 3.10–3.12 show how the events are traced between each object class.

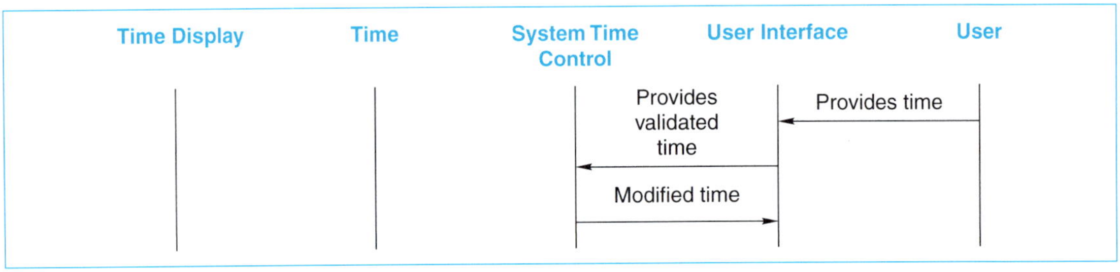

Fig. 3.10 Event Trace for Scenario 2

Source: Adapted from SITARA Process JewelBox™ © SITARA Technologies Pvt. Ltd. 2002 with permission [SITARA Technical Reports: SITARA 2001b]

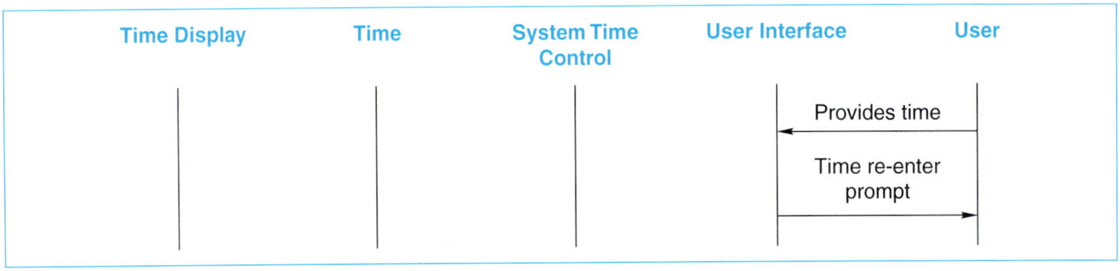

Fig. 3.11 Event Trace for Scenario 3

Source: Adapted from SITARA Process JewelBox™ © SITARA Technologies Pvt. Ltd. 2002 with permission [SITARA Technical Reports: SITARA 2001b]

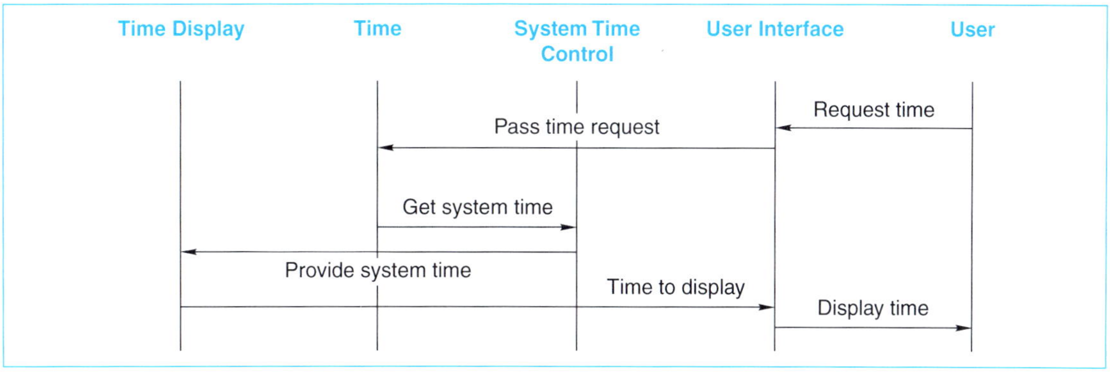

Fig. 3.12 Event Trace for Scenario 4

Source: Adapted from SITARA Process JewelBox™ © SITARA Technologies Pvt. Ltd. 2002 with permission [SITARA Technical Reports: SITARA 2001b]

Step 3: Build State Diagrams

A state diagram is made for each object that shows considerable dynamic behavior. State diagrams help in tracking operations on the objects. Figure 3.13 is a state diagram for time display. Figure 3.14 presents the dynamic behavior of update time.

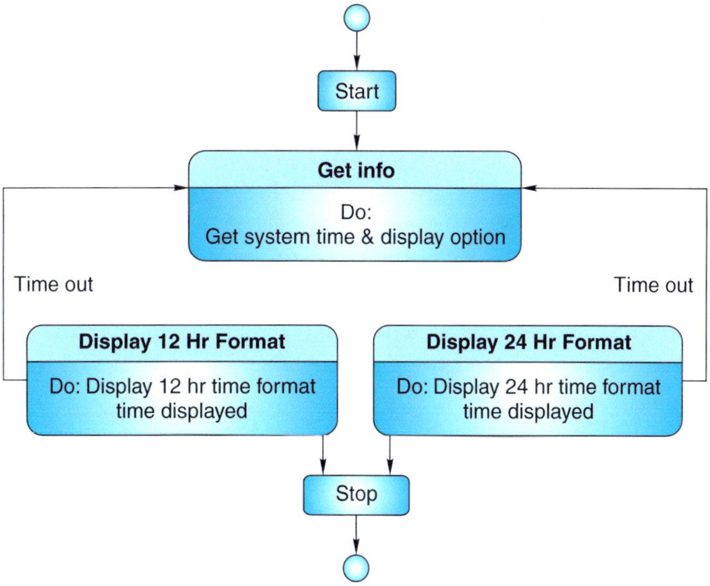

Fig. 3.13 State Diagram for Time Display

Source: Adapted from SITARA Process JewelBox™ © SITARA Technologies Pvt. Ltd. 2002 with permission [SITARA Technical Reports: SITARA 2001b]

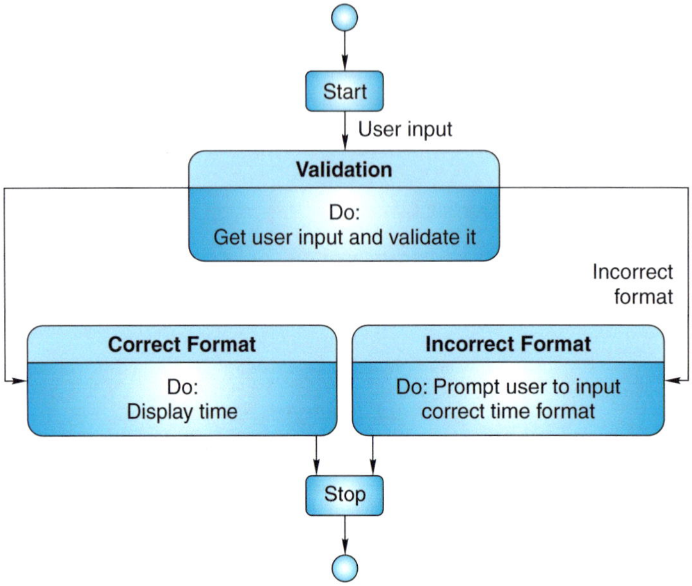

Fig. 3.14 State Diagram for Update Time After Validation

Source: Adapted from SITARA Process JewelBox™ © SITARA Technologies Pvt. Ltd. 2002 with permission [SITARA Technical Reports: SITARA 2001b]

The dynamic behavior of other classes is trivial and hence does not require any state diagram.

Functional Model

The functional model shows how values are computed independent of the sequencing. Functional dependency is shown through data flow diagrams. Functions are represented through the pseudo-code. The processes drive an object or relationship through its life cycle and can be derived from the dynamic model. Data flow diagrams in their simple DeMarco form are used in this step. The processes on the data flow diagrams will correspond to activities or actions in the state diagrams of the classes. The flows on a data flow diagram will correspond to objects or attribute values in an object diagram. The following steps will result in the dynamic model:

1. Identify input and output values
2. Develop data flow diagrams
3. Add operations

Step 1: Identify Input and Output Values

Figure 3.15 shows the input and output values to the time display system. It also shows where the inputs come from and where the outputs go.

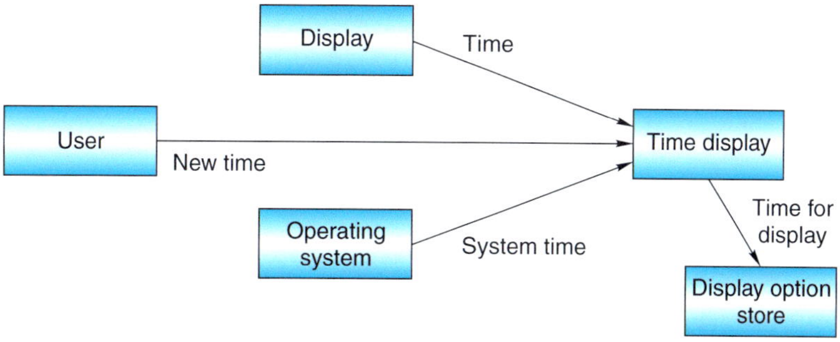

Fig. 3.15 Input–output Values for Time Display System

Source: Adapted from SITARA Process JewelBoxTM © SITARA Technologies Pvt. Ltd. 2002 with permission [SITARA Technical Reports: SITARA 2001b]

Step 2: Develop Data Flow Diagrams

We start with making a top-level data flow diagram. Top-level diagrams give the details about the input of data and how it is processed and converted by the top-level processes. The next level diagrams expand each of the bubbles in the top-level diagrams and explains how processing is done as we go deeper into hierarchy [Hatley 1988]. Flow of data and related processing for display of time is shown in Figure 3.16.

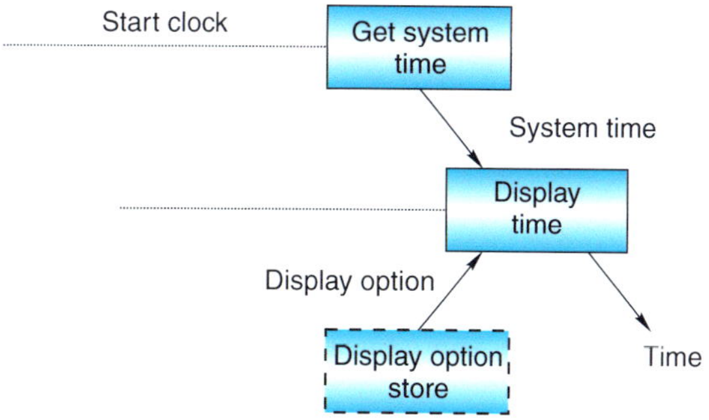

Fig. 3.16 First Level Dataflow Diagram for Display Time

Source: Adapted from SITARA Process JewelBox™ © SITARA Technologies Pvt. Ltd. 2002 with permission [SITARA Technical Reports: SITARA SE/JUNE2001]

Flow of data and related processing for changing the display time is shown in the Figure 3.17.

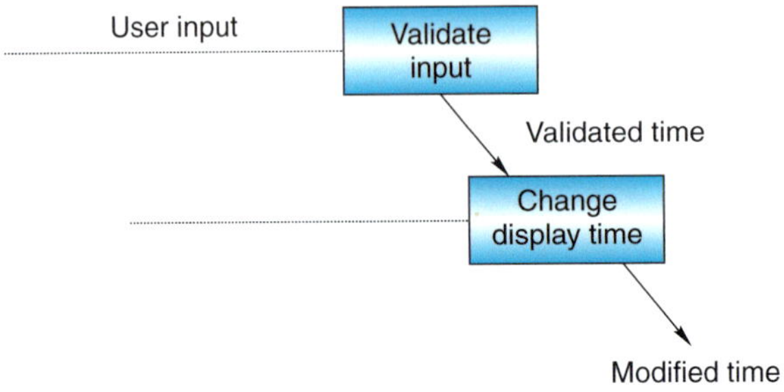

Fig. 3.17 First Level Data Flow Diagram for Update Time After Validation

Source: Adapted from SITARA Process JewelBox™ © SITARA Technologies Pvt. Ltd. 2002 with permission [SITARA Technical Reports: SITARA SE/JUNE2001]

Step 3: Add Operations

In this step, we find all the possible operations traced in the object, dynamic and functional models. These operations are listed in Table 3.2 along with their identifying models:

Table 3.2 Operation name and the identifying model

Operation Name	Identifying Model
Initialize User Interface()	Object Model
Initialize System Time Control()	Object Model
Initialize Time()	Object Model
Initialize Time display()	Object Model
Handle Display Option()	Dynamic Model
Validate User Input Time()	Dynamic Model
Change System Time()	Dynamic Model
Get System Time()	Functional Model

The relevant CMMI process area that corresponds to the activities in this phase belongs to the Requirements Development process area and can be reviewed in Chapter 5.

Detailed Design using Functional Decomposition Method

Continuing with the functional analysis method, a quite probable structure chart is illustrated in Figure 3.18.

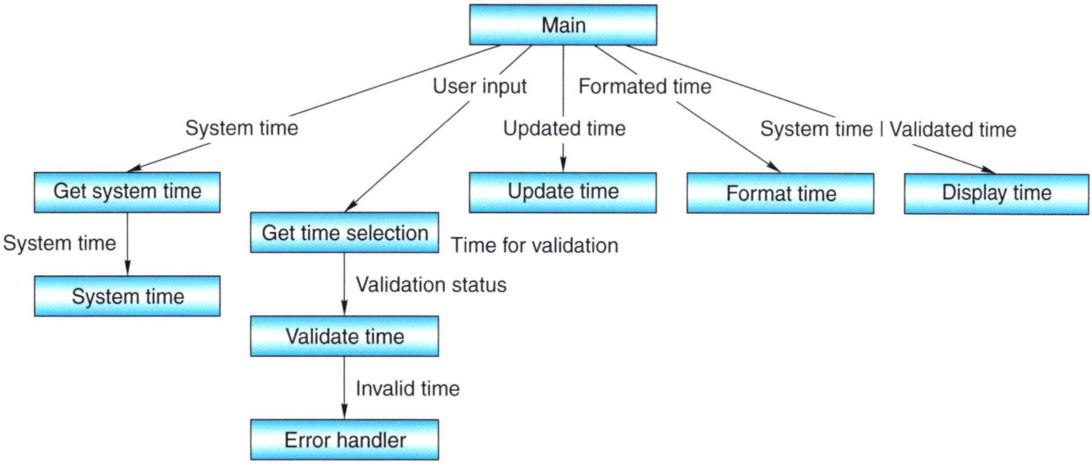

Fig. 3.18 Structure Chart for Time Display System

Source: Adapted from SITARA Process JewelBox™ © SITARA Technologies Pvt. Ltd. 2002 with permission [SITARA Technical Reports: SITARA 2001b]

In this phase, processes identified in the previous phase are grouped into logically related modules. These modules are then arranged in a logical sequence from left to right—the sequence in which they will be invoked. There are many approaches to good design strategies and all of them merit a mention. However, in order to restrict the concerns to good software engineering practices, this essay describes the structured methods approach to design. The strategies available for detailed design and how to do it using the OMT will be illustrated subsequently.

The module specification (MSpec) will elaborate upon the functionality of the architecture/module that will be accomplished. It will elaborate the logic to the maximum extent possible. Ideally, the translation from the MSpec to the code should be in a 1:1 ratio. The MSpec for ValidateTime could look like the following:

```
ValidateTime (Time_for_Validation) RETURNS either VALID_TIME or INVALID_TIME
BEGIN
    IF time format is in 24 Hours format
    THEN
        Validate time against 24 Hours 0 Minutes.
    ELSE
        Validate time against 12 Hours 0 Minutes.
    ENDIF.
        IF time is VALID
    THEN
        return VALID_TIME
    ELSE
```

(*Contd*)

```
            CALL ErrorHandler() with severity value.
            return INVALID_TIME
      ENDIF
END
```

The end-of-phase configuration items which are inputs to the coding phase are as follows:

1. Module specification (MSpec)
2. Structure charts
3. Interface design description
4. Data dictionary entries which can become header files

Design using Object Modeling Technique

The design phase builds on the analysis phase. Information obtained in the analysis phase will be used to design architecture for the time display system. The following steps will result in object design:

1. Implement control
2. Combine the three models
3. Explain classes, including attributes and operations

Step 1: Implement Control

One important step that we have delayed so far is the implementation of control. The implementation of control, including the concurrency control, is shown in Figure 3.19.

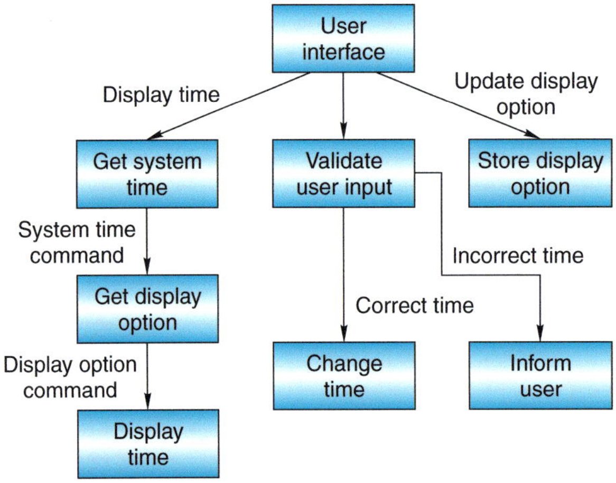

Fig. 3.19 Concurrency Control

Source: Adapted from SITARA Process JewelBox™ © SITARA Technologies Pvt. Ltd. 2002 with permission [SITARA Technical Reports: SITARA 2001b]

Step 2: Combine the Three Models

The most important step in the object design phase is to combine the three models to obtain operations on classes. This will provide us with the final object-oriented model, which will serve as the architecture of the time display system. In the functional model, we found the operations from the three models and in step 1 of object design, we found the control operations. These operations are combined with others required so as to give a complete look to the objects and develop the final design (Figure 3.20).

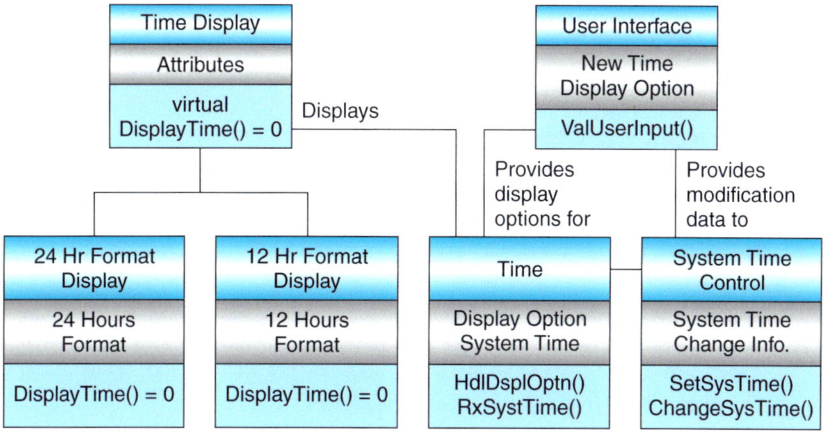

Fig. 3.20 Combine the Three Models

Source: Adapted from SITARA Process JewelBox™ © SITARA Technologies Pvt. Ltd. 2002 with permission [SITARA Technical Reports: SITARA 2001b]

Step 3: Explain Classes, Including Attributes and Operations

Class ***Time***

Attribute Descriptions

Display Option

Origin Class: Time

Purpose: This attribute keeps the information regarding what format user needs time to be displayed.

Possible Values: {12 Hr Format, 24 Hr Format}

Value Provider: Display Option Store (In fact, this value is provided by the user and written to this store)

Description: To find which display format user has specified, time display system looks into the Display Option store and inputs the value into this attribute. Every time, the time has to be displayed, the display format is determined by the information provided by this attribute.

System Time

Origin Class: Time

Purpose: To store the time obtained from operating system.
Possible Values: Any value of time
Value Provider: Operating System
Description: This attribute is used to store the time obtained from the operating system.

Operation Descriptions

HdlDsplOptn()
Origin Class: Time
Description: This operation is used to handle the display option provided by the user. This information is written to persistent storage called Time Display Store.
Input: Display option
Returns: OK flag, which is a character

Algorithm:

get *display option from user()*
write *display option to the Display Option Store()*

RxSystTime()
Origin Class: Time
Description: This operation is used to get the system time from class System Time Control, which in turn gets it from the operating system
Input: Void
Returns: OK flag, which is a character

Algorithm:

send *get time message to system time control ()*
write *system time to local attribute()*

The relevant CMMI process area that corresponds to the activities described in the design phase is the Technical Solution process area and can be reviewed in Chapter 5.

Coding or Implementation Phase

Once the detailed design is baselined, its implementation is rendered in the programming language of preference. Besides maintainability, portability, code readability, comment to non-comment ratio and ease of understandability (noncryptic coding), code structuring is an important consideration in the implementation phase that should be ensured in code walkthrough and inspections.

One of the most important inputs to this phase is the coding standards document. Every language has its unique features and a fairly independent style. If code walkthrough and inspections must happen in a coherent fashion, it is very important to establish a set of rules in a coding standards document that is based on best practices in the industry. This document could be as elaborate as to include *variable naming conventions* (Hungarian notation for instance). Coding standards must be documented in such a way as to help the automation process of the code standardization phase. Coding standards can specify any additional requirements that the code must fulfill, for example, all code must pass lint prior to integration. Coding standards must also detail the code header formats to bring in uniformity to the way the code is structured. The configuration item at the end of coding phase is the code unit that might require code standardization and unit testing.

Code Standardization and Unit-Testing Phase

Code standardization is necessary to bring in uniformity to the manner in which code is developed in the organization. Among other things, code standardization involves formatting the code. Many tools are available in the UNIX environment such as the C beautifier (cb) and indent. One of the advantages of using integrated development environments (IDEs) during implementation is that such coding standards are normally built into the tool functionality. Unit testing of code modules can be carried out as both a white box activity emphasizing structural correctness, and a black box activity, emphasizing functionality. In order to ensure learning and continuous improvement, it is very appropriate to suggest the use of a Red Book and a White Book. The Red Book documents the pitfalls encountered during the phase of unit testing and the White Book contains the lessons learnt from the earlier phases (presented as recommended best practices or practice papers). It is in this phase that most of the project understanding reaches a very stable maturity but is also forgotten because nobody bothered to document the lessons that were learnt and things that could have been done differently but were not done! Unit testing and subsystem integration testing are very useful phases to learn from mistakes. A well-documented Red Book will tremendously aid in the next phase, namely system integration and system-testing phase. A key input to the organizational metric collection effort from these two phases is statistical measures for:

1. Computational errors
2. Logic errors
3. Input and output errors
4. Data-handling errors
5. Interface errors
6. Data definition and database errors

The configuration items at the end of this phase are:

1. Debugged code units
2. Unit-testing report
3. Unit test cases
4. Red Book
5. White Book

The relevant CMMI process area that corresponds to the activities in this phase belongs to process and product quality, Measurement and Analysis, Technical Solution and Verification process areas and can be reviewed in Chapters 4 and 5.

System Integration and System-Testing Phase

System integration can now continue with debugged code units as inputs in a truly bottom-up fashion. This process of system integration can be perceived as being made up of many smaller integration steps.

Finally, after the system is built in this incremental fashion, it is subjected to a system test. Ideally, the input to the system test phase is the user's manual for the system to bring out the end user's perspective to testing.

In systems where bug fixes begin to take place in the system integration phase, it is very likely that the overall system behavior would have to be stressed over and over again to gain confidence in the solution. Here, regression tests would have to be conducted and the results must be well documented. Automating the regression test cycles is a very good opportunity that can be pursued to minimize the cycle time. Red and White Books must be updated. Configuration items at the end of this phase are:

1. System-testing report
2. System test cases
3. Traceability of system test cases with the original requirements
4. Updated Red and White Books
5. Regression test report

The relevant CMMI process area which corresponds to the activities in this phase can be reviewed in Chapter 5. Practices belong to the following process areas: product integration, Verification and Organizational Process Focus.

Alpha and Beta Testing and Customer Approval

Inputs to this phase are the system test reports and system test cases along with the requirements book and user's guide. The scope of activities in this phase corresponds to validation of the system to prove that the system works like how it was designed to work. The developed product is tested in the actual environment of intended use. The objective of testing during validation is to establish confidence in the product when it is subjected to the actual use. This phase is also called end-user testing. The relevant CMMI process area which corresponds to the activities in this phase can be reviewed in Chapter 5. Practices belong to the following process areas: Technical Solution, Verification and Validation.

Continuous Process Improvement

The most important inputs to this phase are the Red Book and the White Book. One of the key points in quality management is to improve constantly. This means never allowing the software development process to remain static, but to improve quality and productivity constantly. Software development methodology, standards and practices must constantly be revised to accommodate newer technologies. An organizational process engineering group (PEG) must be constituted—with a strong management presence—to revise and expand the scope of software development while embracing high-maturity practices of establishing process prediction models, goal setting and innovations, while at the same time emphasizing *production of near-zero defect products with reduced cycle time and increased productivity*. It may not be out of place to stress again the importance of automation and that the process should be a learning opportunity. As experience shows, it is possible to automate as many of the more formal phases of the software development process, and every effort must be made to automate. Process automation holds the key to making the development process a truly optimizing process. The relevant CMMI process area which corresponds to the activities in this phase can be reviewed in Chapters 5–7. Practices belong to the following high-maturity process areas: Organizational Process Focus, Organizational Process Definition, Quantitative Project Management, Organizational Process Performance, Causal Analysis and Resolution and Organizational Innovation and Deployment.

We have seen with the Synergy Approach that testing is an essential part of any development method and cannot be perceived as an add-on activity. Therefore, the development team does not have a separate identify from the test team in the Synergy Approach. Establishing a development process or a life cycle helps to break down complexity. Though not a silver bullet, it is still the only available option for structured development because even our finest people cannot perform at their best when the process is not understood or is operating at its best. In that sense, having a development process is a necessary but not sufficient condition to operate at high maturity. Having the right, processes may be considered as the glue that unifies other aspects of a system. If execution outcomes have to become process dependent and less person dependent (meaning: independent of who executes the tasks), process variation arising out of both common and special causes needs to be addressed. We will review these concepts at length in the subsequent chapters. An ideal software development process has in it the virtues of being an optimizing process that ensures end-of-phase deliverables and is correct, complete, consistent and testable. In order to make the process of developing software repeatable with consistent results, automation of the software development process could be explored. Repetition of the development process knowing enough about the domain is one of the major enablers to minimize variation in execution outcomes. The CMMI practices which will be explored in subsequent chapters describe what is needed to establish a mature software development process. Hallmarks of a mature software development process that make execution outcomes predictable provide for:

- Good configuration management or version control mechanisms
- Metrics collection and analysis
- Reuse of competency assets and lessons learnt from execution after archival

The software engineering concepts explored so far are addressed in the engineering category process areas of the CMMI-DEV constellation. Since the CMMI framework appears in its *triumvirate avatar* of CMMI-DEV (addressing the development aspects), CMMI-ACQ (addressing the acquisition aspects) and CMMI-SVC (addressing the services aspects), we will review a process life cycle that addresses the majority of CMMI-ACQ practices in what follows. The relevance of the triumvirate avatar of the CMMI holds good for all organizations. Even if an organization believes that the acquisition face of the CMMI does not apply to them since they do not acquire any products or services, they are bound to be a provider organization to someone. Such organizations would be much better able to comply with the acquisition organization's requirements if they are knowledgeable about the best practices and expectations of a typical acquisition organization. The same reasoning applies to the services face of the CMMI. Every organization is a service provider and a receiver of services during the course of executing their business. Understanding the expected best practices from a services dimension would be a much desirable process competency to build. We will establish an understanding of the CMMI-SVC while interpreting the relevant process areas of the constellation.

SITARA'S PACKAGE SELECTION AND INTEGRATION PROCESS—ESSAY ON COTS (COMMERCIAL OFF-THE-SHELF) SOFTWARE INTEGRATION

Description of an ETVX (Entry–Task–Verification–eXit) representation of a process involving acquisition of commercial off-the-shelf (COTS) software packages is described in what follows. Since acquisition of products and services is central to the CMMI-ACQ constellation and evaluation of acquired products plays an important role in the Technical Solution process area of the CMMI-DEV, a process description addressing such needs, released from the SITARA Process JewelBox™, is presented in what follows.

Introduction

Package Selection and Integration Process involves the use of effective strategies in COTS evaluation. The most common challenges in COTS-based systems include integration issues and unpredictable interactions with design for change. The marketplace produces a steady stream of products to choose from. COTS evaluation is based on determining the quality of the product in the context of its intended use. Questions that influence COTS evaluation are as follows:

- Why evaluate?
- Who are the stakeholders?
- What is evaluated?
- When to undertake evaluation?
- Where is the interest for evaluation?

COTS evaluation is influenced by a set of factors involving technologies, products, systems, vendors, interfaces, specifications, architectures and the marketplace supporting decision on the COTS software. Or, a completely different set of factors such as risks, return on investment, trends, benefits, compliance and the business health of the COTS software can influence COTS evaluation. The application domain introduces its own characteristic business and technical requirements which also influences COTS evaluation. Therefore, a variety of methods for COTS evaluation based on the application domain are required to be defined. One such repeatable evaluation process that can be used by practitioners—specific to package selection and integration—is described in what follows.

Process Overview

The Package Selection and Integration Process is decomposed into six tightly coupled phases. They are as follows:

Requirements Definition and Requirements Analysis [RDRA]
Product Survey and Market Screening [PSMS]
Vendor Demonstration and Product Ranking [VDPR]
Solution Alternatives and Solution Recommendation [SASR]
Requirements Confirmation and Product Interoperability [RCPI]
Product Development and Rollout [PDRO]

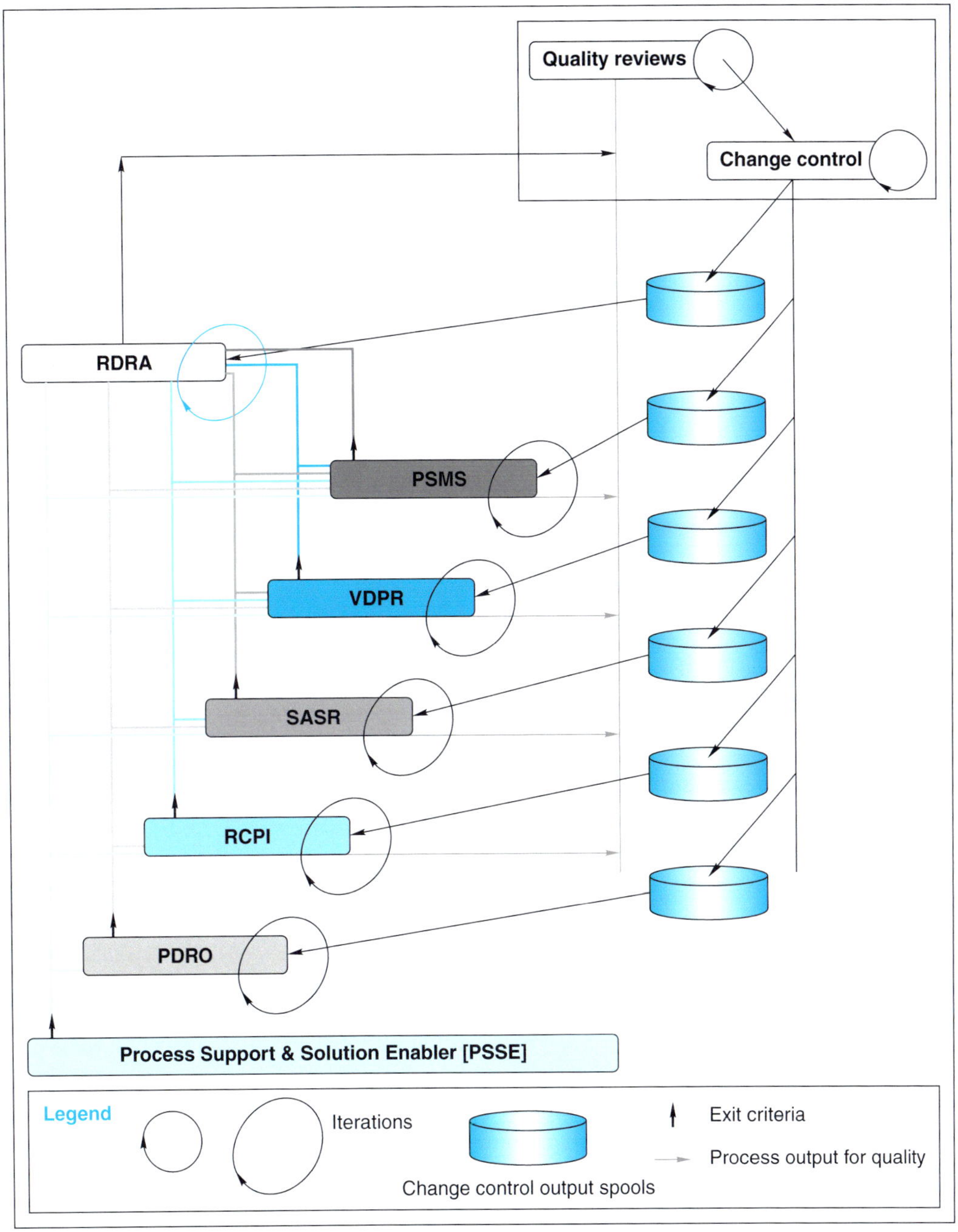

Fig. 3.21 Package Selection & Integration Process Model

Source: Adapted from SITARA Process JewelBox™ © SITARA Technologies Pvt. Ltd. 2002 with permission

Collaborating processes have been clubbed together to have an optimizing effect on each phase as illustrated in Figure 3.21. Repetition and duplication of work is avoided, thereby increasing the effectiveness of each phase. Each phase may feed information backward to the previous phases, eventually culminating in the final customer approval. End-of-phase deliverables are subjected to a thorough review prior to establishing a baseline. Reviews of end-of-phase deliverables are essential to remove errors and defects from configuration items. Changes to the configuration item as a result of changed customer requirements or a changed business scenario are made using a well-defined version control mechanism, under the control of the SCM. The SCM of a software development team can also be the technical lead of the project. The project manager (PM) for the team should ensure that project plans are defined.

RDRA–Requirements Definition and Requirements Analysis

Objectives

- To identify the business, technical, architectural and security requirements of all concerned stakeholders who will be affected by the packaged systems solution
- To document project constraints and technical risks in as detailed a manner as possible
- To identify the long-term and short-term plans of the customer

Entry Criteria

- An executed (signed) work order from the customer along with a project proposal
- An established billing mechanism (e.g., monthly billing invoice giving a breakup of cost elements and the schedule)
- A letter of intent describing customer expectations from the execution of the project
- Management approval to go ahead on the project
- Organization chart giving organization-to-function matrix

Tasks

T1.1 **Feasibility Study**

In RDRA, the management and the technical team conducting the project feasibility study evaluate the customer's wish list. The nature of activities in this phase will involve project staffing and project schedule estimation.

Identification of the right staff profile and the training that will have to be imparted to the staff are also to be evaluated in this phase.

The configuration item or the end-of-phase deliverable from this phase would be the Functional and Business Requirements Specification [**FBRS**][1] and the Package Selection and Integration Plan [**PSIP**]. In the feasibility study, the present system, if any, is also

[1] Configuration items that the SCM has to archive in a suitable configuration management system are identified within square brackets in bold font.

reviewed to understand the current capability of the system and should be documented in the Current System Analysis Report [**CSAR**].

This study will provide inputs to conduct an impact analysis of the new system on the present capability. It will help to understand the business needs of the customer and summarize the cost implications of having to modify the existing system.

T1.2 Develop Functional and Business Requirements Specification

An important point to be emphasized in the FBRS is *what* will the system do rather than *how* it will be done. What is equally important to document is *what the system will not do.* Prioritizing the customer requirements is important. All requirements should therefore be identified as *core* and *non-core*. This would help in assigning weights to product features that would ultimately decide the ranking of the product. Assignment of weights could be based on ease of accomplishment (cost effectiveness), productivity improvement and the business reason for the requirement.

Failure to recognize these implicit requirements will result in rework later on, thereby increasing the cycle time. The focus of this phase is on functionality that would have to be realized given the performance objectives that would have to be achieved under known constraints of operation based on the data or information flow and content.

The FBRS document is a logical and functional breakup of the overall system behavior. These logical or functional units will state the objectives that would be accomplished from a functional unit in as detailed a manner as possible. These logical units will then be decomposed into sub-requirements, which when put together will accomplish the overall requirement of the unit.

When this process is continued to encompass the entire system, the product's functional and business requirements specification can be drawn up.

Role of Configuration Manager

The purpose of configuration management throughout the package selection and integration process is to ensure that changes to project baselines are controlled and correct versions of all baselines are maintained. Configuration manager ensures that the team works on the latest version of configuration items. All releases to the customer must happen through the configuration manager. A person with good technology and business skills can perform this role best. The configuration manager must collaborate with the project manager to ensure that the team is doing the job correctly. In other words, the configuration manager ensures proper execution of the work product. The location of all major deliverables that would require a daily backup should be maintained in a separate document called the Configuration Management Plan [**CMP**]. The configuration management plan will also contain the identification of all emerging project assets that will eventually form the project binder (archive of all configuration items from the project).

T1.3 Develop Package Selection and Integration Plan (PSIP)

One of the major inputs to the PSIP for the project is the Package Selection and Integration process itself, since it lays out the mechanisms for package selection and integration. Besides the FBRS, historical data on similar exercises provide very useful insights into the percentage of time spent on each phase.

PSIP will undergo modification in the Requirements Confirmation and Product Interoperability (RCPI) phase when more realistic project deadlines can be determined.

The PSIP at the end of requirements phase should also detail the need to either have a phased delivery of the product or to determine whether the project is 'doable' in the time constraints imposed by the customer. In addition, the PSIP will make an assessment of the adequacy of resources available to conduct the project.

Role of Project Manager

The role of project management, throughout the package selection and integration process, is to ensure a balanced management of resources by providing adequate management and supervision of team personnel. The PM must track and resolve issues as they happen, clearly define the scope of work, monitor progress and ensure adequacy of risk abatement procedures to contain risks. The PM must collaborate with the configuration manager to ensure that the overall progress of the project is in keeping with the agreed contract. Together with the quality assurance manager, if one is assigned to the project, or with the configuration manager, if the quality assurance role is combined with configuration management, the PM must ensure that the right job is being done. In other words, the PM ensures that the right work products are being developed. Joint Application Development (JAD) sessions are good Process Support and Solution Enablers (PSSE) in this phase. JAD sessions would have to be planned for in the PSIP. It is extremely important to be able to differentiate between the customer needs and customer wants.

T1.4 Major Considerations and Activities

Stakeholder Concerns

Each of the different stakeholders in the COTS-based package selection and integration projects has their own needs and expectations. Hence, the requirements in the RDRA phase come in two flavors—business and technical requirements—keeping in mind the different interests in COTS evaluation. Good documentation standards that would cater to different audiences are an absolutely desirable and essential PSSE to have in this phase. It would serve to document the requirements in multiple flavors, as per need. The PSIP must make sure that sufficient resources and time are allocated for this job.

Derive Detailed Requirements

The high-level FBRS should be used as an input to develop a detailed list of requirements. If we are using the current system as a baseline, then the general practice of reuse, buy and/or build will govern these requirements. *Current system analysis* would have to be carried out while determining the detailed requirements. Decision to reuse the current system would mean that a migration strategy has to be explored and the corresponding migration requirements should be identified. The decision to buy a COTS package would involve an early identification of all the licensing requirements. In the current system analysis, the existing solution is studied in depth to understand the potential impact of changes to the current system on the overall solution. During this analysis, it is also possible to categorize the importance and relevance of the new technical and business requirements to the application domain (e.g., web applications) that are being developed. It is extremely important to identify the relationship between the requirements and its correlation to the application domain for early validation of feasibility. Such a relationship would help in the next phase (Product Survey and Market Screening).

Verification

V1.1 Organization Chart and Organization-to-Function Matrix

Verify whether the organization chart for the project exists with well-defined roles and responsibilities. If such an organization-to-function matrix does not exist, it is important to develop it in the RDRA phase. *This matrix maps out the COTS vendor or solution provider to the assigned product component.*

V1.2 Formal Requirements Definition

Using business needs and requirements as input generates a comprehensive set of functional requirements that are *implementation independent.*

The only acceptable implementation dependencies are those that apply to system linkages and components that are already part of the production environment, and are assumed not to change.

V1.3 Conceptualization

Conduct a preliminary survey of products and/or implementations to get an idea, as how the requirements might be satisfied. Consult with domain experts in applicable technologies. Research product features and possibly contact vendors. Revise the formal requirements to reflect evolution in understanding of what can be implemented. Conceptualization is an informal process, but nonetheless must be documented. Conceptualization is inherently flexible; approaches will differ based on domain, products, participants, resources and such considerations.

V1.4 Package Types List

Identify types of packages available, using conceptualization, research and requirements as input.

V1.5 Obtain Sign-Off

It is crucial to begin the next phase after obtaining customer commitment to the package selection and integration process. In case of absence of management commitment from the customer to a packaged system solution, the project would have to be terminated right at this stage. It is also important to understand the management perspective of the customer to the following:

- Issues concerning technologies
- Preferences, if any, for products, systems and vendors
- Constraints on the interfaces, specifications, architectures and the marketplace

Other major points of consideration to be discussed with the customer requiring a sign-off are as follows:

- Risks
- Return on investment

- Trends in the application domain
- Benefits to the customer from the solution
- Compliance and the business health of the COTS software to the stated and implied requirements

The application domain introduces its own characteristic business and technical requirements that can influence COTS evaluation. All these can be documented in a Quality Assurance Plan [**QAP**].

Guidelines to Conducting RDRA Effectively

G1.1 Do not make changes to the team composition

Package selection and integration projects are quite unique in that changes to the team composition would adversely affect project completion. Considerable amount of insight is gained into the project over time which would be lost to team reshuffles.

G1.2 Know the customer base

It is important to understand the different stakeholders in the COTS-based package selection and integration project. Identify customer preferences and build on prior experience within the organization. The quality assurance manager along with the PM and configuration manager should identify expectations from the customer. This has to be communicated to the package selection and integration team.

G1.3 Know who the key players are

Each of the different stakeholders in the COTS-based package selection and integration project has their own needs and expectations. Understanding the key players in the project such as the customers, competing organizations, vendors, policy makers, procurement agents, system architects, program managers, end users and domain specialists is important.

G1.4 Know the short-term and long-term plans of the customer

The package selection and integration initiative normally involves a long-term plan that is larger and grander in scope than the short-term plan. A good understanding of both the short-term and long-term benefits from executing the project will go a long way in effective mentoring of the team.

From such knowledge, derive the structure of the program carefully. Lay out the urgent and important things as top-priority concerns of the customer and very diligently go about attending to them. The not urgent and not so important items should be tackled last.

G1.5 Resolve issues in a timely manner

Resolve any open issues in a timely manner, and effectively communicate these and their resolutions to all stakeholders. Communication must perforce happen in a disciplined and controlled manner. A single point of contact from either side has to be established early on in this crucial phase. Preferably, the point of contact in this case should be the person with the configuration management responsibility.

G1.6 Develop product list in parallel

A preliminary product list can be developed in parallel while the FBRS is being developed. Elicitation techniques that might help in streamlining stakeholder needs and expectations include use of questionnaires and interviews, operational concepts developed or obtained from end-user surveys, feasibility studies, use of prototypes, qualify function deployment, use cases and demonstrations.

Exit Criteria

Obtain sign-off on the following major configuration items from RDRA phase:

- Current System Analysis Report
- Organization chart
- Organization-to-function matrix
- Preliminary product list
- FBRS: Functional & Business Requirements Specification
- PSIP: Package Selection & Integration Plan
- QAP: Quality Assurance Plan
- CMP: Configuration Management Plan

PSMS–Product Survey and Market Screening

Objectives

- To identify business, technical, architectural and security requirements of all concerned stakeholders in relation to the products that would be on survey
- To document product screening criteria from the identified project constraints and technical risks from the previous phase (RDRA)
- To conduct a market survey of all available products fulfilling the requirements
- To identify clearly the context of the new solution in relationship to the marketplace and the existing system

Entry Criteria

- FBRS: Functional & Business Requirements Specification
- PSIP: Package Selection & Integration Plan
- QAP: Quality Assurance Plan
- CMP: Configuration Management Plan
- Product catalogs
- Research reports & product reviews
- White paper evaluation

- Inputs from site representatives already using the product
- Past experience from knowledgeable individuals

Table 3.3 Template for FBRS

REQUIREMENT ID:
DEFINITION:
AS IS:
TO BE:
NET CHANGE:
BENEFITS:
CONSTRAINTS:
DEGREE OF IMPORTANCE:
STAKEHOLDER:

Source: Adapted from SITARA Process JewelBox™ © SITARA Technologies Pvt. Ltd. 2002 with permission

Tasks

T2.1 Requirements-to-products matrix

Create a traceability matrix for each one of the products vis-à-vis the requirements from the FBRS.

T2.2 Study RDRA deliverables in relation to products

Create a matrix of requirements versus the products that are being evaluated. Understand the mechanisms by which the stated and implied requirements will be fulfilled. Study the product virtues in relation to other competing products. Include market analysis, if available, of the product in the study. Obtain a measure for the size of the product base in the market and age of the product, i.e., whether it has withstood the test of time. Study the viability of the company, and the product, after sales support from the vendor and any other prior experience in using the product serving the application domain. To narrow down the sample of the final evaluation to three products, it is imperative that we start with an initial product list that is at least three times bigger. Note that there is no clear starting point for this exercise. The mix of this product space should include the top performers in the application domain that can be short-listed from the known resources that are mentioned above. The narrowing down process itself is refined from some sort of market survey/analysis activity whereby a number of feasible products are identified. From this set, a certain number are selected, and prepared for integration by means of adaptation, wrapping and so forth. These are, ultimately, integrated into a larger system. Finally, products are replaced as their new versions are released, as superior products are identified and as the underlying technologies are replaced.

Table 3.4 Template for the traceability matrix of requirements in FBRS to the product mix

	Product A	***Product B***	***Product C***
List of Functional Requirements			
1. FR-<UTILITY NAME><#>			
2. FR-<UTILITY NAME><#> • • •			
n. FR-<UTILITY NAME><#>			
List of Security Requirements			
1. QR-<UTILITY NAME><#>			
2. QR-<UTILITY NAME><#> • • •			
n. QR-<UTILITY NAME><#>			
List of Quality Requirements			
1. QR-<UTILITY NAME><#>			
2. QR-<UTILITY NAME><#> • • •			
n. QR-<UTILITY NAME><#>			
List of Product-Specific Features			
1.			
2.			

Source: Adapted from SITARA Process JewelBox™ © SITARA Technologies Pvt. Ltd. 2002 with permission

T2.3 Understand design decisions and tradeoffs

Which design constraints should be used to impose a feasibility litmus test on the marketplace of COTS products? Once the feasible products are identified, how are design tradeoffs quantified so that a measure of fitness for use can be computed? Answers to such questions often involve making tradeoffs among requirements, design and the products selected to implement the design. Consequently, we can expect to see (and we do see) COTS software evaluation being applied not only to select products, but also to support design decisions which are made before and after the products are selected.

T2.4 Archive product reports

Obtain product referrals from vendors. Contact site representatives and obtain references for the product, using which create a product binder from archives resulting from study of product catalogs, research reports, white paper evaluations, product reviews and reports of past experience from knowledgeable individuals.

T2.5 Conduct preliminary screening

Conduct a preliminary screening of the products after completing an evaluation of similar products. The preliminary screening process would include preparation of the evaluation criteria for the product by categorizing the importance and relevance of detailed requirements to the evolving scenario of the application domain (e.g., web applications). In order to improve the coordination of all concerned stakeholders, it is important to generate a glossary of terms that will explain the key topics concerning the application domain.

T2.6 Prepare evaluation questionnaire

Prepare an elaborate questionnaire to quiz the vendor during the demonstration of the product based on both business and technical requirements as documented in the FBRS. The questionnaire should include security, information integrity and integration issues. Technology concerns of the application domain should also be addressed. The PSIP must ensure that this exercise is broken down into different levels of abstraction. Use a demo evaluation questionnaire to get an insight into what the product has to offer.

T2.7 Run a product race

Divide the team into groups representing the different products that stand a good chance to make up the final three and run an internal product race. Short-list the candidate products and prepare a product-specific questionnaire. Choose specific people from the evaluation team to perform vendor demonstrations: the larger the perspectives, the better it would be. Send the questionnaire to the vendor for a self-evaluation test. Plan and conduct vendor demonstrations.

Verification

V2.1 Adequacy of number of products under evaluation

During product study in the PSMS phase, it would become abundantly clear whether the sample space of products being evaluated is sufficient to make up the final selection.

If the number of products in the sample space is not enough, it is important to reopen the initial product list from the RDRA phase and conduct the PSMS phase on any additional products.

V2.2 **Assessment of product capability**

It is important to obtain 'separate' assessment reports for the product from as many viewpoints as possible on:

- Technology considerations
- Database connectivity
- Integration with legacy systems
- Security and control
- Learning curve
- Product adherence to standards in the application domain

V2.3 **Requirements to package mapping**

Using the package types, list and functional requirements as input, create an approximate mapping of functional requirements to package types. This provides a concise, tabular representation of what types of products can support each requirement (if any).

V2.4 **Package identification**

Using package types and functional requirements as input, identify packages within each type. Both the vendor list and product list should be maintained, along with pertinent contacts and product information. At this stage, such packages are considered candidates.

Guidelines to Conduct PSMS Effectively

G2.1 **Make adjustments to project plans**

If required, it is better to make any changes to project plans.

G2.2 **Requirements support matrix**

Package solutions are one approach to satisfying functional requirements in the design proposal. This information should be reflected in a comprehensive matrix that identifies *how* all the requirements would be met, regardless of whether they entail package selection or not. The requirements support matrix is out of scope for package selection; nevertheless, the package selection process may generate input to the creation of this matrix. For example, analysis of requirements for a complete project (during the project planning phase) may indicate that most needs can be met through a package selection process. In contrast, if analysis indicates that only a small proportion of needs are satisfied by package selection, then a different project path may be selected, but one which includes package selection as in analysis and design activities.

G2.3 **Preliminary package screening—platform & security**

Using security and infrastructure standards, eliminate any unacceptable packages from the list of candidates. This applies to platform issues as well as security (e.g., will it run under our production operating system, web servers and similar checks). If the vendor is likely to release an acceptable product in the immediate future, and if the current product is unacceptable, then such products might be excluded from integration at this stage (if timelines can be met and the risk of non-delivery is acceptable, for example, when no acceptable product is available). Develop a Platform & Security Alignment Report [**PSAR**].

G2.4 **Requirements-to-products matrix**

Create a package evaluation matrix by selecting rows from the requirements support matrix for each package type, that is required. For example, for a web personalization package, all of the requirements that pertain to web personalization should be copied onto a separate list. Columns in the matrix will consist of products within the package type. If multiple package types are sought for the project then several matrices are needed (refer to Table 3.4).

G2.5 **Internal Standards Alignment**

Standards from appropriate standards groups should be consulted to identify any recommendations or requirements for products within the desired package types. If there is no standard, then the process may proceed without such considerations. If there is more than one acceptable standard, then proceed with final package selection, using the acceptable standards as candidates. If there is no acceptable standard, then proceed, but be prepared to request an exception (which might be denied, and therefore becomes a risk). Develop an Internal Standards Alignment Report [**ISAR**].

G2.6 **Preliminary Package Screening—Business and Technical Requirements**

Using the requirements-to-products matrix as input, do a preliminary screening of candidate products to produce a smaller number of viable candidates that will be evaluated in greater depth. This process will start with an almost empty matrix and will fill in enough cells to be able to perform a preliminary package screening (not all the cells in the matrix must be populated). Ideally, one package may be selected if it appears the best in class, is representative of the industry best practices, and has a demonstrated usage history in enterprises that have similar functional requirements and similar operating environments (including volume and reliability). It may be desirable to extend the package evaluation matrix further, by introducing weighting criteria (based on business need), and possibly including non-product-related selection criteria such as cost, support, corporate stability, reputation and similar attributes.

Exit Criteria

Obtain sign-off on the following major configuration items from the PSMS phase:

- Product archive
- Requirements-to-products matrix
- Demo evaluation questionnaire
- Nondisclosure agreement

- Final product list for vendor demonstration
- Updated RDRA deliverables
- Platform & Security Alignment Report
- Internal Standards Alignment Report

VDPR—Vendor Demonstration and Product Ranking

Objectives

- To conduct a rain check of whether vendor self-evaluation meets product capabilities vis-à-vis solution requirements
- To arrive at the final list of one to three packages for further probing and evaluation
- To maintain consensus on the final selection from all stakeholders
- To identify the hardware and software requirements to study alternatives before finalizing the selection criteria

Entry Criteria

- Product archive
- Requirements-to-products matrix (package evaluation matrix)
- Demo evaluation questionnaire
- Nondisclosure agreement
- Final product list for vendor demonstration
- Updated RDRA deliverables
- Platform & Security Alignment Report
- Internal Standards Alignment Report

Tasks

T3.1 **Technical evaluation business, architecture, security**

Evaluate the business, architecture and security requirements based on the PSAR.

T3.2 **Exception criteria documentation**

Formalize the exception criteria from the PSAR and ISAR.

T3.3 **Archive nondisclosure agreement (NDA) cover**

Archive all the NDAs obtained from the vendors. It might be necessary to solicit sensitive technical papers and position papers from the vendor.

T3.4 **Vendor demonstration of products**

This exercise may have to be conducted several times to ensure that all perspectives on product evaluation are represented in the final selection.

T3.5 Product references from vendor

Obtain product references from sites that are currently using the vendor's product. Talk to site representatives to ascertain whether the product meets the required criteria.

T3.6 Hardware and software evaluation

'What are the different hardware and software requirements?' for the final solution to work effectively, either as a single-product solution or as a suite of products. This question has to be answered from different perspectives to have meaningful tradeoff rules. The key issues involved are the networking protocols that are supported, host computer requirements, server requirements, software licensing requirements, support software requirements, OS and multiple-OS support for the product.

T3.7 Select people for demonstration

In order to make vendor demonstrations effective, organize the team into sub-teams, with each team assigned specific responsibilities to study product features in relation to the requirements to product matrix.

T3.8 Rank the products

After evaluating the demonstration, rank the products according to the coverage obtained on the FBRS and any additional evaluation criteria for the specific application domain.

T3.9 Update product data sheet

Update the product data sheet after the demonstration.

T3.10 Final package selection

Using the smaller list of candidates that passed prior screening, conduct a formal evaluation that includes a prototype or pilot, and which completes all of the entries in the requirements-to-products matrix. Use a weighting criteria, additional requirements and additional criteria, as available at this stage, to identify the final package. License agreement negotiations should be initiated as soon as possible. Evaluate the enterprise architecture, application architecture, information integrity and security. If the package is still acceptable after these additional checks, then it should be licensed and used. All information accumulated in this stage must be documented. The selected package should be added to the pertinent investment matrix of the appropriate standards group. The resultant documentation from the standards group should reference all the pertinent deliverables from the package selection process. If no product has been selected, then the criteria may be readdressed for an additional stage of package selection, or the functional requirements must be addressed differently (presumably cost-justified for custom development). Generate an exhaustive *product evaluation report*. After a product has been selected as the final choice, obtain proposals from the vendor for fine-tuning the product to meet solution requirements.

T3.11 Package customization

Understand any solution-specific customizations that would have to be rendered in the final package mix, should the products by themselves not support the solution completely.

Verification

V3.1 Ensure requirements coverage

It is important to dedicate a few individuals to make sure that at the end of product demonstration, adequate coverage on the requirements has been obtained. If coverage of 80 per cent or over cannot be obtained, then this phase has to be conducted again with a fresh sample of products. In such a situation, a 'build' versus 'buy' option would seem more reasonable. Establishing exception criteria for a make-do arrangement with products that are available in the market is also an alternative if the solution has to be made available to address a window of market opportunity.

V3.2 Reports from vendor referrals

Conduct an exhaustive study of all inputs obtained from site representatives using the product, with a view to eliminate the product early on.

V3.3 Review vendor proposals

Review proposals against established selection criteria. If additional data are required from the vendors to conduct this exercise, it has to be communicated now. Develop an implementation strategy report that will highlight a preliminary assessment of how the solution is going to be developed. Rework the project completion plans after conducting detailed micro-level assessment of time required for completing the solution. Document the different *vendor proposals*.

V3.4 Review results with sponsor and management

Results of demonstration should be reviewed with the sponsor and management. Create an *adjusted project plan*.

Guidelines to Conduct VDPR Effectively

G3.1 Ensure that changes to requirements are minimal

Changes to requirements at this stage have to be negotiated with the customer. Indiscreet changes to requirements would result in nonclosure of this phase.

G3.2 Provide advance notice to all stakeholders

For vendor demonstrations to be successful, it is important for all concerned stakeholders to be represented. Adequate notice about the demonstration must be given for adequate participation and objective evaluation of the demonstration.

Exit Criteria

Obtain sign-off on the following major configuration items from the VDPR phase:

- Update product data sheet
- Product evaluation report
- Vendor proposals
- Adjusted PSIP

SASR–Solution Alternatives and Solution Recommendation

Objectives

- To document solution alternatives and propose a final solution

Entry Criteria

- Update product data sheet
- Product evaluation report
- Vendor proposals
- Adjusted project plan

Tasks

T4.1 **Work out solution recommendation**

Following a detailed understanding of all the products, it is important to put together a solution recommendation involving the minimal number of products from the short list that would effectively provide the solution. Develop scoring criteria with the objective of achieving the maximum score. If there are any conflicts vis-à-vis the scoring criteria, review the scoring process with all concerned stakeholders and reassign weights. The scoring criterion is to be determined based on the importance and classification of the priority on the requirements.

T4.2 **For all the demonstrated products work this out in parallel**

The above permutations and combinations should be worked out in parallel.

T4.3 **Apply solution provided by the product to the requirements**

Establish enough vendor support to fine-tune the product to meet the stated and implied requirements.

T4.4 **Build an integration strategy for different products**

This strategy has to be used simultaneously for all selected products to make sure that pilots are effective.

T4.5 **Conduct price negotiations**

The project team must evaluate costs based on the following:

- Package cost including license fees
- Design and installation cost
- Selling price and maintenance fees
- Operating costs
- Training costs and on-site assistance costs
- Other costs such as travel and overheads

T4.6 **Take a re-look at the products**

If a product or a combination cannot fulfill at least 80 per cent of the stated and implied requirements, then the selection criteria may have to be readdressed for an additional stage of package selection, or the functional requirements must be addressed differently (presumably, cost-justified for custom development). Solicit alternative proposals from the vendor and document them in review recommendations.

T4.7 **Final recommendations document**

After examining the solution alternatives from the point of view of product interoperability, a final product recommendation can be given to the customer. The project team must justify and quantify the benefits of each of the solution alternatives. The team should group the solution space to accommodate the best-fit solution providing for good interoperability. This can best be done at the vendor location with numeric weights. Prepare a Final Solution Recommendation Report [**FSRR**].

Verification

V4.1 **80 per cent or more coverage**

It is important to determine if 80 per cent or more coverage is obtained from the recommended solution on the stated and implied requirements.

Guidelines to Conduct SASR Effectively

G4.1 **Work the permutations and combinations in parallel**

To reduce cycle time and to maintain objectivity in solution assessment, it is important to conduct the alternative solution pilots in parallel.

Exit Criteria

Obtain sign-off on the following major configuration items from the SASR phase:

- Review recommendations
- Selection Criteria and Coverage Report
- Final Solution Recommendation Report

RCPI–Requirements Confirmation and Product Interoperability

Objectives

- To perform acceptance testing of the solution recommendation and to ensure product interoperability

Entry Criteria

- Review recommendations
- Selection Criteria and Coverage Report
- Final Solution Recommendation Report

Tasks

T5.1 Integration and acceptance testing

The FSRR might contain certain features that were stubbed out. When the final solution is put together, these stubs have to be replaced with working alternatives from the chosen products that have the exhibited and demonstrated capability to accomplish the goals of the solution. The different testing strategies that will be adopted for final package integration have to be documented. Develop the Integration Test Report [**ITP**].

T5.2 Create the feasibility test matrix

This matrix will contain traceability of the solution to the requirements. It will have to verify that at the end of the demonstration, 100 per cent coverage on the stated and implied requirements is accomplished by putting together the different products forming a solution alternative. It might be necessary to build wrappers where the products themselves do not fully satisfy the requirements.

T5.3 Test environment setup

T5.3.1 Rent, purchase or lease considerations

Evaluate the above options to establish the test environment setup.

T5.4 Contract for the product

After a thorough investigation, when product suitability has been established from the above process, award the contract for the product to the vendor. This must include payment terms and conditions, penalty clauses and legal considerations.

T5.5 Revised project plan

Update the project plan to reflect the current project status.

Verification

V5.1 Integration testing report

This report must achieve 100 per cent coverage on the requirements from the proposed solution.

V5.2 Legal considerations

Make sure that the legal implications of using the solution alternatives have been thoroughly whetted by legal experts before signing the contract.

Guidelines to Conduct RCPI Effectively

G5.1 Obtain legal contract from the vendor on similar exercise

Vendors normally have a legal contract that is generally exhaustive. Obtain legal counsel on the final contract that will be executed to ensure that the legal language of the contract does not affect technical intent in any manner.

G5.2 Good inter-group coordination

The role of program management throughout this exercise is to ensure that all the focus groups are aligned and organization/function matrix is serving the purpose in both letter and spirit. Avoiding repetition of work is significantly important.

Exit Criteria

Obtain sign-off on the following major configuration items from RCPI phase:

- Legal approvals
- Contract
- Integration Test Report
- Revised project plan

PDRO–Product Development and Rollout

Objectives

- To define the final product from a suite of products

Entry Criteria

- Legal approvals
- Contract
- Integration Test Report
- Revised project plan

Tasks

T6.1 Design document for product implementation

Document the final design of the solution based on the product mix. This document must consider all interoperability issues and hardware and software support requirements.

T6.2 Simulate all usage situations

This exercise can be done in several ways: simple data flow diagrams, entity relationship diagrams and use-case or any other traditional object-oriented approaches involving the use of depicting event-trace diagrams or preparation of scenarios.

T6.3 Migration and conversion

In preparation for the final rollout of the product, data migration from any existing legacy systems should be worked out. If data retrieval and modification is possible with the final solution without changing the legacy system, wrappers that will facilitate this should be developed. File-to-file conversions may be required for manipulating data elements.

T6.4 Customization and final rollout

It might become necessary to customize the product if it has to interoperate with the existing legacy system before the final rollout.

Verification

V6.1 Verify project milestones

Ensure that additional customizations for the final rollout are planned in advance without affecting project milestones.

V6.2 Verify product compliance

Verify whether the product meets all the stated and implied requirements as it is being built. Document any deviations and have them resolved by the vendor.

Guidelines to Conduct PDRO Effectively

G6.1 Identify wrappers early

In order to simulate all usage situations, it becomes imperative to identify all the wrappers.

Exit Criteria

Obtain sign-off on the following major configuration items from PDRO phase:

- Mulation results
- Final product

PSSE–Process Support and Solution Enablers

Objectives

- To assist in performing the package selection and integration process effectively.

Tasks

Coding standards

Establish coding standards for the different development languages that will be used in the project. Code walkthroughs and reviews can be effective when the code adheres to a documented standard.

Continuous knowledge update on product/solution space

The project team should continuously update its understanding of customer requirements and seek out appropriate solutions to serve the purpose.

Documentation standards

To address the different requirements of the many stakeholders, it would become necessary to have different documentation standards catering to the specific needs of the project.

Formalized review process

Reviews must be conducted in a formal manner. A moderator who has significant experience in conducting similar projects must ensure that all perspectives are represented in the review. The work product that is being reviewed must adhere to standards.

CASE tools

The use of CASE tools for version control and configuration management will help tremendously. Other CASE tools for documentation, developing project plans and performing verification and validation activities must also be explored.

Training

Training of the project team on the package selection and integration process, vendor management and customer management would go a long way in executing the project with little or no risks.

JAD sessions

Joint Application Development sessions help to synchronize the concerns of all stakeholders.

SME inputs

Subject matter experts are domain experts with considerable exposure to the application domain. Their inputs are of tremendous value in proper execution of the project.

Author's Musing

A strategic long-term approach for building a process improvement program is necessary if it has to become a core competency; even a street-side vendor has a strategy when it comes to selling his wares.

4

Managed Level—Interpreting the Level 2 CMMI Process Areas

AUTHOR'S MUSING

What constitutes real management leadership is best quoted from whom I heard it for the first time ...

"Give me one reason to prove that what you say will help you do your job better; then I will do whatever it takes to make it possible!"—George Smith, former Managing Director of Motorola India Electronics Pvt. Ltd.

CHARACTERISTICS OF A LEVEL 1 (OR INITIAL) PROCESS

A level 1 process is also called the 'initial' process, characterized by *ad hoc* practices and large degrees of process variation resulting from insufficient or inadequate project management support. Successful execution of projects in an *ad hoc* culture is largely due to individual heroics and competencies. So long as things work, there is no problem, but the moment they start to go wrong, the blame game begins. A lesser known characteristic of a level 1 process is poorly established roles and responsibilities, with little regard for developing good interpersonal relationships. What lacks in a level 1 process is a governing mechanism that builds and establishes organizational accountability. Management setup in a level 1 organization is basically not concerned with creating an environment that is conducive to nurturing talent and competencies. It mostly feeds and thrives on one-upmanship among individuals. It is important to note that such process characteristics exist in real organizations, mostly because of the way the senior management thinks and acts.

Establishing software engineering practices or having a development process is the least important of the concerns a level 1 process must address. The place to start is to first of all improve interpersonal relationships with a good sense for knowing who is in command and building the necessary discipline to obey simple instructions. Followership is more important than leadership. It is only when conditions necessary to establish commitment management are established that institutionalizing basic project management should be attempted.

The hallmark of a level 1 process is that there is very little visibility, if any, with respect to progress being made on project objectives. It is generally true that a level 1 process is also least concerned with providing a work environment conducive to generating satisfactory work outputs. Hence, it is also useful to view the level 1 process purely from a People CMM perspective [Curtis 2002] [Nandyal 2003]. It might be useful to review some of the issues with a level 1 process, which the People CMM more than adequately addresses.

There is absolute disregard for personal productivity factors at this level of maturity. When appropriate work environment standards and procedures are not institutionalized, overtime is a rule rather than an exception. Organizational infrastructure is not conditioned enough to support individual work commitments. One of the major distractions in a level 1 environment is time wasted on frivolous activities and unproductive meetings. Environmental conditions are often inadequate to support and motivate individual performance. Distractions and continuous interruptions to work are perceived as the single most de-motivator. There is very little scope for team building, because individuals belonging to a product development team are seldom aggregated in a common area. They may be distributed all over the place which leaves very little scope for negotiating and understanding individual commitments.

Examples of a typical Level 1 work environment include situations where multiple contractors with no common understanding of the organizational process work alongside the organizational program managers to deliver on commitments! In such a situation, it is almost impossible to know who is working on what part of the problem. Each individual is free to define the technical architecture without an overriding organizational process, or architecture. As a result, tools used are not common across the project. Assumptions made are purely individualistic and the place where the final product is tested is invariably the field. There is great imbalance of workload on the team; some are overworked while others play Solitaire. The workforce defines its own work rules including the hours they work. One of the main deficiencies in a level 1 work environment is the absence of a structured process or an articulated method to develop software and related artifacts. There is an absence of the very crucial management tracking and oversight process to ascertain closure of committed work. The problem gets compounded with varying personal styles and preferences which lead to waste of both individual time and productivity.

There is yet another reason for such a display—and it is the customer. Many projects that the author has personally supervised as a practitioner are to a large extent influenced by the customer. If the customer cares less for a process orientation, but *wants the solution his way*, then irrespective of how well one plans execution, it will *be the customer's way*. It better be! Such influences are particularly applicable to engineering practices. Note that both the engineering practices adopted and tools used on projects are heavily dependent on the customer's process; many times the site has to align with the customer's engineering practices. Most projects have a tendency to execute their engineering practices, as required and expected by the customer. This is most definitely the reason why some projects have difficulty in answering: 'Should we do it the customer's way, or our way?' If the customer is an internal customer who is on the same process value system, it is generally a lot easier for the process improvement to highlight benefits falling under one of these general categories:

- improved schedule and budget predictability
- improved cycle time
- increased productivity
- improved quality (as measured by defects)
- increased customer satisfaction
- improved employee morale
- increased return on investment
- decreased cost of quality

Process adherence is more difficult and challenging in a level 1 work culture if the customer is an external customer that has a homegrown process which is different and mandates adherence to its methods.

So how do we get out of the trap of which method to use? The answer to this question requires a management decision. Working on two different process mind-sets, one that aligns with the organizational process and the other which aligns with the customer's process, is a real problem. Knowing the process discontinuities between the two approaches should be the initial starting point. Besides, having a process is only a means to the end, and not an end in itself. One of the most important catalysts for jump-starting a process improvement program is to encourage *critiquing the process*. If the process does not work, project teams know what is right and what is wrong about the process right away. Therefore, the best person to suggest a process improvement is the person who is actually having the problem. As George, the author's software engineering guru at Motorola India, would put it: if any one complained that the process was not right or did not align with the customer expectations, he would say—"you are appointed the chair person to solve this problem since you know the problem best! And you have my support, if required." And pronto! Individuals immediately felt empowered to solve their problems within a strong supporting management infrastructure which was mature enough to permit problems to surface so that effective solutions could be rendered. Little wonder then that Motorola India became the first commercial level 5 organization in the world on the Software CMM in 1993. In this sense, a *culture of professionalism* needs to prevail first. The CMMI practices at the managed level (or level 2) can then facilitate the much-needed organizational transformation.

CHARACTERISTICS OF A LEVEL 2 PROCESS (MANAGED PROCESS)

A level 2 process is called a managed process because process improvements address the core issues concerning effective project management by instilling process discipline within the workforce. We will explore the practices contained within the seven process areas at level 2 of the CMMI-DEV. CMMI-ACQ has three process areas and CMMI-SVC has one process area. We shall review these constellation-specific process areas in the following sequence:

- Requirements Management (REQM) (CMMI-DEV, CMMI-ACQ, CMMI-SVC)

- Project Planning (PP)[1] (CMMI-DEV, CMMI-ACQ, CMMI-SVC)
- Project Monitoring and Control[2] (PMC) (CMMI-DEV, CMMI-ACQ, CMMI-SVC)
- Configuration Management (CM) (CMMI-DEV, CMMI-ACQ, CMMI-SVC)
- Measurement and Analysis (MA) (CMMI-DEV, CMMI-ACQ, CMMI-SVC)
- Process and Product Quality Assurance (PPQA) (CMMI-DEV, CMMI-ACQ, CMMI-SVC)
- Supplier Agreement Management (SAM) (CMMI-DEV, CMMI-SVC)
- Agreement Management (AM) (CMMI-ACQ)
- Solicitation and Supplier Agreement Development (SSAD) (CMMI-ACQ)
- Acquisition Requirements Development (ARD) (CMMI-ACQ)
- Service Delivery (SD) (CMMI-SVC)

We will use the following template while exploring interpretations for each process area:

- How does a process area look when it operates at a capability level 1 (or the performed level)?
- How does a process area transform its capability when the transition to capability level 2 (or the managed level) is made?
- How does a process area transform its capability when the transition to capability level 3 (or the defined level) is made?
- How does a process area transform its capability when the transition to capability level 4 (or the quantitatively managed level) is made? Meaning: **How does a process area demonstrate a high maturity measurement and analysis capability?**
- How does a process area transform its capability when the transition to capability level 5 (or the optimizing level) is made? Meaning: **How does a process area demonstrate a high maturity measurement and analysis capability?**

REQUIREMENTS MANAGEMENT (REQM) CMMI-DEV, CMMI-ACQ AND CMMI-SVC

How does Requirements Management process area look when it operates at a capability level 1 (or the performed level)?

The purpose of Requirements Management is to manage the requirements of the project's products and product components and to identify inconsistencies between those requirements and the project's plans and work products. Requirements Management belongs in the engineering category of the continuous representation of the CMMI-DEV and in the project management category of the CMMI-ACQ and CMMI-SVC. The minimum expectation as per the CMMI at a capability level 1 for this process area is that the project manages its requirements. The manner in which individual projects manage their requirements may vary widely. On the whole, requirements are captured and any changes to the original

[1] Renamed as Work Planning only in CMMI-SVC version 1.3.

[2] Renamed as Work Monitoring and Control only in CMMI-SVC version 1.3.

requirements are managed. The project plan and intermediate work products are based on requirements and are kept consistent with the stated and implied expectations.

Projects use a set of work practices that help to ensure, at the very least, consistency of intermediate work products. The development plan with project requirements is maintained. An understanding of the project requirements and commitment from individuals responsible to execute on such requirements is generally visible. Whenever requirements change, an impact analysis is done in order to understand the underlying changes and their implications along with a documented log of changes using some form of change control procedures. In its simplest form, such control can be established using Microsoft Excel worksheets maintained as a workbook, where each sheet is named by the date stamp which records the requirements relevant to that date. A more rigorous approach could be tool driven. This practice may vary within the same organization with other projects maintaining a document that is continuously updated to reflect the day-to-day changes to the original requirements, using a version history section.

When done well and adequately, it is often possible to establish traceability between high-level and detailed requirements. The supporting mechanism that is employed is a traceability or a requirements allocation matrix. A typical structure for a traceability matrix is a table or an Excel workbook that lists high-level requirements and the associated low-level or detailed requirements. Any change to either of these requirements can easily be traced and navigated back and forth using a set of hyperlinks. Hyperlinks are also maintained to other project areas such as project plans and impact analysis documents which detail the overall project context within which the requirements' churn is managed. Any inconsistencies between the most current requirements and the supporting project work products are recorded and appropriate corrective actions taken.

The biggest challenge at the managed capability level is that these practices are project-centric, and therefore highly dependent upon the individual performing the role of leading the project during its technical life cycle. Normally, a systems engineer or project leader responsible for establishing the project requirements and its continuous revision is identified. There is often a great degree of variation resulting from personal styles employed to ensure the execution of project tasks. The CMMI practices and the specific goal that help to establish a level 1 capability are as follows:

SG1 Manage Requirements

- **SP1.1 Obtain an Understanding of Requirements**[3]
- **SP1.2 Obtain Commitment to Requirements**
- **SP1.3 Manage Requirements Changes**
- **SP1.4 Maintain Bidirectional Traceability of Requirements**
- **SP1.5 Identify Inconsistencies between Project Work and Requirements**[4]

[3] Practice title appears as "Understand Requirements" in version 1.3 across all three constellations. There is no noticeable/perceptible change to the informative content associated with this practice and therefore to its interpretation.

[4] Practice title appears as "Ensure Alignment between Project Work and Requirements" in version 1.3 across all three constellations. There is no noticeable/perceptible change to the informative content associated with this practice and therefore to its interpretation.

A quick note on the numbering scheme followed within the CMMI continuous representation would be in order. SP stands for 'specific practice'. The very first numeric value is the corresponding specific goal that the practice addresses. Therefore, all of the above specific practices address the specific goal 1. The second number is the running sequence of practices, from numbers 1 to 5. These five specific practices address the intent behind the specific goal 1 of Requirements Management.

The practical sides to Requirements Management as experienced with some of the author's best professional associations are shown as follows:

Requirements Management

1. List all the requirements from multiple stakeholders
2. Prioritize requirements using Joint Application Development sessions with the customer and the stakeholders
3. Obtain team consensus on feasibility of requirements
4. Establish rough-order magnitude of work along with optimistic and pessimistic estimates
5. Explore multitasking options and/or phased delivery and negotiate a solution
6. If the negotiation does not result in ownership, escalate the matter to senior management

Display 4.1 Interpreting Requirements Management

Source: Adapted from SITARA Process JewelBox™ © SITARA Technologies Pvt. Ltd. 2002 with permission

Author's Musing

Note that the purpose that senior management escalation serves in a level 2 work culture is to sensitize the management enough about project issues and obtain the necessary management commitment and sponsorship. It is not with a view to subvert or overwhelm the situation.

An organization that demonstrates a good degree of learning orientation would explore alternative practices that are both practical and have served their purpose well within the organizational context. It is the author's suggestion to the process champions and process innovators within the organization, such as the process engineering group, to explore as many alternative practices within projects as meet the intent behind the specific goals of the process areas of the CMMI. They will be pleasantly surprised at how many best practices they may already have! This would then spur the momentum toward the establishment of the capability level 2, or the managed level.

How does Requirements Management process area transform its capability when the transition to capability level 2 (or the managed level) is made?

The fundamental shift from level 1 to level 2 happens because of a learning orientation and a desire to formalize an otherwise informal process based on best practices which are unique to projects. Such institutionalization happens because of an underlying policy that offers insights into how the specific practices have to be executed. 'This is way we do things here' philosophy guides the establishment of a policy. The minimum expectations from having followed a structured method to enacting the practices of Requirements Management are established with a guideline stating who does what and when, based on individual roles and responsibilities. The policy also offers a guideline on the choice of tools to be used for capturing requirements. Requirements Management policy also defines the necessary conditions whereby the activities performed in a project qualify as being sufficient and acceptable.

Organizations must articulate a response to the expected practices for Requirements Management described under capability level 1 that is consistent across a wide range of projects. Individuals who are responsible for establishing requirements must be trained on elicitation methods and negotiation skills. They must be trained in the necessary soft skills such as good communication and presentation methods wherein they are able to interact with all stakeholders of the customers (including end users) in a professional manner. Ability to look ahead and establish possible scenarios which the customer might have overlooked ensures documentation of the implicit requirements and obtaining customer consensus to the same. Constantly probing for potential risks based on the knowledge of internal operations of the organization is an added responsibility which the software systems engineer or technical leader of the project who is typically assigned the Requirements Management role carries. Sufficient time and effort should be planned within the project to ensure sufficient understanding is gained and transferred to all relevant stakeholders of the project. Typically a document of understanding (DoU) is established as an initial understanding document to train the remaining team members on the domain, technical aspects of the project and delivery expectations of the customer. Commitment from all team members is obtained during the project kickoff for the entire duration of the project. Should requirements change during elicitation or during the course of the project, well-defined configuration and change management techniques are applied after an impact analysis. Senior management oversight on issues affecting resource availability, costs, internal infrastructure required to execute the project and overall readiness to execute the project during the Requirements Management phase of the project must be ensured to preempt risks before they become issues.

A capability level 2 process area in general has the following building blocks of ten 'generic practices' which require to be institutionalized. Being the very first process area being interpreted, the practices are listed as under. To avoid needless repetition, future references to these set of 10 generic practices will be made by reference to a mnemonic we will explore soon.

GP2.1 **Establish an Organizational Policy**

GP2.2 **Plan the Process**

GP2.3 **Provide Resources**

GP2.4 **Assign Responsibility**

GP2.5 **Train People**

GP2.6 **Manage Configurations**

GP2.7 **Identify and Involve Relevant Stakeholders**

GP2.8 **Monitor and Control the Process**

GP2.9 Objectively Evaluate Adherence

GP2.10 Review Status with Higher-Level Management

The mnemonic for the generic practices at capability level 2 is EPPAT MIMOR (pronounced 'eepat-mimor'). By memorizing eepat-mimor, one can commit almost 60 percent of the CMMI framework to memory! Keeping this mnemonic in mind enables a practitioner to execute the requirements of the CMMI from a cognitive map—one of the most useful features of the CMMI that goes a long way to minimize common cause variation. This is one of the several reasons why the CMMI qualifies as a DFSS process for software and systems engineering—a framework that is designed to minimize both special and common causes of variation.

Requirements Management is institutionalized to a good degree within projects based upon these ten generic practices. A capability level 2 Requirements Management process clearly identifies practices that establish a consistent system of repeatable practices across projects, though it is a few steps away from being recognized as a defined process.

How does Requirements Management process area transform its capability when the transition to capability level 3 (or the defined level) is made?

The Requirements Management process or procedure is based on the aggregate experience from several projects which have successfully executed on project commitments. Recognition of best practices actually begins to apply at the capability level 2. Such best practices are however at the *techniques* level specific to the project characteristics. An example of a structured process that qualifies as a defined process for Requirements Management is the use of Quality Function Deployment (QFD) or the House of Quality (HOQ) approach. Definitions for the different elicitation strategies, planning strategies for obtaining requirements in the most effective manner, conducting project reviews and feasibility studies for requirements and such are defined at the organization level to ensure minimal variation to the Requirements Management practices.

> **AUTHOR'S MUSING**
>
> Quality Function Deployment (QFD) is an excellent mechanism to track activities and results right from requirements all the way to release. Software engineering researchers credit Dr. Genichi Taguchi with the first QFD model used in Mitsubishi's Kobe shipyard (Creech 1994).

Another example could be the use of an elicitation process that is based on a questionnaire along with a Requirements Management template that has placeholders, to collect the necessary inputs in order to apply the development or maintenance process to. Traditionally a defined Requirements Management process would have templates for the requirements book, software functional requirements specification, systems functional requirements specification, and a well laid out guideline offering the 'how to develop requirements'. The process of Requirements Management elicitation is through a JAD session, where multiple stakeholders representing the different perspectives work out the details of 'what needs to be done'. The abstraction at which Requirements Management operates is to understand 'what the system will do' rather than 'how the solution should be rendered'. The implementation details are seldom explored. Getting the problem definition correct is the first step—the details of the 'how to do it' can wait.

Author's Musing

The biggest challenge in a JAD session is eliciting requirements from a subcontractor who was previously supporting the customer with the solution and has been transitioned out of the project and the cause for such transition is—you! Getting to know the functionality or features of the previous work product during a knowledge transfer or knowledge-sharing session as part of the JAD session is the most challenging and difficult part. It requires more than just good technical competency to absorb the knowledge; it also requires an exercise of both tact and business savvy to do it right. I have noticed that the task of knowledge transfer can be a very daunting and challenging process if poor program management tactics are used. And many times one could be setting oneself up for failure without good program management.

While eliciting information on what the product should do, it is very important for the process to have a mechanism to also document 'what the product will not do'. The Requirements Management procedure would also offer techniques using surveys and questionnaires to arrive at the implicit requirements. The list of mandatory features that the product should support is typically documented in a needs document.

After all is said and done, a level 3 Requirements Management process area should be prepared to face up to the real life challenges—volatile requirements. Requirements will change. Therefore a defined process should have a mechanism that supports handling major and minor requirements changes. A structured and consistent mechanism to conduct an impact analysis distinguishes a capability level 3 Requirements Management process from its level 2 variant. For minor errors and projects with small team size (less than three individuals), the use of a process known as the test-analyze-and-fix or the TAF process is quite common. Normally the project lead along with the concerned stakeholders review the minor changes, establish traceability and allocate a development person to render and offer a fix using the defined development process. For the major changes and projects with a large team size (over ten people), a board, such as the configuration control board (CCB), which is composed of multiple stakeholders, studies the fan-out of a changed requirement using a defined change control process.

A defined Requirements Management process also provides a structure that permits measurement of the process and analysis of information in a meaningful way. It is only when a development framework is defined well that the key work products from the development process become worthy of quantitative analysis.

As is evident from the above description, a process is not a *one-size-fits-all*. So, a considerable amount of tailoring and use of alternative practices have to be defined based on recognition of the best practices. Recognition of best practices would itself serve as a tool to improve the defined process. Multiple definitions and acceptable ways of executing the process are documented and approved for use on projects. Where there is a need, a tailoring guideline would also be made available to ensure that the process is *fit for use*. It is only when this stage—*process to derive a process* (tailoring guideline)—lends itself well to measurement, can one confidently claim that a defined Requirements Management process is established.

From the perspective of the CMMI constellations two generic practices are expected to support the intent of a capability level 3 process area:

GP3.1 **Establish a Defined Process**

GP3.2 **Collect Improvement Information**

All future interpretations of process areas will make references to these two generic practices instead of repeating them.

AUTHOR'S MUSING

It is extremely important to recognize the importance of institutionalizing a good capability level 3 process area of the CMMI and its impact on minimizing common cause variation. An essential prerequisite to enable a higher-capability process area (CL4 or CL5) begins with a strong CL3 foundation. A process definition that is consistently applied across the organization is the first step to minimize common cause variations. It is easy to overlook this point.

How does Requirements Management process area transform its capability when the transition to capability level 4 (or the quantitatively managed level) is made? Or, how does Requirements Management demonstrate a high maturity measurement and analysis capability?

At the capability level 4 or the quantitatively managed capability level, quantitative data are the primary driver for process improvement. Since the Requirements Management process separates what is known as the *voice-of-process (VOP)* from the *voice-of-customer (VOC)*, use of a tool such as the QFD goes a long way to make sure that they both speak the same language. When they do not, the Requirements Management process must be mature enough to take note and do something about it. One of the most common metrics that is collected and tracked is to understand the 'requirements churn'. The metric itself is referred to differently in different work cultures: requirements volatility index (RVI) and requirements stability index (RSI). This number is used to define a threshold which serves as a trigger for management decisions such as replanning, renegotiation, reallocation of resources, and so on.

The traditional definition for RVI is

$(\Delta MAD\ R + \delta MAD\ R)/R$ as a percentage.

R: Original requirements at the time of baseline

ΔMAD R: Major changes to requirements identified as Modified, Added, Deleted

δMAD R: Minor changes to requirements identified as Modified, Added, Deleted

Important note: Make sure that there are no double counts.

RSI is computed as (1-RVI), as a percentage.

Since RVI and RSI numbers are simply dependent upon the number of modification/addition/deletion change requests, irrespective of whether the change is major or minor, based on an analysis of the complexity, the face value of RVI or RSI in itself is by no means an indicator of the extent of rework required. RVI is oftentimes used to trigger a management decision process such as re-estimation of Project Planning parameters.

One of the flaws with the way RVI is used in practice requires attention. In the $[\Delta MAD\ R + \delta MAD\ R]/R$, what happens if the delta is because of δMAD R, i.e., a large number of minor change requests, and has little or no impact on the project. According to the trigger a process may have established, and irrespective of whether the change is major or minor, the process expects a replan if it exceeds the threshold. Then, of course, there is another side to it: what if you get just one major change that is significant enough to actually blow the project away! The trigger threshold for re-estimation may not be reached, but it actually results in a lot of unplanned activities impacting the original project plan itself, meaning that this one major change actually calls for replanning, as otherwise it would lend a deathblow to the project.

AUTHOR'S MUSING

The requirements churn happens as a result of external and internal factors; the process improvement program must ensure that it minimizes effects of the internal factors.

The author's view is to use the RVI in such a way that one can also factor in the complexity of the change involved based on whether it is a high-level requirement that has changed (oftentimes, such changes have a significant fan-out and are invariably major changes) or a low-level requirement that has changed (since fan-out from such a change is minimal, these are normally minor changes), and to normalize the RVI on a scale of 1–10, where 1 is the least complex and 10 is highly complex. So, let us say we have a 30 percent RVI value due to a lot of minor changes, and therefore the team determines the complexity to be 1 (this is always subjective based on how much the team knows, and it is acceptable to go with a wideband Delphi approach to determine the complexity number; after all, professional judgment has to be applied). The team should use this complexity indicator and not just the RVI value alone to define whether a replanning exercise is required or not.

Then how is the measure for RVI *actually* to be used? If anything, it could be used to trigger a Decision Analysis and Resolution process to arrive at the complexity of the change involved. RVI can also tell us whether the artifact is ready for a baseline or not and whether or not to proceed to the next phase. A high RVI value, irrespective of whether it is because of major changes or minor changes, tells us something about the readiness of the Requirements Management work product (the requirements book or software functional requirements specification) for scheduling either a peer review or for establishing a formal baseline. Besides, one could use the RVI to establish a customer profile, i.e., whether you have a confused customer or a customer who is clear in his thinking. There is another way to look at the RVI, which will be described when we explore the establishment of Requirements Management at a capability level 5: to understand whether the RVI is resulting from a common cause variation on account of the *voice-of-process (VOP)* or due to special cause variation resulting from the *voice-of-customer (VOC)*. This insight can be had when a formal causal-analysis review of the RVI measure is done.

One of the other uses of RVI is to use this measure while using a COnstructive COst MOdel (COCOMO) to determine which of the three project classes—organic mode, semi-detached mode and embedded mode—to classify a project into. COCOMO begins with making such a decision for the class of the project. We will explore COCOMO at length while dealing with Project Planning at capability level 4.

This leads us to an interesting question: *Is this metric worth having?* It all depends upon what purpose it would serve and how generic is the extrapolation to understand special causes of variation (meaning external influences). No matter what is done, it is impossible to eliminate special causes of variation in a highly human-intensive process such as software development. You could only minimize their impact. Having minimized the impact of special causes (read it as *voice-of-customer (VOC)*) the next step in this continuous progression is to build robust practices for Requirements Management to understand the implications from the common causes (read it as *voice-of-process* (*VOP*)).

Author's Musing

I would like to give my point of view on the interpretation of special and common causes of variation in relation to software engineering. In a sense both these types are assignable causes. Whereas a special cause of variation is 'determined and assigned' objectively to a source external to the development process, a common cause of variation is 'determined and assigned' objectively to a known source or cause which is internal to the development process.

Examples of special causes: changing customer requirements, lack of access to the validation environment, coordination issues with multiple stakeholders (customers, end users, and so on), interoperability issues with a legacy application, lack of adequate process documentation from the legacy, improper coding techniques employed on the legacy, escape defects from the legacy, and so on.

Examples of common causes: lack of domain understanding, lack of appropriate tools, first-time execution of a project with no organizational memory, lack of individuals with adequate competency, internal churn resulting from people leaving midway, inability to capture the implicit requirements, lack of budgets and resources, lack of historical data for establishing estimates for effort, size and cost, and so on.

The advantage of this view of special causes and common causes *vis-à-vis* software engineering is that it neatly segregates all causes of variation to fall into two classifications or buckets—external to the process (*voice-of-customer (VOC)* or special cause) and internal to the process (*voice-of-process (VOP)*). Clearly, very little process control can be exercised with the first category of causes. And the answer to many of the causes in the second category is effective management practices using a well-defined development process.

From the perspective of the CMMI constellations, two generic practices are expected to support the intent of a capability level 4 process area:

GP4.1 Establish Quantitative Objectives for the Process

GP4.2 Stabilize Sub-Process Performance

These generic practices should be applied to the practices that define the Requirements Management process.

The way to understand the above generic practices is as follows: Quantitative objectives can be established for either specific goals or specific practices. It would be meaningless to set a quantitative objective for generic goals or generic practices. One should first study the possibility of establishing a quantitative goal for the specific goal or the specific practice, based on a review of its applicability in a vast majority of the projects. It is always useful to ask the questions 'why are we collecting this measure?' and 'what insights does the measure offer?' If there are no clear answers, then the stakeholders should take a re-look at the measure itself. Metrics and measurement is a serious business and costs a lot of money (time spent by professionals collecting data). Mature processes offer significant opportunities for metrics collection at every work product–development process intersection. A wise and an informed decision has to be made as to what are the critical measurement points.

Collecting time spent on Requirements Management as a percentage of the total effort on the project at the time of project closure makes a good measure. So, one must definitely collect the time and effort spent on Requirements Management. It would also be instructive to learn how many defects were due to poor Requirements Management review in the execution of the development process. So, collecting defect data attributed to Requirements Management in what is known as phase containment effectiveness (PCE) for the Requirements Management Review process is useful.

PCE is defined for a phase as

$$(\text{PCE})_{\text{Phase}} = \frac{(\text{Errors})_{\text{Phase}}}{(\text{Errors} + \text{Defects})_{\text{Phase}}}$$

What is the problem with this measure? The problem is that there is an implicit assumption that defect and error counts are disjoint. Meaning, errors in the current phase have nothing to do with defects from earlier phases. Quite practically, errors in the current phase have deep links or connections to undetected errors from earlier phases (also known as escape defects or simply as defects). Such defect analysis also assumes that one can clearly tell apart a requirements defect from an analysis defect or a design defect. In fact the PCE measure actually throws light on the review effectiveness only when we have a stable set of requirements. So, one should read meaning into PCE only when it is correlated to a very low RVI (ideally 0 percent) or to a very high RSI (ideally 100 percent). Unless PCE is correlated to RVI or RSI, it does not offer any insightful information. Therefore an insight the author would like to offer is that the PCE measure makes sense only in the context of the requirements phase, or, at the most, up to the analysis phase. Beyond the requirements and analysis phases, it is very difficult to tell a defect type resulting from one phase apart from those because of the rest of the phases.

Actually stopping here—knowing just these numbers—does not make for practical wisdom. We will need to know the causes behind these numbers and objectively segregate the special causes from the common causes and have a process response that addresses the unique distinctions that make up for the variation. Here is where we should decide whether a process area lends itself to be scaled up to a capability level 5 or not.

Author's Musing

The only measure that is worthy of being placed under a control chart and, as a result, has a distinctive advantage to offer is the error and defect count. Placing any other metric on a control chart is, in my considered opinion, meaningless. After all, the use of a control chart is to know the capability of the development process in statistical terms (sigma terms) *to contain defects.* For most other types of metrics collected in software engineering, as the only 'consumable' in a literal sense of the term is 'time', the applicability of run charts to understanding the behavior of a project parameter would be my preferred

(Contd)

choice. Establishing control limits in most cases actually makes no sense. Tracking the performance of such metrics against a goal would be a much better way to understand the performance of a process. I will give an example: How does one establish control limits for code size, effort variation, schedule variation and the like, and draw meaningful insights from such analysis?

Let us take the code size: How could I say that the final executable should be within ±10 percent of 1 MB? Knowing the goal of 1 MB (in embedded applications, memory is a constraint) and tracking the growth of executable code size as features are added makes for practical sense. Needless to say, code optimization depends to a large degree on individual abilities to comprehend and realize logic in a computer language. Further, if a feature has to be supported since it is a customer requirement, it has to be rendered only in code! How would I cut out code to fit the control limit of ±10 percent? Not possible.

Say, effort variation has to be within ±10 percent and the customer changes his mind and cuts out 50 percent of the features! Then the effort variation would go down proportionately and show a decrease of say–60 percent (increase of 60 percent)! Is this a good thing or a bad thing? On the contrary, let us say that the customer added features to its original list of requirements with no scope to negotiate the end date, and this causes effort variation to now go up by 70 percent. (Which means, if a smart team was putting in 10 hours a day, it now has to put in 17 hours a day to accomplish the project objectives since the end date is inflexible. Or, add equally smart team members from the buffer team which has also absorbed the project objectives) Is this a good thing or a bad thing? No insights can be had. Having a band such as ±10 percent for schedule variation also has the same explanation. If the project is far ahead of its schedule (and therefore shows a–50 percent variation), is it not a nice thing to have? There is another useful insight to note. On fixed deadline projects, when the customer adds functionality, effort variation has to be a ridiculously high value if the schedule variation has to have low impact. Obviously I would add more effort to meet the schedule.

I would like to restate a point I made earlier and leave you with a thought: Tracking the performance of most metrics against a goal would be a much better way to understand the performance of a process.

How does Requirements Management process area transform its capability when the transition to capability level 5 (or the optimizing level) is made? Or, how does Requirements Management demonstrate a high maturity measurement and analysis capability?

The same RVI and PCE measures could be looked at from another perspective. What could be the common causes for the RVI index to be high? Or, what could be the common causes of variation resulting in a low PCE measure? We could conduct a Pareto analysis to determine the root causes which contribute the major reasons behind the numbers to understand the role played by both the common causes such as deficiency in articulating the Requirements Management process, templates for requirements capture, domain training provided to individuals on Requirements Management, and so on, as well as the special causes, such as first-time execution of such projects, unclear list of expectations from the customer, pioneering type of work, and such. Using a Pareto chart, one could draw meaningful conclusions based on the identification of the *critical few from the trivial many* conditions leading to the manifestation of the problems.

It is required of any learning process to have a good Causal Analysis and Resolution process for every process discontinuity. It is equally important to use the Pareto to actually highlight whether it is a recurring pattern happening month after month with no resolution or is it just a false alarm. In case of a false alarm, even though the thresholds or limits set for normal conditions of operation may have been exceeded, it is not productive to conduct an exhaustive analysis. Typically, only an automated system lends itself to such analysis of out-of-bound data points, as in such automated systems out-of-bound conditions are indicative of a problem.

In human-intensive activities, false alarms (cancelled change requests, individuals putting in their papers and withdrawing them, and the like) are so very common. What would be more useful is to understand the context or the sufficiency conditions which must exist for the process to depict an inbound tendency. From the many high-maturity CMMI implementations the author has participated in, such context information that must exist does not get spelt out and this is where there is a serious loss of valuable information. A non-software example to highlight this point: if I am asked how long it takes to go from my home to the airport, I could give you a quantitative *forecast* based on a *trend* which is based on past experience and I could say, 30 minutes. Now, this estimate is actually based on several factors (the sufficiency conditions): I use the same horsepower car, use the same route, know exactly how many signal lights I will encounter, approximately know the traffic density, know that there are no major road repairs, etc. These are the things that would form the *sufficiency conditions* that must exist if the *necessary conditions*—that I drive at an average of 60 km/hr and use a defined process to drive the car—are fulfilled. The importance of knowing the sufficiency conditions actually leads to a very important process attribute, which is to be able to recognize common causes from the special causes of variation.

From the perspective of the CMMI constellations, two generic practices are expected to support the intent of a capability level 5 process area:

GP5.1 Ensure Continuous Process Improvement

GP5.2 Correct Root Causes of Problems

These generic practices should be applied to the practices that define the Requirements Management process.

Author's Musing

I would like to leave you with a thought: Requirements Management is known for its instability due to the very nature of the task. The level of abstraction in Requirements Management is to determine what the product should do and not how it will be done. Needless to say, in many situations where the marketing personnel drive the Requirements Management process, the needs analysis (which happens only in the requirements analysis phase) is the best place in the life cycle to bring a sense of stability to the development life cycle. And unless the phase is stable, there is no great value to be derived from measurement! We need to have a stable process before meaningful measurements can be carried out, using which one could attempt to build a capable process. With this insight as background, it would be useful to introspect whether the Requirements Management process is a good opportunity for quantitative analysis of measurement data. In case of Qualitative analysis, the answer is yes!

PROJECT PLANNING (PP)[5] CMMI-DEV, CMMI-ACQ AND CMMI-SVC

How does Project Planning process area look when it operates at a capability level 1 (or the performed level)?

The purpose of Project Planning is to establish and maintain plans that define project activities. Project Planning belongs to the project management category of the continuous representation of the CMMI. The purpose of Project Planning at capability level 1 involves activities that help fundamentally to establish reasonable estimates based on project requirements and develop an execution plan to which the relevant stakeholders endorse their commitment.

The project establishes estimates for the tasks necessary to evolve the work products based on a defined scope. Inputs for such estimates come from the explicit and implicit requirements of the project, based on gathered requirements. A high-level work breakdown structure (WBS) is put in place to understand the project's critical paths and associated risks. The project establishes a development life cycle that best addresses the constraint of operation for the project, based on history of successful execution. Such information typically comes from past planning data and successful life cycles in use, as well as experience gained from project execution. A point to note: in an offshore development setting, where multiple types of projects are executed for multiple types of customers, generalizing a method for establishing estimates is very difficult. In many cases, there is even a situation where such project execution is unprecedented in the organization's history. And there is no organizational memory in the form of a planning database and experience to rely on. Such projects would most definitely have only a 'guesstimate' at best to start with and as project understanding improves, these guesstimates are refined to become estimates. One often resorts to the use of buffer team members as a strategy to abate any risks that might be encountered. The buffer team absorbs the learning along with the actual team and supplements or augments project capacities to meet customer deadlines. It is very useful to look at such projects as having an effective alternative practice to minimize the impact from risks resulting from incorrect 'establishment of estimates', rather than saying that these projects are outliers and eliminating them from the scope of process improvements. First-time executed projects indeed demonstrate excellent best practices simply because individuals on such projects are generally highly geared to demonstrate to the customer a 'we can do it' attitude! This positive mental attitude is also due to the fact that most first-time executed projects lead to follow-on business. A purely psychological factor that is associated with a never-done-before type of project is that the learning orientation comes from *survival anxiety* [Coutu 2002]. Whereas learning anxiety is an organizational disability coming from the individual's fear of change that often threatens individual identity and self-esteem, survival anxiety is what truly contributes to learning due to the fundamental trait of coercive persuasion [Nandyal 2003]. Under such conditions, complacency is generally low because the motivation is toward demonstrating success, even if the team is set up to fail. The corresponding goal that is addressed by the capability level 1 process is as follows:

---

[5] In version 1.3, Project Planning is renamed to Work Planning only in the CMMI-SVC constellation. It will still remain a core process area since the nature of change is only renaming the word 'project' to 'work' which is more relevant in the context of services.

SG1 Establish Estimates

- **SP1.1** **Estimate the Scope of the Project**
- **SP1.2** **Establish Estimates of Work Product and Task Attributes**
- **SP1.3** **Define Project Life Cycle**
- **SP1.4** **Determine Estimates of Effort and Cost**

Note the difference to the goal and practice titles in CMMI-SVC V1.3.

SG1 Establish Estimates

- SP1.1 Establish the Service Strategy
- SP1.2 Estimate the Scope of the Work
- SP1.3 Establish Estimates of Work Product and Task Attributes
- SP1.4 Define Lifecycle Phases
- SP1.5 Estimate Effort and Cost

Author's Musing

Establish the Service Strategy—how should this practice be interpreted? Whether, this practice addresses only the larger program or should it be worked upwards to a program in a recursive manner?

The key here is: A good way to look at service strategy is: to simulate the different approaches and possibilities that a service might encounter 'even' before it is executed by answering the several 'what-if' situations. The strategy might also involve risk identification, assessment and developing a suitable response to mitigate the impact. This practice has more to do with readying a service for execution; which includes studying the ramifications due to all the remaining process areas. In quantitatively managed environments/cultures, use of Crystal Ball with OptQuest can engage the project to determine the 'certainty' value quantitatively for a given 'what-if' condition related to say, a reduced effort estimate or increased schedule estimate and such.

Planning data from similar projects which have been executed successfully drives the creation of a project plan. Typically, the project establishes the necessary budgets and resources along with a schedule that is derived from the practitioners' experience, if historical measures from similar projects are not available. Every project is unique and therefore the risks that a project could potentially encounter vary. A list of project risks along with appropriate abatement procedures are drawn up. Risks could be technical or nontechnical. Many times, instead of a process issue, it could be management issue resulting from wrong business decisions. It is important to draw a distinction between management issues and process issues.

Author's Musing

It is my belief that more than anything else, software projects are successful simply because teams displayed a positive mental attitude which makes even the impossible,

(Contd)

possible. When such a positive attitude does not exist—it does not matter how good the plan is—even successful projects up until now are bound to fail! A common-sense approach to resource allocation would be 'don't risk the chances of success by enrolling the support of the "nay-sayers"!' Beginning the project with a 'not possible' orientation makes the possible, impossible!

It is best to delegate the execution of high-risk projects to risk takers; risk avoiders are obviously a poor choice. The minimal expectations for a project plan are to ensure that stakeholders are involved, with necessary commitments in terms of allocation of budgets, schedule, buffer resources and crucial competencies. Doing so fulfills the following goal:

SG2 Develop a Project Plan

- SP2.1 **Establish the Budget and Schedule**
- SP2.2 **Identify Project Risks**
- SP2.3 **Plan for Data Management**
- SP2.4 **Plan for Project Resources**
- SP2.5 **Plan for Needed Knowledge and Skills**
- SP2.6 **Plan Stakeholder Involvement**
- SP2.7 **Establish the Project Plan**

Note the difference to the goal and practice titles in CMMI-SVC V1.3.

SG2 Develop a Work Plan

- SP2.1 Establish the Budget and Schedule
- SP2.2 Identify Risks
- SP2.3 Plan Data Management
- SP2.4 Plan the Resources
- SP2.5 Plan Needed Knowledge and Skills
- SP2.6 Plan Stakeholder Involvement
- SP2.7 Establish the Work Plan

Given the right resources, chances of success in execution of the project are high. Project plans are reviewed with the involvement of the project team to ensure buy-in from the multiple constituencies that determine successful project execution. Typically a project kickoff meeting is held, along with the senior management, with a well-defined accountability structure for the project. A well-structured project typically runs on twin engines—a technical lead and a project lead. The role of the technical lead is to ensure that requirements are correct, consistent, complete and testable. And the project lead ensures that the team marches forward in step with the established project plan. Periodic team meetings are conducted to track and monitor the plan. Should there be a deviation, corrective actions are taken to eliminate the risk factors and to ensure successful execution of the project. The specific practices that support this goal are given below:

SG3 Obtain Commitment to the Plan

- SP3.1 **Review Plans That Affect the Project**
- SP3.2 **Reconcile Work and Resource Levels**
- SP3.3 **Obtain Plan Commitment**

Note the difference to the goal and practice titles in CMMI-SVC V1.3.

SG3 Obtain Commitment to the Plan

- SP3.1 **Review Plans That Affect the Work**
- SP3.2 **Reconcile Work and Resource Levels**
- SP3.3 **Obtain Plan Commitment**

When all of the above 14 specific practices in the three specific goals of Project Planning are supported in intent and true spirit, the project's capability is said to operate at the 'performed level' or capability level 1 for Project Planning.

The practical sides to Project Planning as experienced with some of the author's best professional associations are as follows:

Project Planning

1. List execution options available for consideration based on a study of the requirements and available organizational competencies
2. Determine the constraint of operation (cost, quality, schedule or scope)
3. For multiple constraints of operation, rank them in order of priority and significance and establish a Risk Management procedure
4. Use brainstorming sessions with customers and stakeholders to decide if the available prioritized options result in ownership
5. Establish a work breakdown structure along with work allocations and project schedule
6. Establish a staffing profile showing ramp-up and ramp-down for the project based on complexity analysis and an assessment of the domain competencies
7. If ownership does not result, escalate the matter to senior management

Display 4.2 Interpreting Project Planning

Source: Adapted from SITARA Process JewelBox™ © SITARA Technologies Pvt. Ltd. 2002 with permission

How does Project Planning process area transform its capability when the transition to capability level 2 (or the managed level) is made?

Remember eepat mimor? The process needs the support of these ten generic practices to institutionalize a formal mechanism for Project Planning. An organizational policy defines the need for a project plan and establishes the criteria that projects should adopt for enabling project management. Standard tools for Project Planning are identified and made available for projects. A general note on the choice of tools at a capability level 2: it is dictated by the customer. So, projects could use more than one tool to institutionalize a project management competency. In fact this genetic diversity is what instills the notion of best practices in a capability level 2 process within which there is an inherent oversight mechanism that is called for through the process of stakeholder reviews and senior management reviews. In a sense these generic practices seed the realization of project monitoring and the initiation of appropriate project control mechanisms to remedy any potential deviation.

The policy also establishes the criteria whereby individuals can assume critical project roles, such as that of the project manager or technical leader. It also defines the necessary training that is necessary for project managers and program managers to enhance their knowledge, skills and process abilities. Such training must also impart a thorough working knowledge of process models, for example, the CMMI-DEV, CMMI-SVC, CMMI-ACQ, ITIL and methodologies such as Six Sigma. The requirements churn most definitely influences the effort distribution and reallocation of resources. Under such circumstances, the project plan is monitored through the use of well-defined techniques for managing the creation and release of the most current project plan. When such changes are made, the project plan has to be reviewed with all concerned stakeholders to obtain their commitment to the newer objectives and goals.

In summary, the same ten generic practices we explored in Requirements Management would apply. We will restate them just once more to facilitate recollection. Going forward, this set of ten generic practices will be abbreviated as EPPAT MIMOR with fewer references to the complete practice titles.

GP2.1 **Establish an Organizational Policy**

GP2.2 **Plan the Process**

GP2.3 **Provide Resources**

GP2.4 **Assign Responsibility**

GP2.5 **Train People**

GP2.6 **Manage Configurations**

GP2.7 **Identify and Involve Relevant Stakeholders**

GP2.8 **Monitor and Control the Process**

GP2.9 **Objectively Evaluate Adherence**

GP2.10 **Review Status with Higher-Level Management**

While it is easy to say 'follow the eepat mimor and you will have institutionalization', it is nevertheless quite a challenge! If it were that simple, most organizations would easily demonstrate a capability level 2. Some of the challenges the author has faced as a practitioner are as follows:

- **How does one embrace a customer's process if it is different from what the organizational policy expects?**
- *In what ways would an onsite-offshore model adapt to the CMMI where the offshore process gets to operate in a 'hands-off' mode on Project Planning?* Meaning: the onsite determines the estimates, schedules and the plan, and the offshore process only has to deliver upon these expectations. In such cases how does one tailor the CMMI?

There are common-sense answers to these questions: 'Do what it takes to get the job done!' and 'know that a plan is good only until the battle begins'. The limitation with a capability level 2 type of project plan is that when the project gets into trouble, the ones who are burnt out are the engineers—the ones who had nothing to do with the planning process! The realization of the importance of these two statements results in a mind-set that builds the level 3 or the defined capability.

How does Project Planning process area transform its capability when the transition to capability level 3 (or the defined level) is made?

When a *do-what-it-takes* spirit exists, it is but natural to explore alternative practices which adequately accommodate the requirements of real life and at the same time meet the expectations of the CMMI practices. It is here that a sense of process ownership resulting from a proactive mind-set—customer is the one who gets me my paycheck and not my employer—ensures the possibility of defining a process that is proactive to accommodating change and realizing a value proposition that is tangible even when the deadlines are aggressive. There is no harm in having aggressive but meaningful deadlines. As is well said, 'a goal without a deadline is a dream'. Stretched goals actually serve the purpose of infusing a certain sense of process innovation to enable the realization of the impossible. But, the lesson that is learnt well in the process of making a transition to the level 3 capability is to say 'no!' to an unreasonable request. Project management matures at capability level 3 into a competency and plays an influencing role in customer decisions. A capability level 3 process establishes a sense of credibility for the organizational baselines on estimates of schedule, effort, cost and quality for a defined project complexity and plays an influencing role while deciding these for the customer.

A culture of best practices, which a capability level 3 process area enables, permits stakeholders to take note of both the successful and mistake-prone processes in the OSSP in order to effect appropriate corrections to them. The defined project management process details activities necessary for conducting periodic retrospectives and end-of-project postmortems to help analyze *what went right* and *what went wrong*. The process improvement framework is used to permit problem recognition and mistake-proof the Project Planning process. When a problem is identified or when a process fails, the word is spread around so that all other projects might take note of this and prevent such an occurrence. Likewise, when good practices become evident, the good word goes around too, so others might follow in the same footsteps, leading to success.

Improvements to Project Planning parameters can be known in quantitative terms with the use of measures such as schedule performance index (SPI), cost performance index (CPI), effort variation (EV), and schedule variation (SV). These measures can be tracked periodically during the execution of the project. For the realization of a capability level 3, generic goal 3 and the related generic practices have to be institutionalized. Recollecting them:

GG3 Institutionalize a Defined Process

GP3.1 **Establish a Defined Process**

GP3.2 **Collect Improvement Information**

Author's Musing

Schedule and effort variation offer a good management perspective to understand how good the estimation accuracy is. Typically, deviation is calculated as

[Actual-Estimated] expressed as a percentage of the Estimated value

Therefore, Deviation = [Actual-Estimated]/ [Estimated]

Note: In practice, variation and deviation are used interchangeably and they both mean the same thing. I personally favor the use of the term 'deviation'.

How does Project Planning process area transform its capability when the transition to capability level 4 (or the quantitatively managed level) is made? Or, how does Project Planning demonstrate a high maturity measurement and analysis capability?

The quantitative understanding of the Project Planning process area is dependent upon the accuracy of the base metric and the effectiveness of the metrics collection process. We will restrict the discussion here to understanding how CPI, SPI, SV, and EV are useful.

CPI is a ratio of the budgeted cost to the actual cost. The CPI number ideally should be 1, but then, with CPI as 1, from the finance manager's point of view the project would not make much profit! So, a goal for a CPI value could be established based on profitability concerns and by considering other humanistic aspects such as employee burnout, at say 1.2 (actual costs are 20 percent below the budget), and the projects' CPI performance could be tracked against such a goal—also called the bull's-eye. Tracking CPI with a bull's-eye could be established as a run chart.

It would be meaningless to use a control chart for reasons explained earlier in the chapter. Another reason could be that establishing a control chart helps understand the importance of *what was done* to bring a value closer to the average value (accepted quality level or a goal that is used, such as CPI being 1.2). In an endeavor such as software development, it is extremely difficult if not impossible to list down everything that a project manager did to bring the CPI value closer to the ideal. Besides, between two points in the project execution which are spaced out in time, numerous factors, which do not have a direct cause–effect relationship, come into play. What appears to be a common cause variation due to the *voice-of-process (VOP)* based on studying the 'effects' part of the cause–effect equilibrium may in fact have a cause that is external to the process, arising due to the *voice-of-customer (VOC)* when analyzed using the causes. One of the reasons for this dichotomy is that the process governing development and the process controlling execution typically are distributed between the development site (offshore) and the customer site (or onsite). But, the responsibility or ownership of the product or outcome is shared between both sides of the process development and process control. This makes the absolute assignment of the cause of variation to either the *voice-of-process (VOP)* (common cause) or the *voice-of-customer (VOC)* (special cause) difficult.

Author's Musing

This leads to another interesting find from personal research: when analyzing a variation pattern, it is useful to do a separate analysis of the 'effects' and the 'causes' before one can gain meaningful insights. Conducting a Causal Analysis and Resolution is useful if and only if both the cause and effect have the same source (either the *voice-of-process (VOP)* or the *voice-of-customer (VOC)*). If the sources of cause and effect are different, then conducting a full-scale causal analysis in software engineering is not recommended. This problem has a very high incidence since software development initiatives are globally and geographically distributed with no clear demarcations for what is in process and what is outside the process.

Of course, such analysis can be driven from historical data to speed it up and would have to be maintained as a live record by the process assurance personnel.

SPI is the ratio of planned schedule (in chronological days) versus the actual schedule (in chronological days). SPI is best tracked at a project level by the project manager on the high-level tasks of the WBS, with the necessary empowerment of engineers to track their own low-level tasks. To give an example: if the planned schedule for a project was 100 chronological days, and it took just 50 days to complete the project (actual schedule), then the SPI is 2. On the other hand, if the planned schedule was 100 days and it took 150 days to complete the project, there would be a schedule overrun now, and the SPI would be 0.66. An ideal value for SPI is 1. However, for projects which are of the fixed-bid type it is more profitable to have high SPI values, provided other quality-related and humanistic aspects can be accounted for.

SV is a related topic. It describes how closely the scheduled end date of a task is living up to its expectations. The schedule deviation is known in terms of chronological days and is indicative of how far ahead or how far behind a task is from completion. And when this deviation is expressed in terms of the estimated value, schedule variation is expressed as a percentage of the estimated value. This measure is a good indicator of the progress being made on the project.

EV is related to understanding how the person-day effort that was planned for a project varies over the execution. A good level 4 project plan recognizes a staff ramp-up and ramp-down process that is based on both practical and planned realities. The effort in person-days even with the COCOMO is a subjective decision—though based on certain parameters which we review next.

The COCOMO by Barry Boehm is a hierarchy of three models which is based on an assessment of the project characteristics [Boehm 1981]. COCOMO classifies a project to be of one of the three types or modes—organic, semidetached and embedded.

Organic mode refers to projects which have small teams that execute the project from experience and for which the requirements are well established. Semidetached refers to a project with intermediate levels of complexity and calls for team competencies which have a mix of both experts and the apprentice level of individuals. Both these classes have relatively low RVI since requirements are usually fixed and do not change much. The embedded mode of a project classification usually has multiple operational constraints with tight deadlines and quality requirements. In other words, the embedded mode projects can be considered to be critical projects with extremely high expectations.

Effort and the chronological months are then computed using the established a–b–c–d parameters based on historical project data and current project characteristics using a basic regression formula. These parameters are fixed according to the type of software project. For more insights into how these numbers are fixed one is referred to Boehm (1981).

Project Type	a	b	c	d
Organic	2.4	1.05	2.5	0.38
Semidetached	3.0	1.12	2.5	0.35
Embedded	3.6	1.2	2.5	0.32

Estimation could be based on either the approximate number of lines of code (LOCs) that have to be developed or the number of function points (FPs). Such size estimates get accurate only after sufficient clarity is obtained toward the completion of low-level design. Therefore, effort and schedule estimation accuracy using COCOMO improves only after low-level design, an unfortunate practical reality since sufficient project time would have elapsed by then. For projects which have a history of execution, the COCOMO probably serves its purpose well.

Software engineering literature is replete with translation of FP to LOC count (e.g., 128 LOCs in C language are 1 FP, 29 LOCs in an object-oriented language are 1 FP, and so on). Using such an approximate value for the FP or the LOC value, the estimates for effort and chronological months is determined using COCOMO model 1 in its most basic form. A research initiative on the COCOMO from SITARA Technologies establishes, after repeated trials, that COCOMO results are accurate only when the LOC count is in the 2000 to 50 million lines of code range. Below 2000 LOC, and above 50 million LOCs, the COCOMO does not yield any insights for effort or chronological months' determination (SITARA SET V2.0)[6].

6 SITARA Software Engineering Tool: SET V2.0 is based on an award-winning tool at the Motorola Software Engineering Symposium and Tools Fair 1994, called the Integrated Software Engineering Toolkit (ISET) developed by the author. ISET attempted to automate the development life cycle using a suite of collaborative tools. I would like to acknowledge the work of a research student of mine, Mr. Somu Patil, in the creation of Software Engineering Tool SET V1.0.

When the COCOMO model 2 or the intermediate COCOMO is used, then in addition to the number of lines of code, cost drivers based on project attributes, hardware attributes and personnel attributes are also taken into consideration. SITARA's research has used the following information from classical software engineering literature on this topic to describe the cost drivers. The sequence of steps along with the corresponding screenshots from the SITARA Software Engineering Tool, SITARA SET Version 2.0, are described in what follows.

STEP 1:

Invoke SITARA Software Engineering Tool.

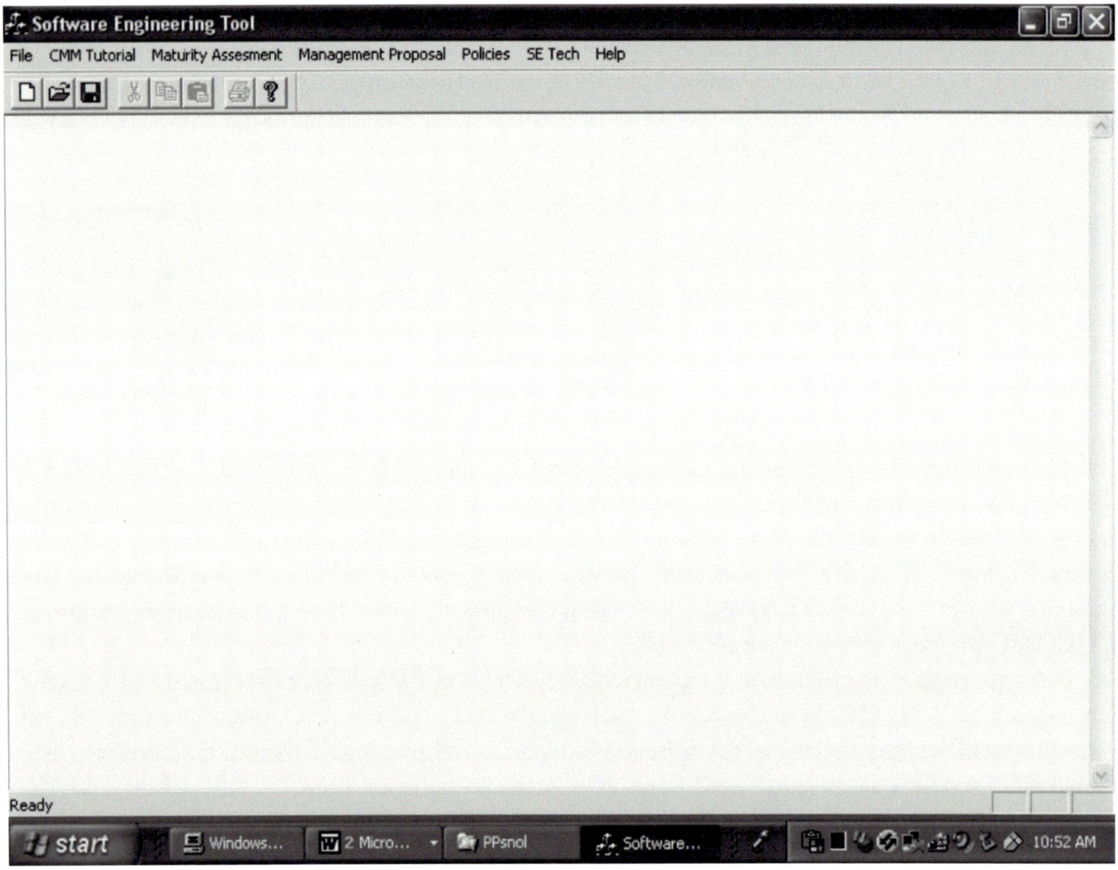

STEP 2:

Decide the class of the project as organic, semidetached or embedded and choose between the LOC or FP estimate.

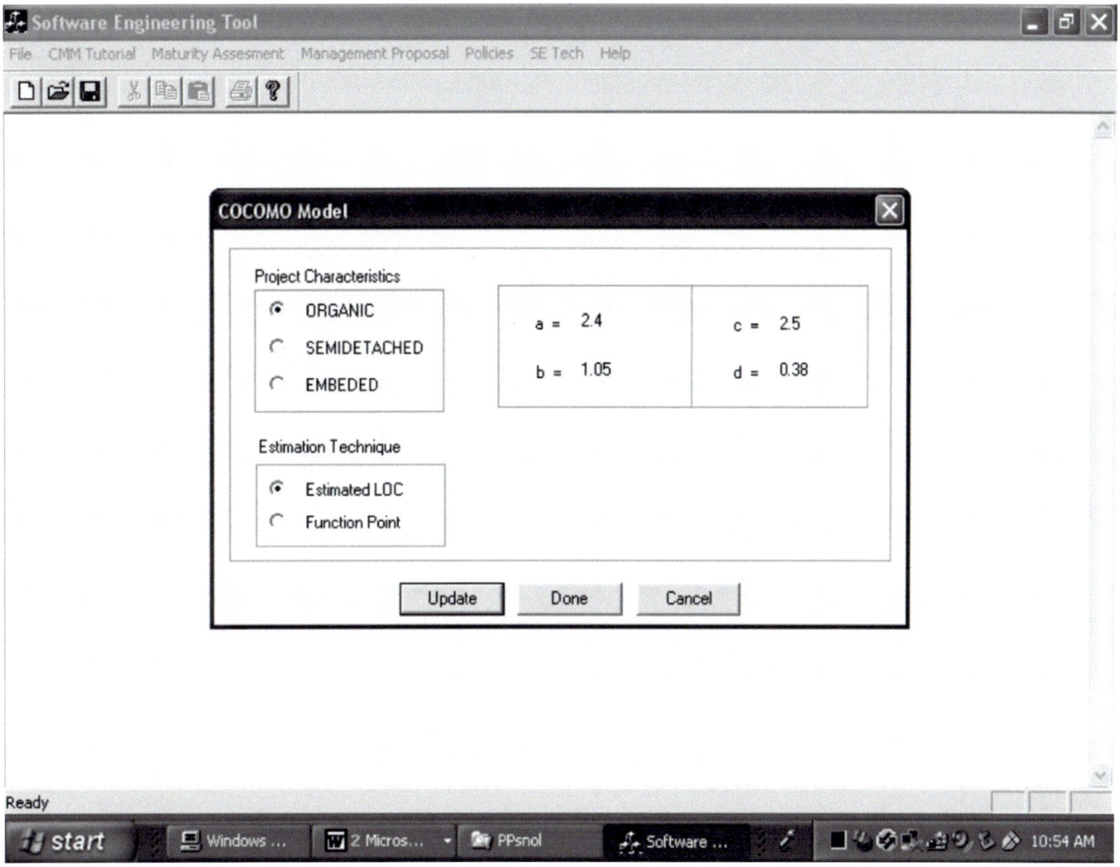

STEP 3:

Enter the approximate value for LOC. Consider the weighted average of three values for the LOC (optimistic, pessimistic and most likely) using the formula Estimated LOC = [Optimistic Estimate + 4 × (Most Likely Estimate) + Pessimistic Estimate]/6.

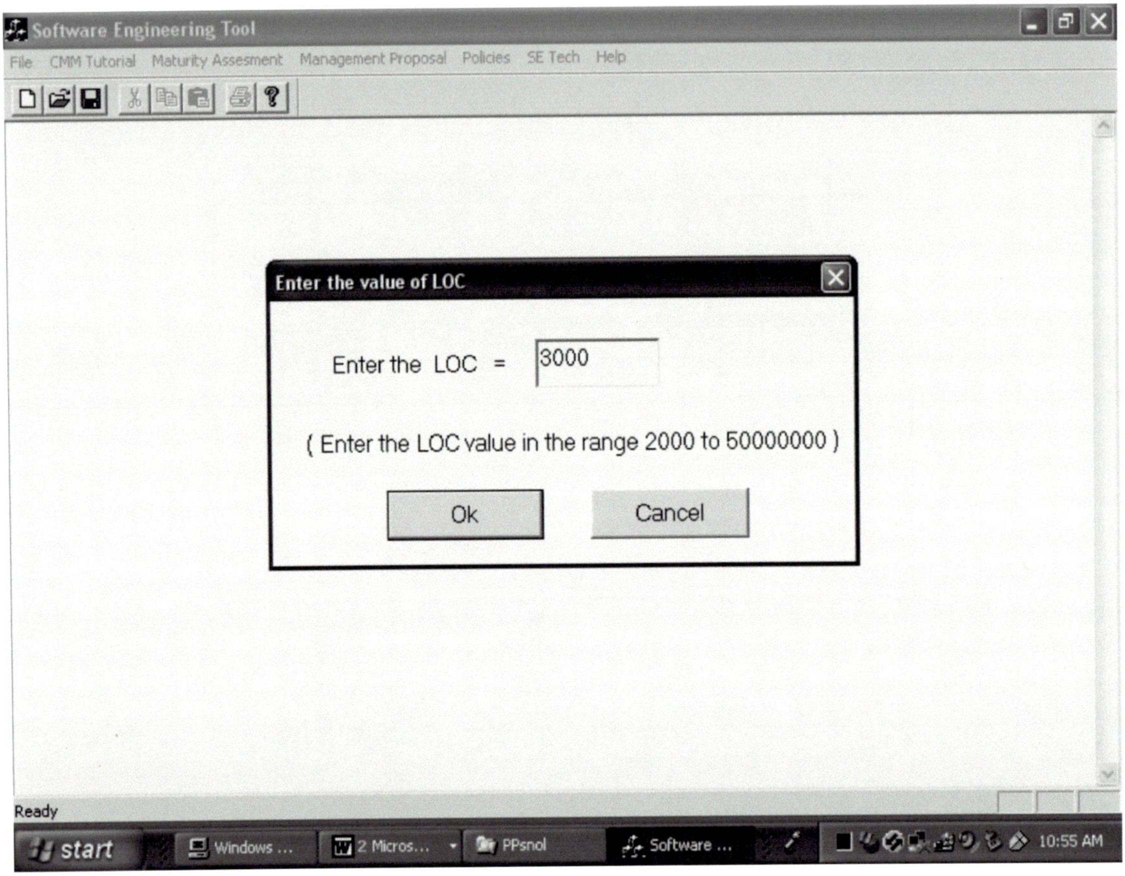

STEP 4:

Obtain team consensus on the 15 project attributes cost drivers on the parameters shown on the screen. These parameters are ranked on a *low–average–high* scale relying on experience: required software reliability, database size, product complexity, execution time constraints, main storage constraints, virtual machine volatility, computer turnaround time, analyst capability, application experience, programmer capability, virtual machine experience, programming language experience, modern language experience, use of software tools and required development schedule.

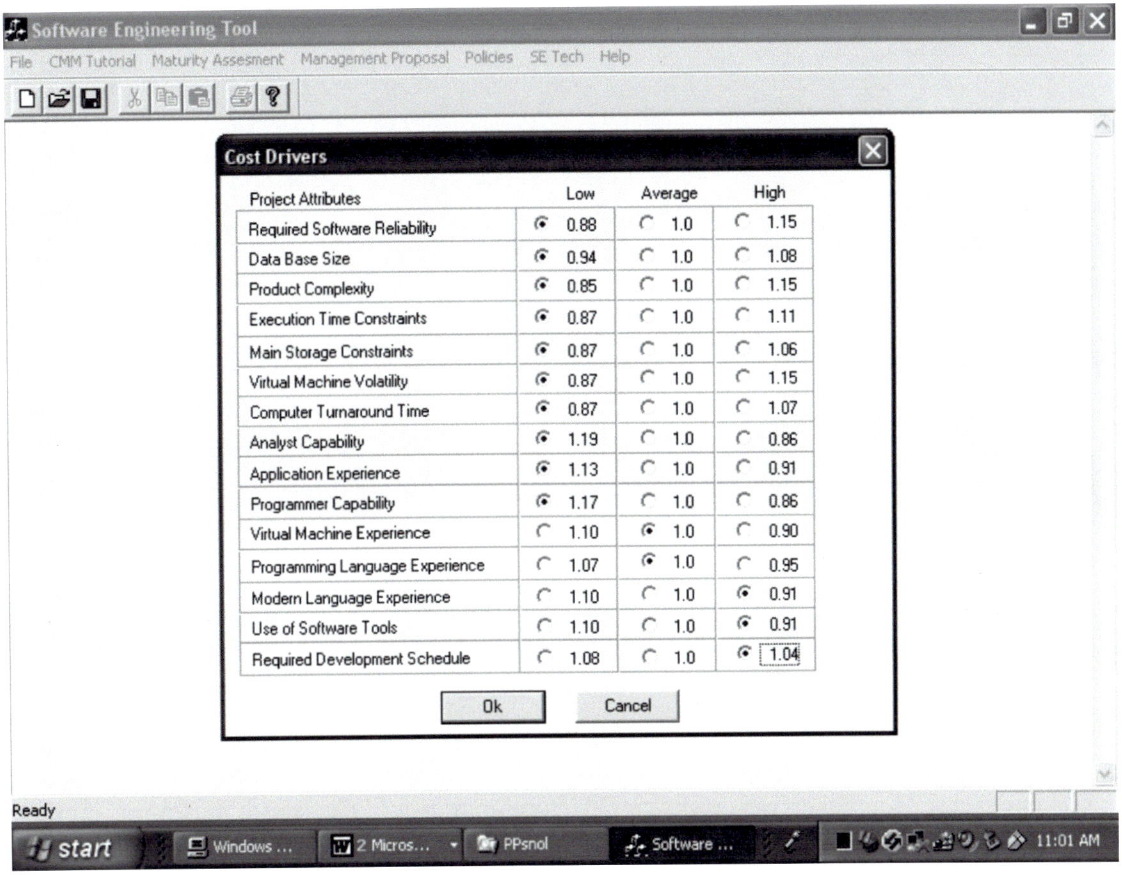

STEP 5:

The SITARA SET Version 2.0 calculates both the initial and the final effort based on well-published effort adjust factors (EAFs). EAFs range from 0.9 to 1.4 and SET takes the average value from using 0.9 and 1.4 and reports the final effort value, which is the most practical effort in person-months that a project can consider. Duration in chronological months is also provided by the tool using the final effort value. Based on the final effort and duration, it is possible to determine the number of resources that are required. In this screenshot below, for the selections made, approximately 1 person is good enough to work for about 4.2 chronological months.

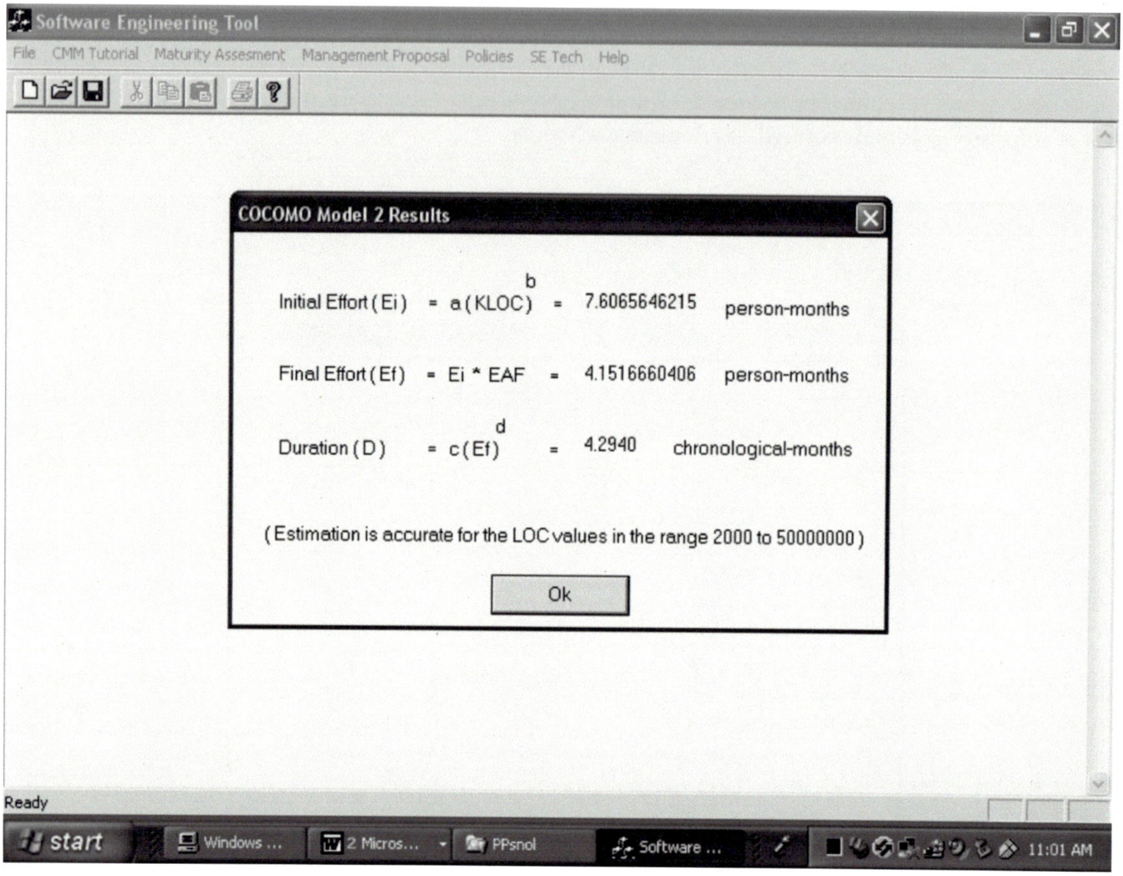

On a closing note, it is useful to take note of the fact that the use of internal tools such as the SITARA SET Version 2.0 for establishing estimates for effort and development time is a mechanism to minimize the common cause of variation (*voice-of-process (VOP)*, or more specifically voice of the Project Planning process). Organizational Innovation and Deployment (OID), which is a level 5 process area, encourages the use of such innovations resulting from technology and tools research to build a foundation of practices which enables a process area to operate at the next capability level, which is level 5.

From the perspective of the CMMI constellations, two generic practices are necessary to support the intent of a capability level 4 process area:

GP4.1 Establish Quantitative Objectives for the Process

GP4.2 Stabilize Sub-Process Performance

These generic practices should be applied to the practices that define the Project Planning process.

How does Project Planning process area transform its capability when the transition to capability level 5 (or the optimizing level) is made? Or, how does Project Planning demonstrate a high maturity measurement and analysis capability?

The only known technique for minimizing common cause variation in a Project Planning process is to know more and learn more about the project with a keen, discerning eye for detail. Repetition and honing the art of Project Planning and program management into a competency is the only sure-shot formula for minimizing the impact of common cause variation. Validated historical data and a rich project information base, along with the use of formal methods such as the COCOMO, most definitely go a long way in enabling Project Planning to operate at a capability level 5.

From the perspective of the CMMI constellations, two generic practices are necessary to support the intent of a capability level 5 process area:

GP5.1 **Ensure Continuous Process Improvement**

GP5.2 **Correct Root Causes of Problems**

These generic practices should be applied to the practices that define the Project Planning process.

It may be useful to point out that the specific practices of PP in general enable the realization of GP2.2 ('Plan the Process'), GP2.3 ('Provide Resources'), GP2.4 ('Assign Responsibilities') and GP2.7 ('Identify and Involve Relevant Stakeholders') across the 22 process areas of the CMMI-DEV, six process areas of the CMMI-ACQ constellation and seven process areas of the CMMI-SVC constellation.

PROJECT MONITORING AND CONTROL (PMC)[7] CMMI-DEV, CMMI-ACQ AND CMMI-SVC

How does Project Monitoring and Control process area look when it operates at a capability level 1 (or the performed level)?

The purpose of Project Monitoring and Control is to provide an understanding of the project's progress so that appropriate corrective actions can be taken when the project's performance deviates significantly from the plan. Project Monitoring and Control belongs to the project management category of the continuous representation of the CMMI. The Project Planning process area establishes a mechanism to develop a project plan based on project requirements, whereas Project Monitoring and Control helps to maintain the plan using a defined tracking mechanism. In a sense, Project Planning and Project Monitoring and Control go hand in hand.

When significant deviation from the planned events takes place, appropriate corrective actions are taken to minimize the impact on the project. Project Monitoring and Control involves establishing a structured process to monitor the Project Planning parameters such as size, effort, cost and schedule. It also enables a project to ensure that commitments are renewed periodically with the project stakeholders.

[7] In version 1.3, Project Monitoring and Control is renamed to Work Monitoring and Control only in the CMMI-SVC constellation. It will still remain a core process area since the nature of change is only renaming the word 'project' to 'work' which is more relevant in the context of services.

From the execution standpoint, a list of risks that could potentially impact the project and those that arise as a result of certain decisions made in relation to the project are documented and understood. Implications of the risk are normally assessed on the basis of a decision analysis process and monitored using periodic project reviews.

Information required for project execution such as engineering specifications, engineering standards, algorithms, reuse of legacy information and standard data structures are also monitored in order to ensure that it is current and can be used on changing project needs. At important project transition points such as when a critical milestone is encountered, a milestone review to take stock of the health of the project is conducted through a process of management oversight. Progress reviews leading to the attainment of milestones and those tasks which are on the critical path are also conducted with an intention to minimize the impact of potential risks and increase the probability of expected closure.

The corresponding specific goal and specific practices that should be fulfilled are as follows:

SG1 Monitor Project against Plan

- SP1.1 **Monitor Project Planning Parameters**
- SP1.2 **Monitor Commitments**
- SP1.3 **Monitor Project Risks**
- SP1.4 **Monitor Data Management**
- SP1.5 **Monitor Stakeholder Involvement**
- SP1.6 **Conduct Progress Reviews**
- SP1.7 **Conduct Milestone Reviews**

Note the difference to the goal and practice titles in CMMI-SVC V1.3.

SG1 Monitor the Work Against the Plan

- SP1.1 **Monitor Work Planning Parameters**
- SP1.2 **Monitor Commitments**
- SP1.3 **Monitor Risks**
- SP1.4 **Monitor Data Management**
- SP1.5 **Monitor Stakeholder Involvement**
- SP1.6 **Conduct Progress Reviews**
- SP1.7 **Conduct Milestone Reviews**

The next set of specific practices helps to ensure that corrective actions are rendered in a timely manner befitting the circumstances in the context of the existing project needs. Any project would have to face up to the challenges of the real-life drawbacks resulting from either 'common causes' (*voice-of-process (VOP)*) or 'special causes' (*voice-of-customer (VOC)*). When corrective actions have to be rendered, all concerned stakeholders are involved in the decision process following a thorough analysis of the issues at hand.

The capability level 1 practices that enable this vision within the CMMI help to achieve the following specific goal:

SG2 Manage Corrective Action to Closure

- SP2.1 **Analyze Issues**
- SP2.2 **Take Corrective Action**
- SP2.3 **Manage Corrective Action**

Note the difference to the goal and practice titles in CMMI-SVC V1.3.

SG2 Manage Corrective Action to Closure

- SP2.1 Analyze Issues
- SP2.2 Take Corrective Action
- SP2.3 Manage Corrective Actions

When the above ten specific practices of Project Monitoring and Control are supported in intent and spirit, the project's capability is said to operate at the 'performed level' or capability level 1.

The practical sides to Project Monitoring and Control as experienced with some of the author's best professional associations are as follows:

Project Monitoring And Control

1. Track the high-level and detailed tasks as percentage completed through a project plan using a tool that supports such capability
2. Assess the progress on a periodic basis with the team, by reviewing the completion status of tasks in the project plan
3. Update the risk list of the project based on a team assessment of project volatility
4. Use a brainstorming session with the customer and stakeholders to decide if a new prioritization of the options on the plan need to be established
5. Understand the plan of events ahead of the project and establish accountability structure and staffing structure
6. If ownership to the renewed commitments does not result, escalate the matter to senior management

Display 4.3 Interpreting Project Monitoring and Control

Source: Adapted from SITARA Process JewelBoxTM © SITARA Technologies Pvt. Ltd. 2002 with permission

How does Project Monitoring and Control (PMC) process area transform its capability when the transition to capability level 2 (or the managed level) is made?

PMC is a proactive approach to identifying the course of action necessary for executing the project based on real-time feedback. Real-time decisions have to be taken from the frontline and the practices contained within PMC enables project leaders to establish a vision for the project based on an assessment of ground reality. A policy should therefore support and empower the project leaders with tools and infrastructure that help to make such real-time decisions.

When institutionalized at capability level 2, PMC serves the purpose of establishing the necessary infrastructure such as project management and project tracking tools, configuration management tools, and the like, along with requisite training on how to use them to effectively monitor and control the execution of the project. Progress reviews are normally used at level 2 to ensure that the process allows for both corrective and preventive actions so as to contain gross deviations within the project which might lead to risks.

Monitoring the Project Planning parameters of schedule, cost, time, effort and scope is done using a metrics database. Besides, other related measures such as cost of quality, productivity, maturity indicators for the project, process and overall delivery are also monitored using quantitative definitions for the measures. The goals established for these measures are monitored periodically and appropriate corrective actions are taken when the thresholds are exceeded. The metrics information itself is reviewed and sanitized using the most current project performance baselines during baseline reviews.

In order to establish a capability level 2 PMC process area, the generic practices which go by the mnemonic eepat mimor have to be institutionalized in order to fulfill a required generic goal—GG2. Within the EPPAT MIMOR, it might be mentioned that GP2.8—Monitor and Control the Process—is enabled across the process areas of the three CMMI constellations by institutionalizing the specific practices of PMC.

How does Project Monitoring and Control (PMC) process area transform its capability when the transition to capability level 3 (or the defined level) is made?

At level 3, a process definition for consistent application of practices within the PMC is established. Such procedures include criteria for conducting milestone reviews, end-of-phase reviews, baseline reviews and release reviews. In a sense, practices contained within Verification can be reused to enact the PMC practices to a good degree. The purpose of PMC is to ensure enough checks and balances within the project life cycle for its successful execution.

In order to institutionalize a capability level 3 for PMC, GG3 and the related practices have to be established within the process infrastructure. They are as follows:

GG3 Institutionalize a Defined Process

GP3.1 **Establish a Defined Process**

GP3.2 **Collect Improvement Information**

How does Project Monitoring and Control (PMC) process area transform its capability when the transition to capability level 4 (or the quantitatively managed level) is made? Or, how does Project Monitoring and Control demonstrate a high maturity measurement and analysis capability?

PMC complements Project Planning from a quantitative perspective. Deviations for CPI, SPI, SV and EV can be quantitatively monitored to understand the impact due to special cause variations. From the perspective of the CMMI constellations, two generic practices are necessary to support the intent of a capability level 4 process area:

GP4.1 Establish Quantitative Objectives for the Process

GP4.2 Stabilize Sub-Process Performance

These generic practices should be applied to the practices that define the PMC process.

How does Project Monitoring and Control (PMC) process area transform its capability when the transition to capability level 5 (or the optimizing level) is made? Or, how does Project Monitoring and Control demonstrate a high maturity measurement and analysis capability?

Project Planning and PMC practices are highly interdependent. PMC is a good candidate process area to operate at higher capability levels. Some of the practical issues which PMC may not handle effectively are the schedule slippages due to delays resulting from the *voice-of-customer* (*VOC*). While PMC is a good candidate process area to be understood using quantitative techniques and rendered using control charts, special cause variations are highly probable with assignable causes to customer dependencies. Since planning parameters are mostly congruent when the *voice-of-process* (*VOP*) is consistent with the *voice-of-customer* (*VOC*), it is nevertheless useful to understand the characteristics of PMC using statistical techniques. PMC can also play a very effective role in the process if these practices are used to understand the effectiveness of other screening process areas such as Verification and Validation. Questions such as 'Are the right people doing peer reviews?' and 'How well are the peer reviewers prepared and knowledgeable about the work product being reviewed?' would get adequate responses if PMC is institutionalized at a capability level 4 or 5. From the perspective of the CMMI constellations, two generic practices are necessary to support the intent of a capability level 5 process area:

GP5.1 Ensure Continuous Process Improvement

GP5.2 Correct Root Causes of Problems

These generic practices should be applied to the practices that define the PMC process. Refer to the interpretations on enabling Project Planning process area at higher capability levels.

It may be useful to point out that the specific practices of PMC in general enable the realization of GP2.8 ('Monitor and Control the Process') and GP2.10 ('Review Status with Higher-Level Management') across the 22 process areas of the CMMI-DEV, six process areas of the CMMI-ACQ constellation and seven process areas of the CMMI-SVC constellation.

CONFIGURATION MANAGEMENT (CM) CMMI-DEV, CMMI-ACQ AND CMMI-SVC

How does Configuration Management process area look when it operates at a capability level 1 (or the performed level)?

The purpose of Configuration Management is to establish and maintain the integrity of work products using configuration identification, configuration control, configuration status accounting and configuration audits. Configuration Management belongs to the support category of the continuous representation of the CMMI. The purpose of Configuration Management is to establish and maintain the integrity of work products as they evolve during the course of development. Typical work products that govern the execution of a project requiring configuration management are the requirements specification, project plan, requirements analysis or need analysis document, high-level and detailed design, code, unit test cases and test logs, system test cases and test logs, acceptance test cases and test logs and finally release notes and end-user documentation.

A baseline refers to a formal archival process that establishes a point of reference which a project can roll back to, if necessary. Therefore a certain sense of traceability, both within a phase and across phases, is expected to synchronize and stabilize a rollback decision.

Identification of the intermediate work products that define the overall execution of the project is the first important activity that needs to be executed under Configuration Management. An appropriate configuration management system based on project needs to serve as a repository for storing project information with appropriate levels of access restriction is the next step. A formal mechanism to create and release baselines establishes the protocol for how project information can be accessed, used and improved. In doing so the following specific goal at a capability level 1 of the Configuration Management process area is achieved:

SG1 Establish Baselines

- SP1.1 **Identify Configuration Items**
- SP1.2 **Establish a Configuration Management System**
- SP1.3 **Create or Release Baselines**

After establishing such a minimal precondition or a prerequisite for conducting Configuration Management activities, the next set of activities is designed to keep track of the evolution of the work product. Change is a continuous process in the lifeline of a project. Hence, it is impossible to eliminate special causes of variation. In order to minimize the degree of impact, a formal process such as configuration management helps to track changes and to establish a mechanism for conducting an audit to take stock of the execution. These activities are enabled through the following two specific goals and related specific practices:

SG2 Track and Control Changes

- SP2.1 **Track Change Requests**
- SP2.2 **Control Configuration Items**

SG3 Establish Integrity

- SP3.1 **Establish Configuration Management Records**
- SP3.2 **Perform Configuration Audits**

When the above seven specific practices of Configuration Management are supported in intent and spirit, the project's capability is said to operate at the 'performed level' or capability level 1 for Configuration Management.

The practical sides to Configuration Management as experienced by the author with some of his best professional associations are as follows:

Configuration Management

1. Identify the intermediate work products that the project will develop in order to realize project objectives
2. Establish a formal configuration management and version control system for archiving project information
3. Ensure that access to project information and release of project information is assigned to a defined role on the project
4. Establish a mechanism for conducting an assessment of impact of change and internalize the change, as appropriate
5. Should the volatility cause the configuration audit to flag a risk, escalate the matter to the senior management attention

Display 4.4 Interpreting Configuration Management

Source: Adapted from SITARA Process JewelBox™ © SITARA Technologies Pvt. Ltd. 2002 with permission

How does Configuration Management process area transform its capability when the transition to capability level 2 (or the managed level) is made?

Process support policies define the acceptable Configuration Management practices in baseline management as well as release management process. Configuration management and version control tools are made available within the process infrastructure to establish consistency within and across projects. Functional configuration audits (FCAs) and physical configuration audits (PCAs) are conducted on all configuration items within a defined periodicity. The purpose of FCA is to ascertain whether the functionality is being built into specs. FCAs also serve a useful purpose as the progress indicator 'Just how much of what we were supposed to build has been completed and how much more is pending?' is a question that is often the focus of senior management during milestone reviews. Checkpoint reviews planned in the configuration management plan facilitate the conduct of FCAs and PCAs. PCAs ensure that the configuration item is located where it was meant to be. Corrective actions are initiated with appropriate monitoring of corrections to remedy any slips in either the integrity or correctness of configuration items in the configuration management system/database. Backup and retrieval of project data and information with appropriate levels of access control and rights of use is ensured. Rollback of changes and other maintenance functions such as cleanup of unwanted configuration items are handled without compromising the integrity and availability of baseline data. Configuration management assumes a significant importance in the CMMI-SVC constellation to ensure service continuity and minimize interruptions. Necessary training on the right use of configuration management practices and tools is provided to individuals. Depending upon the complexity and size of the project, dedicated configuration and release managers are assigned the responsibility of Configuration Management. Within the EPPAT MIMOR, it might be useful to note that GP2.6 (Manage Configurations) is enabled across the process areas of all three constellations of the CMMI by institutionalizing the specific practices of Configuration Management.

How does Configuration Management process area transform its capability when the transition to capability level 3 (or the defined level) is made?

Best practices across projects and within the industry are reviewed for organizational applicability. Such practices are documented into organizational standards for Configuration Management and revised based on practitioners' experiences. Constellation-specific definitions for configuration and change management activities are defined in relevant process standards and guidelines. A defined Configuration Management process establishes a capability level 3 rigor for Configuration Management, and in the process GG3 and related practices are institutionalized. They are as follows:

GG3 Institutionalize a Defined Process

GP3.1 **Establish a Defined Process**

GP3.2 **Collect Improvement Information**

It is very difficult to demonstrate and justify Configuration Management at a capability beyond level 3. It would also require enough business justifications and customer mandates to do so. However, purely from the CMMI perspective, GG4 and the related generic practices, GP4.1 and GP4.2, need to be established for enabling CM at capability level 4:

GG4 Institutionalize a Quantitatively Managed Process

GP4.1 **Establish Quantitative Objectives for the Process**

GP4.2 **Stabilize Sub-Process Performance**

And to enable CM at capability level 5, GG5 and the associated generic practices, GP5.1 and GP5.2, need to be institutionalized:

GG5 Institutionalize an Optimizing Process

GP5.1 **Ensure Continuous Process Improvement**

GP5.2 **Correct Root Causes of Problems**

It may be useful to point out that the specific practices of CM in general enable the realization of GP2.6 ('Manage Configurations') across the 22 process areas of the CMMI-DEV, six process areas of the CMMI-ACQ constellation and seven process areas of the CMMI-SVC constellation.

MEASUREMENT AND ANALYSIS (MA) CMMI-DEV, CMMI-ACQ AND CMMI-SVC

How does Measurement and Analysis process area look when it operates at a capability level 1 (or the performed level)?

The purpose of Measurement and Analysis is to develop and sustain a measurement capability that is used to support management information needs. Measurement and Analysis belongs in the support category of the continuous representation of the CMMI. Its main purpose is to serve the needs of the project by highlighting the execution with verifiable data, using which management information can be rendered. As observed earlier, process measurement is a serious business and costs a lot of money. While a mature process offers significant opportunities at the work product baseline stage in the development life cycle for metrics collection, a wise and an informed decision has to be made as to what these critical measurement opportunities are at a minimum. Measuring anything that moves is a gross mistake! Not measuring enough is also a gross mistake!

Importance of institutionalizing robust Measurement and Analysis practices can be best understood with the following illustration. Adequate samples of measurement data are an essential prerequisite for subsequent analysis of process performance. Given the nature of project execution in software, a project will at most go through the life-cycle phases at least once from requirements to release and, if well managed, will probably iterate within the life cycle a few times. Therefore, the only measurement opportunities one can conceive are at the time of creation of a baseline or reopening of a baseline. So, for any given phase the number of measurement opportunities and therefore sample points is extremely limited (the author has not seen more than five to ten baseline sample points per work product per phase). Even if similar projects are grouped (which is highly debatable since complexity levels and clarity levels are seldom the same), one can stretch such baseline measurement opportunities to no more than 15–20 points per analysis cycle (which could be between 6 months and 1 year). *Dilemma:* If you wait long enough to get sufficient data points, then the relevance of the analysis no longer holds good! Unless smart measures are taken at appropriate stages within the software life cycle by highly experienced measurement champions, there is good reason to believe that such opportunities will be lost for all time to come.

Measurement and Analysis activities have to align with the overall business objectives. The key question is not 'What do we measure?' but 'What information do we want about the process and product in order to make informed decisions?' Measurement decisions are influenced both by organizational as well as people characteristics. A good measurement program should insulate the risks of making personal judgments on individuals who are tasked to produce work. Easier said than done! The scale of measurement tilts from being in a proactive mode of discovery to a highly reactive mode of behavior modification the moment a project gets into rough weather! It is useful to steer project understanding away from behavior modification to uncovering facts about the process that were not known earlier—and to stay in the discovery mode [DeMarco 1995].

The goal–question–metric paradigm credited to Victor Basili is a very useful technique to address the effectiveness of the measurement program [Basili 1984]. Asking the right questions and knowing the goals of the process area is a good way to work the intent of the CMMI framework into the organizational process design. Asking a question in this new way may be worth a dozen answers—of both quantitative and qualitative nature.

Clarifying the business objectives in an organizational scorecard is a useful first step that actually serves as an input for defining the measurement objectives. Specifying the measure that best characterizes the process, follows. Establishing the mechanism for data collection, defining the most appropriate time for data collection in the execution cycle and defining the mechanism to store and analyze data to produce insightful information for management use is the next logical step. Typically, this would include the types of measurement procedures that would be used to interpret process and product information. We will further discuss such data representation tools when we explore the level 4 process area of Quantitative Project Management. The following practices enable the realization of the specific goal:

SG1 Align Measurement and Analysis Activities

- SP1.1 **Establish Measurement Objectives**
- SP1.2 **Specify Measures**
- SP1.3 **Specify Data Collection and Storage Procedures**
- SP1.4 **Specify Analysis Procedures**

The next set of activities deals with establishing a mechanism for collecting data, analyzing the measurement data, storing the results of such analysis and communicating the insights from measurements to all concerned stakeholders. These practices serve to:

SG2 Provide Measurement Results

- SP2.1 **Collect Measurement Data**[8]
- SP2.2 **Analyze Measurement Data**
- SP2.3 **Store Data and Results**
- SP2.4 **Communicate Results**

When the above eight specific practices of Measurement and Analysis are supported in intent and spirit, the project's capability is said to operate at the 'performed level' or the capability level 1 for Measurement and Analysis.

AUTHOR'S MUSING

A parametric model is one where measurements are conducted using well-defined parameters addressing a measurement need. Metrics must reveal the additional changes that are required, and also the specific training programs that must be provided. And shared vision from having an effective metrics program must shed light on all the three important aspects of project management, process management and engineering.

The flow diagram in Figure 4.1 is an example that illustrates the point that a picture is sometimes worth a thousand words. It captures the spirit of Measurement and Analysis best [Florac et al. 1997].

[8] Practice title appears as "Obtain Measurement Data" in version 1.3 across all three constellations. There is no noticeable/perceptible change to the informative content associated with this practice and therefore to its interpretation.

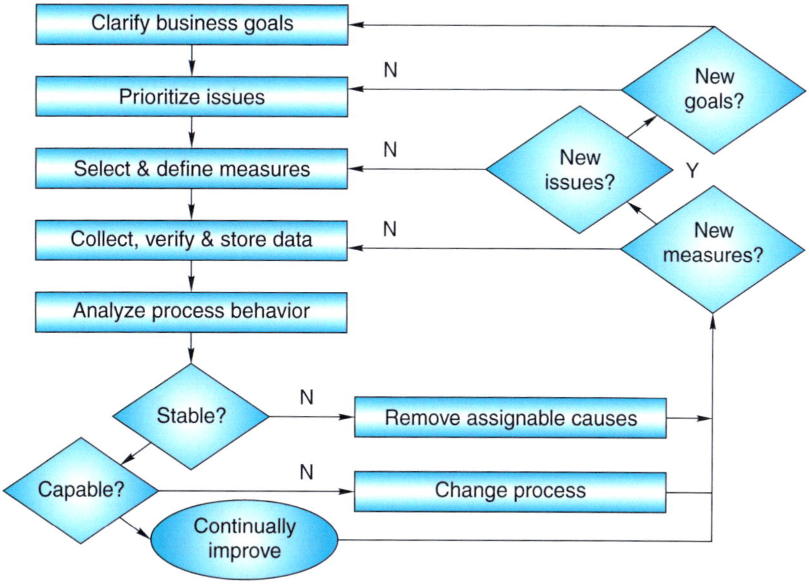

Fig. 4.1 Practical Software Measurement: Measuring for Process Management and Improvement

Source: Adapted from guidebook published by the Software Engineering Institute CMU/SEI-97-HB-003

The practical sides to Measurement and Analysis as experienced by the author with some of his best professional associations are as follows:

Measurement and Analysis

1. List issues that come up month after month in the management review exercise
2. Determine if these are business issues or process issues. If they are business issues, then resolve them through a management process. Otherwise, establish measures based on clarifying and prioritizing the issues
3. Explore a nonintrusive mechanism to collect metrics data; if the level of intrusion has a detrimental side effect on productivity and other humanistic aspects 'after trial', discontinue the metric collection
4. Establish a measurement criteria for each phase of the development life cycle to ensure quality of the intermediate work products
5. Analyze measurement results to arrive at a process solution
6. Revise metrics collection based on insights the process improvement has to offer
7. Should improvement effects result in nonresolution of the issues that surfaced during management review, escalate the matter to the senior management's attention

Display 4.5 Interpreting Measurement and Analysis

Source: Adapted from SITARA Process JewelBox™ © SITARA Technologies Pvt. Ltd. 2002 with permission

How does Measurement and Analysis process area transform its capability when the transition to capability level 2 (or the managed level) is made?

Organizational policy establishes the data management policy including a fair use of process measurement information. Mature processes recognize the fact that if there is a problem it is a process problem, because the right talent was hired for the right reasons. The process improvement framework is put to best use by ensuring that the problem does not recur. If it does, then there is a problem with the process improvement process. Such mature thinking encourages and builds a work culture that is sensitive to providing measures—both good and bad.

Projects establish metrics collection and analysis plans along with the necessary analytical procedures. In order to establish consistency with the techniques employed for data collection, analysis and their representation, definitions for derived metrics are made within a process measurement guideline. Measurement objectives are established to understand the performance of both the process and work products based on quality parameters.

Project-level data capture and analysis is supported with the help of necessary tools, training and infrastructure, such as a metrics database. Data are reviewed in periodic project and management reviews. In cases where gross deviations are found, remedial measures are employed to bring the process or product attribute to within acceptable levels of quality. An essential training requirement which the author has found to be of tremendous value in organizations who manage their process well is training on Six Sigma methodology leading to certifications (Green Belt, Black Belt and Master Black Belt). It is only when the importance of quantitative assessment of process and project performance is ingrained in every individual contributing such information can something meaningful come out of the process of Measurement and Analysis. Representation of process performance and its interpretation to meeting organizational business objectives is the responsibility of the entire rank and file of the organization.

Senior management engagement in the process of goal setting, driving change based on quantitative feedback, and improving the process capability based on actual performance results is an essential prerequisite to enable high-maturity CMMI practices. Measurement and Analysis practices using some form of cascading business goals down to the last person in the organization serve an essential purpose in laying a firm foundation to meet this objective. Balanced scorecards described in Chapter 7 while interpreting the practices of OID are typically used to serve this purpose. In other words, if Measurement and Analysis is not solid even at a capability level 2 rigor, subsequent process improvements are rendered useless. Individuals who are sensitive to measurement and analysis of their own work are essential if the overall organizational maturity/capability has to be improved. After all, the capability of an organization is the collective capability of the individuals making up the organization. What better way to know this, if not quantitatively?

In order to establish Measurement and Analysis at level 2 capability, generic goal 2 and the ten generic practices with the mnemonic EPPAT MIMOR have to be institutionalized.

How does Measurement and Analysis process area transform its capability when the transition to capability level 3 (or the defined level) is made?

Since Measurement and Analysis is a support process area, a set of defined practices for the remaining process areas helps to establish objective measurement and analysis criteria. Data definitions for project and process parameters are provided in a metrics guideline. Periodic review of measurement information across the organization and sanitizing project data ensures data integrity. In order to establish a capability level 3 for Measurement and Analysis, the following have to be institutionalized:

GG3 Institutionalize a Defined Process

GP3.1 **Establish a Defined Process**

GP3.2 **Collect Improvement Information**

Author's Musing

I would like to make a general observation here about my interpretation of 'how to know whether a process area is operating beyond capability level 3'. A crucial test to know this is to identify whether the specific practices contained in the process area have enabled either of these two desirable conditions:

1. Do the practices show a reduction of overall cycle time? 2. Do the adopted practices show a reduction in post-release defects?

If the answers to any of these two questions can be proved to be positive, with supporting data to justify, then the process area can be considered to demonstrate influences of having reached higher capability levels. It would be difficult, if not impossible, for most support process areas to operate beyond a defined capability level. Measurement and Analysis is a support process area. Having a robust set of Measurement and Analysis practices enables quantitative management and scaling up the capability levels for process areas in the other categories.

Software measurement cannot be automated and is still very much an intrusive process. It requires individuals to be sensitive to collect the right metrics at the right time (mostly before formal baselines can be established). However, one might justify that Measurement and Analysis has attained a capability level 4 with the mere use of consistent metrics templates and tools. In a sense, common cause variation (due to the *voice-of-process (VOP)*) could very well be contained using these steps. However, the very act of measurement cannot be automated. What about analysis? Maybe, maybe not! Therefore it requires a different interpretation to know whether a process area has scaled up to higher capability levels. One example is illustrated of how analysis of the Risk Management process area using a consistent template as in Template 4.1 might minimize common cause variations.

It is very difficult to demonstrate and justify Measurement and Analysis at a capability beyond level 3. Being a support category process area common to all three constellations of the CMMI, it would also require enough business justifications and customer mandates to do so. However, purely from a theoretical perspective, the generic goal 4 and the related generic practices 4.1 and 4.2 need to be established for enabling OID at capability level 4. And to enable OID at capability level 5, the generic goal 5 and the associated generic practices 5.1 and 5.2 need to be institutionalized:

GG4 Institutionalize a Quantitatively Managed Process

GP4.1 **Establish Quantitative Objectives for the Process**

GP4.2 **Stabilize Sub-Process Performance**

Project Management–Risk Priority Number

Purpose: To understand the degree of change within a project's execution context and plan for the necessary abatement

Inputs	• Likelihood of occurrence [L] • Impact [I] • Phase of occurrence/detection [P]
Outputs	• Risk priority number [RPN]
Calculation	RPN = L × I × P
Typical Use	1. Each of the inputs can have a number ranging from 1 to 10 using the following: Likelihood: Low (1–3), Medium (4–6), High (7–10) Impact: Low (1–3), Medium (4–6), High (7–10) Phase: Early life cycle (1–3), Mid-life cycle (4–6), End life cycle (7–10)
	2. RPN is the product of Likelihood, Impact and Phase. If RPN < 30, then the individual assigned the issue will document the necessary abatement procedure and resolve the issue If 35 < RPN < 215, the team will evolve the best abatement strategy using a brainstorming session and diffuse the issue If 250 < RPN < 1000, the team along with senior management will diffuse the issue along with the other categories impacting decision making 3. Also to determine if SITARA DAR guidelines have to be employed to plan an alternative course of actions or abatement steps (refer to Decision Analysis and Resolution Process Area)

Template 4.1 Template for Defining Software Metrics with an Example Definition for Risk Priority Number in the Project Management Category

Source: Adapted from SITARA Process JewelBox™ © SITARA Technologies Pvt. Ltd. 2002 with permission

GG5 Institutionalize an Optimizing Process

GP5.1 Ensure Continuous Process Improvement

GP5.2 Correct Root Causes of Problems

It may be useful to point out that the specific practices of Measurement and Analysis in general enable the realization of GP2.8 ('Monitor and Control the Process') across the 22 process areas of the CMMI-DEV, six process areas of the CMMI-ACQ constellation and seven process areas of the CMMI-SVC constellation.

PROCESS AND PRODUCT QUALITY ASSURANCE (PPQA) CMMI-DEV, CMMI-ACQ AND CMMI-SVC

How does Process and Product Quality Assurance (PPQA) process area look when it operates at a capability level 1 (or the performed level)?

The purpose of PPQA is to provide staff and management with objective insight into processes and associated work products. Process and Product Quality Assurance belongs in the support category of the continuous representation of the CMMI. While there is no need for a separate group of individuals such as the quality assurance to conduct the PPQA activities, objectivity has to be ensured. This is absolutely justified given the rich domain content that needs to be understood for building effectiveness and efficiencies with such PPQA activities. Project leaders from related domains working on other projects or modules could very well conduct PPQA activities. This mechanism is very useful, because when project leaders also become process champions, the process improvement program has a good chance to get into the autopilot mode. Besides, multiplexing project leaders from other projects working on similar domains to render the PPQA activities on a related project has the high probability of seeding and growth of best practices, since such a critiquing exercise now becomes a *value-added* activity. The most desirable quality attributes for a product have been popularized with acronyms such as FURPS of Hewlett Packard and CUPRIMDSO of IBM [Kan 1995]. FURPS stands for functionality, usability, reliability, performance and serviceability. CUPRIMDSO is an acronym for capability, usability, performance, reliability, install-ability, maintainability, documentation, service and overall. Reliability ranks among the most critical quality attributes according to popular surveys of most products and applications. The objective evaluation of both the process and the work product with such an enablement leads to the following:

SG1 Objectively Evaluate Processes and Work Products

SP1.1 **Objectively Evaluate Processes**

SP1.2 **Objectively Evaluate Work Products and Services**[9]

A report of events leading to either compliance or noncompliance could be handled on professional terms when such peer-level PPQA practices are encouraged. Noncompliance *per se* is not a bad thing; it is important to understand professionally why it exists and whether it is desirable. Many times, noncompliance to an established process itself seeds best practices! Such understanding is possible only if the PPQA activities are carried out by a peer level. Records of ensuring quality into the intermediate work products based on such an exercise can be maintained.

An example of a recommended PPQA record released from the SITARA Process JewelBox™ is provided in Template 4.2.

When quality records are established and communicated to ensure compliance to the stated and intended quality objectives, the following specific goal and specific practices are realized:

[9] Practice title appears as "Objectively Evaluate Work Products" in version 1.3 across all three constellations. There is no noticeable/perceptible change to the informative content associated with this practice and therefore to its interpretation.

Date		
List of Participants		
Title & Purpose of the Report		
Ppqa Conducted at	☐	End of Phase
(Place a Check Mark)	☐	End of Project
	☐	Event Driven

Highlights Of Activities In Current Phase

Strengths (What Went Right)

Opportunities For Imporvement (Lessons Learnt) And Action Plan

What Should Be Done To Internalize The Learning?

Additional Process Or Tools Required

Phase Look Ahead & Road Map

Associated Risks And Abatement Procedure

Miscellaneous

Template 4.2 Template for Conducting PPQA Activities

Source: Adapted from SITARA Process JewelBox™ © SITARA Technologies Pvt. Ltd. 2002 with permission

SG2 Provide Objective Insight

SP2.1 Communicate and Ensure Resolution of Noncompliance Issues[10]

SP2.2 Establish Records

[10] Practice title appears as "Communicate and Resolve Noncompliance Issues" in version 1.3 across all three constellations. There is no noticeable/perceptible change to the informative content associated with this practice and therefore to its interpretation.

The practical sides to PPQA as experienced by the author with some of his best professional associations are as follows:

Process And Product Quality Assurance

1. Establish a need and periodicity for a third party or objective review of the process and work product quality as being end of phase, end of project or event driven
2. Use a formal checklist to guide the process of identifying strengths and opportunities for improvement based on phase of execution
3. Establish an action plan to internalize the learning from the project
4. Record the phase look ahead and road map providing activities planned for the next phase
5. Establish a risk list based on peer-assessment of project status
6. Escalate unresolved issues if necessary to obtain senior management commitment

Display 4.6 Interpreting Process and Product Quality Assurance

Source: Adapted from SITARA Process JewelBox™ © SITARA Technologies Pvt. Ltd. 2002 with permission

How does Process and Product Quality Assurance (PPQA) process area transform its capability when the transition to capability level 2 (or the managed level) is made?

The ten generic practices of EPPAT MIMOR establish the minimum criteria for PPQA to qualify as a managed process at capability level 2. A quality management plan is defined for the project based on the organizational quality policy. This plan identifies the review schedule, the quality audit schedule and the governing baseline criteria for each end-of-phase work product. The project plan is used to define the overall responsibility and accountability structure for the project, and the quality assurance plan addresses specific steps taken in the project to assure quality of services and products. Specific procedures which address how process noncompliance is handled, periodicity of customer feedback, senior management escalation and the modus operandi for communicating the quality audit status reports for the organizational stakeholders is established.

The periodicity of process audits and formal process assessments is also established in the quality assurance plan for the organization. Individuals who conduct such appraisal and audit activities are trained using specific industry-accepted techniques such as the SCAMPI (Standards CMMI Appraisal Method for Process Improvement). A psychologically safe organizational work culture is created and established to ensure that mistakes are recognized and reported by the project personnel early, so that corrective and preventive actions can be rendered with an enduring process response.

Quality management tools which are useful in collecting and analyzing data to serve management information needs on process and product quality are also established. Such tools render the acceptable quality limits for project parameters (both planning and execution) and define specific controls that should be used to bring out-of-bound conditions into the normal process. It is useful to point out that the specific practices of PPQA in general enable the realization of GP2.9 ('Objectively Evaluate Adherence of the Process') across all the process areas of the three CMMI constellations.

How does Process and Product Quality Assurance (PPQA) process area transform its capability when the transition to capability level 3 (or the defined level) is made?

A defined PPQA process at capability level 3 has to address a very crucial need of establishing a structured problem recognition process. Definitions of process evaluation and product reviews are based on audit procedures and guidelines. Supporting process templates and forms are defined in the process asset library—also known as the OSSP. Operational process descriptions for how to perform PPQA activities and the different types of reviews and audits, such as incremental, checkpoint, milestone and baseline, that are supported within the stated organizational policy for causal analysis and process improvement are also defined.

There are actually a number of different inputs that could enable causal analysis at the organizational level. If the quality of the product depends upon the quality of the process used to develop it, one could consider doing a causal analysis of the process and fix the process. Product-level causal analysis at the organizational level is also doable, provided such analysis scales up to address requirements from other projects as well. The same holds true for a product line as well.

1. *Process retrospectives:* These are normally conducted once every 6 months to take stock of the process and to review its relevance to the organizational business objectives. If the business objectives have changed or if new goals based on customer requirements are established, then causal analysis of the relevant process is conducted to identify what is necessary and sufficient to support the new goals. This is more of a proactive causal analysis—something that is done in order to meet stretched objectives. These could result from external influences as well, such as embracing industry best practices, published reports from benchmarking exercises, and so on.
2. *Process postmortems:* These are, as the name indicates, a reactive mechanism to understand the discontinuities in the process *vis-à-vis* the delivery objectives which project(s) may have failed to accomplish.
3. *Best practices review:* These are mechanisms to force an organization to get into a reflective mode to understand both the relevance of emerging best practices at the project level and its impact on the entire organization.

Typical techniques for a product line could still be the same as that for a single product, such as the use of Pareto analysis and fishbone diagram or even a structured review—and these could be defined as PPQA practices. In order to establish a capability level 3 for PPQA the following have to be institutionalized:

GG3 Institutionalize a Defined Process

GP3.1 **Establish a Defined Process**

GP3.2 **Collect Improvement Information**

How does Process and Product Quality Assurance (PPQA) process area transform its capability when the transition to capability level 4 (or the quantitatively managed level) is made?

How does Process and Product Quality Assurance (PPQA) process area transform its capability when the transition to capability level 5 (or the optimizing level) is made? Or, how does Process and Product Quality Assurance demonstrate a high maturity measurement and analysis capability?

One way to render PPQA at capability level 4 or 5 is to define specific audit checklists that monitor and control the project execution using quantitative definitions for the project planning and other execution parameters. The use of checklists as a mechanism to minimize both special and common cause variation can be the basis for rendering PPQA at CL 4 or CL 5. Other statistical techniques include the use of test of hypothesis, or the classical method using the *p*-value method or using confidence intervals for PPQA measures of cost of poor quality and cost of quality. The same conclusion can be reached no matter which of the three methods is used.

Examples of all three types of analysis for COPQ are illustrated in Figures 4.2–4.3.

Hypothesis testing is a statistical technique to rule out randomness or the hand of Dame Luck in an outcome based on data arising out of ambiguous circumstances. The *null hypothesis*, H_0, is the default possibility that will be accepted unless convincing evidence to the contrary is presented. The research or alternative hypothesis, denoted H_1, is the convincing contrary evidence which rules out the null hypothesis as a reasonable possibility. Application of hypothesis testing involving software processes essentially deals with addressing two circumstances: first, drawing two or more random samples of process data from a population to prove or disprove that there is no difference in the behavior (null hypothesis) at, say 95% confidence level. And so the process is in control. Meaning, there is still a 5% possibility for an error of judgment to occur where we reject a true null hypothesis when in fact we should have ruled that the difference is not statistically significant—a type I error. By tradition, this is set to 95%; values lower than this level increase the chance of committing a type I error and higher than this level increase the chance of committing a type II error, which is not rejecting a false null hypothesis (we never say, accepting a

Ho *p*> 0.05: Sample1 Mean COPQ% = Sample2 COPQ%
Ha *p*< 0.05: Sample1 Mean COPQ% ≠ Sample2 COPQ%

Two-sample t-test and CI: Sample1, Sample2

Two-sample T for Sample1 vs Sample2

	N	Mean	StDev	SE Mean
Sample1	7	1.231	0.121	0.046
Sample2	7	1.1943	0.0447	0.017

Difference = mu (Sample1) – mu (Sample2)
Estimate for difference: 0.0371
95% CI for difference: (–0.0690, 0.1433)
t-test of difference = 0 (vs not=): T-Value = 0.76 P-Value = 0.460 DF = 12
Both use Pooled StDev = 0.0911

Fig. 4.2 [MIMOS 2009]: *p*-Value Method: *p*-Value of 0.46 Is Greater Than $\alpha = 0.05$, So Unable to Reject the Null Hypothesis

Classical Method: T-Value = 0.76 Which Does Not Fall in the Reject Region of T < -1.96 or > 1.96, So Unable to Reject the Null Hypothesis

Source: Q3 2009 Process Capability Analysis Report MIMOS Berhad, Malaysia, a site appraised by SITARA Technologies at CMMI-DEV V1.2 Level 5 (Continuous Representation) in October 2009. Reproduced with permission.

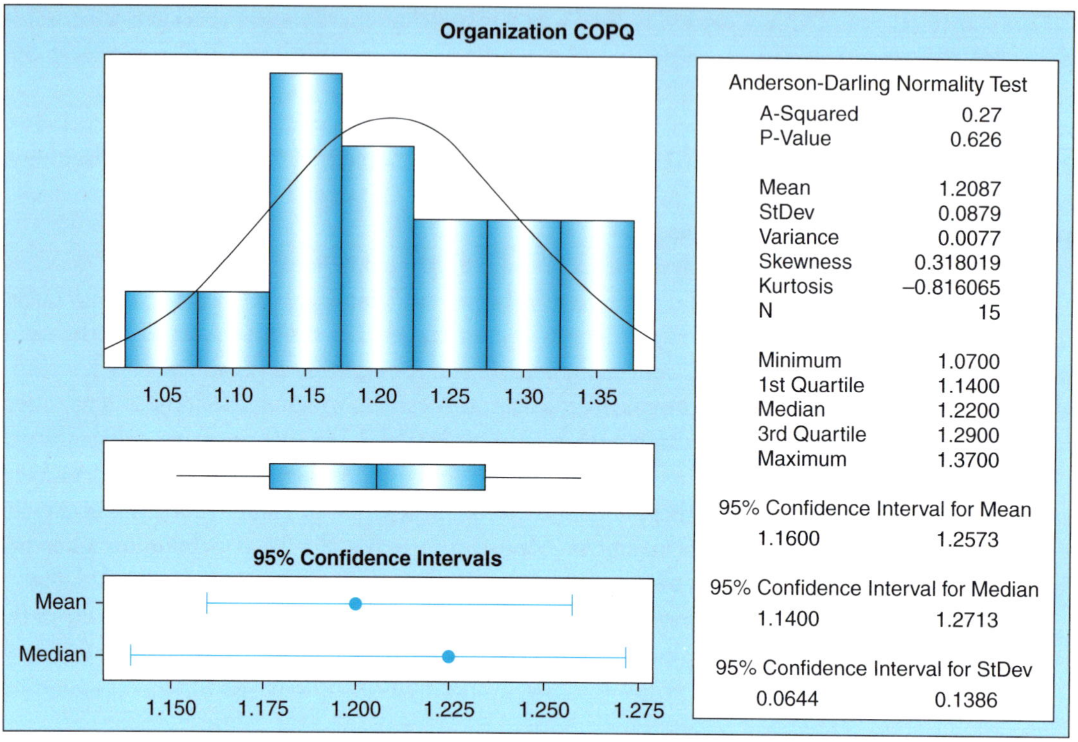

Fig. 4.3 [MIMOS 2009]: Confidence Interval Method: Using 95% Confidence Interval for Mean Yields Population Mean of COPQ to Fall in the 1.16–1.273 Range, and As COPQ = 1.2087 Is Contained in This Interval, Unable to Reject the Null Hypothesis

Source: Q3 2009 Process Capability Analysis Report MIMOS Berhad, Malaysia, a site appraised by SITARA Technologies at CMMI-DEV V1.2 Level 5 (Continuous Representation) in October 2009. Reproduced with permission.

false null hypothesis even though the two are equivalent, simply because of the favored status of the null hypothesis as the default). The second is to prove statistically that a pilot improvement or innovation indeed had an effect on the process outcome, for good or for worse, before large-scale process changes are made.

Confidence interval gives probable upper and lower bounds for the unknown quantity that is being estimated. In the above example, the estimated COPQ falls between 1.16 and 1.273, as if to say that while the definite value is not known, one can safely presume it to lie in this range. From the range, one can say how reliable an estimated value actually is. Confidence interval therefore puts the estimate in the right perspective by defocusing the importance of treating it as a single number when such single value precision can never be guaranteed. Stated differently, *the probability that the population mean for COPQ is within 1.96 standard errors from the sample average COPQ (1.2087) is approximately 0.95.*

From the perspective of the CMMI constellations, two generic practices are necessary to support the intent of a capability level 4 process area:

GP4.1 **Establish Quantitative Objectives for the Process**

GP4.2 **Stabilize Sub-Process Performance**

These generic practices should be applied to the practices that define the PPQA process.

From the perspective of the CMMI constellations, two generic practices are necessary to support the intent of a capability level 5 process area:

GP5.1 **Ensure Continuous Process Improvement**

GP5.2 **Correct Root Causes of Problems**

These generic practices should be applied to the practices that define the Process and Product Quality Assurance process.

It may be useful to point out that the specific practices of PPQA in general enable the realization of GP 2.9 ('Objectively Evaluate Adherence') across the 22 process areas of the CMMI-DEV, six process areas of the CMMI-ACQ constellation and seven process areas of the CMMI-SVC constellation.

Refer Project Planning, Project Monitoring and Control, Verification and Validation process areas for a more thorough interpretation of the probable project and process parameters that could be established within the PPQA checklists.

SUPPLIER AGREEMENT MANAGEMENT (SAM)[11] CMMI-DEV, CMMI-SVC

How does Supplier Agreement Management (SAM) process area look when it operates at a capability level 1 (or the performed level)?

The purpose of SAM is to manage the acquisition of products from suppliers. SAM belongs to the project management category of the continuous representation of the CMMI-DEV and CMMI-SVC as a shared process area. The purpose that the SAM process area serves is to enable a managed acquisition of products from suppliers after establishing a formal agreement. A point to note is that if the personnel from the supplier work as an integrated team with the development site using the same site practices (or the process), then the practices covered under SAM would not apply. Mechanisms established within the Project Planning process area and related practices for establishing the necessary oversight would themselves prove useful in such situations.

Other situations, which cannot be addressed within the scope of SAM even though formal agreements might be in place, are as follows:

- Where the solution provider (supplier) is the only known source for the competency
- Where the solution provider (supplier) uses a third party team of experts, whose word is final and binding on the product

[11] SAM is classified in v1.3 as a shared process area between CMMI-DEV and CMMI-SVC. A shared process area is common to only two of the three CMMI constellations.

- Where the customer preselects the vendor with whom the project team needs to work collaboratively

Instead of ruling the entire SAM process area out of scope, it would be more appropriate to rule only those specific practices that are not applicable to the site as being out of scope. Based on the type of agreement, establish an accountability structure as to *who does what and when* in a contract that binds the supplier to a commitment. Different sourcing strategies such as COTS, products through contractual agreements, custom development and in-house vendor, in any combination, might be employed. Select the suppliers after an evaluation of their capabilities and competencies. The Product Screening and Market Survey phase of the SITARA Package Selection and Integration Process (Chapter 3) describes the typical entry criteria, tasks and verification and exit criteria to enable the following specific practices which realize SG1:

SG1 Establish Supplier Agreements

SP1.1 **Determine Acquisition Type**

SP1.2 **Select Suppliers**

SP1.3 **Establish Supplier Agreements**

The above practices help to render an evaluation of the acquired product using a well-defined criterion. Acquire the product for integration according to the established supplier agreement in order to ensure product quality. Transition the acquired product for the final development of the solution. A more comprehensive approach could involve CMMI-ACQ practices and the COTS integration process described in Chapter 3. We shall review the related practices of Agreement Management and Solicitation and Supplier Agreement Development process areas, which help in the institutionalization of the following specific goal and specific practices:

SG2 Satisfy Supplier Agreements

SP2.1 **Execute the Supplier Agreement**

SP2.2 **Monitor Selected Supplier Processes**

SP2.3 **Evaluate Selected Supplier Work Products**

SP2.4 **Accept the Acquired Product**

SP2.5 **Transition Products**

Note the simplification rendered to the goal and practice titles in version 1.3 of CMMI-DEV and CMMI-SVC.

SG2 Satisfy Supplier Agreements

SP2.1 Execute the Supplier Agreement

SP2.2 Accept the Acquired Product

SP2.3 Ensure Transition of Products

The practical sides to SAM as experienced by the author with some of his best professional associations are as follows:

Supplier Agreement Management

- SAM process has a high relevance in a PSIP, where the use of COTS products is a standard way to shrink-wrap the development life cycle.
- SITARA's version of a PSIP is released from the SITARA Process JewelBox™ and is provided as a quick reference model to ensure that the practices contained in the SAM process area have practical relevance from a 'business standpoint'. Please refer to Chapter 3 for details.

Display 4.7 Interpreting Supplier Agreement Management

Source: Adapted from SITARA Process JewelBox™ © SITARA Technologies Pvt. Ltd. 2002 with permission

How does Supplier Agreement Management (SAM) process area transform its capability when the transition to capability level 2 (or the managed level) is made?

The ten generic practices represented by EPPAT MIMOR establish the minimum criteria for SAM to qualify as a managed process at capability level 2. A capability level 2 process area in general has the following building blocks which ought to be supported with practices called generic practices:

GP2.1 **Establish an Organizational Policy**

GP2.2 **Plan the Process**

GP2.3 **Provide Resources**

GP2.4 **Assign Responsibility**

GP2.5 **Train People**

GP2.6 **Manage Configurations**

GP2.7 **Identify and Involve Relevant Stakeholders**

GP2.8 **Monitor and Control the Process**

GP2.9 **Objectively Evaluate Adherence**

GP2.10 **Review Status with Higher-Level Management**

Refer Chapter 3 on SITARA's PSIP for details on how these practices can be institutionalized.

How does Supplier Agreement Management (SAM) process area transform its capability when the transition to capability level 3 (or the defined level) is made?

Refer Chapter 3 for details. From the CMMI perspective, it is necessary for SAM to demonstrate the attainment of generic goal 3, through generic practices 3.1 and 3.2, which are as follows:

GG3 Institutionalize a Defined Process

GP3.1 **Establish a Defined Process**

GP3.2 **Collect Improvement Information**

It is difficult to justify and demonstrate the SAM at a capability beyond level 3. Being a support category process area, having a defined process would be more than adequate. From a theoretical perspective, the generic goal 4 and the related generic practices 4.1 and 4.2 need to be established for enabling SAM at capability level 4:

GG4 Institutionalize a Quantitatively Managed Process

GP4.1 **Establish Quantitative Objectives for the Process**

GP4.2 **Stabilize Sub-Process Performance**

And to enable SAM at capability level 5, the generic goal 5 and the associated generic practices 5.1 and 5.2 need to be institutionalized:

GG5 Institutionalize an Optimizing Process

GP5.1 **Ensure Continuous Process Improvement**

GP5.2 **Correct Root Causes of Problem**

AGREEMENT MANAGEMENT (AM) CMMI-ACQ

How does Agreement Management (AM) process area look when it operates at a capability level 1 (or the performed level)?

The purpose of AM is to govern supplier and acquirer relationship as per the terms of a supplier agreement. Supplier agreements typically establish a legal framework that binds the acquirer and supplier in a relationship of mutual understanding. Contractual requirements of the supplier are baselined in the supplier agreement. Such contractual requirements are derived from the solicitation package. As viewed from the acquirer's end the supplier agreements must be executed to cover monitoring of supplier processes, acceptance of delivered products and management of supplier invoices. The project management team must be aware of all legal aspects.

The specific goal of AM expects the terms of the supplier agreement to be met by both the acquirer and supplier. After the execution of the supplier agreements, the alignment of supplier's processes to acquirer's processes must be ensured. The acquired product must be in line with the supplier agreement prior to acceptance by the acquirer. Nonconforming products must be handled in accordance with the supplier agreement. Supplier must be compensated per the payment process defined in the supplier agreement for handling invoices.

SG1 Satisfy Supplier Agreements

SP1.1 **Execute the Supplier Agreement**

SP1.2 **Monitor Selected Supplier Processes**

SP1.3 **Accept the Acquired Product**

SP1.4 **Manage Supplier Invoices**

It might be useful to note that this specific goal is directly extracted out of specific goal 2 of the CMMI-DEV V1.2, Supplier Agreement Management (SAM) process area. To bring in this perspective from the CMMI-DEV V1.2, the appropriate specific goal is as follows:

SG2 Satisfy Supplier Agreements

SP2.1 **Execute the Supplier Agreement**

SP2.2 **Monitor Selected Supplier Processes**

SP2.3 **Evaluate Selected Supplier Work Products**

SP2.4 **Accept the Acquired Product**

SP2.5 **Transition Products**

Even though the statements bear a striking similarity, the intent is quite different. First, these practices are interpreted from the 'acquirer' perspective, not supplier's. The other difference to the specific practices in the context of AM is the inclusion of management of supplier invoices and elimination of the evaluation of selected supplier work products since its scope in SAM was restricted to only custom-made products. Even though 'Transition Products' is not a specific practice in AM, its relevance is built into the context of validation prior to acceptance of the acquired product.

Supplier agreement covers internal and external communication besides information regarding the relationship, performance, results and impact on the business that is shared on a routine basis. Emphasis on a documented acceptance criteria leads to establishment of the necessary approval reports and acquirer-initiated validation strategies prior to acceptance. Transitioning of the solution into a live environment is the supplier's responsibility with acquirer oversight. Invoice handling is based on accepted billing cycle and payment terms and conditions in the contractual agreement, which could be any one of the following: statement of work, contract, licensing agreement, service level agreement and memorandum of agreement.

The practical sides to AM as experienced by the author with some of his best professional associations are as follows:

Agreement Management

- AM process has a high relevance in a PSIP, where the use of COTS products is a standard way to shrink-wrap the development life cycle.
- SITARA's version of a PSIP is released from the SITARA Process JewelBox™ and is provided as a quick reference model to ensure that the practices contained in the AM process area have practical relevance from a 'business standpoint'. Please refer to Chapter 3 for details.

Display 4.8 Interpreting Agreement Management

Source: Adapted from SITARA Process JewelBox™ © SITARA Technologies Pvt. Ltd. 2002 with permission

How does Agreement Management (AM) process area transform its capability when the transition to capability level 2 (or the managed level) is made?

The ten generic practices represented by EPPAT MIMOR establish the minimum criteria for AM to qualify as a managed process at capability level 2. A capability level 2 process area in general has the following building blocks even in the CMMI-ACQ constellation which ought to be supported with practices called generic practices. They are as follows:

GP2.1 **Establish an Organizational Policy**

GP2.2 **Plan the Process**

GP2.3 **Provide Resources**

GP2.4 **Assign Responsibility**

GP2.5 **Train People**

GP2.6 **Manage Configurations**

GP2.7 **Identify and Involve Relevant Stakeholders**

GP2.8 **Monitor and Control the Process**

GP2.9 **Objectively Evaluate Adherence**

GP2.10 **Review Status with Higher-Level Management**

Where commonality across constellations can be exploited, it should be attempted without duplication. Such scope exists between the SAM process of CMMI-DEV and CMMI-SVC and AM of CMMI-ACQ. Refer Chapter 3 on SITARA's package PSIP for details on how these practices can be institutionalized.

How does Agreement Management (AM) process area transform its capability when the transition to capability level 3 (or the defined level) is made?

Refer Chapter 3 for details. From the CMMI perspective, it is necessary for AM to demonstrate the attainment of generic goal 3, through the generic practices 3.1 and 3.2, which are as follows:

GG3 Institutionalize a Defined Process

GP3.1 **Establish a Defined Process**

GP3.2 **Collect Improvement Information**

It is difficult to justify and demonstrate AM at a capability beyond level 3. From a theoretical perspective, the generic goal 4 and the related generic practices 4.1 and 4.2 need to be established for enabling AM at capability level 4:

GG4 Institutionalize a Quantitatively Managed Process

GP4.1 **Establish Quantitative Objectives for the Process**

GP4.2 **Stabilize Sub-Process Performance**

And to enable AM at capability level 5, the generic goal 5 and the associated generic practices 5.1 and 5.2 need to be institutionalized:

GG5 Institutionalize an Optimizing Process

GP5.1 Ensure Continuous Process Improvement

GP5.2 Correct Root Causes of Problem

SOLICITATION AND SUPPLIER AGREEMENT DEVELOPMENT (SSAD) CMMI-ACQ

How does Solicitation and Supplier Agreement Development (SSAD) process area look when it operates at a capability level 1 (or the performed level)?

The purpose of SSAD is to prepare a solicitation package, select one or more suppliers to deliver the product or service and establish and maintain a supplier agreement. Supplier agreements are developed and managed (control of changes and amendments, if any) within the scope of SSAD to serve as a legal framework that binds the acquirer and supplier in a relationship of mutual understanding. This relationship is fostered using Agreement Management practices. Ground rules for the relationship including communication, documentation of decisions and conflict resolution through the life of the agreement is the acquirer's responsibility.

Solicitation package is established using the requirements and design constraints of Acquisition Requirements Development process area or other performance criteria spelt out in Measurement and Analysis. Potential suppliers are identified from a variety of sources. The acquirer can also determine to pursue a *sole-source* acquisition rather than a competitive bid based on supplier credentials or other documented criteria. Solicitation package might expect a response to a standard request for proposal to enable comparisons of proposed solutions by suppliers, while encouraging alternative proposals in a separate document. Such standard proposals might adhere to a statement of work (SoW) format with typical line items that include objectives, requirements, design constraints, list of deliverables and rights of use, supplier expectations of support during product transition into live environment, collaterals such as development and administration of the training material by the supplier to ensure hand-over of solutions, validation strategies and post-project support. The SoW can modify and revise its content as it moves through solicitation and negotiation and as supplier agreements are established. Minutes of meetings where decisions of such changes are recorded are useful and must be signed on by all parties prior to acceptance of changes. Supplier evaluation criteria (both milestone and ongoing) are established by the acquirer. The proposal content might also be defined by the acquirer so as to facilitate comparison of competitive bids maintaining equity in proposal reviews and assessments. The following specific goal and specific practices have to be met in intent:

SG1 Prepare for Solicitation and Supplier Agreement Development

SP1.1 Identify Potential Suppliers

SP1.2 Establish a Solicitation Package

SP1.3 Review the Solicitation Package

SP1.4 Distribute and Maintain the Solicitation Package

Proposed supplier solutions are evaluated with stakeholders to ensure alignment of proposals with overall requirements of the solicitation package. Clarifications of proposed solutions are sought from suppliers prior to evaluating the results of selection where candidate suppliers are identified. Negotiations on the contract and inclusion of any additional terms and conditions, such as nondisclosure agreements, payment terms and conditions, onsite-offsite work schedule and handling of the general execution of the items in the SoW, must be ironed out. The negotiation team typically includes legal experts, purchase personnel, financial analysts, program managers and key witnesses from both supplier and acquirer sides to sign on relevant documents that form the basis for contract execution. Suppliers are finally selected based on the evaluation of their ability to meet specified requirements using the established criteria. The following CMMI-ACQ goal and practices should be met in intent:

SG2 Select Suppliers

SP2.1 **Evaluate Proposed Solutions**

SP2.2 **Establish Negotiation Plans**

SP2.3 **Select Suppliers**

Supplier agreements are established, containing the initial scope of reference within the SoW, subsequent addendums, nondisclosure agreements, work orders and records of minutes of meetings. Specific references to the use and handling of confidential proprietary information of both the acquirer and supplier have to be addressed within the scope of the supplier agreement. In doing so, the following specific goal and practices must be met in intent:

SG3 Establish Supplier Agreements

SP3.1 **Establish an Understanding of the Agreement**

SP3.2 **Establish the Supplier Agreement**

It might be useful to note that specific goals SG2 and SG3 share some commonality with SG1 of the CMMI-DEV V1.2, Supplier Agreement Management (SAM) process area. Instead of duplicating effort, it might be useful to leverage commonality between SAM and SSAD.

The practical sides to SSAD as experienced by the author with some of his best professional associations are as follows:

Solicitation And Supplier Agreement Development

- SSAD process has a high relevance in a PSIP, where the use of COTS products is a standard way to shrink-wrap the development life cycle.
- SITARA's version of a PSIP is released from the SITARA Process JewelBox™ and is provided as a quick reference model to ensure that the practices contained in the SSAD process area have practical relevance from a 'business standpoint'. Please refer to Chapter 3 for details.

Display 4.9 Interpreting Solicitation and Supplier Agreement Development

Source: Adapted from SITARA Process JewelBox™ © SITARA Technologies Pvt. Ltd. 2002 with permission

How does Solicitation and Supplier Agreement Development (SSAD) process area transform its capability when the transition to capability level 2 (or the managed level) is made?

The ten generic practices represented by EPPAT MIMOR establish the minimum criteria for SSAD to qualify as a managed process at capability level 2. Refer to Chapter 3 on SITARA's PSIP for details on how these practices can be institutionalized.

How does Solicitation and Supplier Agreement Development (SSAD) process area transform its capability when the transition to capability level 3 (or the defined level) is made?

Refer to Chapter 3 for details. From the CMMI perspective, it is necessary for SSAD to demonstrate the attainment of generic goal 3, through the generic practices 3.1 and 3.2, which are as follows:

GG3 Institutionalize a Defined Process

GP3.1 **Establish a Defined Process**

GP3.2 **Collect Improvement Information**

It is difficult to justify and demonstrate Solicitation and Supplier Agreement Development at a capability beyond level 3. From a theoretical perspective, the generic goal 4 and the related generic practices 4.1 and 4.2 need to be established for enabling SSAD at capability level 4:

GG4 Institutionalize a Quantitatively Managed Process

GP4.1 **Establish Quantitative Objectives for the Process**

GP4.2 **Stabilize Sub-Process Performance**

And to enable SSAD at capability level 5, the generic goal 5 and the associated generic practices 5.1 and 5.2 need to be institutionalized:

GG5 Institutionalize an Optimizing Process

GP5.1 **Ensure Continuous Process Improvement**

GP5.2 **Correct Root Causes of Problem**

ACQUISITION REQUIREMENTS DEVELOPMENT (ARD) CMMI-ACQ

How does Acquisition Requirements Development (ARD) process area look when it operates at a capability level 1 (or the performed level)?

The purpose of ARD is to develop and analyze customer and contractual requirements. While the focus of practices contained in Requirements Development of the CMMI-DEV essentially focuses on customer and product requirements, ARD focuses on contractual requirements as well. Such requirements are typically established in a solicitation package which is used to evaluate proposals. Both technical and nontechnical requirements such as expectations from progress reviews, logistics support during and after readiness reviews, warranty compliance and minimizing the total cost of ownership are documented. Only approved changes to requirements are maintained in the scope of ARD; requirements changes due to internal and external volatility are controlled using Requirements Management practices. Requirements analysis documents are the equivalent baseline configuration items where CMMI-DEV is involved in articulating lower-level product definitions using the functional requirements specification as basis. Except for a specific goal in ARD that addresses contractual requirements, much of the techniques and methods involved in the analysis of requirements using Requirements Development practices of the CMMI-DEV still apply in the context of ARD. Hence, a combination of both CMMI-DEV practices of Requirements Development described in Chapter 5 and acquisition-related analysis described under the Requirements Definition and Requirements Analysis (RDRA) phase of the SITARA package selection and integration process in Chapter 3 should be institutionalized to fulfill the following specific goals and specific practices:

SG1 Develop Customer Requirements

SP1.1 **Elicit Stakeholder Needs**

SP1.2 **Develop and Prioritize Customer Requirements**

SG3 Analyze and Validate Requirements

SP3.1 **Establish Operational Concepts and Scenarios**

SP3.2 **Analyze Requirements**

SP3.3 **Analyze Requirements to Achieve Balance**

SP3.4 **Validate Requirements**

The contractual requirements are the precise set of requirements which establish the operational concepts of the customer after necessary alternative solutions are developed. The evaluation of alternative solutions applies to a broad context of requirements instead of taking just a narrow design or functional requirements focus by including performance, interface, verification and validation requirements as well. Such requirements are established in a solicitation package; allocation matrix is typically used to maintain traceability with supplier deliverables. *In a multi-vendor acquisition strategy, the organization-to-function matrix maps out the COTS vendor or solution provider to the assigned product component.* While requirements are evolved throughout the life cycle of the project, it is desirable to minimize such changes after the ARD phase (refer to requirements confirmation and product interoperability phase of the SITARA PSIP in Chapter 3). Otherwise, it is bound to impact timely completion of the project and make validation of the final product difficult. When a stable set of functional and nonfunctional requirements is established and allocated, the following specific goal is institutionalized. ARD and SSAD together define the contents of a solicitation package.

SG2 Develop Contractual Requirements

SP2.1 **Establish Contractual Requirements**

SP2.2 **Allocate Contractual Requirements**

It might be useful to note that specific goals SG1 and SG3 of ARD share a significant commonality with SG1 and SG3 of the CMMI-DEV V1.2, Requirements Development (RD) process area. Instead of duplicating effort, it might be useful to leverage commonality between the two process areas while taking contractual requirements into consideration.

The practical sides to ARD as experienced by the author with some of his best professional associations are as follows:

Acquisition Requirements Development

- ARD process has a high relevance in a PSIP, where the use of COTS products is a standard way to shrink-wrap the development life cycle.
- SITARA's version of a PSIP is released from the SITARA Process JewelBox™ and is provided as a quick reference model to ensure that the practices contained in the ARD process area have practical relevance from a 'business standpoint'. Please refer to Chapter 3 for details.

Display 4.10 Interpreting Acquisition Requirements Development

Source: Adapted from SITARA Process JewelBox™ © SITARA Technologies Pvt. Ltd. 2002 with permission

How does Acquisition Requirements Development (ARD) process area transform its capability when the transition to capability level 2 (or the managed level) is made?

The ten generic practices represented by EPPAT MIMOR establish the minimum criteria for ARD to qualify as a managed process at capability level 2. Refer to Chapter 3 on SITARA's PSIP for details on how these practices can be institutionalized.

How does Acquisition Requirements Development (ARD) process area transform its capability when the transition to capability level 3 (or the defined level) is made?

Refer to Chapter 3 for details. From the CMMI perspective, it is necessary for ARD to demonstrate the attainment of generic goal 3, through the generic practices 3.1 and 3.2, which are as follows:

GG3 Institutionalize a Defined Process

GP3.1 **Establish a Defined Process**

GP3.2 **Collect Improvement Information**

It is difficult to justify and demonstrate ARD at a capability beyond level 3. From a theoretical perspective, the generic goal 4 and the related generic practices 4.1 and 4.2 need to be established for enabling ARD at capability level 4:

GG4 Institutionalize a Quantitatively Managed Process

GP4.1 **Establish Quantitative Objectives for the Process**

GP4.2 **Stabilize Sub-Process Performance**

And to enable ARD at capability level 5, the generic goal 5 and the associated generic practices 5.1 and 5.2 need to be institutionalized:

GG5 Institutionalize an Optimizing Process

GP5.1 Ensure Continuous Process Improvement

GP5.2 Correct Root Causes of Problem

SERVICE DELIVERY (SD) CMMI-SVC

How does Service Delivery process area look when it operates at a capability level 1 (or the performed level)?

The purpose of Service Delivery is to deliver services in accordance with service agreements. Service agreements establish and maintain a written agreement with customers by defining the level of support between the service provider, the customer and end users. Such agreements are called service-level agreements (SLAs) or statement of work (SoW), or, in their simplest form, they can be a catalog of services with indicative prices. Service agreements are akin to supplier agreements of the CMMI-ACQ, wherein they set forth the contractual terms that bind the service provider and those affected by the service into a relationship of mutual understanding, good faith and positive disposition. Practices in the Service Delivery process area enable best practices for preparation, operation, monitoring and continuous maintenance of the service system. Operation of the service system is the manner in which the service provider responds to service requests which can be of two types: continuous or scheduled as established in service agreements and those that are *ad hoc* which are developed over time to better service the recipients of service. Example of a continuous or scheduled service: within a pizza delivery service, the normal delivery time is defined as 40 minutes from the time the order has been received, or else the pizza is free. Example of an *ad hoc* service request: flash delivery of a drycleaner service can define 1 hour as the latency to service a rush order and might establish a surcharge of double the price of normal service published in the service catalog. Such ground rules that govern the operations of a service provider under normal and special circumstances are established in service agreements.

The status of service requests must be tracked in a request management system which records, keeps track and updates as time progresses until final resolution of the service requests (also known as closure of tickets).

Essentially, the motivation should be to continuously improve the service quality without getting overwhelmed or exasperated by the situation even when such situations are bound to occur. A typical example that one can cite is how an airline steward is able to maintain a cheerful disposition amidst growing resentment among travelers on long-distance flights even as service quality starts to deteriorate. Service levels become far from expectation as the flight wears into the final hours before touchdown—yet an exceptional airline service makes efforts to mask such service inadequacies by constantly improving the service quality in real time, by say, keeping toilets clean to the most extent possible, mopping up spilled food in the aisles, ensuring timely delivery of meals and distracting the attention of the recipients of service with some good-quality onboard entertainment! If complaints are expressed despite best efforts, then to get such statements recorded in service feedbacks is an option. Service discrepancy reports providing useful service data have to be recorded as well in the request management system, analyzed and redressed with appropriate handling mechanisms defined in the service policies, say crediting every accepted complaint with 5000 miles or such. Service data from customers and end users are useful to resolve concerns of Service Delivery and support personnel and to redesign the service system to better respond to service requests. For example: if the constant feedback is to empower the air traveler to preselect seats, then web check-in must offer a traveler such self-service features and subsequent change control until check-in is completed. Such improvements might also be driven by reviewing competition information and should be reflected in the service agreements as improvements become institutionalized. In doing so, the following specific goal and specific practices must be met in intent:

SG1 Establish Service Agreements

SP1.1 **Analyze Existing Agreements and Service Data**

SP1.2 **Establish the Service Agreement**

The necessary preparation that is essential to deliver a service requires to be established prior to delivery. Such preparation should include ability to deliver services under both normal and abnormal conditions while ensuring that the consumables required by both the product and service are available on hand. An example of service failure under abnormal conditions is the all too familiar prerecorded telephone message which repeats as follows *ad nauseam*: 'All of our agents are busy attending to other customer calls. Your call is important to us; please continue to hold and the first available agent will answer your call in the order it was received.' If the customer's call were so important, why not hire sufficient agents to support calls within a realistic response time within the service delivery strategy? It would be more appropriate to treat consumables as any resource which is not available once it is utilized—including service agents. Such a broadening of this term would then imply elapsed time in a project that is ticking, committed human resources, committed software tools, committed network bandwidth and quite literally a consumable as in the following example. Example: a pizza shop must ensure that the requisite dough to make different sizes of pizza is on hand before taking a service request. Should a service request for a medium pizza be taken when the requisite dough to make a medium pizza is not on hand then a Service Delivery approach must make amends for the same by say, upgrading the pizza size to large at no extra cost. It is imperative within the Service Delivery approach to communicate such information to all operations staff and management, assign and transfer responsibility for resolving service requests and informing the service recipient of the resolution for consistent Service Delivery. In doing so, the following specific goal and practices have to be met in intent:

SG2 Prepare for Service Delivery

SP2.1 **Establish the Service Delivery Approach**

SP2.2 **Prepare for Service System Operations**

SP2.3 **Establish a Request Management System**

Multiple mechanisms to receive service requests must be ensured within the service system. Service tickets are opened over a telephone call, over a fax, over a web-based form or using a ticket management system. Ultimately, all such ticket handling, tracking and processing must converge into one request management system. Information required for processing service requests such as time of receipt of service request, name and contact information and information appropriate to track service requests to closure must be enabled in the Service Delivery while fulfilling the intent behind the following specific goal and practices:

SG3 Deliver Services

- SP3.1 **Receive and Process Service Requests**
- SP3.2 **Operate the Service System**
- SP3.3 **Maintain the Service System**

How does Service Delivery (SD) process area transform its capability when the transition to capability level 2 (or the managed level) is made?

A policy that is consistent with the SD approach governed by a service agreement is used to process service requests and for SD. The SD plan can be contained within the scope of a larger project plan or can be a simple tactical plan that can be tracked within the request management system for short-duration service life cycles. Resources required to support the service request including consumables must be chartered such that capacity and availability concerns are addressed minimizing service interruptions. Appropriate resource sourcing strategies must be included in the scope when risks due to non-availability of resources are anticipated. Review of the alignment of the actual SD with the established service agreements must be ensured at multiple levels starting with the help desk to the final delivery. Improvement opportunities must be actively sought from the time a service request is opened until its final disposition. Management oversight and resolution of service inadequacies must be addressed using related process area practices after the underlying cause is studied. The ten generic practices represented by EPPAT MIMOR establish the minimum criteria for SD to qualify as a managed process at capability level 2. A capability level 2 process area in general has the following building blocks in the CMMI-SVC constellation as well, which ought to be supported with generic practices:

- GP2.1 **Establish an Organizational Policy**
- GP2.2 **Plan the Process**
- GP2.3 **Provide Resources**
- GP2.4 **Assign Responsibility**
- GP2.5 **Train People**
- GP2.6 **Manage Configurations**
- GP2.7 **Identify and Involve Relevant Stakeholders**
- GP2.8 **Monitor and Control the Process**
- GP2.9 **Objectively Evaluate Adherence**
- GP2.10 **Review Status with Higher-Level Management**

How does Service Delivery (SD) process area transform its capability when the transition to capability level 3 (or the defined level) is made?

Definitions of the standard operating procedures to handle service requests and improvements rendered over the course of SD are established and maintained. From the CMMI perspective, it is necessary for SD to demonstrate the attainment of generic goal 3, through the generic practices 3.1 and 3.2, which are as follows:

GG3 Institutionalize a Defined Process

GP3.1 **Establish a Defined Process**

GP3.2 **Collect Improvement Information**

It is difficult to justify and demonstrate SD at a capability beyond level 3 due to a profusion of special cause variations that cannot be anticipated in advance. Even though process measurements of such special causes or incidents can be made, they serve very little purpose for analysis and subsequent process control. Such special cause variations are best addressed within the scope of practices belonging to Risk Management or Incident Resolution and Prevention. From a theoretical perspective, the generic goal 4 and the related generic practices 4.1 and 4.2 need to be established for enabling SD at capability level 4:

GG4 Institutionalize a Quantitatively Managed Process

GP4.1 **Establish Quantitative Objectives for the Process**

GP4.2 **Stabilize Sub-Process Performance**

And to enable SD at capability level 5, the generic goal 5 and the associated generic practices 5.1 and 5.2 need to be institutionalized:

GG5 Institutionalize an Optimizing Process

GP5.1 **Ensure Continuous Process Improvement**

GP5.2 **Correct Root Causes of Problem**

5

Defined Level—Interpreting the Level 3 CMMI Process Areas

Author's Musing

A high-maturity process must have 'effective' alternative practices that accomplish the same objectives behind the CMMI goals using techniques that are an appropriate response to the project circumstances and the project's critical-to-performance needs. Performance includes quality, cost, scope and time.

CHARACTERISTICS OF A LEVEL 3 PROCESS (DEFINED PROCESS)

A level 3 process is called a defined process because the organization expects the process improvement framework to effect holistic improvements across the organization by building a *culture of best practices*. Such a culture can be established only on a firm foundation which the level 2 maturity provides. The prerequisite for establishing a defined process is that the process infrastructure should first qualify as a managed process. Therefore the process capabilities which establish a defined process are built on top of the capabilities of a managed process.

The formal definition of a defined process is as follows: it is a managed process that is tailored from the organization's set of standard processes according to the organization's tailoring guidelines, has a maintained process description and contributes work products, measures and other process improvement information to the organizational process assets. Inputs that contribute to the definition of the process at the organizational level include practices that have worked well (or best practices) at the project level. Let us review the dynamics that are at play in any project execution and explore how a level 3 process is created.

All projects have requirements: external and internal requirements. External requirements are those which are driven by the specific nature of business and are influenced by the customer. These external requirements include the use of specific process standards, procedures or guidelines and templates. Internal requirements for a project typically would include internal quality standards, procedures and guidelines. Using both the external and internal requirements, a project establishes a project life cycle which governs the execution of the project. Projects render life cycles based on customer dependencies and internal factors such as a need to adhere to process and quality standards. At the level 3 or defined process maturity, the organization institutionalizes a policy to internalize experience reports resulting from such use of diverse life-cycle descriptions which are specific to the project by reviewing their applicability and relevance at the organizational level. Both, best practices and those practices that have not worked well, are brought up to the attention of an organizational group of process specialists such as the process engineering group or the software engineering process group for a review of the applied methods and practices on projects. Those practices and procedures which have an organizational impact are studied by the specialist group and a baseline of the acceptable organizational practices is established in what is known as the OSSP. OSSP at the organizational level then serves as reference for any new project requiring process definition. A process asset library (PAL) is grown over a period of time gaining experience while executing projects. PAL, typically, is a combination of the OSSP, external process benchmarks and the measurement repository/system used to objectively evaluate process effectiveness based on a defined metrics strategy.

Based on customer dependencies, and its uniqueness, a project might also choose to tailor the organizational standard to derive a process that is more applicable in handling the specific project characteristics. Such a tailoring mechanism is available for use in the tailoring guideline. Much of the inputs to the tailoring guideline are again based on experiential reports resulting from quality audits, project postmortems and process retrospectives. The tailoring guideline helps to derive a project-specific process and a project life cycle that best serves the needs of the project after studying its characteristics.

External benchmarks and external best practices are reviewed by the process engineering group before establishing them into the OSSP as reference documents. PAL itself is placed under effective version control and configuration management to establish integrity and access to the most current information by the organizational stakeholders. PAL is deployed in the organization as a tool and is called variously as quality management system, quality information portal and software engineering archives. PAL is a very important competency asset and constitutes intellectual property requiring appropriate access rights.

Execution results from the project are measured using the project's planning and execution parameters such as schedule estimation accuracy, effort estimation accuracy, review effectiveness in terms of phase containment, assessment of defect prevention built into the development practices using in-process fault measures, cost performance index, schedule performance index, cost of poor quality, cost of quality and a host of other metrics that have organizational relevance. All these are compiled, analyzed and controlled in a metrics or measurement database.

Process stability is achieved after a number of iterations of using and fine-tuning the practices. The measurement database and the OSSP now offer a sense of coherence to the process, whose integration, we have observed, is referred to as the process asset library (PAL). PAL now becomes an internal input available for projects to define their life cycle and for establishing project goals required to meet business objectives. Projects begin to take note of the process improvement framework thus established and further improve its effectiveness by proposing technical reports, white papers and practice guides. The establishment of such experience reports enables the growth of a process culture in the organization. In order to improve the cycle time and establish a sense of confidence in the work products that are created, the OSSP builds in a reuse capability wherein

(Contd)

work products that have proven characteristics and known capability are reused. Therefore reuse repositories for design best practices, decisions taken in the past, risk abatement strategies that have worked well for the organization, ready reckoners, guidebooks for technical solutions and the like are also archived. Reuse becomes one of the key drivers for cycle time reduction or productivity improvement.

Author's Musing

An obsession with cutting down on cycle time and using goals for cycle time reduction (CTR) may not leave enough time to absorb what is to be learnt from project execution or for creating learning opportunities on a project. While CTR is a good metric to have and manage, there has to be a good balance vis-à-vis the overall merits resulting from competency development and competency orientation.

Improvements to process, tools and technologies that have greater organizational relevance are archived within the OSSP. Appropriate levels of configuration management and revision control ensure that the objectives of the process improvement program are achieved. In general, a learning orientation among individuals with effective management and engineering practices that establish an environment that proactively manages change using the defined process begins to take hold.

In the process a *culture of best practices* prevails. Practices that ensure sustenance of such a culture are organized into 11 process areas at the level 3 or the defined process maturity level in the CMMI-DEV constellation, 9 process areas in the CMMI-ACQ constellation and 12 process areas in the CMMI-SVC constellation.

Author's Musing

The thing to keep in mind is not to turn the OSSP or organizational process asset library into a dumping ground! Practices and assets that have a limited applicability at the project level could be maintained in project-specific or local definitions of best practices. Only when there is a larger degree of applicability of such practices having an impact at the organizational level would it be best to percolate such changes to the OSSP or the PAL.

With this understanding of the process dynamics required for the creation of a level 3 process maturity, we shall explore the process areas of all three CMMI constellations that establish a level 3 (defined) process. Six process areas at level 3 are common to the three constellations and are contained in CMF. The process areas are:

- Requirements Development (RD) [CMMI-DEV]
- Technical Solution (TS) [CMMI-DEV]
- Product Integration (PI) [CMMI-DEV]
- Verification (VER) [CMMI-DEV]
- Validation (VAL) [CMMI-DEV]

- Acquisition Technical Management (ATM) [CMMI-ACQ]
- Acquisition Verification (AVER) [CMMI-ACQ]
- Acquisition Validation (AVAL) [CMMI-ACQ]
- Service Continuity (SCON) [CMMI-SVC]
- Capacity and Availability Management (CAM) [CMMI-SVC]
- Service System Development (SSD) [CMMI-SVC]
- Service System Transition (SST) [CMMI-SVC]
- Strategic Service Management (STSM) [CMMI-SVC]
- Incident Resolution and Prevention (IRP) [CMMI-SVC]
- Organizational Process Focus (OPF) [CMMI-DEV, CMMI-ACQ, CMMI-SVC]
- Organizational Process Definition [CMMI-DEV, CMMI-ACQ, CMMI-SVC]
- Organizational Training [CMMI-DEV, CMMI-ACQ, CMMI-SVC]
- Integrated Project Management for IPPD[1] [CMMI-DEV, CMMI-ACQ, CMMI-SVC]
- Risk Management [CMMI-DEV, CMMI-ACQ, CMMI-SVC]
- Decision Analysis and Resolution [CMMI-DEV, CMMI-ACQ, CMMI-SVC]

REQUIREMENTS DEVELOPMENT (RD) CMMI-DEV

How does Requirements Development look when it operates at a capability level 1 (or the performed level)?

Requirements Development (RD) belongs in the engineering category of the continuous representation of the CMMI. It is with the practices of RD that the abstraction of development changes from a *what-is-needed* to a *how-will-it-be-rendered* approach. In doing so, the customer requirements, product and product component requirements are analyzed primarily from a feasibility study point of view. In order to understand the feasibility of developing the solution, the elicitation of requirements using a structured questionnaire in a joint application development (JAD) session to elicit requirements by involving all relevant stakeholders is typically adopted.

Author's Musing

A joint application development (JAD) session is typically conducted as follows:

Participating team members include technical and management leaders from the participating subcontractor agencies, key decision makers from the customer site, the marketing team, the program manager and the release manager for the project. They

(Contd)

[1] Renamed as Integrated Work Management only in CMMI-SVC version 1.3. It will still remain a core process area since the nature of change is only renaming the word 'project' to 'work' which is more relevant in the context of services.

engage in a brainstorming exercise to establish a shared vision of the product development activities.

Product requirements are literally mined from the different stakeholders and documented as the first-level requirements specification document. Such elicitation results in the identification of both high-level and detailed requirements without assigning any priorities or establishing differences between the needs and the wants at this stage.

Using this initial list of requirements, the scope of the product development initiative is determined with defined responsibilities among the subcontractors in terms of who-does-what and how-do-the-teams-synchronize. The duration of a JAD session is typically no more than 2–3 days at a stretch.

After the requirements allocation is complete, analysis of how they will be rendered is conducted by the different collaborating parties (subcontractors) who meet again as a team to iron out interface issues, risks, technical limitations, cost and legal issues. This process to synchronize and stabilize the product requirements continues well past into the high-level design phase.

In the process of elicitation of the needs, additional insights into the development life cycle or process to be followed by all collaborating teams would be laid out. Such a process description serves more as a mechanism to establish a common process language and medium of communication among collaborating teams.

In Chapter 3, we have explored three techniques from software engineering principles that define activities involved in the analysis of software requirements. Much of what is stated therein for analysis has to do with the way the product would be realized. A combination of techniques such as structured development, COTS integration and object-oriented methods could also be used depending upon the product development context; all three ideas have been presented in Chapter 3. In this chapter we will explore the use of Quality Function Deployment as an example of functional analysis, which is quite different from structured analysis. The above techniques enable the realization of the following:

SG1 Develop Customer Requirements

SP1.1 Elicit Needs

SP1.2 Develop the Customer Requirements[2]

The important attributes of any requirement are that it should be correct, complete, consistent and testable. Fundamentally, QFD evolves from understanding the customer's needs and wants, and prioritizing them before using a structured development process to realize the product. Thereafter, customer feedback is obtained, and, if required, this basic flow is repeated as many times as necessary to ensure that the *voice-of-customer (VOC)* (customer's needs and wants) are met in the product using a systematic development process (*voice-of-process (VOP)*) that is capable of delivering on customer expectations.

[2] Practice title appears as "Transform Stakeholder Needs into Customer Requirements" in version 1.3 in the CMMI-DEV constellation. There is no noticeable/perceptible change to the informative content associated with this practice and therefore to its interpretation.

AUTHOR'S MUSING

In RD, eliciting customer needs is an extremely important specific practice if the customer is an external customer. Not having enough information during the elicitation stage about the customers' end-user context will result in enormous rework.

Expanding this basic flow, we will now illustrate the essential ingredients of a QFD matrix as applied to software development.

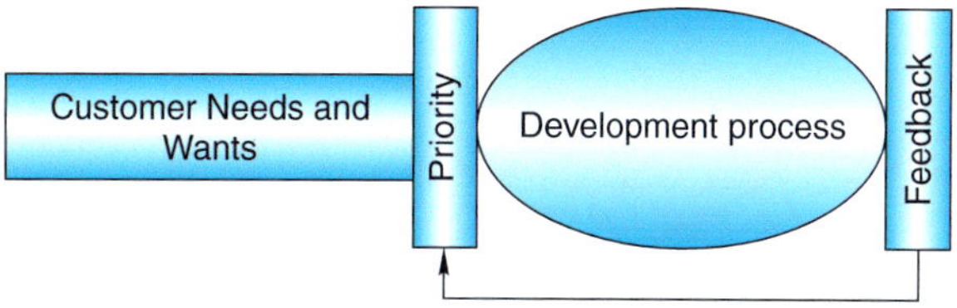

Fig. 5.1 [SITARA 2001c]: The Basics of QFD

Source: Adapted from SITARA 'CMMI as a Second Language' course Version 2.0 © 2001, SITARA Technologies Pvt. Ltd. with permission.

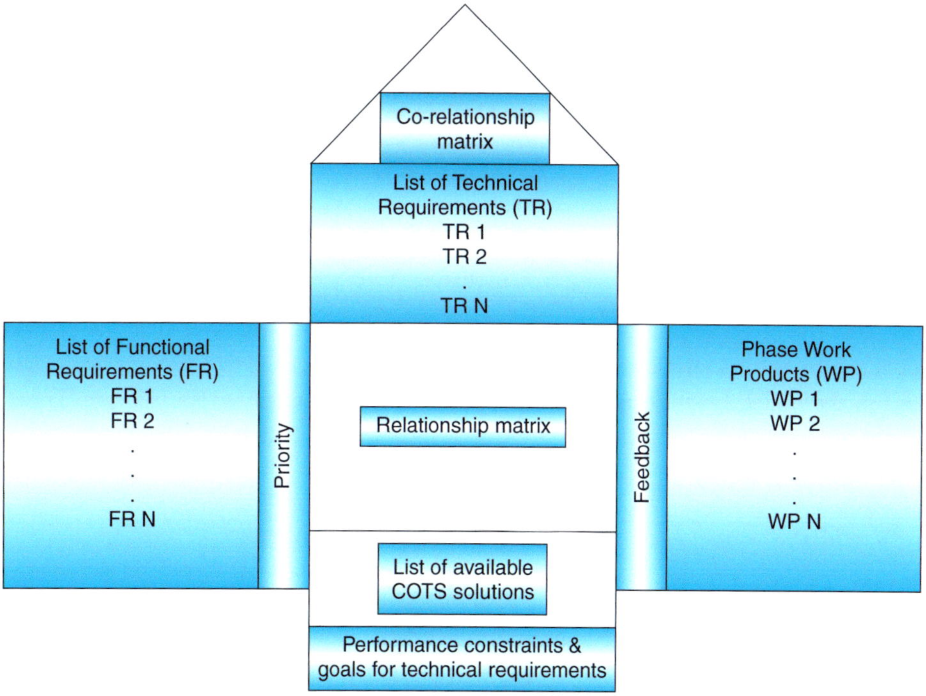

Fig. 5.2 [SITARA 2001c]: Applying QFD to Establish Bidirectional Traceability between Functional and Technical Requirements

Source: Adapted from SITARA 'CMMI as a Second Language' course Version 2.0 © 2001, SITARA Technologies Pvt. Ltd. with permission.

The important features of the QFD approach are the relationship matrix and the co-relationship matrix. The co-relationship matrix establishes the mapping of functional requirements into the technical requirements. It is very likely that one functional requirement may map into more than one technical requirement. In the relationship matrix, based on the priority that is assigned to the requirement from a JAD session, further classification of the requirement as mandatory or hard requirement or optional or soft requirement is done.

Author's Musing

A simple tool that I have found to be useful in establishing such traceability with QFD is Microsoft Excel sheets with the use of hyperlinks. One of its other advantages is that it accommodates and addresses the highly probabilistic event of volatile requirements effectively.

A few links, at worst, are what need to be changed to establish a context to a dynamic functional requirements list. The only limitation though is that it is not possible to render a cell within an Excel sheet to contain more than one hyperlink. Using multiple cells (columns) of an Excel sheet to list the entities shown in the QFD diagram above is an option.

The co-relationship matrix establishes a relationship between the different technical requirements (TRs). Meaning: if TR1 should be supported, then what are the other mandatory TRs that are a prerequisite to TR1? The co-relationship matrix therefore establishes the interface requirements and interoperability of the different technical requirements. It may be useful to highlight the fact that a functional requirement emerging from the *voice-of-customer* (*VOC*) could very well be a testing or performance requirement. Such requirements translate into goal-based technical requirements; that is, technical requirements with performance constraints or goals of operation.

Using the package selection and integration process described in Chapter 3, it would be possible to identify the different COTS solutions or packaged implementations that can be procured and used for product realization. A choice of the COTS solution to render a product feature also establishes the requirements for the wrappers that have to be developed in order to ensure that the solution can be integrated. Techniques for analysis presented in Chapter 3 could be used to develop appropriate levels of abstraction (object model, dynamic model and functional model) to compose the solution. These activities result in the realization of the following:

SG2 Develop Product Requirements

SP2.1 Establish Product and Product-Component Requirements

SP2.2 Allocate Product-Component Requirements

SP2.3 Identify Interface Requirements

One of the most important steps that could be taken is to develop prototypes for the critical technical requirements which can offer a proof-of-concept view of the solution. Technical requirements which have a significant performance constraint and/or are heavily driven by the presentation logic (e.g., graphical user interfaces) are ideal choices for establishing pilots. Besides, such technical requirements invariably end up on the critical path of a project. Using such proof-of-concept pilots, customer feedback can be obtained and used to further refine the requirements. If necessary, a renegotiation of the mandatory requirements within known project constraints is done with the customers and other stakeholders and options of phased delivery are explored.

The technical requirements from this QFD after the proof of concept become the inputs to the Technical Solution process area where the design of the solution is rendered. These activities lead to the fulfillment of the following specific goal:

SG3 Analyze and Validate Requirements

- SP3.1 **Establish Operational Concepts and Scenarios**
- SP3.2 **Establish a Definition of Required Functionality**[3]
- SP3.3 **Analyze Requirements**
- SP3.4 **Analyze Requirements to Achieve Balance**
- SP3.5 **Validate Requirements**

The practical sides to RD as experienced with some of the author's best professional associations are as follows:

Requirements Development

1. Analyze the project requirements obtained from the different stakeholders and categorize them into 'core' and 'non-core' requirements.
2. Identify and document the implicit and explicit requirements.
3. Review and revise the requirements to make sure that they are correct, complete, consistent and testable.
4. Identify and involve project team members in a knowledge transfer exercise to ensure a common understanding of the project expectations.
5. Identify and obtain the necessary project infrastructure such as simulators, emulators and other hardware and software resources to realize the product solution.
6. Establish the necessary documentation that uses a structured analytical technique to break down and simplify complexity.

Display 5.1 Interpreting Requirements Development

Source: Adapted from SITARA Process JewelBox™ © SITARA Technologies Pvt. Ltd. 2002 with permission

How does Requirements Development transform its capability when the transition to capability level 2 (or the managed level) is made?

[3] Practice title appears as "Establish a Definition of Required Functionality and Quality Attributes" in version 1.3 of the CMMI-DEV constellation. There is no noticeable/perceptible change to the informative content associated with this practice and therefore to its interpretation.

Organizational policy is supportive of a structured analysis framework within which the organization develops and maintains an understanding of both the explicit and implicit product requirements that have to be supported in the solution. Such a policy typically commits to the necessary organizational resources, tools and methods that have to be employed by the projects for the realization or rendering of the solution. The policy is also supportive of the training and resource requirements for projects to render analysis in a structured manner.

A well-defined analysis phase (or an acceptable tailoring option such as using a high-level design phase instead of analysis) is planned within the development life cycle of the project. Resource assignment to the project is made based on skill and the most optimal resource levels that should be deployed to enable a clear understanding of project complexity and constraints of operation.

A literal translation of the *what-is-needed* into *how-it-will-be-done* is enabled using objective insights from experienced individuals in the organization who may belong to subject matter expert teams. Such subject matter experts train project resources to render an understanding of the project requirements.

In the process of elicitation of the customer needs, should the requirements change, a well-defined configuration management and monitoring process is used to ensure that functional and technical requirements are traceable. Identification and involvement of all the affected groups who would need the modified view of the requirements is built into the practices with effective management oversight.

Within the CMMI, the ten generic practices of EPPAT MIMOR establish the minimum criteria for RD to qualify as a managed process at capability level 2.

How does Requirements Development transform its capability when the transition to capability level 3 (or the defined level) is made?

An organizational standard defining the acceptable analytical techniques that should be employed on projects for breaking down complexity and for analyzing project requirements is established for projects to either use on as-is basis or exercise the necessary tailoring judgment. Projects that have established best practices within the use of the process framework for defining analysis techniques contribute to the organizational repository of best practices (PAL).

A practitioner's experience with projects based on the constraints of operation is actively solicited in the form of best practice submissions. These submissions are reviewed by a team such as an experts' group or the process engineering group before a pilot is run to study their effectiveness.

The expectations from the CMMI for RD to qualify at capability level 3 are to enable GG3 and the associated practices of GP3.1 and GP3.2, which are as follows:

GG3 Institutionalize a Defined Process

GP3.1 **Establish a Defined Process**

GP3.2 **Collect Improvement Information**

How does Requirements Development transform its capability when the transition to capability level 4 (or the quantitatively managed level) is made? Or, how does Requirements Development demonstrate a high maturity measurement and analysis capability?

RD is a very good candidate process area to be placed under a higher capability level given the virtues and benefits from enabling the engineering process areas to a high degree of fault tolerance.

Besides, some of the specific practices of RD lend themselves to measurement or quantification and for stabilizing of their influences on the overall effectiveness of the process area. Since this is the first process area *at level* 3 in this book that has been identified to operate at capability level 4, a general rule on what constitutes the attainment of generic goal 4 or of the generic practices 4.1 and 4.2 will be provided. This introductory view is common to every process area that is being identified as a candidate for enabling a level 4 capability.

It would be useful to consider the application of the generic practices of GP4.1 and GP4.2 to the specific practices and sub-practices of a process area. In order to do this, it is best to first study the relevance of these generic practices. If it is found relevant to enable the specific practices and sub-practices of a process area at capability level 4 that justifies the return on investment, then it is useful to identify the specific practices and sub-practices that best lend themselves first to quantification and then to stabilization. The way to interpret

GP 4.1 **Establish Quantitative Objectives for the Process**

—is to check if the specific practices and sub-practices of the process area lend themselves well to measurement based on organizational quantitative objectives within the metrics program. If yes, then it is useful to explore the enablement of GP4.1. The way to interpret the relevance of

GP4.2 **Stabilize Sub-Process Performance**

—is to check if the specific practices and sub-practices of a process area can be stabilized. If the specific practices are greatly influenced by special causes of variation which are outside the process control, then the applicability of GP4.2 is limited. If the special cause variations are due to assignable causes within the scope of the development process, then it is most desirable to raise the process area–specific practices to a capability level 4 or the quantitatively managed capability.

Another useful thought would be that even if one of the two generic practices is applicable, it might be worth one's while to consider scaling the capability of a process area to the higher level. There are distinct advantages in doing so, from a process improvement perspective. It is useful to keep in mind that not every specific practice that can be quantified can be controlled and vice versa. With this background, it would be useful to note that specific practices that have a bearing on eliciting customer needs and developing customer requirements are highly susceptible to special causes of variation arising out of the *voice-of-customer* (VOC). Even though such special causes of variation have poor process control, as such special causes are mostly dependent on variations resulting from causes that are outside the context of the process, minimizing impact of variation to a good degree is still possible and therefore it is worth exploring what such techniques could be. Examples of quantitative analysis involving RD practices include statistically validated advantages of including a reverse walkthrough process during analysis, wherein the customer and elicitation roles are reversed to improve understanding of customer requirements and to arrest requirements churn. Requirements churn can be quantitatively managed. Use of control charts, box plots and hypothesis testing to demonstrate the advantages of including feasibility study to reduce cycle time of the development process by collecting process sample data before and after the introduction of the feasibility study is as illustrated in Figures 5.3–5.5.

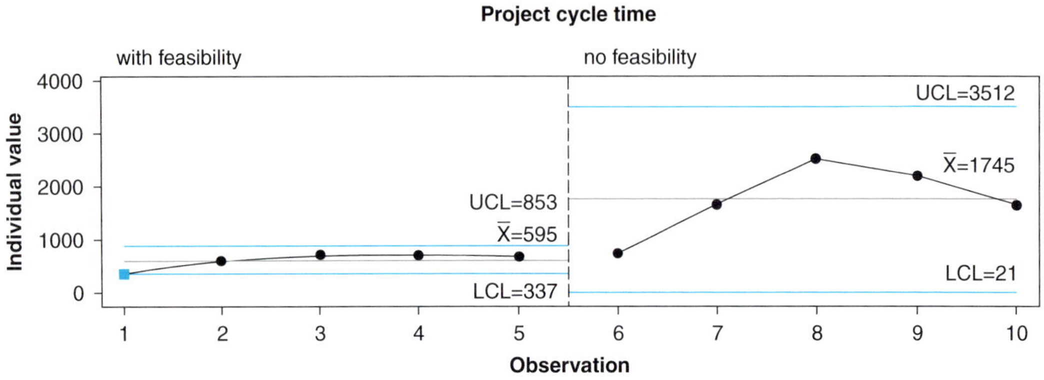

Fig. 5.3 [MIMOS 2009]: Control Charts of Individual Observations Reveal Both a Shifting of the Average Process Performance and Narrowing of Control Limits with the Introduction of Feasibility Study

Source: Q3 2009 Process Capability Analysis Report MIMOS Berhad, Malaysia, a site appraised by SITARA Technologies at CMMI-DEV V1.2 Level 5 (continuous representation) in October 2009. Reproduced with permission.

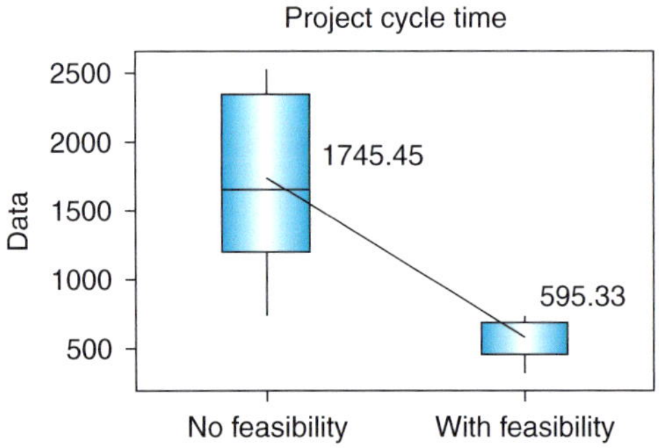

Fig. 5.4 [MIMOS 2009]: Box Plots Reveal a Difference in the Distributions of Cycle Time with and without Feasibility Study; a Shift in Average Process Performance, Improving the Cycle Time, is Evident with Feasibility Study

Source: Q3 2009 Process Capability Analysis Report MIMOS Berhad, Malaysia, a site appraised by SITARA Technologies at CMMI-DEV V1.2 Level 5 (Continuous Representation) in October 2009. Reproduced with permission.

It might be instructive to note that the expectation from a high-capability process is to both quantitatively and statistically demonstrate the effects of improvement. If the effects of improvement minimize special causes, then the process area operates at capability level 4. If improvements address common cause variations, then the capability level of the process area ought to be 5. This understanding is critical in distinguishing whether the process area is operating at capability level 4 or capability level 5.

```
Paired T for No Feasibility - With Feasibility

                     N      Mean     StDev    SE Mean
No Feasibility       5      1745       674        301
With Feasibility     5       595       152         68
Difference           5      1150       539        241

95% CI for mean difference: (481, 1819)
T-Test of mean difference = 0 (vs not = 0): T-value = 4.77 P-value = 0.009
```

The *P*-value of 0.009 indicates that the development cycle times are not the same with and without feasibility study. Feasibility study drastically reduces the cycle time.

Fig. 5.5 [MIMOS 2009]: Two-sample *t-test* for Assessing Impact of Feasibility Study on Drastic Reduction of Cycle Time

Source: Q3 2009 Process Capability Analysis Report MIMOS Berhad, Malaysia, a site appraised by SITARA Technologies at CMMI-DEV V1.2 Level 5 (Continuous Representation) in October 2009. Reproduced with permission.

1. *No conclusions can be made without objective proof.*
2. *The proof is in the data.*
3. *There is no guarantee that a process, howsoever obviously it might appear to improve the process, will indeed contribute to improvements unless verified and validated statistically.*

These three points in the author's opinion are the implicit expectations made by the CMMI of all high-capability process areas.

Measures specific to RD that can be quantified and statistically managed to minimize influence of special cause variations are phase containment effectiveness, cost of poor quality and cost of quality of the analysis phase. The requirements churn or requirements volatility at the time of completion of analysis phase is a commonly used metric to define the degree of stability (or instability) of the customer requirements. However, applicability of this measure alone is, to a very limited degree, indicative of the problem complexity (please refer to the Requirements Management process area for details). Effective deployment of GP4.1 and GP4.2 practices requires the enablement of CMMI level 4 process areas. Please refer to Chapter 6 for a more detailed understanding of the types of statistical methods that should be employed and the types of quantitative analysis that are required to institutionalize a level 4 capability for RD.

Use of a checklist and a questionnaire to guide the elicitation of probable modes of operation of the solution being developed is a good technique that could be applied while realizing the practices contained in the RD process area. Another area that could establish requirements stability is to understand factors that contribute to a high level of requirements clarity. Clarity levels within a team are dependent upon domain exposure and competencies of team members. Therefore, it is useful to use team reflection, brainstorming and other team-based practices such as wideband Delphi process to arrive at a consensus on level of requirements clarity through effective team learning.

AUTHOR'S MUSING

Fundamentally, wideband Delphi (or Delphi method) is a brainstorming technique to strike a common ground concerning team decisions.

The wideband Delphi estimation technique is a heuristics approach for estimating software size, effort and cost. It depends heavily on the expertise of individuals and integrity of the historical database in use. It is generally considered an adequate way to satisfy the CMMI level 2 estimation practices where there is inadequate historical data. In fact, it is a good way to building a historical database. The estimates from wideband Delphi are also extremely site specific. Together with historical data, having a list of prerequisite conditions and known causes of variation tends to make the wideband Delphi technique useful even for higher-maturity practices.

The wideband Delphi estimation process described below is one of the several variants that is homegrown within SITARA Technologies and has been used on a number of exercises including obtaining consensus on time estimates for completing the observations and findings on formal appraisals with assessment team members! The experience with this approach suggests that convergence on the final estimates is quicker and often closer to actual values.

The process of estimating size, effort and cost using wideband Delphi is as follows:

1. A trained subject matter expert or domain specialist serves as the moderator for the estimation process.
2. The domain specialist reviews inputs (project documentation) to the work product that is to be developed and resolves all cross-references if any. An important prerequisite is to ensure that all the 'to-be-decided' items have an adequate resolution.
3. Estimation teams such as the project team is called forth to participate in an opening meeting where the domain specialist provides an overview of the work that is required to be executed.
4. Project documentation is explained to the project team and inputs from historical database for size, effort and cost with similar complexity are provided as *a priori* information to this team.
5. A detailed work breakdown structure is prepared and circulated to the estimation team giving the high-level and detailed tasks necessary to be performed.
6. The estimation team members are asked to make relevant, documented assumptions and develop an estimate for size, effort and cost based on their perceived level of understanding of the complexity involved.
7. Initial estimates for the min (optimistic view), mid (neutral view) and max (pessimistic view) values are now established as a baseline after obtaining inputs from every individual on the estimation team.
8. A meeting where each individual then shares the estimates and explains the rationale is conducted where all assumptions and understanding of the issues involved are shared.
9. A wide variation in the estimates is possible in the very first cycle of the estimation process.

(Contd)

10. Having established a new understanding from collective brainstorming, individuals are now asked to recalibrate their estimates. Clarifications, if any, are provided by the domain specialist.
11. Individuals revise their estimates for size, effort and cost with an attempt to converge to more realistic estimates based on the team's judgment of the shared understanding of the complexity.
12. The team re-assembles to draw a consensus on the effort and cost estimates based on the complexity and clarity level of the project documentation.
13. Normally, the convergence is approached quickly (within two cycles) and better managed by recording decisions taken and through team consensus.
14. Estimated effort and cost for the complexity and clarity levels of project documentation are now stored in the historical database for future tracking with actual values after execution.

Wideband Delphi is better known for arriving at acceptable size, effort and cost estimates for project tasks. Though mostly used for arriving at common estimates, it most definitely can be extended to other areas of software engineering which fundamentally require team consensus, for instance:

- Assessing project risks
- Evaluating alternative design techniques
- Cost projections and progress reviews

How does Requirements Development transform its capability when the transition to capability level 5 (or the optimizing level) is made? Or, how does Requirements Development demonstrate a high maturity measurement and analysis capability?

Common cause variation with causes assigned to what is 'in process' offers a good opportunity to explore a cause–effect relationship. A general rule on what constitutes the enablement of generic goal 5 or of the attainment of generic practices 5.1 and 5.2 is provided. This introductory view is common to every process area that has been identified as a candidate for enabling a level 5 capability, and, therefore, would not be cited again to avoid needless repetition.

It would be useful to consider the application of the generic practices GP5.1 and GP5.2 to the specific practices and sub-practices of a process area. In order to do this, it is best to first study the relevance of these generic practices. If it is found relevant to enable the specific practices and sub-practices of a process area at capability level 5 that justifies the return on investment, then it is useful to identify the specific practices and sub-practices that best lend themselves first to quantification and then to stabilization. The way to interpret

GP5.1 **Ensure Continuous Process Improvement**

—is to check if the specific practices and sub-practices of the process area lend themselves well to continuous improvement based on an organizational analysis of the common causes. If yes, then it is useful to explore the enablement of GP5.2. The way to interpret

GP5.2 Correct Root Causes of Problems

—is to check if the specific practices and sub-practices of a process area lend themselves to root causes that are within the scope of the development process (or in-process variation). If the specific practices are naturally influenced by common causes of variation, then there is much meaning in knowing these causes or factors before applying GP5.2.

Another useful thought would be: just as with CL4 practices, even if one of the two generic practices is applicable, it might be worthwhile to consider scaling the capability dimension of a process area to this higher capability level. There are distinct advantages in doing so, from a process improvement perspective. Understanding the dependencies of the causes of requirements' volatility and analyzing the influences of both special and common causes of variation to minimize their influence and impact using the process improvement framework would render RD to a higher capability. Use of instruments such as requirements checklist, elicitation questionnaires, review checklists and guidelines could serve as effective process instruments to minimize variation. It may be useful to note that procedure definitions, process guidelines, forms, ready-to-use templates, development checklists, audit checklists and the like are all useful when it comes to minimizing the impact of both special and common causes of variation. However, for a process area to demonstrate a capability level 4 or level 5 rigor, an expectation placed by the CMMI is that some form of statistical analysis (preferably use of control charts where possible) of causes of variation is rendered.

The same measures that were chosen to understand the influence of special causes can be used to study the effects of common cause influence. Examples illustrated in Figures 5.3–5.5 apply equally well here; *only the cause of variation being studied would be common cause instead of special cause*. This understanding is critical in distinguishing whether the process area is operating at capability level 4 or capability level 5. Effective deployment of GP5.1 and GP5.2 practices requires the enablement of CMMI level 5 process areas. Please refer to Chapter 7 for a more detailed understanding of the types of statistical methods that should be employed and the types of quantitative analysis that are required to institutionalize a level 5 capability.

AUTHOR'S MUSING

Simulation is normally a choice available to establish 'user experiences' and therefore they are more relevant while developing user interfaces during usability analysis. Simulations of actual functionality of a product are normally undertaken to establish a proof of concept using prototypes.

TECHNICAL SOLUTION (TS) CMMI-DEV

How does Technical Solution look when it operates at a capability level 1 (or the performed level)?

Technical Solution (TS) belongs to the engineering category of the continuous representation of the CMMI. The focus within TS is to develop, design and implement the solution. The development of the low-level design in what is known as module specifications involves writing *pseudo*-code to capture the logical propositions along with proper definitions of the data structures. In a nutshell, data structures + algorithms = programs. At this level of abstraction, data structures along with the necessary logic in the form of algorithms are developed in order to realize the implementation in code. The challenges of real life impose an iterative mode of developing the logic. This might entail the creation of appropriate prototypes of components or modules that are the critical logic blocks to prove in the solution. For instance, while choosing structured methods to realize the solution, it would be useful to keep the depth of modules to no more than four levels deep. This structure helps a lot when getting into testing activities involving unit, integration and system testing.

TS or developing good-quality design is at the heart of enabling good-quality software solutions, and, therefore, it may be useful to digress here to the topic of testing and get a perspective on what is being suggested. The author would like to call it a personal software process for testing, since the techniques proposed in what follows have worked well on all of the product development initiatives undertaken by him. Understanding of the process areas on product integration and verification would need supporting ideas that are to be found in the following essay on a personal software process for testing.

Fencing Technique: Essay on Personal Software Process for Testing

Abstract:

This essay provides an understanding of how to manage and handle testing of software products in practical and real-life scenarios such as with ever-changing product requirements with unclear expectations of the user interface. How to effectively manage the testing process by separating the testing of application code and the user interface code in such a scenario is described with the help of an example. After testing the application code and the user interface code separately, the process of integrating the two is addressed.

It highlights the use of language constructs in C to effectively narrow down the bug in what is termed the 'fencing technique'. This technique has been put to use in numerous software product development and testing initiatives that the author has been involved with. Two of the products which were developed using concepts found in this essay were award-winning tools in the Motorola Tools Fair in 1993 and 1994.

A product development initiative in Windows environment using C language for application development is used as an example to explain the process. However, this process could be applicable to product development initiatives in other environments as well. Native language constructs and environment features would then have to be exploited to gain full benefits from what is presented in this essay.

INTRODUCTION

Before delving into the PSP for testing, a brief introduction to the software testing process would be in order. Software testing has consistently evolved with the changing paradigm to software development. White-box testing to emphasize structural integrity and black-box testing to emphasize functional integrity were relevant and applicable when structured methods was the most acceptable way of problem decomposition [Beizer 1990, 1995]. With the maturing of object-oriented methodologies and solutions seeking to be object focused, classes having built-in-self-test (BIST) features similar to digital hardware design could become a reality. This is primarily possible due to the high degree of modularization of function and associated data into classes. So, the BIST functions or methods could be developed to potentially stress the class methods.

(Contd)

Metrics collection itself assumes a new meaning when we are also able to qualitatively assess the test strategy rather than merely predict defects and effort. Fencing technique is one such strategy, which can potentially trap run-time and application errors in a systematic manner.

Test strategy: The test strategy adopted in this PSP for testing is to perform independent testing of the application code and the user interface code and defer the integration of the two until after requirements stability is gained. The application code developed can be exercised to check completion and correctness as described in the next section, on application code testing. User interface testing is described separately in Section 3. The final integration and the fencing technique to rule out the possibilities of run-time errors are described in Sections 4 and 5.

APPLICATION CODE TESTING

Testing of software is very much a process of systematic elimination of the reasons for failure. A broad classification of bugs or failure conditions is functionality failures (bugs local to functions or modules), interface failures (bugs between two communicating modules due to incorrect data-reference pass by value versus pass by reference) and global parameter failures (bugs due to incorrect data initializations and settings) [Nandyal 1993]. These failure conditions are not dependent upon the method employed to build software. The application code developed using structured methods is just so much more prone to having the third category of failures. Real-life product testing effort would require that testing be planned with *design for change*, in mind.

Unit testing of the application code is iterative and is performed by tracing the branching of the logical paths that the code can potentially take. Test cases are identified to ensure 100% line coverage (note: *not path coverage*). Unreachable code, if any, and bugs due to exercising the different lines of code can be uncovered with these test cases. Black-box testing of modules or units can then be adopted to determine functional correctness at the unit level to contain all functional defects [Nandyal 1993]. Black-box testing of a unit would mean that each unit or module is considered to be the system and it is ensured that adequate test cases are employed to highlight the unit behavior. Ideally, such tests should be conducted in a bottom-up fashion. In a structured methods approach, for instance, we start module testing with the module specification, which cannot be decomposed further. With reference to Figure 5.6, testing begins with Function_1_AtLevel3() and the other functions at this level. When testing is complete, the incidence of functional and structural defects/bugs due to this module is practically zero. After all the modules which are at this final level of decomposition are tested in both a white-box and black-box sense, the module which is immediately higher in the hierarchy is tested. With reference to Figure 5.6, Function_1_AtLevel2() would be tested after all the functions at level 3 are individually tested. What is accomplished by this manner of bottom-up integration is that zero interface errors or defects would exist after testing the integrating module in a white-box and black-box sense. This approach is continued all the way up until the system is completely integrated. With reference to Figure 5.6, the system is complete after integrating all the modules from the main() function which is at level 1. A detailed elaboration of this method can be found in Nandyal [1997].

The virtue of such an application integration process is that modifications to requirements can be handled with relative ease. With reference to Figure 5.6, let us assume that a change to requirement resulted in the creation of New_Function_AtLevel3(). With the above testing strategy, this would be tested after all dependencies such as Function_1_AtLevel4() and Function_2_AtLevel4() are tested both in a white-box and black-box sense.

It is useful to mention that functions or modules can be effectively tested using driver functions. Development of these driver functions to exercise the behavior is a very useful step in the process of integration of the

(Contd)

application code with the user interface. Suffice it to say here, that drivers are recommended and were used in this PSP strategy to stress the functionality of each one of the modules. For a more detailed elaboration, refer to Nandyal [1993].

USER INTERFACE TESTING

Figure 5.7 is a sample user interface (UI) structure chart, which will be used as an example to develop the idea further.

In a Windows environment the GUI begins with the development of WinMain() function. Several initialization functions are called before windows commands begin to get interpreted by WndProc() function. The WM_COMMAND message of WndProc() is where all the action happens. A parameter called the wParam contains the menu activation. It is here that dialogs get popped up and user inputs are received. After sufficient information to process the request is made available, the application is called using callback functions. The UI testing is restricted to doing a thorough job of ensuring functional and structural correctness of this much of the final product. The next few paragraphs describe testing of what was briefly presented to be the UI of the product.

WinMain() in Figure 5.7 is the GUI equivalent of main() in Figure 5.6. In a manner similar to the testing of the application code (Section 2), testing of the UI begins in a bottom-up manner. So, the message loop handling the processing of windows messages in function WndProc() is tested in both a white-box and black-box sense.

Use of stubs comes in very handy. Stubs are what the application code will eventually replace. The Windows commands dispatched from the WinMain() function are checked for recognition and acknowledgment in the UI-testing process. Stubs could be dummy dialogs which say that when a message called IDM_OPEN is received, a PopOpenFileDialog(), say, is called. It could just be a modal dialog which can be dismissed as having fulfilled the requirements of the functionality behind the FileOpen() function, the behavior of which is delegated to the application code development and tested during the application code testing. Stubs are mere informational dialogs, which are acknowledgments to the occurrence of an event.

When the UI is tested in this manner, what is possible to eliminate is all known causes for UI malfunctioning. Since the user input capture involves designing dialog boxes which in itself is quite an involved process, segregating the development of UI as a parallel activity to the application code development results in significant cycle time reduction and defect elimination, thereby leading to a good chance of building a quality product on time—which is every developer's dream in a real world that involves unstable and numerous changes to both application specs and UI design.

INTEGRATION PROCESS

After the application code and UI are independently tested and known to be of proven quality, the integration process can be indulged in. If the strategy adopted for testing the application code is through a driver and that adopted for testing the UI is through a stub, the integration process is a mere replacement of the driver with the UI event handler and the stub with the application callback function. This is an extremely useful step in further eliminating possibilities of defects due to *ad hoc* integration!

At this stage of development, the only possible causes for application failure are *run-time errors or defects*. Practically, there is no reason for the application code or for the UI to have any defects. Here is where the fencing technique I developed, and will illustrate next, comes in handy.

(*Contd*)

FENCING TECHNIQUE

The good old #ifdef, #endif pair is all that it boils down to! For languages that do not support preprocessor directives, there are numerous other ways to achieve the same effect. What is important is to understand the technique of applying them, which is elaborated below.

In the integration process, what is done is that the event handler of the UI replaces the driver of the application code. The stub in the UI is replaced by the application code. The only modifications necessary are to ensure that the application callback functions are called using the right UI parameters after taking proper care to ensure their initialization. Here again, beginning the integration process with application code involving simple processing logic is a good starting point. The executable generated after the stub is replaced by the application callback, and is known to potentially harbor defects which would occur only during run time.

When the executable is run and the event working, the application callback is exercised, and if all goes well, then that is the end of integration of this feature of the application code with its corresponding UI. Other application callbacks can then be integrated.

If, however, there are run-time errors, then it is best to block out the entire application callback with #ifdef 1, #endif statements. Regenerate the executable with all of the application code blocked out in this manner by putting a fence around the application callback (*the fencing technique*). When this executable is exercised, obviously there will be no run-time errors. This is because the run-time errors are *always* due to the application code *after* integrating with the UI. Since all of the application code is blocked out using the fence, the executable will stay without causing run-time errors. Now, the fence (#ifdef 1, #endif pair) has to be relaid so that we get to the sticky part in a systematic manner.

In the fencing technique this is done block by block, beginning with the outermost logic block and converging rapidly to the logic block, causing the problem in a series of executable generations.

So, we relay the fence by blocking out most of the logic blocks inside the next largest logic block, and continue. With this technique it is extremely easy to locate the cause in the application code that is causing the run-time failure to occur. After the logic block is isolated in this manner, the fix mostly seems to suggest that the reason for failure is improper reference to the manner in which variables are interpreted.

CONCLUSION

Identifying and eliminating run-time errors in products is a nightmare if a systematic approach to testing of the application and the UI is not undertaken. Ideas in this essay describe a very practical and a personal software-testing process that seems to have worked very well for me in numerous product development initiatives.

The fencing technique introduces with the help of an example the application of ideas in this book to large product development initiatives. From the tone set in the essay, it is clear that this technique is not restricted by the methodology employed. In fact, it is very clear that the methodology employed or the manner in which the specifications are handled is immaterial when it comes to identifying certain fatal application failures, which are so very common.

What is described is a very systematic bottom-up testing and integration approach of the application code and the UI code. When done in parallel, significant cycle time reductions have been seen to result. Additionally, a controlled and systematic process of eliminating all known causes of failure in the application code and the UI code as separate activities helps to build confidence in the integration process.

During the integration of the application code and the UI code, the fencing technique is the only effective saving grace to rapidly converge on the application logic block which is prone to run-time errors. A useful technique resulting from years of developing and testing products is presented in this essay.

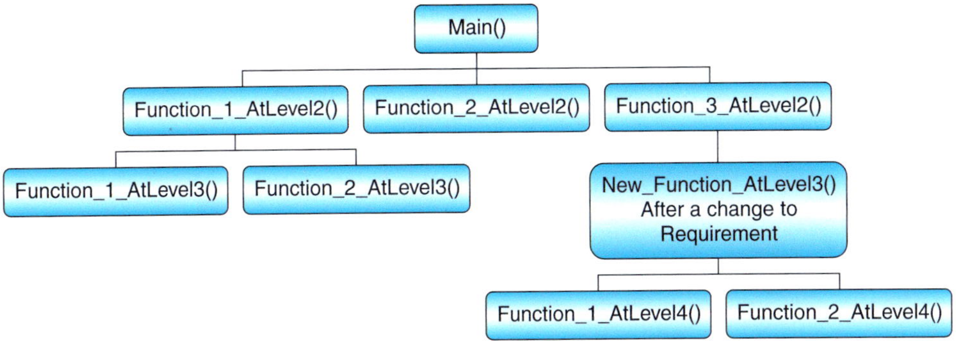

Fig. 5.6 Example Structure Chart of the Application Code

Source: Adapted from SITARA Process JewelBox™ © SITARA Technologies Pvt. Ltd. 2002 with permission

A good technical design considers and isolates modules susceptible to large degrees of churn from the more stable and predictable application features using partitioning of design. Containing the effects of changes or requirements churn with the use of design partitions helps to render the process of verification effectively.

Design alternatives have to be explored based on the product or application requirements. From the above essay, one of the proposed alternatives was to separate the presentation logic from the application logic and develop them separately until each of them is verified independently. Delaying the integration of application and presentation logic to after proving in fault tolerance of both independently is one of the several techniques that an evaluation of alternatives must consider.

Much of what is needed to enable the practices of TS at a capability level 1 is described in the above essay. In addition refer to Chapter 3 for a more elaborate treatment of what constitutes design in a traditional sense of a development process. The practical side of what constitutes design in both structured methods and object modeling technique has also been described in Chapter 3.

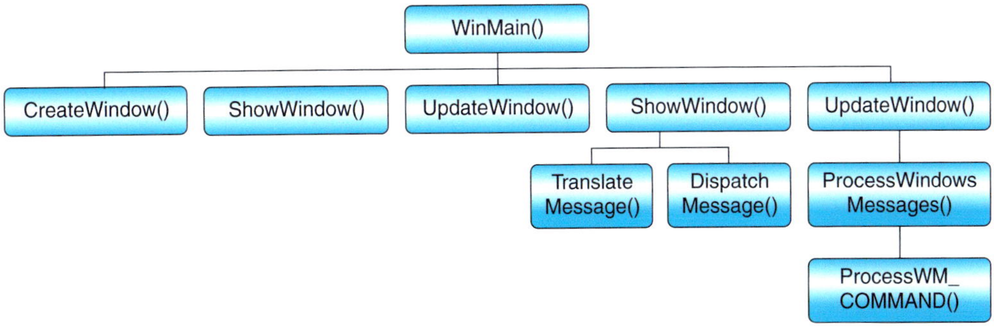

Fig. 5.7 Example Structure Chart of the User Interface

Source: Adapted from SITARA Process JewelBox™ © SITARA Technologies Pvt. Ltd. 2002 with permission

When the following specific goals and specific practices are coupled with practices defined in Decision Analysis and Resolution, a capability level 1 or the performed level of capability for TS is enabled:

SG1 Select Product Component Solutions

SP1.1 **Develop Alternative Solutions and Selection Criteria**

SP1.2 **Select Product-Component Solutions**

SG2 Develop the Design

SP2.1 **Design the Product or Product Component**

SP2.2 **Establish a Technical Data Package**

SP2.3 **Design Interfaces Using Criteria**

SP2.4 **Perform Make, Buy or Reuse Analyses**

SG3 Implement the Product Design

SP3.1 **Implement the Design**

SP3.2 **Develop Product Support Documentation**

The practical sides to TS as experienced with some of the author's best professional associations are as follows:

Technical Solution

1. Use the analysis specifications for the product to drive design choices based on an assessment of both the 'core' and 'non-core' requirements.
2. Establish the component and module logic in pseudo-code along with definitions for the data structures.
3. Ensure traceability of pseudo-code to the component specifications describing the functionality.
4. Implement the modules in the programming language with applicable standards.
5. Conduct appropriate levels of preliminary testing to ensure module integrity and revise module logic and data structure definitions as necessary.
6. Update changes to the documented logic and data structures within the design specifications.
7. Establish the necessary documentation that uses a structured design technique to represent module or component functionality.

Display 5.2 Interpreting Technical Solution

Source: Adapted from SITARA Process JewelBox™ © SITARA Technologies Pvt. Ltd. 2002 with permission

How does Technical Solution transform its capability when the transition to capability level 2 (or the managed level) is made?

When transition to capability level 2 is made for design, one of the key enablers for establishing consistency of design practices is a policy that governs and defines the minimum expectations for the design process. The organizational policy supports available options within the established organizational standards for rendering design with appropriate design tools, makes provision for the necessary training of the domain specialists and often resorts to using the services of design champions who mentor and support the design.

Design champions who are well versed in both the project domain and the influencing technologies evaluate the available options and make the final selection using the practices contained in the Decision Analysis and Resolution process area. Appropriate module-level roles and responsibilities for developing the design into code are assigned after providing the necessary orientation and training. Since design is an iterative process between conceptualization and realization of logic, forward and backward traceability between code and design and design and analysis is maintained in order to keep intermediate work products correct, complete, consistent and internally traceable. Such forward and backward traceability is maintained within a configuration management system and monitored through appropriate corrective steps. Should the design method be influenced by the customer's process or by the design used to conceive a legacy, such decisions are documented and a waiver process is used to ensure compatibility among interoperating designs.

Within the CMMI, the ten generic practices of EPPAT MIMOR establish the minimum criteria for TS to qualify as a managed process at capability level 2. And in doing so, the generic goal 2 is established. A refresher of the mnemonic EPPAT MIMOR and the affected generic goal would be in order.

GG2 Institutionalize a Managed Process

- GP2.1 **Establish an Organizational Policy**
- GP2.2 **Plan the Process**
- GP2.3 **Provide Resources**
- GP2.4 **Assign Responsibility**
- GP2.5 **Train People**
- GP2.6 **Manage Configurations**
- GP2.7 **Identify and Involve Relevant Stakeholders**
- GP2.8 **Monitor and Control the Process**
- GP2.9 **Objectively Evaluate Adherence**
- GP2.10 **Review Status with Higher-Level Management**

It might be useful to note that both RD and TS are related process areas whose practices are highly interdependent. Quite often, practices belonging to both the analysis and design process are governed by the choices and decisions made by the customer. Even the tools and techniques that have to be employed on the project are driven by the customer. In such a case, the transition to capability level 3 at the defined level would first have to consider the *project context*. And when generalizations of the practices into what could be termed best practices at the project level can be made, a transition to the defined capability for TS becomes possible.

It is also possible that even when the governing design is within the project's control, most level 2 practices consider project-level constraints and define a project life cycle that may be unique to the characteristics of that project. Design techniques adopted at the project level may however establish a commonality of practices aligning with the organizational mandates, and, therefore, it is appropriate and expected that TS cannot operate at capability level 2 for too long. As soon as projects define their design techniques and realize best practices which might be local to the project's context, practices belonging to Organizational Process Focus and Organizational Process Definition are used to establish an organizational baseline of best practices for design. Of course, there has to be a dedicated focus within the organizational process improvement infrastructure that is sensitive to such recognition and seeding of organizational practices. It is only when such thinking is in place that the process improvement framework can be successfully used as a leverage to define the organizational standards for TS and the transition to capability level 3 can be made.

How does Technical Solution transform its capability when the transition to capability level 3 (or the defined level) is made?

At the defined capability, organizational choices for enabling and articulating acceptable design representations are identified and documented within the OSSP. Such a rendering of acceptable design methodologies and standards influences the available choices for projects. Within the process infrastructure, other necessary process aids such as tailoring guidelines may be used to make the organizational design methodology applicable within the project's context.

The expectations from the CMMI for TS to qualify at capability level 3 are to enable GG3 and the associated practices of GP3.1 and GP3.2. They are as follows:

GG3 Institutionalize a Defined Process

- GP3.1 **Establish a Defined Process**
- GP3.2 **Collect Improvement Information**

How does Technical Solution transform its capability when the transition to capability level 4 (or the quantitatively managed level) is made? Or, how does Technical Solution demonstrate a high maturity measurement and analysis capability?

TS is an excellent candidate process area to be placed under a higher capability level given the virtues and benefits from enabling the engineering process areas to a high degree of fault tolerance. Some of the specific practices within TS which lend themselves to measurement or quantification and therefore for stabilizing their influences to improve the overall effectiveness of the process area itself are as follows:

- SP1.1 **Develop Detailed Alternative Solutions and Selection Criteria**
- SP1.2 **Evolve Operational Concepts and Scenarios**
- SP2.4 **Perform Make, Buy or Reuse Analyses**
- SP3.1 **Implement the Design**

The two generic practices at capability level 4 may be applied to study the influences of special causes of variation on these practices. Design quality attributes for the product components can drive the choices used to define available alternatives. Quantitative goals defining code complexity can be tracked using tools. Along with a robust set of practices belonging to the verification process area, data from design reviews and code walkthroughs could be used to study attainment of quality objectives for intermediate work products. Both historical data and competition analysis can drive the establishment of quality and performance goals for the design work products in terms of response time, code complexity, usability features, and so on. Quantitative goals for in-process faults resulting from an analysis of historical data using design verification data can drive the goal setting and tracking of the attainment of design objectives for work product quality measures. Since design is at the heart of enabling product quality measures, TS can be considered an excellent candidate process area for establishing a level 4 capability.

How does Technical Solution transform its capability when the transition to capability level 5 (or the optimizing level) is made? Or, how does Technical Solution demonstrate a high maturity measurement and analysis capability?

When the practices of Causal Analysis and Resolution are rendered to understand the robustness of design, TS can scale up the next capability level at level 5. Pareto analysis of verification data can highlight the potential issues with design that most commonly occur as patterns of design failure. Studying the common cause influences of design failure and isolating the root cause and rendering an insulation with a process fix would be possible for the practices of TS. It is therefore possible to conceive a level 5–capable TS process area. The expectations from CMMI in order to render a capability level 5 TS process area are as follows:

GG5 Institutionalize an Optimizing Process

GP5.1 **Ensure Continuous Process Improvement**

GP5.2 **Correct Root Causes of Problems**

AUTHOR'S MUSING

On face value, it might appear that the CMMI is prescriptive of a waterfall model wherein you do practices belonging to RD, then do practices in TS, and so on, whereas real-life development contexts are not quite the same due to lots of iterations. Note that there is no imposition of a sequence of specific practices to be followed within either the RD or TS. You might need to perform a few RD-specific practices, then step into a few TS-specific practices, and then go back to RD practices, and so on. In that sense, the CMMI is most definitely accommodative of a real-life situation.

PRODUCT INTEGRATION (PI)
CMMI-DEV

How does Product Integration look when it operates at a capability level 1 (or the performed level)?

Product Integration (PI) belongs to the engineering category of the continuous representation of the CMMI. It might be useful to note that practices within the engineering process areas cannot be treated disjointedly. There is a very significant dependence on both the rigor and effective performance of all practices identified to belong to the six different process areas in the engineering category.

Given such a high degree of overlap, what has been observed by the author when teaching the 'Introduction to CMMI' course is that a practitioner is often confused as to why something is categorized as being part of the TS process area when it actually belongs to the PI, or vice versa! Instead of thinking that the practices within a process area are sequenced and have to be performed in that order, it is useful to note that no such sequencing is intended either implicitly or explicitly within a process area. It is very likely that some practices of RD have to be performed prior to conducting a few practices within TS and then it might require invoking the remainder of RD prior to including some from PI and iteratively evolve the solution. It is very useful to note that the spirit and purpose behind a process area is contained within the specific practices. Both the intent and the precept parts have to be equally emphasized if the right interpretations have to be rendered.

Within the scope of PI, the different modules or components conceived in the design are aggregated so as to ensure that the sub-assemblies are built to specification. Determining the integration sequence has a dependency on the extent of legacy integration and, therefore, the creation of stubs and drivers. The integration sequence can be bottom-up or top-down, as described in the essay on personal software process for testing.

The use of appropriate integration environment (such as integration tools and operational environment) is a prerequisite for ensuring that the intermediate work products can be verified along with integration activities. Building the intermediate work products has a dependency on good version control of software code within a configuration management system. Good configuration management systems support a wide variety of build options, including the use of branched code and code residing in a geographically distributed development environment.

In one of the author's very early exposures (early 1990s) to a configuration management and build tool called Domain Software Engineering Environment (DSEE), it was evident that support for distributed code development was prevalent much before the CMMI thought process existed! DSEE was one of the best tools till date, used by the author wherein multiple builds could be triggered with rules (as in a makefile used in C language), to include pre-built libraries. One could distribute the load of final product integration by setting up build rules on idle machines within a networked environment to speed up the build process. Eventually, the complied code had to be translated into proprietary target platform executables (such as the Motorola S-records).

When code has to be debugged on the target platform, the PI process becomes a serious business. Each build cycle can last from 6 to 8 hours at a minimum. Considerable amount of time is involved in downloading the final builds onto the target platform, say an EPROM (erasable programmable read-only memory). In such a case, it is important to ensure that all the necessary components are proved in using simulators and emulators before the executable is built to operate on the target platform. One of the product integration strategies that can be employed in such cases is to exercise a suite of related functions within a build cycle. What merits emphasis is that depending upon the complexity of the product that is to be developed, product integration itself needs thorough planning and execution. It is not as simple as it might appear.

Testing the functionality of the sub-modules in both a black-box and white-box sense constitutes the main purpose behind PI. In doing so, the following specific goals and specific practices are realized with the attainment of a capability level 1 for PI:

SG1 Prepare for Product Integration

SP1.1 Determine Integration Sequence[4]

SP1.2 Establish the Product Integration Environment

SP1.3 Establish Product Integration Procedures and Criteria

SG2 Ensure Interface Compatibility

SP2.1 Review Interface Descriptions for Completeness

SP2.2 Manage Interfaces

SG3 Assemble Product Components and Deliver the Product

SP3.1 Confirm Readiness of Product Components for Integration

SP3.2 Assemble Product Components

SP3.3 Evaluate Assembled Product Components

SP3.4 Package and Deliver the Product or Product Component

The practical sides to product integration as experienced with some of the author's best professional associations are as follows:

Product Integration

1. Establish the necessary product integration environment along with the necessary hardware.
2. Develop a well-tested and peer-reviewed product integration script which exercises the necessary build sequence for components and libraries that have to be included to develop the final executable.
3. Assemble the work products using the integration sequence and exercise the sub-components in both a black-box and white-box sense to ascertain functional and structural accuracy.
4. Redo or modify the design should the verification and validation of the sub-assembly result in errors.
5. Implement the design in code and verify the build conditions for which a fix has been rendered.
6. Test the functionality on the target platform with necessary test cases and document the product integration test report.

Display 5.3 Interpreting Product Integration

Source: Adapted from SITARA Process JewelBox™ © SITARA Technologies Pvt. Ltd. 2002 with permission

[4] Practice title appears as "Establish an Integration Strategy" in version 1.3 of the CMMI-DEV constellation. There is no noticeable/perceptible change to the informative content associated with this practice and therefore to its interpretation.

How does Product Integration transform its capability when the transition to capability level 2 (or the managed level) is made?

When the necessary core practices of PI are in place, it is now possible to build the next layer of capability at level 2, much like the peel of an onion, on top of the core practices. The EPPAT MIMOR generic practices of level 2 are what support a capability level 2 product integration process area.

An organizational policy defines the support available at the organizational level for PI activities, which includes support for both hardware and software infrastructure to render product integration and support activities. The policy is inclusive of procurement and support of specific tools along with their deployment with necessary training. The policy has to support any customer-specific choices and dependencies of tools to support PI activities.

It is important for the integration tool and the configuration management tool to interoperate with the development tools being used (such as code compilers) so that the development and integration activities can happen in a seamless manner. Necessary training and orientation to these activities is provided to the concerned stakeholders within the process context.

Build cycles and the code fragments that are exercised are established within a configuration management system with logs of product integration testing, demonstrating the sufficiency and adequacy conditions of the built functionality. PI activities are monitored using a product integration plan and attainment of product quality goals are ascertained using 'as-run' or 'run-in' logs.

How does Product Integration transform its capability when the transition to capability level 3 (or the defined level) is made?

Best practices resulting from projects are evaluated for a larger organizational applicability. Organizational development and integration standards are established within the OSSP to enable projects to adopt or adapt a tailored PI process that is best deployed on projects with similar characteristics. In doing so, a capability level 3 or defined process capability can be established for PI using the following generic goal and associated generic practices:

GG3 Institutionalize a Defined Process

GP3.1 **Establish a Defined Process**

GP3.2 **Collect Improvement Information**

It is the author's opinion, given the fact that the PI practices are highly dependent on tool capability, that it is very difficult to demonstrate and justify product integration at a capability beyond level 3. Stated differently, if the tool has built-in capability to isolate, mitigate and eliminate special and common causes of variation associated with PI such that they do not occur to begin with, then such capability is already institutionalized within the definition of PI by the tool. Specific opportunities to further minimize special/common cause variations are therefore very minimal. If a dedicated focus on identifying and controlling such instances has to be established nevertheless, it would require sufficient business justifications and customer mandates to do so. From a theoretical perspective, generic goal 4 and the related generic practices 4.1 and 4.2 need to be established for enabling PI at capability level 4.

GG4 Institutionalize a Quantitatively Managed Process

GP4.1 **Establish Quantitative Objectives for the Process**

GP4.2 **Stabilize Sub-Process Performance**

For enabling PI at capability level 5, the generic goal 5 and the associated generic practices 5.1 and 5.2 need to be institutionalized.

GG5 Institutionalize an Optimizing Process

GP5.1 Ensure Continuous Process Improvement

GP5.2 Correct Root Causes of Problems

VERIFICATION (VER) CMMI-DEV

How does Verification look when it operates at a capability level 1 (or the performed level)?

Verification (VER) belongs to the engineering category of the continuous representation of the CMMI. It includes activities governing peer reviews and almost all of the testing activities such as unit testing, integration testing, system testing and regression testing. The purpose of Verification is to ensure that selected work products meet their specified requirements—both stated and implied requirements. Where code is involved, the purpose of Verification is to ascertain that the code functions as it was designed to function.

A technical review refers to the IEEE Standard for Software Reviews and Audits (IEEE-STD-1028), which contains prescriptive process definitions for five types of best-in-class software management and technical reviews. The five major types of reviews are the Management Review Process, Technical Review Process, Software Inspection Process, Walkthrough Process and Audit Process. In an offshore–onsite development initiative, a sixth type of review, called the Joint Reviews, is often encountered. Joint reviews held between onsite and offshore teams at predefined points in time are principally referred to as life-cycle, end-of-phase or milestone reviews. Joint reviews are considered formal reviews, to solicit feedback and approval to proceed and to provide assurance to customers that the final product will eventually meet its requirements.

Verification could include both incremental and regressive mechanisms to build sufficiency criteria to establish operational requirements for the work product. Verification activities typically govern the exit criteria from a phase before a baseline of the work product is established. Development initiatives include an objective verification of the work product from a fitness-of-use point of view. Inspections and walkthroughs are examples of a peer-review process.

It is necessary to identify critical components or work products of the development life-cycle phase that should be objectively verified. One example of a critical component is a module such as the graphical user interface (GUI). GUIs are prone to modification and change requests catering to end-user requirements. Localization of the presentation layer helps to improve inspection efficiency.

Establishment of a verification environment could include setting up of either a simulated environment or the use of emulators if the target environment is not available for testing. The verification steps necessary to exercise the work product are executed using a documented procedure for either peer reviews or structured walkthroughs. In doing so the objectives of the following specific goal is achieved:

SG1 Prepare for Verification

SP1.1 Select Work Products for Verification

SP1.2 Establish the Verification Environment

SP1.3 Establish Verification Procedures and Criteria

Perspective-Based Peer Review Process

The perspective-based peer review process from the SITARA Process JewelBox™ set forth here is an *exhaustive* peer-review process. It fulfills the practices on the CMMI V1.2 Level 3 Process Area on Verification. *Tailoring of this process is necessary.*

DEFINITION: TAILORING

The purpose of tailoring is to eliminate tasks that add unnecessary costs, cycle time and data without adding value to the process or for the definition of the product. Tailoring of a standard takes the form of deletion of wasteful steps, alteration of activities to more explicitly reflect the application to a particular context or addition of activities to satisfy program requirements. Sound engineering judgment is necessary to ensure that tailoring does not contribute any additional risks. Tailoring a process is the responsibility of the development team in consultation with the process champion or software quality assurance who actually owns the development process.

OBJECTIVE

The objective is to describe in detail the mechanisms that shall govern the review process.

- To document the necessary preliminary activities that shall be executed before calling for a review.
- To provide the review process mechanism.
- To provide details on the review meeting.
- To document the activities that shall govern the review disposition.
- To provide the post-review meeting activities.
- Templates for facilitating the review process.

PURPOSE

The purpose is

- To conduct the business specification reviews, technical specification reviews and test readiness reviews using a structured approach;
- To document a formal, well-defined process to conduct reviews of all deliverables/policies/baselines at the site;
- To establish a quality checkpoint ensuring the creation of defect-free deliverables using systematic screening mechanisms; and
- To encourage the development process to embark on an internal process improvement initiative by continuously improving the review process mechanism itself.

(Contd)

PRELIMINARY ACTIVITIES

- The document/deliverable shall be correct, complete and consistent with respect to interrelated artifacts before the author calls for a review. The author and a review leader/review facilitator shall conduct such a preliminary investigation.
- Any information, which the author does not already possess to make the deliverable correct, complete and consistent, shall be solicited by the author from people competent to provide such information. This shall happen much before actually documenting the deliverable and would ideally happen at the point of entry to each phase.
- The author shall choose a review leader/review facilitator well in advance and appraise this person about the nature of the review and provide the person the document/deliverable that will be reviewed using which a baseline will be formed. Typically, this should happen several days prior to the actual review. For short-duration projects, engineering judgment is to be exercised.
- If the review leader/review facilitator decides that the document is fit for a review, then he will put together a review panel that will be comprised of between 4 and 9 people, who will review the document/deliverable keeping their perspective in mind.
- If the review leader/review facilitator decides that the document is not fit for a review, then this person will suggest that the document/deliverable be modified/rewritten by the author before a formal review is conducted. This decision will have to be communicated to all concerned people, for example, the project manager.
- The review panel assembled together to conduct the review shall comprise people having a good exposure to the domain that is being captured in the document/deliverable and in the whole review process mechanism itself.
- After conducting this readiness check, a representative from the software quality assurance (SQA) department shall authorize the conduct of the review. The review leader/review facilitator shall appraise the concerned SQA representative on the worthiness of the document/deliverable for a review.
- The SQA representative shall then allow the review leader/review facilitator to distribute the deliverable/document in a formal manner.
- The review document/deliverable will be in the possession of the review leader/review facilitator and no requests from the author to modify or change or append new material to the review material shall be entertained.
- The review leader/review facilitator shall conduct a preliminary estimate of the time required for completely reviewing the document and make sure that the estimated time is made available for the review panel. However, a minimum of 2 working days shall be made available for the review material of 150 pages in size (including all references/support literature) to be reviewed.
- The review leader/review facilitator shall then raise a duly completed review meeting notice form and distribute the review material.

Use electronic mail to reduce cycle time and improve effectiveness of coordination activities wherever possible.

(Contd)

REVIEW PROCESS MECHANISM

- After the review panel gets the review material, the members shall review the document keeping in mind their assigned perspective. While it is not important to limit the perspective, it is important to do a thorough job of the assigned perspective. The reviewer can however examine the review material from an unassigned perspective as well.
- These perspectives are as follows:

Author	The person who is responsible for creating the document/deliverable
Quality Assurance and Recorder	An SQA representative from support organization or a project member given this role
Testing	Testing perspective shall ensure that all the requirements are testable
Analysis	Analysis perspective shall ensure that the requirements are correct, complete and consistent
Design	Design perspective shall ensure that the requirements are verified and validated to maintain internal cohesion and are mutually supportive
Code/ implementation	Implementation perspective shall ensure that the requirement can be implemented with the given constraints
Observers	Observers are allowed by the review leader/review facilitator to sit and observe the review process. Such people shall not participate in the review itself. But they can be present to learn the review dynamics. Example: Fresh recruits

- After completing the review, the reviewers shall fill in the review details section of the review meeting notice form.
- All the inputs on the review material shall be made available to the review leader/review facilitator through a reviewer form.
- The reviewer form shall contain comments of the reviewers that will be discussed between the reviewer and the author moderated by the review leader/review facilitator much before coming into the review meeting.
- Errors/defects that do not require any discussion and that get accepted by the author shall be removed as discussion items from the review. The author shall ensure that any accepted errors/defects will be fixed.
- If there are any contentious issues that cannot be resolved outside the review meeting, they shall be brought up during the review meeting by the review leader/facilitator.
- The review leader/review facilitator shall have the final say on any unresolved issue either outside a review meeting or during a review meeting.

REVIEW MEETING

- All the reviewers, the author and the review leader shall meet on the assigned day for the review meeting 10 minutes before the actual review.
- The review meeting shall be facilitated by the review leader/review facilitator who will also be the moderator. All decisions taken by the review leader shall be final.

(Contd)

- The review meeting shall not be used as a forum to air suggestions, better ways of doing things, better approaches and the like. The review meeting shall restrict the scope of examination to add value to the document/deliverable, as it exists. The review leader/review facilitator shall reserve the right to request a person to leave the review if personal attacks on the author are indulged in.
- The review leader/review facilitator shall also reserve the right to dismiss a person from the review panel if the reviewer is found to be unprepared for the review. Such incidents shall be dealt with firmly by a suitable senior management decision on the reviewer's ability to perform again on reviews.
- Any voluntary submissions of inability to perform on the review panel after accepting the review perspective shall be dealt with firmly and would affect the reviewer's performance appraisal. When this is repeated more than thrice, a warning shall be issued to the reviewer and this warning shall form a part of the personnel records of the reviewer.
- All reviews shall be restricted to a maximum duration of 2 hours. Any deliverable/document requiring more than 2 hours for reviewing shall be broken up into manageable pieces and reviewed separately.
- No reviewer shall sit on more than two reviews per day. It is the duty of the review leader/facilitator to ensure that such incidents do not happen and that there are no clashes with other reviews. It is, however, the responsibility of the reviewer to ensure that such information is communicated to the review leader/facilitator well in advance.
- The review shall begin on time and end on time and latecomers shall not be entertained. A maximum tolerance of 5 minutes, again at the discretion of the review leader/facilitator, can be allowed.
- During the meeting the SQA perspective and Recorder shall record all the important decisions arrived at during the review.

REVIEW DISPOSITION AND POST-REVIEW MEETING ACTIVITIES

- The review leader/facilitator shall conclude the decisions arrived at after completing the review meeting through a formal review disposition.
- The review disposition could be one of the following:

Accepted	If the document/deliverable has no known defects/errors.
Conditionally Accepted	If the document is not fit to form a baseline. A few errors/defects pointed out by the review panel must be removed and appropriate changes must be incorporated before it is accepted. The review leader/review facilitator shall ensure that a Closure Action Team (CAT) comprising of a few important reviewers is formed to assist the author to complete the deliverable. The CAT and the author shall review the changes and make a formal announcement to the review leader/facilitator that the document is fit to form a baseline. The reviewer leader/facilitator shall then announce the formation of a baseline. The Configuration Manager will own the baseline. All the review metrics shall be owned by the SQA.
Not Accepted	The document has major defects/errors and the document has to be rewritten. Such situations should be extremely rare if the review leader/facilitator has the competence to serve in this position.

(Contd)

- The SQA representative in consultation with the project manager shall complete a review disposition and quality assurance form.
- All deliverables forming a project baseline shall have the authorization from the SQA perspective that participated in the review with the sanction of the moderator.
- No document/deliverable shall be allowed to go out of the development process to the customer unless the moderator approves the document to conform to the development process practices.
- No document/deliverable shall be baselined without having appropriate metrics information.
- Such authorizations shall carry the signature and stamp of approval of the moderator. The author and the individuals assisting the author in the CAT shall sign off the deliverable. Sign-off serves to ensure a 'collective responsibility' to any problems that would arise after sending the deliverable to the customer.*
- Any such post-release issues shall be documented using a problem tracking report form.

* IMPORTANT: Obtaining a formal sign-off from all relevant stakeholders is mostly symbolic. It should not be 'overdone' so as to affect team harmony.

Peer reviews are typically conducted using perspectives. One such procedure is described here. Data from peer reviews typically include error classification by type, by origin and by identification of cause. In doing so, the following specific goal and specific practices are built into the process capability:

SG2 Perform Peer Reviews

SP2.1 Prepare for Peer Reviews

SP2.2 Conduct Peer Reviews

SP2.3 Analyze Peer Review Data

Verification is conducted either as a peer review or as a testing activity on the work product. When results deviate from expectations, corrective actions are rendered to bring the work product within the specifications. In doing so, the following specific goal and related specific practices are built into the process:

SG3 Verify Selected Work Products

SP3.1 Perform Verification

SP3.2 Analyze Verification Results and Identify Corrective Action[5]

[5] Practice title appears as "Analyze Verification Results" in version 1.3 of the CMMI-DEV constellation. There is no noticeable/perceptible change to the informative content associated with this practice and therefore to its interpretation.

The practical sides to Verification as experienced with some of the author's best professional associations are as follows:

Verification

1. The work product for peer review or walkthrough is determined to be correct, complete and consistent by the author and the review moderator before calling for a peer review.
2. The moderator and the author decide the composition and the perspectives for the review team that would objectively verify the integrity of the work product using a structured peer review or walkthrough.
3. The work product is reviewed using multiple perspectives with a view to uncover all known errors.
4. Errors, and defects from prior phases, are captured in a 'peer-review log' with appropriate classifications by type, phase of origin and cause.
5. The verification is concluded with a review disposition for the work product as accepted, conditionally accepted and rejected.
6. For work products which are conditionally accepted, a closure action team comprising of the moderator, the author and a few key review members is assigned to verify that the work product is rectified to adhere to specifications.

Display 5.4 Interpreting Verification

Source: Adapted from SITARA Process JewelBox™ © SITARA Technologies Pvt. Ltd. 2002 with permission

How does Verification transform its capability when the transition to capability level 2 (or the managed level) is made?

Practices within Verification are governed by an organizational policy which may include directives to use process capability baselines for inspection and peer reviews. Policy could also define the use of customer specifications where necessary. The peer review policy is indicative of supporting process infrastructure such as peer review guidelines, procedures (as described in SITARA's perspective-based peer-review process) and review checklists. Most high-maturity practices also include review readiness checklists to verify if the work product is ready for a peer review or walkthrough.

Training on the organizational standards for peer reviews, code walkthroughs, inspection techniques and testing strategies is provided to all relevant stakeholders. A peer review plan defining the review schedule and tasks associated with testing activities with well-defined entry and exit criteria is used to govern activities leading to the establishment of a baseline. Peer-review metrics are analyzed using quantitative techniques to objectively verify the status of the work product with senior management oversight in periodic management reviews. If necessary, the work product review results are shared with the customer in order to obtain a sign-off before the next phase is commenced.

The ten generic practices of EPPAT MIMOR establish a level 2 process capability for Verification practices.

How does Verification transform its capability when the transition to capability level 3 (or the defined level) is made?

Best practices both across projects and within the industry are identified to ensure that Verification practices are dependable. A well-defined process is articulated for the multiple types of work product reviews with a view to reduce escape defects, increase phase containment effectiveness and build a quality work product. The two generic practices which enable the realization of generic goal 3 and in doing so establish Verification at the capability level 3 are as follows:

GG3 Institutionalize a Defined Process

GP3.1 Establish a Defined Process

GP3.2 Collect Improvement Information

How does Verification transform its capability when the transition to capability level 4 (or the quantitatively managed level) is made? Or, how does Verification demonstrate a high maturity measurement and analysis capability?

Well-defined goals are established for acceptable *defect density* measures and peer review rates. The notion of establishing a peer review rate has to take into account program complexity based on code branching. Performance testing can happen only after code is put into system test mode. Many times such flaws cannot be caught during unit testing; much worse, such logical propositions are unthinkable in design (number of open connections to a database, for instance). Run-time failures which have nothing to do with the developed application but on the operating system it runs on are also typical. It is with issues such as being unable to think through all possible logical propositions and combinations that the software can operate with that make software development and verification a challenging business.

Peer reviews are planned based on historical performance and quantitative goals for preparation rate and inspection rate. Quantified goals based on historical data for phase containment effectiveness are used in a manner so as to establish an objective basis to plan for defect prevention activities. At the end of life-cycle iteration prior to establishing a baseline of the associated work products and associated process measures, an analysis of the review effectiveness is conducted with a view to understand the pattern of escape defects despite process controls. It is useful to note that escape defects are bound to exist since what is unknown remains unknown. Unknown errors which are caught outside the process controls constitute escape defects. A graphical representation of the cumulative system test cases exercised and the number of defects or bugs identified and eliminated over time is plotted to ensure that reliability of code is guaranteed using an objective verification of the extent of test coverage.

The emphasis on enabling a capability level 4 process for Verification is primarily due to the fact that the highest leverage for a process orientation comes from identifying potential faults, isolating them using a process improvement framework and eliminating them from the system of practices using appropriate process definitions. At the level 4 capability, cost of poor quality (cost of rework) commands major emphasis. Since rework needs to be minimized, a capability level 4 consciously measures and monitors the cost of poor quality. Within the scope of the CMMI, the necessary goal to be supported with the expected generic practices is as follows:

GG4 Institutionalize a Quantitatively Managed Process

GP4.1 Establish Quantitative Objectives for the Process

GP4.2 Stabilize Sub-Process Performance

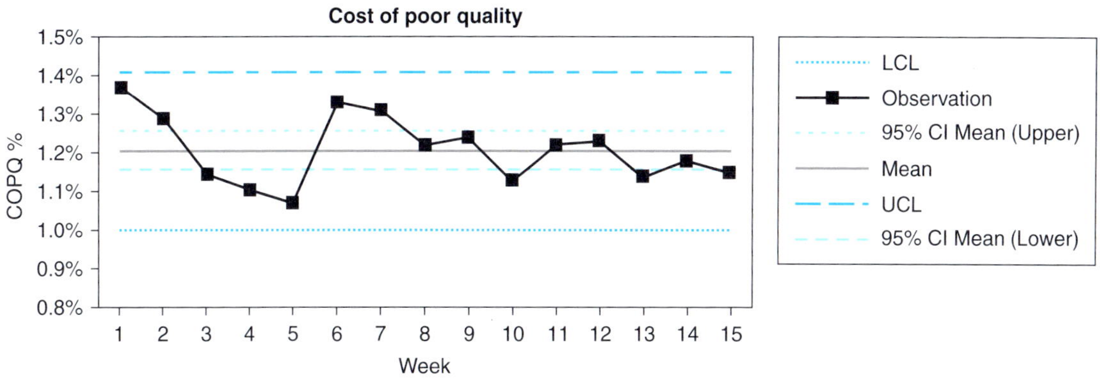

Fig. 5.8 [MIMOS 2009]: Monitoring COPQ in a Time Series Chart

Source: Q3 2009 Process Capability Analysis Report MIMOS Berhad, Malaysia, a site appraised by SITARA Technologies at CMMI-DEV V1.2 Level 5 (Continuous Representation) in October 2009. Reproduced with permission.

How does Verification transform its capability when the transition to capability level 5 (or the optimizing level) is made? Or, how does Verification demonstrate a high maturity measurement and analysis capability?

Pareto charts are typically used to understand the types of errors that are being encountered in practice. Both common cause variations (due to the development process) and special cause variations (due to the *voice-of-customer (VOC)* or for reasons lying outside the process control) are analyzed with a view to render corrective actions. Tools that effectively address issues concerning common cause variations such as lint, static and dynamic testing tools are used to ensure that problems related to the software code are addressed in the early stages of development (before code integration).

Practices contained within Verification typically contribute toward what is known as cost of quality, which is traditionally conceived to be a sum of appraisal, detection and prevention costs. It is always desirable to keep the total cost of quality to a small percentage of the overall costs (also expressed as a percentage of effort). It is to be noted that test-intensive projects are bound to have a high cost-of-quality measure. A well-defined capability level 5 Verification process enables a stratification of projects by type (development, testing or maintenance) along the cost-of-quality dimension. Knowing the Verification practices in terms of cost of quality is a useful basis to establish a capability level 5 for the Verification process area. For Verification to operate at capability level 5, generic goal 5 and the associated generic practices have to be institutionalized as follows:

GG5 Institutionalize an Optimizing Process

GP5.1 **Ensure Continuous Process Improvement**

GP5.2 **Correct Root Causes of Problems**

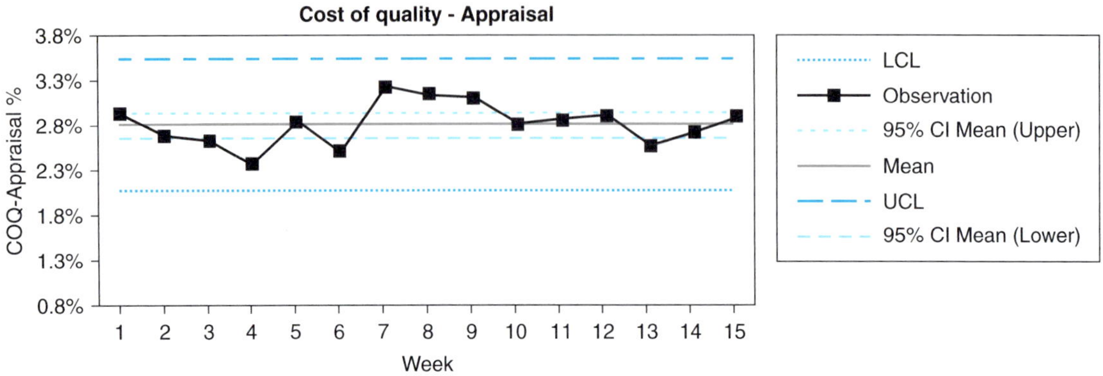

Fig. 5.9 [MIMOS 2009]: Monitoring COQ Appraisal in a Time Series Chart

Source: Q3 2009 Process Capability Analysis Report MIMOS Berhad, Malaysia, a site appraised by SITARA Technologies at CMMI-DEV V1.2 Level 5 (Continuous Representation) in October 2009. Reproduced with permission.

VALIDATION (VAL) CMMI-DEV

How does Validation look when it operates at a capability level 1 (or the performed level)?

Validation (VAL) belongs to the engineering category of the continuous representation of the CMMI. Much along similar lines of interpretation rendered for Verification process area, Validation practices too can be established at the capability level 4 and 5. While Verification practices could be rendered in a simulated or emulated environment, Validation practices involve testing of the product in the actual end-user environment. While much of the principles of testing in the end-user environment would remain the same, the objectives behind the testing process would be different. It is important to point out that if the objectives behind Verification are the same as those of Validation, then, there is no value addition. Validation should not turn into conducting Verification twice!

Besides the involvement of testing in the real end-user environment, Validation includes multiple types of testing such as destructive testing, stress testing, load testing and also endurance testing. Moreover, there is an element of time involved when it comes to actually studying the behavior of the system over elapsed time.

Certain product components in the final solution have a critical-to-performance characteristic which needs a thorough study. One example of performance characteristic involves validating system behavior at the boundary values. Such components are selected from the product suite for validation activities. Where destructive testing is involved, a sample is used. Destructive testing in the case of embedded software applications is to see how abuse patterns are handled. Famous among them are when a single input is expected: what if the user jams the keyboard or a car CD player, or what if the user jams in a stack of CDs into the CD player of a car? How does the microcontroller react? In embedded applications for automobiles, where a cluster of microcontrollers defines the behavioral characteristics of a car, validation involving destructive testing might involve identification of test cases to actually enact an air bag deployment upon a crash or having all four tires flat (a highly improbable event) or checking for multiple failure conditions that either singly, or in a combination, constitute a catastrophic event.

In one of SITARA's instructions of the SEI's 'Introduction to CMMI', an interesting discussion came up with respect to the practical sides of what is verification and what constitutes validation in the context of software development. Think of verification as peer reviews of all work products, unit testing of software modules, and integration testing of software parts. While still working on the development process, think of validation as system testing, user-acceptance tests and end-user testing. When the product is out of the development process (post-release), validation is stress testing and failure testing. Actually, validation starts with identifying and analyzing *escaped test cases* resulting from field reports.

It goes without saying that software applications are finite state machines and are subject to failure over extended periods of use (which involves time) without resetting the application back into a known start state. One can easily relate to situations and circumstances where one needs to give a three-finger salute or reboot the machine because the OS just hangs indefinitely. That is exactly the elapsed time it takes based on the number of non-responsive tasks, which is a valid test case that was probably not thought of while system-testing, for a software system to fail. A systems example that can be cited is that of an unresponsive cell phone to key press events including the power-off button. The only way to bring the cell phone back from an unknown zombie state to the start state is to cut off the power completely by pulling out the battery and reinserting it back.

It is in such failure analysis and subsequent fixing of the system that validation assumes importance. Validation requires the product to *run in* enough before one can recognize the failure patterns.

A non-software example to illustrate validation could be designing an automatic vending machine which is to vend a candy that costs $1. Users of the vending machine can insert coins in denominations of 10 cents to a quarter. Each time the user inserts a coin, till this amount does not total up to $1, a product from the vending machine cannot be dispensed. System testing in such an *in-process validation* is to put both valid coins and slugs, and test the vending machine to dispense the product. When slugs are used, the vending machine must have enough processing logic (being a finite state machine) to reject them. Since the vending machine is working just fine in the test environment, it is placed in its intended environment of use for an operational test such as in a school campus. Let us suppose that a student (the actual user) wanting to dispense a candy puts a few valid coins and a few slugs. Since the vending machine was designed right, it rejects the slugs. Out of sheer frustration, the student gives two kicks to the vending machine and out come a dozen candies! And let us suppose that this phenomenon is a reproducible event with repeatable results. Has the vending machine been validated enough? The answer is no! We never thought that *giving the vending machine two kicks in the reproducible sequence in the test environment* was a valid input! Taking this new test case and putting it back to system testing while still in the development process constitutes *revalidation* of the system. Building such a system of Validation practices enables a process capability level 1, with the realization of the following specific goals and specific practices:

SG1 Prepare for Validation

SP1.1 **Select Products for Validation**

SP1.2 **Establish the Validation Environment**

SP1.3 Establish Validation Procedures and Criteria

SG2 Validate Product or Product Components

SP2.1 Perform Validation

SP2.2 Analyze Validation Results

The practical sides to Validation as experienced with some of the author's best professional associations are as follows:

Validation

1. Use the high-level requirements specification and end-user testing criteria defining the acceptance-testing requirements to exercise the product in the end-user environment.
2. Explore both explicit and implicit test conditions which objectively determine the pass–fail conditions for the work product or the final product.
3. Exercise each function or feature over prolonged periods of iterative test cases to find out any terminal states that either results in the system to hang or core dump with run-time failures.
4. Log the sequence of test cases and system responses to ensure that the failure conditions and patterns of failure can be regenerated.
5. If the failure conditions can be re-created, then such conditions need to be reported as field failures and need to be fixed within the system with a modification or change notification.
6. After the system is fixed, try out the failure conditions and perform validation as a regression activity to ensure that the fix did not cause new defects or faults.

Display 5.5 Interpreting Validation

Source: Adapted from SITARA Process JewelBox™ © SITARA Technologies Pvt. Ltd. 2002 with permission

How does Validation transform its capability when the transition to capability level 2 (or the managed level) is made?

The fundamental requirements of establishing Validation at a capability level 2 would be to institutionalize the EPPAT MIMOR practices. An organizational policy establishes and governs the conditions when Validation is out of scope along with how such situations need to be handled with management support. Such a situation is typical in an offshore development context where the end-user environment is seldom replicated. When Validation is in scope, the management policy defines the practices that ensure the enactment of Validation steps along with explicit steps for the creation of the end-user environment. In a COTS integration process, program management policies are established to ensure vendor participation in validation activities besides infrastructure overheads.

Individuals who are trained to conduct validation activities and who support both the management and engineering activities to ensure that the product functions the way it was designed to function are made available in what is termed as SWAT (skilled with advanced technology) teams. An architecture evaluation team is also available to ensure that validation errors due to poor architecture are minimized.

Management oversight during validation activities includes active participation during field trials and field testing with necessary and visible support to the development teams to ensure timely fixes of problem reports resulting from the field. Where corrective actions have to be taken, Validation practices enable a reasonable resolution to the available options or alternatives. Validation records are established to ensure that product delivery and handover is based on objective criteria. Release notes along with necessary end-user documentation are also validated to ensure consistency of support documentation with the overall product behavior.

How does Validation transform its capability when the transition to capability level 3 (or the defined level) is made?

At the capability level 3, a defined process is established based on best practices resulting from iterations of product validation procedures employed on projects with differing performance expectations. Much of the process documentation includes procedures to handle the different testing methods that are best employed to validate the behavioral characteristics of products with differing performance constraints. The two generic practices which enable the realization of generic goal 3 and in so doing establish Validation at the capability level 3 are as follows:

GG3 Institutionalize a Defined Process

GP3.1 **Establish a Defined Process**

GP3.2 **Collect Improvement Information**

How does Validation transform its capability when the transition to capability level 4 (or the quantitatively managed level) is made?

How does Validation transform its capability when the transition to capability level 5 (or the optimizing level) is made? Or, how does Validation demonstrate a high maturity measurement and analysis capability?

Validation is a good candidate process area that can be rendered with a level 4 or level 5 rigor. A good process performance model that can be considered is to establish a defect prediction model for post-release defects. While it is possible to establish regression models based on fault or defect removal efficiencies across life-cycle phases and *review and inspection effectiveness* as common cause factors, an example will be highlighted here to appreciate how quantitative management can be kept simple. Regression modeling will be elaborated in Chapters 6 and 7 while interpreting the level 4 and 5 process areas.

If there is a good enough process to estimate the size in lines of code and if the average post-release defect density from past performance is known, then it is possible to estimate/predict the number of post-release defects even before the first line of code is written. Example: If the estimated number of lines of code (LOC) is 10,000 and the average post-release defect density is 10 defects/kLOC, then the estimated/predicted number of post-release defects is 100. Further, if we know the defect distribution by phase from past performance as 2 out of 10 defects/kLOC were due to requirements phase, analysis phase and design phase each, and 4 out of 10 defects/kLOC were due to coding, then it is possible to bring visibility of the prediction to the phase level. In this example, requirements, analysis and design phases contribute 20 defects each, and the coding phase contributes 40 defects, making up the total at 100 predicted post-release defects. Since competency levels within an organization and individual capability do not change drastically, these measures are good for some time. Revision of these baselines and improvement of the size estimation technique are obvious ways to improve the prediction capability. This simple, yet useful prediction technique without the use of traditional prediction models based on regression analysis is a good starting point to establish an appreciation for quantitative management of a defined process.

The interpretation offered for Verification while dealing with the level 4 and level 5 capability holds equally well for Validation. The same sense of conducting Pareto analysis and stabilizing the sub-process characteristics of the specific practices that constitute Validation is required to be established in practice. In doing so, the generic goals 4 and 5 and the associated generic practices can be rendered. A capability level 4 or level 5 is attained when these practices are institutionalized.

GG4 Institutionalize a Quantitatively Managed Process

GP4.1 **Establish Quantitative Objectives for the Process**

GP4.2 **Stabilize Sub-Process Performance**

GG5 Institutionalize an Optimizing Process

GP5.1 **Ensure Continuous Process Improvement**

GP5.2 **Correct Root Causes of Problems**

Author's Musing

Troubleshooting in a development environment is very different from troubleshooting in real life.

ACQUISITION TECHNICAL MANAGEMENT (ATM) CMMI-ACQ

How does Acquisition Technical Management look when it operates at a capability level 1 (or the performed level)?

The purpose of Acquisition Technical Management (ATM) is to evaluate the supplier's TS and manage selected interfaces. Practices of ATM dovetail with those of TS belonging to the CMMI-DEV from an acquisition perspective. Therefore, this process area involves review of the TS (design) of the supplier. Such reviews are used to confirm the designs to match contractual requirements and confirm the progress made by the suppliers toward realization of the final product. When supplier solutions have to interoperate with existing solutions from either the acquisition organization or from other suppliers who the acquisition organizations might employ, interfaces have to be managed. This process area also involves use of supplier demonstrations of solutions using prototypes, simulations and technology demonstrations. It might be useful to review the VDPR phase of the SITARA COTS Integration process described in Chapter 3. Typically, ATM is performed in conjunct with other technical and Agreement Management processes including but not limited to Requirements Management, Risk Management, configuration management and data management.

Conducting technical reviews of solutions is done to gain confidence that the supplier is able to offer solutions that minimize risks of failure. Such reviews can be similar to the types discussed in the Verification process area under the heading 'Perspective Based Peer Review Process'. Stakeholder needs, expectations and constraints can be verified during such reviews. Samples of candidate solutions, detailed designs and implemented design can be selected for analysis based on criteria defining their importance, probability of failure and the risks involved. Reviews can verify conformance to standards, adherence to the allocated requirements and early validation of the solution. Reviews can also ensure that the entry and exit conditions in a phased development match up to expectations.

Interfaces can be both internal to a solution and external when subsystems have to be put together. Interface failures are highly probable if good product integration strategies are not employed. An example of a proven integration approach is described under the TS process area called 'Essay on Personal Software Process for Testing'. The reader is encouraged to read this again to gain a perspective of how to minimize interface faults using the fencing technique.

When the following specific goals and specific practices are coupled with practices defined in Decision Analysis and Resolution, a capability level 1 or the performed level of capability for TS is enabled:

SG1 Evaluate Technical Solutions

SP1.1 **Select Technical Solutions for Analysis**

SP1.2 **Analyze Selected Technical Solutions**

SP1.3 **Conduct Technical Reviews**

SG2 Perform Interface Management

SP2.1 **Select Interfaces to Manage**

SP2.2 **Manage Selected Interfaces**

The practical sides to ATM as experienced with some of the author's best professional associations are as follows:

Acquisition Technical Management

1. Conduct a rain check of whether vendor self-evaluation meets product capabilities vis-à-vis solution requirements.
2. Arrive at the final list of solutions for further probing and evaluation.
3. Maintain consensus on the final selection from all stakeholders.
4. Identify the hardware and software requirements to study alternatives before finalizing the selection criteria.
5. Ensure requirements coverage in the supplier solutions.

Display 5.6 Interpreting Acquisition Technical Management

Source: Adapted from SITARA Process JewelBox™ © SITARA Technologies Pvt. Ltd. 2009 with permission

How does Acquisition Technical Management transform its capability when the transition to capability level 2 (or the managed level) is made?

The fundamental requirements of establishing Validation at a capability level 2 would be to institutionalize the EPPAT MIMOR practices. When transition to capability level 2 is made, a consistent policy defining acquisition of Technical Solutions that is in line with the policy for TS process area of the CMMI-DEV is established. Many of the practices described for the institutionalization of the CMMI-DEV process areas of TS, Verification, PI and Validation are institutionalized from an acquirer's perspective emphasizing reviews, inspections and other auditing techniques. For example, in the implementation phase of the supplier TS, the acquirer may examine a product to determine if it is ready for production and if the supplier has accomplished adequate production planning. The analysis would determine if production or production preparations incur unacceptable risks that might compromise schedule, performance, cost, or other established objectives. The acquirer might evaluate the full, production-configured product to determine if it correctly and completely implements all contractual requirements. The acquirer could also determine whether the traceability of the final contractual requirements to the final production-configured product has been maintained. Since these practices are not much in variance with the CMMI-DEV, the relevant level 2 capability descriptions provided for these process areas might be used. Readiness reviews at different stages of acquisition might include initial technical review, alternative solutions review, system requirements review, security review, critical design review, test readiness review, release readiness review and physical configuration audits. Functional configuration audit verifying the functionality of the subsystems or solutions being built is the responsibility of the supplier which the acquirer might oversee.

How does Acquisition Technical Management transform its capability when the transition to capability level 3 (or the defined level) is made?

At the capability level 3, a defined process is established based on best practices resulting from iterations involving Agreement Management of several suppliers in different contexts. COTS solutions might be involved in the acquisition strategy. In such a case, a process similar to the one described in Chapter 3 under the heading 'Essay on COTS integration' must be established. The integration strategy to manage interfaces involving multiple methods of solution integration has to be defined with a focus on minimizing risk to the solution when it is place in the intended environment of use. The two generic practices which enable the realization of generic goal 3 and in so doing establish Acquisition Technical Management at the capability level 3 are as follows:

GG3 Institutionalize a Defined Process

GP3.1 **Establish a Defined Process**

GP3.2 **Collect Improvement Information**

How does Acquisition Technical Management transform its capability when the transition to capability level 4 (or the quantitatively managed level) is made?

How does Acquisition Technical Management transform its capability when the transition to capability level 5 (or the optimizing level) is made? Or, how does Acquisition Technical Management demonstrate a high maturity measurement and analysis capability?

Where ATM practices involve the deployment of the full-fledged TS capability of the CMMI-DEV, it would make best sense to consider improving its capability to a 4 or 5. Refer to the descriptions offered in the TS process area of the CMMI-DEV. Otherwise, the business justifications and business objectives ought to be studied before considering quantitative enablement of techniques using the high-maturity practices described in Chapters 6 and 7.

ACQUISITION VERIFICATION (AVER) CMMI-ACQ

How does Acquisition Verification look when it operates at a capability level 1 (or the performed level)?

The purpose of Acquisition Verification (AVER) is to ensure that selected work products meet their specified requirements. The practices of Acquisition Verification dovetail with those of Verification belonging to the CMMI-DEV from an acquisition perspective. Typical verification activities include the review of the solicitation package, supplier agreements and plans, requirements documents, design constraints developed by the acquirer and other acquirer-developed work products. To a significant extent, the practices required for the preparation of verification activities, performing them and identifying corrective and preventive actions closely associate themselves with the Verification process area of the CMMI-DEV constellation. Acquisition Verification reuses most of the concepts contained in the Verification process area of the CMMI-DEV. Verification belongs to the engineering category of the continuous representation of the CMMI-DEV, whereas Acquisition Verification is an Acquisition Category process area of the CMMI-ACQ constellation in the continuous representation. These practices must be interpreted from the acquirer's perspective, while the intent behind the goals and practices remains the same—verify whether we are building the product right. Since the specific goals and specific practices appearing below are exactly the same as those of the Verification process area, refer to the interpretation provided under the Verification process area of the CMMI-DEV.

SG1 Prepare for Verification

- SP1.1 **Select Work Products for Verification**
- SP1.2 **Establish the Verification Environment**
- SP1.3 **Establish Verification Procedures and Criteria**

SG2 Perform Peer Reviews

- SP2.1 **Prepare for Peer Reviews**
- SP2.2 **Conduct Peer Reviews**
- SP2.3 **Analyze Peer Review Data**

SG3 Verify Selected Work Products

- SP3.1 **Perform Verification**
- SP3.2 **Analyze Verification Results**

ACQUISITION VALIDATION (AVAL) CMMI-ACQ

How does Acquisition Validation look when it operates at a capability level 1 (or the performed level)?

The purpose of Acquisition Validation (AVAL) is to demonstrate that an acquired product or service fulfills its intended use when placed in its intended environment. The practices of Acquisition Validation dovetail with those of Validation belonging to the CMMI-DEV from an acquisition perspective. Since the acquisition context might involve a product, or a service or both, validation involves demonstration of the performance of acquired entity in the intended environment of use. Early validation considerations that are incremental right from the time of Acquisition Requirements Development through to Acquisition Validation is the best known mechanism to build robustness into the practices. From an acquirer's perspective, setting up of the required validation environment might become a limitation from a cost consideration if the end-to-end solution is being conceived and developed by the solution provider (supplier). Collaboration of the acquirer's validation team with the system test team of the supplier must be explored. Acquisition initiatives might involve any combination of COTS, or custom development, or joint development between the acquirer and supplier. Acquisition Validation must conceive appropriate procedures to handle all such situations involving all the relevant stakeholders. The intent behind the goals and practices remains the same as that of the Validation process area of the CMMI-DEV—verify whether we are building the right product. Since the specific goals and specific practices appearing below are exactly the same as that of the Validation process area, refer to the interpretation provided under the Validation process area of the CMMI-DEV.

SG1 Prepare for Validation

- SP1.1 **Select Products for Validation**
- SP1.2 **Establish the Validation Environment**
- SP1.3 **Establish Validation Procedures and Criteria**

SG2 Validate Selected Products and Product Components

- SP2.1 **Perform Validation**
- SP2.2 **Analyze Validation Results**

SERVICE CONTINUITY (SCON) CMMI-SVC

How does Service Continuity look when it operates at a capability level 1 (or the performed level)?

The purpose of Service Continuity (SCON) is to establish and maintain plans to ensure continuity of services during and following any significant disruption of normal operations. A certain amount of redundancy has to be built into the service operations such that critical functions are not affected. Non-critical functions have to prioritized, and should be available based on agreements which require to be supported. The plan must identify a catalog of services which cannot be degraded and those which can be allowed to perform in a degraded manner. A catalog of services typically lists out the services being provided, a summary of their characteristics and details of the customers and maintainers of each. The plan must detail the duration up to which such degraded performance is allowed for those services which can be rendered in a degraded fashion and must track the status of return to normal operation. Such a Service Continuity plan must be developed, tested and maintained to ensure disaster recovery and must serve adequately as a mitigation and handling mechanism for any service outage. The focus of Service Continuity can be at the project level or at the organizational level or both. Since such a plan can only be made robust as experience is gained, it must be documented based on information previously collected with tests to validate effectiveness and appropriate revisions to training material for carrying out the Service Continuity plan. Such training material and delivery must address all stakeholders who will either be impacted or those who are required to execute the Service Continuity plan. Prior to setting up the Service Continuity plan, it must be reviewed with relevant stakeholders and validated using repeated trials to ensure that the continuity plan is effective at handling all the what-if conditions, at all times. The Service Continuity plan must clearly establish the escalation mechanism with defined roles and responsibilities and execution authority. Typically such roles and responsibilities are established for supervisors and staff (negotiate services, perform required service functions, develop and operate the standard operating procedures), management (responsible for maintaining contract for services, reviews and providing assurance of service quality), senior management (manage service profiles while communicating and maintaining awareness of service deliverables) and the board (set policy, direct and authorize).

When the above are addressed within the service establishment and delivery process, the following specific goals and specific practices are likely to result. Service Continuity will then operate at capability level 1.

SG1 Identify Essential Service Dependencies

- SP1.1 **Identify and Prioritize Essential Functions**
- SP1.2 **Identify and Prioritize Essential Resources**

SG2 Prepare for Service Continuity

- SP2.1 **Establish Service Continuity Plans**
- SP2.2 **Establish Service Continuity Training**
- SP2.3 **Provide and Evaluate Service Continuity Training**

SG3 Verify and Validate the Service Continuity Plan

- SP3.1 **Prepare for the Verification and Validation of the Service Continuity Plan**
- SP3.2 **Verify and Validate the Service Continuity Plan**
- SP3.3 **Analyze Results of Verification and Validation**

How does Service Continuity transform its capability when the transition to capability level 2 (or the managed level) is made?

The policy on Service Continuity must consider the following: what are the service continuity measures in place while the service provider is involved in upgrading the service either due to improvement efforts or introduction of new processes and technologies? How is Service Continuity ensured to handle disasters and outages? How are impacts to operational-level agreements (OLAs)—the internal operational translation of service-level agreements (SLAs) established with customers or end users—handled? SCON policy sets expectations for the Service Continuity plan to resume key services following a major disruption, along with training, verification and validation of the plan.

Typically established in a Service Continuity plan, a contingency plan establishes the process of recovery of failed systems or system components based on the service profiles maintained in the catalog of services, especially to handle significant disruptions. Special training and preparation required for handling such disruptions with assigned management and technical responsibilities for a highly specialized team such as SWAT must be considered. Resources required for maintaining uninterrupted service ensuring continuity while adhering to the SLA (and OLA) with the intention of achieving business and user satisfaction must be planned and provided for.

In a recent personal experience, a major cellular service provider in India was involved in upgrading their billing and other service systems around July 11, 2009. I lost my mobile while on travel. Most system applications during the upgrade were disabled to an extent that even though the loss of the mobile was recorded in voice, nothing could be done to deactivate the SIM card for over 4 days. In the meanwhile, the stolen mobile was used to make calls all over the world for approximately $8,000. Additionally, I was burdened to report the loss of mobile in an e-mail, so that I would have a recorded proof of the report since the service provider did not assure me with any guarantees that the complaint would be recorded or attended to, until all systems were up again. Complicating matters, the call center management was outsourced to third parties who were not aware of the cellular service provider's uptime strategies. Once the systems were back again, demands were made of me to cough up the payment when my mobile was compromised since their systems had not recorded the reported loss! Thankfully, the e-mail sent to the customer care and the automated reply acknowledging the receipt saved me from the mediocre service of this cellular service provider. Clearly, the service continuity of the service provider neglected to conduct an impact analysis of the potential damage or loss that may result, leading to financial loss, damage to reputation or regulatory breach, had the mobile been used to perpetrate illicit activities.

From this anecdote, it is useful to look at service continuity from a perspective of what should be done when the service usage is compromised. In this case a prompt disconnection of the services to the lost mobile would have been in order and must have also figured in the service continuity process. On the contrary, every second week for two months, after their billing systems were up again, the cellular service provider disconnected their services to my mobile which had a new SIM card. It took over 3 months for the issue to be resolved. Considerable ill-will and customer dissatisfaction could have been avoided.

From the anecdote we understand the importance of having good configuration management and change management while the recovery from service disruption is happening. Change management in the context of services assumes a very broad scope and includes management of any addition, modification or removal of a configuration item. Configuration items are the approved, supported or baselined service components. Relevant stakeholders including any outsourced entities and business partners should be involved in the training, education and maintaining awareness of the status of the service restoration. Constant review and testing of the service restoration process and specific training requirements for those involved in executing the Service Continuity process were also missing. Probably the service provider had no Service Continuity strategy in place. The fundamental requirements of establishing Service Continuity at a capability level 2 would be to institutionalize the EPPAT MIMOR practices.

> **AUTHOR'S MUSING**
>
> Importance and the need for institutionalizing robust processes become evident only when things go wrong! Unfortunately, it is such situations that teach the importance of having a process orientation best, but painfully so. When situations are handled with a 'business as normal' face instead of a crisis staring the organization in its face, one must commend the efforts of the process designers that have put a working process in place.

How does Service Continuity transform its capability when the transition to capability level 3 (or the defined level) is made?

At the capability level 3, a defined process is established based on a foundation of best practices resulting from similar circumstances handled in the past. Best practices could also result from studying and utilizing the most appropriate technology and supporting tools to enable the end-to-end business processes. Maintaining service continuity of all business processes operating as a network is important and typically they include procurement of raw material, utilization of inventory, receiving orders, selling finished goods, handling customer complaints and compliments, learning and feedback on capacity and availability mismatches, invoicing for services, accounting for money received and such. Evidently, improvement information must be collected on all interoperating processes which are designed to collaboratively ensure uninterrupted service.

The two generic practices that enable the realization of generic goal 3 and in so doing establish SCON at the capability level 3 are as follows:

GG3 Institutionalize a Defined Process

GP3.1 **Establish a Defined Process**

GP3.2 **Collect Improvement Information**

How does Service Continuity transform its capability when the transition to capability level 4 (or the quantitatively managed level) is made?

How does Service Continuity transform its capability when the transition to capability level 5 (or the optimizing level) is made? Or, how does Service Continuity demonstrate a high maturity measurement and analysis capability?

Stability of service continuity is affected both by special and common cause variations. There are sufficient quantifiable causes that can be identified, controlled and monitored while enabling a high process capability for Service Continuity. As Service Continuity is at the very heart of ensuring user and business satisfaction, this process area can justifiably operate at higher process capability. Like every other CMMI process area that qualifies for high-capability institutionalization, business justifications and business objectives ought to be studied before considering quantitative enablement of techniques using the high-maturity practices described in Chapters 6 and 7.

CAPACITY AND AVAILABILITY MANAGEMENT (CAM) CMMI-SVC

How does Capacity and Availability Management look when it operates at a capability level 1 (or the performed level)?

The purpose of Capacity and Availability Management (CAM) is to ensure effective service system performance and ensure that resources are provided and used effectively to support service requirements. In the continuous representation, CAM is a project management category process area. CMMI-SVC defines capacity as the degree to which one thing may support, hold, process, or produce another thing. Availability is the degree to which something is accessible and usable when needed. Service agreement defines the different types of services and service systems, the measurement criteria for capacity and availability with respect to a fixed time period. The practices contained in CAM ensure that a service provider establishes and maintains capacity and availability at justifiable cost with efficient use of resources. There has to be a proper balance between capacity and availability such that service continuity is ensured at acceptable levels of performance for all the services in the catalog. Special service situations such as surges or spikes in service requirements or unanticipated long durations of low demand must be addressed within the CAM strategy. Market conditions and the dynamics impacting the very business strategy of the service provider have to be constantly monitored in order to fine-tune the CAM strategy. Simultaneous production and consumption of services is a unique challenge which is experienced in a service offering as against traditional product development. Example: a restaurant serving food is simultaneously consuming raw material while producing finished products. The elasticity in this context is a question of studying supply–demand equilibrium besides maintaining and understanding of fluctuations in service demands. Peak hour and slack hour demands make up the special cause influencing the service quality. Such special causes need to be studied constantly so that the necessary resources such as chefs, servers, cleaners and dish handlers are scheduled into shifts to meet the service demand.

> The best example to illustrate the dynamic elasticity involving CAM is that of the daily wage earner selling vegetables in a pushcart in India. He borrows money in the morning from a moneylender at a 10% or so daily interest rate. This means that in the time available from dawn to dusk, he has to put the borrowed money to best use. Whether he makes money or not, he has to be conscious that he owes 10% interest to the moneylender. He has to buy just the necessary quantities of vegetables from the wholesale market which he is confident of selling by dusk—not more, not less. The quality and quantity of the vegetables he sources should be appropriate to the demand and profile of customers he normally sells them to. He must establish a strategy regarding which streets he should cover first while maximizing the prospects of selling the vegetables quickly. His strategy must also include the prospects of selling out his first consignment quick enough so that he can make a second and possibly a third trip to the wholesale market to procure the necessary quantities of maybe more vegetables or fruits this time round, and rotate his profits by reinvesting appropriately in just the necessary quantity so he is able to service his market. He must mark up the prices such that he is left with something more than what he owes to the moneylender. The supply–demand and cost–capacity balance must be made on a daily basis.

Adjustments to service levels as necessary to maintain an acceptable level of quality even when influenced by special cause variations must be handled as part of Service Delivery. In order to prevent a complete breakdown of service, resilience, security and reliability, requirements must be built into CAM strategy. Security includes issues related to confidentiality, integrity, availability of data, hardware and software components, documentation and standard operating procedures as the service transitions from pre-production to the production environment while undergoing transition through multiple quality assurance stages before the service goes live.

Data can be *business data,* which answers the question *how many types of what is needed to keep the business operations going?* It can be *service data,* which answers the question *how can we establish proof for delivery of service per the level of service agreed to?* It can be *technical data,* which answers the question *what are the mechanisms with which alerts can be raised and exception reports provided when thresholds or limits of the service are hit?* It can be *financial data,* which answers the question *what information is required to sustain and manage future business requirements?* Finally, data could be *utilization data,* which answers the question *how can a system or system component be accounted for being put to use within defined time slices?* Answers to these questions establish the key performance indicators or KPIs which define the critical success factors for the service provider.

CAM includes planning, decision making, establishing corrective actions, negotiation of service agreements and allocation of resources to meet the current and future demands ensuring elasticity. Bench management involving gainfully employing idle capacity must be explored using Strategic Service Management (STSM). Example: A provider of on-call taxi service might end up in situations with significant idle capacity of both taxies and drivers. STSM must explore alternative deployment strategies for gainfully employing such capacity by building collaborations and partnerships with allied service providers such as travel desks of major hotels in the area, public transport agencies requiring such services or committing a certain number of vehicles for a completely different profile of customers, say a school for pickup and drop-off of school-going children from home at specific times.

ITIL defines best practices for capacity management separate from availability management within the scope of Service Delivery. While capacity management answers the question *'how much capacity should be provided?'* based on the *strategic business plans* of the service provider in a cost-effective manner, availability management decides the same from a *user satisfaction* perspective. Capacity planning is influenced by studying situations leading to non-availability of a system or system component when capacity management provided assurances of its availability.

When the above are addressed within the project management process, the following specific goals and specific practices are likely to result. Service continuity will then operate at capability level 1.

SG1 Prepare for Capacity and Availability Management

- SP1.1 **Establish a Capacity and Availability Management Strategy**
- SP1.2 **Select Measures and Analytic Techniques**
- SP1.3 **Establish Service System Representations**

SG2 Monitor and Analyze Capacity and Availability

- SP2.1 **Monitor and Analyze Capacity**
- SP2.2 **Monitor and Analyze Availability**
- SP2.3 **Report Capacity and Availability Management Data**

How does Capacity and Availability Management transform its capability when the transition to capability level 2 (or the managed level) is made?

Policy that is forward looking and is able to forecast business impacts before they happen is the hallmark of a good CAM policy. The policy must be able to enable Service Delivery, the level 2 process area, while ensuring current and future capacity and availability requirements in the most cost-effective manner. Policy must support evaluation of new technology/tools and systems and make necessary financial commitments to such research activities. As both consumable and non-consumable resources come under the purview of CAM, the level 2 generic practices of EPPAT MIMOR must address the following at a minimum: hardware, networking equipment, communication equipment, infrastructure, peripherals, software, human resources and procurement network. CAM policy must also address the more tactical aspects of the steps that have to be taken to monitor resources and system performance, or say, how the data in Capacity Database (CDB) will be kept up to date and used. CAM can also be strengthened at level 2 capability by addressing *business capacity management* for future-proofing the delivery, *service capacity management* for the live operational demands and *resource capacity management* for the components that make up the service and service system. When configuration changes are required to resolve problems, impact of such changes on existing capacity and availability must be studied prior to releasing the change. Periodically updated CAM plans identify both the forward-looking capacity and availability forecasts of demands using the strategic business plans to provide for sufficient procurement lead times. The most important aspect of CAM is constant monitoring of components for each service, collection of data and analysis of usage levels against established thresholds. Optimal use of resources on an ongoing basis while service levels are achieved is the key. Typical monitors in an IT service required for CAM include the following: hardware utilization, storage utilization, network utilization, transaction density, transaction response time, number of concurrent service requests handled and call drops and terminations. This list is quite exhaustive and a comprehensive documentation involving all types of IT services is beyond the scope of this book. Health and safety monitors, for instance, are important in services where compromising health and safety would lead to severe business impact. Monitors must be established for all operational parameters whose compromise leads to issues (incidents and problems). These monitors yield useful improvement information on the appropriateness of the capacity and availability during Service Delivery and for tuning the service system to better deliver on expectations. Typically, a capacity database (CDB), which is a subset of configuration management database (CMDB), is used to store service data (business, service, technical, financial and utilization) and serves as a historical database used by sub-processes involved in CAM process. The distinction between CDB and CMDB is that while CDB stores capacity data, CMDB stores all configuration items pertaining to all attributes of the service. Information provided by CDB required by other processes is made available through the CMDB. A review of the current tools, resources and responsibilities assigned for CAM is typical to establish management oversight at all levels—supervisor/staff, management, senior management and board. Capacity and availability audit reports are established.

How does Capacity and Availability Management transform its capability when the transition to capability level 3 (or the defined level) is made?

At the capability level 3, a defined process to conduct the following are essential: trend analysis, analytical modeling, simulation procedures and baseline modeling of current performance achievement.

Improvements to CAM could result from incident and problem management addressed within IRP while identifying, diagnosing and resolving capacity- and availability-related events. Improvements can also result from studying mismatch between expected and actual capacity and availability requirements, cost of improving the capacity and availability and return on such investments and conducting failure impact assessments of a few critical components or of the entire system. The two generic practices which enable the realization of generic goal 3 and in so doing establish CAM at the capability level 3 are as follows:

GG3 Institutionalize a Defined Process

GP3.1 **Establish a Defined Process**

GP3.2 **Collect Improvement Information**

How does Capacity and Availability Management transform its capability when the transition to capability level 4 (or the quantitatively managed level) is made?

How does Capacity and Availability Management transform its capability when the transition to capability level 5 (or the optimizing level) is made? Or, how does Capacity and Availability Management demonstrate a high maturity measurement and analysis capability?

Significant from being a process area that is subject to both common and special cause variations with good opportunities to quantify both, CAM must be considered for quantitative enablement using the high-maturity practices described in Chapters 6 and 7. Examples for a typical measure that can be quantitatively and statistically managed are percentage availability and percentage non-availability of a service component (instead of the entire service). These metrics can be tracked and reported against the established service level targets of uptime.

SERVICE SYSTEM DEVELOPMENT (SSD)-ADDITION CMMI-SVC

How does Service System Development look when it operates at a capability level 1 (or the performed level)?

The purpose of Service System Development (SSD) is to analyze, design, develop, integrate, verify and validate service systems, including service system components, to satisfy existing or anticipated service agreements. As one might imagine, all of the engineering process area practices of the CMMI-DEV get involved in services involving product development scenarios. Therefore, this entire process area is marked as a CMMI 'addition' to emphasize a particular aspect of its use as relevant to the services constellation. Such emphasis in the CMMI-SVC constellation is summarized in what follows. The focus of SSD is on building the infrastructure required to provide services and processes required to support services.

The requirements for SSD are established from various sources such as service agreements, customer feedback from delivering existing services, defects and problem reports during Service Delivery and Incident Resolution and Prevention. Focus of SSD is on collecting, coordinating, analyzing, validating and allocating stakeholder requirements for service systems. Prior to designing and building solutions, evaluation of alternative service system solutions that meet service requirements and verifying and validating service system conformance to stated and implied requirements during actual Service Delivery must be performed. In product development scenarios, since there is a very strong dependency on the engineering process areas of CMMI-DEV, it might be useful to build practices contained in CMMI-DEV in tandem with CMMI-SVC. Operational concepts and scenarios of Service Delivery are elicited and appropriate alternative solutions are explored prior to designing the service system. Service system architecture, components and consumables (that which ceases to exist or modifies its identity as a result of the service) are designed together with appropriate interface descriptions and control documents. Both the options of reusing existing service systems or service components and make-or-buy analysis are explored. External and internal interfaces required by the service system are identified for activities such as report generation. Several verification and validation techniques such as peer reviews, walkthroughs, audits, simulations, testing and demonstrations are used to verify and validate the service system, service system components and the environment using defined procedures and criteria. Verification and validation reports of the service system are established with appropriate involvement of end users. Instead of repeating the interpretations here, the reader can refer to Verification and Validation process areas of the CMMI-DEV.

When the above are addressed within the service establishment and delivery process, the following specific goals and specific practices are likely to result. Service System Development will then operate at capability level 1.

SG1 Develop and Analyze Stakeholder Requirements

- SP1.1 **Develop Stakeholder Requirements**
- SP1.2 **Develop Service System Requirements**
- SP1.3 **Analyze and Validate Requirements**

SG2 Develop Service Systems

- SP2.1 **Select Service System Solutions**
- SP2.2 **Develop the Design**
- SP2.3 **Ensure Interface Compatibility**
- SP2.4 **Implement the Service System Design**
- SP2.5 **Integrate Service System Components**

SG3 Verify and Validate Service Systems

- SP3.1 **Prepare for Verification and Validation**
- SP3.2 **Perform Peer Reviews**
- SP3.3 **Verify Selected Service System Components**
- SP3.4 **Validate the Service System**

How does Service System Development transform its capability when the transition to capability level 2 (or the managed level) is made?

Institutionalization of the ten EPPAT MIMOR capability level 2 practices requires consideration of all service life-cycle phases. SSD policy sets expectations at the organizational level to address collection of stakeholder needs, allocating them to service components, analyzing and validating requirements, designing service system components and establishing interface requirements to ensure compatibility, integration, verification and validation while ensuring peer reviews of selected work products. One can take advantage by the striking similarities of practices described under the engineering category process areas of CMMI-DEV to establish the required process mind-set. A more useful point to note in the context of SSD is a consistent policy with necessary support for *post-implementation review*. Just as the proof of the pudding is in the eating, much of the proof of the effectiveness of deploying a service solution comes after implementation is complete. Service quality parameters must be checked for operational correctness that ensures a balanced approach. A balanced scorecard described under Organizational Innovation and Deployment can be used to significantly improve the capability level 2.

How does Service System Development transform its capability when the transition to capability level 3 (or the defined level) is made?

A full life cycle for developing a service starting with requirements management, analysis, design, integration, verification and validation is established within the scope of policies related to Service Delivery. Taking an ITIL definition for a service process as *a connected series of actions, activities, changes performed by agents with the intent of satisfying a purpose or achieving a goal*, process orientation with a defined service life cycle can be established. Based on this definition, there is sufficient room to define and take corrective actions of all things that make up the service process. Institutionalization of a defined process in the CMMI requires generic goal 3 and the two generic practices listed below to be addressed within the process scope.

GG3 Institutionalize a Defined Process

GP3.1 **Establish a Defined Process**

GP3.2 **Collect Improvement Information**

How does Service System Development transform its capability when the transition to capability level 4 (or the quantitatively managed level) is made?

How does Service System Development transform its capability when the transition to capability level 5 (or the optimizing level) is made? Or, how does Service System Development demonstrate a high maturity measurement and analysis capability?

While it might appear that SSD involves analysis, design, development, integration, verification and validation of service systems, significant planning is called for. Activities encompassing SSD must be executed like any time-bound project with *identified measureable improvements* within a specified service area. *What should be measured and how they should be analyzed and used* is a decision up to the service organization. Demonstrating that a process solution is effective in addressing and controlling the quality of service solution offered requires that measures of before–after be made and analyzed statistically to understand the significance of the difference the change has made. SSD is one such process area which is rich in quantifiable opportunities, where techniques using the high-maturity practices described in Chapters 6 and 7 can be institutionalized to reap significant advantages.

SERVICE SYSTEM TRANSITION (SST) CMMI-SVC

How does Service System Transition look when it operates at a capability level 1 (or the performed level)?

The purpose of Service System Transition (SST) is to deploy new or significantly changed service system components while managing their effect on the ongoing Service Delivery. The focus is on getting the new system into operational use by transitioning into/retiring a system that might not be needed and making adjustments to service system and enable Service Delivery.

Planning, communicating, managing, deploying and confirming that service system components effectively transition to the delivery environment refers to the comprehensive process of preparing for, executing and confirming a deployment of service system component to a fully functional state while maintaining operation. Deployment might involve new installation, replacement or retirement of an existing service system/component after checking compatibility. Critical aspects of SST include configuration control, management of internal and external interfaces, deployment of service system components into delivery environment, acceptance of new or revised system and management of impact of transition. Appropriate rollback strategies without disruption of operations must be planned. For example: using staging servers, quality servers, pre-production servers and production servers to ensure smooth transition. Configuration management, management of internal and external interfaces and stakeholder acceptance of new or revised service system are important practices to be considered. Studying the as-is service system and the to-be service system along with compatibility analysis of current and post-transition system ensures risk identification and risk mitigation associated with the transition. Transition notification and transition training strategies should be evolved. The effectiveness of the service system in the delivery environment based on the transition plan and assessments should be systematically deployed and evaluated.

Service transition might involve outsourcing of Service Delivery and developing vendor partnerships after a build-versus-buy decision is made. An effective service transition should ensure a seamless integration of third parties and their solutions making the integrated working relationships so efficient that it should be difficult for an end-user or a customer to tell the difference between the services provided by a full-time employee and a contracted staff. When the above are addressed within the service establishment and delivery process, the following specific goals and specific practices are likely to result. SST will then operate at capability level 1.

SG1 Prepare for Service System Transition

- SP1.1 **Analyze Service System Transition Needs**
- SP1.2 **Develop Service System Transition Plans**
- SP1.3 **Prepare Stakeholders for Changes**

SG2 Deploy the Service System

- SP2.1 **Deploy Service System Components**
- SP2.2 **Assess and Control the Impacts of the Transition**

How does Service System Transition transform its capability when the transition to capability level 2 (or the managed level) is made?

SST policy sets the expectations for planning, implementing and managing the transition of service system components into the live environment. SST could be the result of making the necessary changes to the configuration while resolving a problem. Or, it could be a temporary fix using a work-around until such time that the problem management team can review the most appropriate lasting solution. In which case, practices of configuration management, change management and release management processes significantly influence the effectiveness of SST. Configuration management activities encompass a whole range of activities starting with planning, identification, control, status accounting and verification and audits of configuration items. Change management arises as a result of finding permanent solutions to problems. Change management involves evaluation of RFC (request for change) or forward schedule of changes (FSC), their authorization and implementation, approval, registration and classification of configuration items into a configuration management database (CMDB). Such functions are typically designated and assigned to a change manager presiding over a change advisory board (CAB). In mature processes, change management is not involved in the actual identification of configuration items and updating of change records; this is the job of configuration management. Neither is change management involved in the actual release of working solutions; this is the job of release management. The principal role of change management within SST is to assess the impact of change and authorize changes. Configuration management addresses the identification of areas impacted and updating configuration records. Release management controls the release of new versions of software/hardware necessary to implement the change. Capacity management might be useful to assess impact on business and IT performance. RFCs are normally evaluated by a CAB to approve and prioritize changes. Regular summaries of changes and impact on SST are recorded and communicated to ensure stakeholder coordination and management review. A number of measurement opportunities are exploited to ensure thorough monitoring and control of the process. Some of the typical measures that could yield value within the gamut of SST process are as follows: number of configuration changes, number of emergency or urgent change requests, number of regular change requests, number and percentage of changes made, backlog status of change requests, business and service impact of changes and cost summaries. When a collection of new or changed validated configuration items has to be released or transitioned into the live environment, a governing release policy must guide the type of release: full release, incremental or delta release, package release of configuration items from the appropriate hardware/software archives/libraries. Tested rollout plans along with back-out plans which do not affect normal operations of the service system during the transition have to be established. The transition management staff should be given requisite management and technical training: both operational users who release the service to the business and business users who use the new service ought to be oriented and trained appropriately. The anecdote presented while describing service continuity serves as a useful illustration to bring out the importance of the above considerations. The fundamental requirements of establishing SST at a capability level 2 would be to institutionalize the EPPAT MIMOR practices.

How does Service System Transition transform its capability when the transition to capability level 3 (or the defined level) is made?

Practices described to institutionalize a capability level 2 rigor for SST must be defined as standard operating procedures and continuously improved. In doing so, the two generic practices which enable the realization of generic goal 3 and in so doing establish Service System Transition at the capability level 3 are as follows:

GG3 Institutionalize a Defined Process

GP3.1 **Establish a Defined Process**

GP3.2 **Collect Improvement Information**

How does Service System Transition transform its capability when the transition to capability level 4 (or the quantitatively managed level) is made?

How does Service System Transition transform its capability when the transition to capability level 5 (or the optimizing level) is made? Or, how does Service System Transition demonstrate a high maturity measurement and analysis capability?

Even though SST is influenced by both common and special cause variations that can be quantitatively understood, the actual rendering of service establishment and delivery functions are handled by other CMMI-SVC process areas. If such distinction is made, it is very difficult to demonstrate and justify SST at a capability, beyond level 3. It might be a better option to address the higher-capability enablement of process areas that actually do the work for SST.

STRATEGIC SERVICE MANAGEMENT (STSM) CMMI-SVC

How does Strategic Service Management look when it operates at a capability level 1 (or the performed level)?

The purpose of Strategic Service Management (STSM) is to establish and maintain standard services in concert with strategic needs and plans. Practices in this process area ensure that the set of services provided by the service provider aligns with the long-term business objectives. Standard services which are maintained in a service catalog serve to ensure service continuity during disruptions. STSM extends the practices of Organizational Process Focus, Organizational Process Definition and Organizational Process Performance by broadening their focus to the actual service instead of the process of delivering the service. Therefore improvements to service offering must focus on gathering and studying competition information and service data such as market segmentation, requirements of customers and end users in different segments, market research, customer satisfaction surveys, service review data and strengths, weaknesses, opportunities, threats (SWOT) analysis. Service-level agreements (SLAs) are established based on competency analysis and delivery capability of the service provider. SLAs document the agreement between the service provider and customer with agreed service levels for a service. Such agreements must consider the following service parameters: maximum acceptable continuous period of lost service, maximum acceptable period of degraded service, acceptable degraded performance level during period of service recovery, redundancy and backup requirements, assigned responsibilities during normal and abnormal service conditions, escalation procedure, minimum and maximum reaction time at different escalation stages, key measures to monitor and reporting.

ITIL defines service level management as *the process of defining, agreeing, documenting and managing the levels of customer IT services that are required and cost justified.*

When the above are addressed within the service establishment and delivery process, the following specific goals and specific practices are likely to result. STSM will then operate at capability level 1.

SG1 Establish Strategic Needs and Plans for Standard Services

SP1.1 **Gather and Analyze Relevant Data**

SP1.2 **Establish Plans for Standard Services**

SG2 Establish Standard Services

SP2.1 **Establish Properties of Standard Services and Service Levels**

SP2.2 **Establish Descriptions of Standard Services**

How does Strategic Service Management transform its capability when the transition to capability level 2 (or the managed level) is made?

STSM policy deals with providing the required direction for the establishment and maintenance of standard services across the organization and ensuring their descriptions are available across the organization. Once a decision to deploy enhancements to existing service profile or catalog of services is made, the process of institutionalizing, improving and sustaining them falls on the remaining process areas of the service establishment and delivery category process areas. Relevant sections of SD, SCON, CAM, SSD, SST and IRP have established the criteria to enable STSM at a capability level 2 with the institutionalization of the EPPAT MIMOR practices.

How does Strategic Service Management transform its capability when the transition to capability level 3 (or the defined level) is made?

Definitions to standardize and consistently render the types of activities encompassing STSM described to achieve capability level 1 must be pursued while considering incremental and innovative improvements to them. Operational definitions and process descriptions for a number of service component enablers of the CMMI-SVC constellation, such as service desk operation and management, incident management process, problem management process, change management process, configuration management process and finally release management process along with the six process areas of service establishment and delivery, must be institutionalized. The two generic practices which enable the realization of generic goal 3 and in so doing establish Strategic Service Management at the capability level 3 are as follows:

GG3 Institutionalize a Defined Process

GP3.1 **Establish a Defined Process**

GP3.2 **Collect Improvement Information**

How does Strategic Service Management transform its capability when the transition to capability level 4 (or the quantitatively managed level) is made?

How does Strategic Service Management transform its capability when the transition to capability level 5 (or the optimizing level) is made? Or how does Strategic Service Management demonstrate a high maturity measurement and analysis capability?

STSM depends upon other process areas to actually enact the service requirements after a strategic decision to include such new or enhanced service capability is made. *Per se*, this process area does not offer sufficient quantifiable opportunities for pursuing quantitative enablement techniques using the high-maturity practices described in Chapters 6 and 7.

INCIDENT RESOLUTION AND PREVENTION (IRP) CMMI-SVC

How does Incident Resolution and Prevention look when it operates at a capability level 1 (or the performed level)?

The purpose of Incident Resolution and Prevention (IRP) is to ensure timely and effective resolution of service incidents and prevention of service incidents as appropriate. Incidents are events that may result in breaking service commitments if they are not attended to. IRP practices establish the basis to conduct the following activities: identification of the underlying cause or causes, removing them or minimizing impact of such events, monitoring the conditions that manifest the event and provide temporary work-arounds until a permanent fix is enabled. The definition of incidents in the context of the service industry using other established frameworks such as ITIL (Information Technology Infrastructure Library) is *events which are not part of the standard operation of a service and which cause or may cause an interruption to, or a reduction in, the quality of that service*. ITIL further draws a distinction between incident and a problem by defining a problem as an unknown underlying cause of one or more incidents.

IRP practices are required to troubleshoot the Service Delivery aspects and yield information to improve the capability of the service. For instance: incidents related to shortcomings owing to capacity and availability must inform the CAM process of the required adjustments to proactively prevent problems in the future. The scope of IRP extends itself to address both business and technology processes. Proactive impact analysis of the loss of service components or the service system with a purpose of ensuring service continuity at all times identifies the critical service requirements and risk mitigation strategies. A requirement which is not fully addressed within the CMMI-SVC for effective IRP is problem management—the process of analyzing an unknown underlying cause of one or more incidents for a permanent resolution with configuration and release management or with individual work-around at justifiable cost. SCON and IRP ought to interoperate based on the established service continuity plans. Whereas SCON deals with the more critical service impacts requiring careful consideration, IRP covers technical faults impacting the business from a day-to-day operational management perspective. Such impacts can usually be resolved within an incident management process or problem management process. IRP provides inputs concerning incidents to other processes such as capacity and availability or change and configuration management processes to effect the necessary changes to isolate, mitigate and eliminate the incident.

When the above are addressed within the service establishment and delivery process, the following specific goals and specific practices are likely to result. STSM will then operate at capability level 1.

SG1 Prepare for Incident Resolution and Prevention

SP1.1 **Establish an Approach to Incident Resolution and Prevention**

SP1.2 **Establish an Incident Management System**

SG2 Identify, Control and Address Incidents

- SP2.1 **Identify and Record Incidents**
- SP2.2 **Analyze Incident Data**
- SP2.3 **Apply Work-Arounds to Selected Incidents**
- SP2.4 **Address the Underlying Causes of Selected Incidents**
- SP2.5 **Monitor the Status of Incidents to Closure**
- SP2.6 **Communicate the Status of Incidents**

Note the difference to the goal and practice titles in CMMI-SVC V1.3.

SG2 Identify, Control, and Address Individual Incidents

- SP2.1 Identify and Record Incidents
- SP2.2 Analyze Individual Incident Data
- SP2.3 Resolve Incidents
- SP2.4 Monitor the Status of Incidents to Closure
- SP2.5 Communicate the Status of Incidents

SG3 Define Approaches to Address Selected Incidents

- SP3.1 **Analyze Selected Incident Data**
- SP3.2 **Plan Actions to Address Underlying Causes of Selected Incidents**
- SP3.3 **Establish Work-Arounds for Selected Incidents**

Note the difference to the goal and practice titles in CMMI-SVC V1.3.

SG3 Analyze and Address Causes and Impacts of Selected Incidents

- SP3.1 Analyze Selected Incidents
- SP3.2 Establish Solutions to Respond to Future Incidents
- SP3.3 Establish and Apply Solutions to Reduce Incident Occurrence

How does Incident Resolution and Prevention transform its capability when the transition to capability level 2 (or the managed level) is made?

The IRP policy must ensure ongoing management commitment to maintain the level of service assured at all times, as it is very easy to go off guard when services are being delivered smoothly without a hitch. Performed at several levels in the organization, constant audit and review of the service effectiveness and recovery capabilities from incidents and problems should be planned. Changeover and backup strategies to address different scenarios of service disruption must be planned and appropriate resources including infrastructure should be provided to maintain the minimum support level guaranteed. Where external or third party dependence is involved, all stakeholders are integrated to offer a seamless solution. Risks involving a complete disruption of service must be suitably addressed to minimize loss of or denial of service. Whereas service continuity addresses the more serious city outage, state outage and country outage, operational support must be ensured to handle the day-to-day management by building in redundancy and resilience into the service capability. Constant validation of such operational capability must be fulfilled with appropriate roles and responsibilities. Both the IRP policies and the subsequent operational management have to consider the business impact analysis—*the consequences of damage caused to the business as a result of a disruption to critical business processes*—before embarking on Risk Management strategies and risk reduction measures. Decisions on recovery latency ranging from gradual to immediate must be implemented while ensuring coordination among all stakeholders including partners and outsourced entities. The anecdote citied on a major cell phone service provider while interpreting service continuity again serves as a good example. As observed in this example, training, education, competency development, maintaining awareness and the overall alignment of all interdependent entities in the Service Delivery along with the required infrastructure for knowledge sharing has to be considered within the IRP strategy. The fundamental requirements of establishing IRP at a capability level 2 would be to institutionalize the EPPAT MIMOR practices.

How does Incident Resolution and Prevention transform its capability when the transition to capability level 3 (or the defined level) is made?

At the capability level 3, a defined process is established based on best practices resulting from repeated handling and perfecting the system of practices described for enabling capability level 2. Improvements to IRP are both an inside-out and outside-in approach since a service is not delivered in isolation. All constituencies within the business, the board, senior management, management, supervisors and staff, ought to proactively determine a response to incidents and problems as they occur—the inside-out requirement. On the other hand, technology partners and customers set expectations with technology improvements and raising expectation levels of IRP practices—the outside-in requirement. IRP together with SCON should serve the organizational needs best, for minimizing service disruption. Institutionalization of the CMMI generic practices 3.1 and 3.2 ensures IRP is able to effectively address and limit the chances of unknown incidents cropping up. The two generic practices which enable the realization of generic goal 3 and in so doing establish IRP at the capability level 3 are as follows:

GG3 Institutionalize a Defined Process

GP3.1 **Establish a Defined Process**

GP3.2 **Collect Improvement Information**

How does Incident Resolution and Prevention transform its capability when the transition to capability level 4 (or the quantitatively managed level) is made?

How does Incident Resolution and Prevention transform its capability when the transition to capability level 5 (or the optimizing level) is made? Or, how does Incident Resolution and Prevention demonstrate a high maturity measurement and analysis capability?

IRP yields a lot of measurable process data that can be put to good statistical analysis and subsequent use. Such metrics can be with respect to the maintenance of equilibrium of cost–capacity and demand–supply under adverse conditions (special and common cause influences). There is a considerable scope for process learning to result with which to effectively minimize the impact of incidents and problems with effective process management. Business justifications and business objectives from the points of view of resource utilization, cost, capacity and availability data and the routine validation data ought to be studied in relationship to qualitative impacts such as loss of goodwill, reputation, income and industry standing, before considering quantitative enablement of techniques using the high-maturity practices described in Chapters 6 and 7.

Author's Musing

There seems to be a disconnect in the current thinking of what is level 3 and of what is high maturity. In fact, high maturity is nothing more than a continuity of level 3 practices with quantitative and statistical management. The notion of process stability and process capability getting enabled at the level 3 of the CMMI model due to the relevant practices needs to be emphasized. Noise in the system is minimized because of level 3 practices—an essential prerequisite for high maturity. Unfortunately, it is made out to look that after level 3, there is a 'new' type of process phenomenon that takes hold, which from my personal experience is not true.

ORGANIZATIONAL PROCESS FOCUS (OPF) CMMI-DEV, CMMI-ACQ AND CMMI-SVC

How does the Organizational Process Focus look when it operates at a capability level 1 (or the performed level)?

Organizational Process Focus (OPF) belongs to the process management category of the continuous representation of all three CMMI constellations. The purpose of OPF is to plan, implement and deploy organizational process improvements based on a thorough understanding of the current strengths and weaknesses of the organization's processes and process assets. Being the foundation upon which a successful change management program is built, OPF serves two essential purposes: to plan and implement improvements to the software and systems development framework and to establish consistency and commonality of process assets across the organization. OPF enables an understanding of the strengths and opportunities for improvement. Such understanding comes from multiple sources, some of the most valuable sources being process retrospectives at the completion of major milestones during project execution, project postmortem reports, formal and informal process appraisals and audits and integration of external benchmarking reports and best practices into the process design.

OPF offers visibility to periodically reinforce and engage the practitioners' attention to assessing and evaluating the effectiveness of practices that are used to develop both systems and software. In the initial stages of process improvement, it is best to have a dedicated team of professionals such as the process engineering group or the process engineering council to drive this initiative. Knowing the strengths and opportunities for improvement in relationship to a framework such as the CMMI staged or continuous representations is a useful first step to understand process gaps and discontinuities.

While OPF identifies improvement proposals for the systems or the software development process, a whole gamut of organizational processes could be covered and addressed for best leverage. Improvements ought to be holistic and systemic for sustaining gains with the process program. Such a holistic and systemic view is enabled if, and only if, the process improvement program delivers improvements to the three systemic interactions of *people–process–technology* triad within an operating environmental and business context (Figure 5.10). If the key premise is to build organizational capability, then the three interacting parts of the system—people, process and technology—must improve as a system.

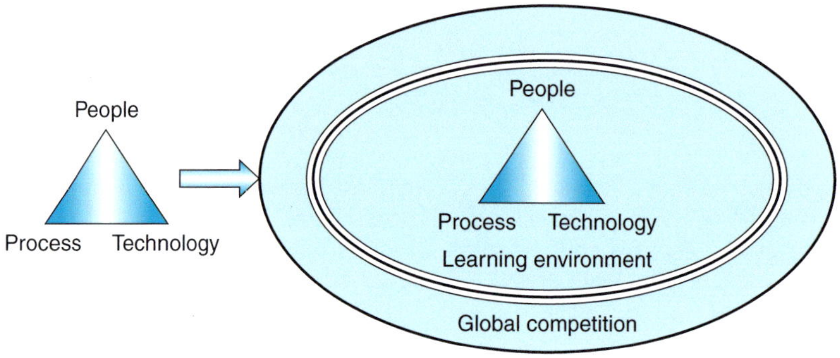

Fig. 5.10 People–Process–Technology Triad

Source: Reused from People Capability Maturity Model [Nandyal 2003]

A well-managed change initiative ought to consider improvements to all three of the above, keeping in mind the need for creating a learning environment as the necessary compeller influenced by global competition. Productivity improvement makes sense only when equal emphasis is placed on all three interacting components. Overemphasizing improvements to just any one of them without suitable adjustments to the other two will yield a lopsided change management program.

Improvements could be engineered through understanding the organizational process imperatives for performance characteristics using a goal-question-metric (GQM) paradigm. GQM could be used to enable the necessary internal dialogue while building the supporting process infrastructure.

Author's Musing

Asking the right questions knowing the specific and generic goals of the process area is a good way to work the intent of the CMMI framework into the organizational design. The goal-question-metric paradigm of Victor Basili is one such useful technique to address the effectiveness of the change program. The only way to confirm the measurement and verification aspects of the change management program works in step and synchronously with changes induced to the process is to ensure that these activities are used to objectively evaluate the quality of the new processes.

A good starting point for the change management program could be from an external appraisal of the process. External appraisals help to expose the obvious flaws in the process design that do not get highlighted due to familiarity and exposure. An external perspective offers a neutral unbiased perspective regarding the merits and the limitations of the process. Process appraisal with necessary rigor serves to prioritize and establish a program of coordinated action to enable the realization of the objectives of the system of practices. Not every process improvement recommendation can be attempted at once. Some may need to be fixed prior to supporting others. In doing so, the following specific practices are incorporated into the process:

SG1 Determine Process Improvement Opportunities

SP1.1 **Establish Organizational Process Needs**

SP1.2 **Appraise the Organization's Processes**

SP1.3 **Identify the Organization's Process Improvements**

For every process recommendation that is worked on, it is important for the respective process owner or the process action teams to answer the question—*'is the change getting better or is it getter bitter?'* SCAMPI Class B/C appraisals and process audits help to establish such understanding [Nandyal 2007]. Every new procedure, standard or tool addressing the improvement must be put through a few iterations of piloting on selected projects. When pilot results prove useful, they can then be deployed across the larger organizational context. The role played by the collection of measures or metrics that directly relates to measuring the efficacy of the change is emphasized based on test of hypothesis (refer Chapters 6 and 7).

Following an objective evaluation of the process change, it is possible to hone the practices into a process by documenting the lessons learnt, revising the scope of implementation and restructuring the process action teams and process engineering groups if business situations have changed. Many times it might become necessary to revise the organizational approach for the next process appraisal. Since process maturity is a journey and not a goal, importance must be given to repeating the cycle of improvement and sustaining the momentum from right process alignment. In doing so, the following specific practices are enabled:

SG2 Plan and Implement Process Improvements Activities[6]

SP2.1 **Establish Process Action Plans**

SP2.2 **Implement Process Action Plans**

SG3 Deploy Organizational Process Assets and Incorporate Lessons Learned

SP3.1 **Deploy Organizational Process Assets**

SP3.2 **Deploy Standard Processes**

[6] Goal title appears as "Plan and Implement Process Actions" in version 1.3 across all three constellations. There is no noticeable/perceptible change to the informative content associated with this goal and therefore to its interpretation.

SP3.3 Monitor Implementation

SP3.4 Incorporate Process-Related Experiences into the Organizational Process Assets[7]

We shall review more of the deployment aspects of OPF required for SG3 fulfillment while interpreting the capability level 2 and capability level 3 institutionalization.

The practical sides to OPF as experienced with some of the author's best professional associations are as follows:

Organizational Process Focus

1. Conduct a process appraisal to understand the distinctions and limitations of the system of practices within the organization.
2. Characterize each gap or discontinuity as a process issue, business issue or a people characteristic, and address these issues appropriately.
3. Prioritize the process recommendations after assessing the impact and degree of change and establish process action teams to work on the recommendations in a coordinated manner.
4. Study the effectiveness of the process changes in periodic intervals to determine the attainment of planned objectives and roll out the practices to make the change applicable to the larger organizational entity.
5. Internalize learning opportunities by enriching the definition and articulation of the process.

Display 5.7 Interpreting Organizational Process Focus

Source: Adapted from SITARA Process JewelBox™ © SITARA Technologies Pvt. Ltd. 2002 with permission

How does the Organizational Process Focus transform its capability when the transition to capability level 2 (or the managed level) is made?

The intent behind process improvement is institutionalized with supporting organizational policies that establish the objectives, periodicity and rigor for process appraisals. Such policies defining the scope are used to plan the implementation objectives across the organization. For example: should the organizational maturity be level 2 or higher? And, whether there is a target profile of the process areas or not?

Establishing and identifying a plan of coordinated action in a process improvement plan with assigned ownership is a key expectation at the managed capability level. Resources needed to make the process intent operational are provided with the necessary supporting infrastructure (such as corporate intranet sites to deploy process assets and ensuring access to information).

Those assigned responsibility to engineer the process have both the exposure and necessary training to ensure that the objectives of the process are grounded in *day-to-day* realities of the business. Rigid postures in relation to the process serve no one's interests. Instead, the organization offers tailoring

[7] Practice title appears as "Incorporate Experiences into the Organizational Process Assets" in version 1.3 across all three constellations. There is no noticeable/perceptible change to the informative content associated with this practice and therefore to its interpretation.

guidelines with the process asset descriptions for projects to resort to and exercise appropriate levels of professional and management judgment while rendering or using the process.

One of the most useful process enablers is the adequate use of necessary tools to render the software and systems engineering methods. Common tools which are relevant and usable by a large number of projects are identified, piloted and deployed in the organizational process. Experience of practitioners working on projects is also collected and actively solicited in process improvement proposals, reviewed by a team of experts and assessed from the perspective of organizational applicability. Studies of such improvement proposals are carried out and internalized after evaluating the degree of impact and the enabling mechanisms available for rendering the process change. Successful life cycles and methodologies that walk the talk are identified and rendered within the OSSP using the practices of a related process area—Organizational Process Definition.

Generic goal 2 and the related practices that serve the establishment of a capability level 2 or the managed level for the OPF are EPPAT MIMOR.

How does the Organizational Process Focus transform its capability when the transition to capability level 3 (or the defined level) is made?

As OPF is an enabling process area for all process areas to attain a capability level 3, establishing OPF at capability level 3 or at the defined level is a necessary condition for the attainment of level 3 process maturity. A useful manifestation of a level 3 OPF capability is to enable the organizational process asset library or the OSSP to serve as a process database capturing the defined process and a compilation of life cycles that have worked well.

The organizational process asset library establishes a tailoring guideline using which projects make the Organizational Process Definitions applicable to their context while addressing the constraints of operation. External benchmarks and known industry best practices are also made available for project use. A metrics database serves the organizational process needs by establishing quantitative and qualitative performance objectives. Such an organizational metrics database is used to track the actual performance of projects against established goals and threshold limits.

Projects that have encountered risks in execution and have responded well with definite abatement procedures that could potentially lend themselves to reuse are captured into a risk repository and a 'lessons learnt' database. Technical risks that have been assessed with successful alternative evaluations and that are known to have value from a reuse perspective are captured into a decision analysis and a resolution repository. A guideline for rendering decisions when technical alternatives have to be explored to accommodate the real-world situations that define the project response is incorporated into the organizational process asset library.

A mature organizational process asset library defines the procedures and standards that should be adopted by the organizational workforce in order to expeditiously render solutions. This would include making available a reuse library or repository for organizational use. Besides, the process asset library is periodically revisited to ensure effective housekeeping and retiring of processes and procedures that have outlived their relevance. The two generic practices that enable the realization of generic goal 3 and in so doing establish Organizational Process Focus at the capability level 3 are as follows:

GG3 Institutionalize a Defined Process

GP3.1 **Establish a Defined Process**

GP3.2 Collect Improvement Information

It may be useful to point out that the specific practices of OPF in general enable the realization of GP3.2—'Collect Improvement Information'—across the 22 process areas of the CMMI-DEV, 6 process areas of the CMMI-ACQ constellation and 7 process areas of the CMMI-SVC constellation.

It is difficult to justify and demonstrate OPF at a capability beyond level 3. From a theoretical perspective, the generic goal 4 and the related generic practices 4.1 and 4.2 need to be established for enabling OPF at capability level 4.

GG4 Institutionalize a Quantitatively Managed Process

GP4.1 Establish Quantitative Objectives for the Process

GP4.2 Stabilize Sub-Process Performance

And to enable OPF at capability level 5, the generic goal 5 and the associated generic practices 5.1 and 5.2 need to be institutionalized.

GG5 Institutionalize an Optimizing Process

GP5.1 Ensure Continuous Process Improvement

GP5.2 Correct Root Causes of Problem

It may be useful to point out that the specific practices of PP in general enable the realization of GP3.2—'Collect Improvement Information'—across the 22 process areas of the CMMI-DEV, 6 process areas of the CMMI-ACQ constellation and 7 process areas of the CMMI-SVC constellation.

ORGANIZATIONAL PROCESS DEFINITION (OPD) CMMI-DEV (+IPPD), CMMI-ACQ AND CMMI-SVC

How does Organizational Process Definition look when it operates at a capability level 1 (or the performed level)?

Organizational Process Definition (OPD) belongs to the process management category of the continuous representation of the CMMI. The purpose of OPD is to establish and maintain a usable set of organizational process assets and work environment standards. For IPPD, Organizational Process Definition + IPPD also cover the establishment of organizational rules and guidelines that enable conducting work using integrated teams. OPD realizes the intent behind OPF by establishing the necessary organizational process assets. Usable sets of process descriptions, life cycles, methods and practices that are employed within the organization to address both engineering and management needs as a result of being identified as best practices within the site's context are continually updated and maintained. Necessary tailoring guidelines as applicable are also rendered to cater to the specific needs of the project. Process capability baselines for specific performance goals met through using the defined process are also maintained within the measurement repository. Process capability baselines define the specific performance measures attained, such as schedule performance index, cost performance index, estimation accuracy, in-process defect measures across phases, phase containment effectiveness, and so on, as a result of using specific organizational practices.

Based on the evaluation of practices within projects, best practices that address the purpose and intent of sound organizational processes are identified. Such practices define standard development, maintenance and support processes, life-cycle models in use, pre-tailored process descriptions, specific methods for analysis, design, construction and testing (for more details, please refer to Chapter 3 on process methods in software engineering) and tailoring guidelines to derive a process.

Mature process descriptions include lessons learnt in the form of what is called a red book and successful design alternatives that have been employed on projects with known results to match those in what is called the white book. Standards and guidelines defining the generally applicable industry-wide known best practices are also captured. A good OPD practice eliminates the need to reinvent the wheel by offering tailor-made solutions to common issues faced by projects operating within the organization's process context. Another useful artifact maintained within the process asset library is a contribution of practitioners to the development of white papers and technical reports. The organization is also sensitive to using the OPF and OPD practices as an effective foundation to leverage its Organizational Innovation and Deployment practices.

Results from studying successful pilot implementations and accepted best practices are transitioned into the design of the organizational process. In doing so, the following specific goals and specific practices are enabled within the organizational process intent:

SG1 Establish Organizational Process Assets

SP1.1 **Establish Standard Processes**

SP1.2 **Establish Life-Cycle Model Descriptions**

SP1.3 **Establish Tailoring Criteria and Guidelines**

SP1.4 **Establish the Organization's Measurement Repository**

SP1.5 **Establish the Organization's Process Asset Library**

SP1.6 **Establish Work Environment Standards**

SP1.7 **Establish Rules and Guidelines for Teams (CMMI-ACQ and CMMI-SVC only. Included in version 1.3 of CMMI-DEV)**[8]

[8] By adding this specific practice, both the CMMI-ACQ and CMMI-SVC constellations have subsumed and therefore eliminated the need to carry a specific goal addressing IPPD aspects i.e., SG2 Enable IPPD Principles. CMMI-DEV v1.3 also adopts the same approach while eliminating the IPPD Addition.

IPPD Addition (Relevant only to CMMI-DEV constellation)[9]

SG2 Enable IPPD Management

- SP2.1 **Establish Empowerment Mechanisms**
- SP2.2 **Establish Rules and Guidelines for Integrated Teams**
- SP2.3 **Balance Team and Home Organization Responsibilities**

The practical sides to OPD as experienced with some of the author's best professional associations are as follows:

Organizational Process Definition

1. Establish acceptable organizational processes based on the use of a defined tailoring guideline for project use.
2. Establish a consistent definition of basic and advanced (or derived) process metrics for process measures.
3. Review effectiveness of practices periodically based on postmortem reports to incorporate improvements to the process assets.
4. Develop a process repository with access controls to enable deployment and use of organizational assets.
5. Revise assets from formal appraisals, as appropriate, and keep the assets current and fresh.

Display 5.8 Interpreting Organizational Process Definition

Source: Adapted from SITARA Process JewelBox™ © SITARA Technologies Pvt. Ltd. 2002 with permission

How does Organizational Process Definition transform its capability when the transition to capability level 2 (or the managed level) is made?

At the managed level, the organizational purpose behind defining and using a consistent system of practices is outlined in a policy, stating the minimal process adherence necessary for acceptable work products and solutions. The policy also establishes how non-compliance to the process would be handled and the criteria that qualify a waiver, when necessary and applicable. Should business reasons dictate a process that is outside the scope of the regular development process, the policy supports a process of exception handling and treats outliers with the necessary management oversight.

Well-defined plans (typically at the end of each quarter) establish the periodicity of best practices review. Accepted best practice submissions are transitioned into the organizational process asset after the necessary proving in of such ideas from examining results attained through pilots.

Adequate and skilled resources are assigned the responsibility to work on best practice initiatives which result in the development of support tools to attain performance objectives. Such a group is typically called the software resource center, knowledge center or the learning laboratory. A team of professionals, who are vested with responsibility to evaluate tools and technologies applicable within the organizational

---

[9] IPPD addition has been removed from the CMMI-DEV V1.3. A new specific practice SP 1.7 with the title "Establish Rules and Guidelines for Teams" has been included instead.

context, are typically called skilled with advanced technology (SWAT) teams. Interoperability and integration of competencies is also explored using practices defined in the process areas of Integrated Project Management.

It is also very useful to explore the practices adopted by the customer. Many times, such a study of customer practices, tools and technologies adopted would itself seed best practices within the local context and serve as an effective process response which addresses specific customer contexts. In doing so, the managed capability level gets institutionalized with the following generic goals and generic practices getting established:

GG2 Institutionalize a Managed Process

GP2.1 **Establish an Organizational Policy**

GP2.2 **Plan the Process**

GP2.3 **Provide Resources**

GP2.4 **Assign Responsibility**

GP2.5 **Train People**

GP2.6 **Manage Configurations**

GP2.7 **Identify and Involve Relevant Stakeholders**

GP2.8 **Monitor and Control the Process**

GP2.9 **Objectively Evaluate Adherence**

GP2.10 **Review Status with Higher-Level Management**

How does Organizational Process Definition transform its capability when the transition to capability level 3 (or the defined level) is made?

At the defined capability level, OPD establishes a consistent system of practices that could be adopted by projects working within the organizational process context. Continuous improvement cycles defined in the process improvement plan revisit the articulated practices to make process descriptions effective. In doing so, the process area enables the institutionalization of generic goal 3 and the related practices as follows:

GG3 Institutionalize a Defined Process

GP3.1 **Establish a Defined Process**

GP3.2 **Collect Improvement Information**

It is difficult to justify and demonstrate OPD at a capability beyond level 3. From a theoretical perspective, the generic goal 4 and the related generic practices 4.1 and 4.2 need to be established for enabling OPD + IPPD at capability level 4.

GG4 Institutionalize a Quantitatively Managed Process

GP4.1 **Establish Quantitative Objectives for the Process**

GP4.2 **Stabilize Sub-Process Performance**

And to enable OPD + IPPD at capability level 5, the generic goal 5 and the associated generic practices 5.1 and 5.2 need to be institutionalized.

GG5 Institutionalize an Optimizing Process

GP5.1 Ensure Continuous Process Improvement

GP5.2 Correct Root Causes of Problem

It may be useful to point out that the specific practices of OPD in general enable the realization of GP 3.1—'Establish a Defined Process'—across the 22 process areas of the CMMI-DEV, 6 process areas of the CMMI-ACQ constellation and 7 process areas of the CMMI-SVC constellation.

ORGANIZATIONAL TRAINING CMMI-DEV, CMMI-ACQ AND CMMI-SVC

How does Organizational Training look when it operates at a capability level 1 (or the performed level)?

Organizational Training belongs to the process management category of the continuous representation of the CMMI constellations. The purpose of establishing Organizational Training is to ingrain the necessary skills, knowledge and competencies for effective realization of products and solutions. Where complementary skills can be integrated and leveraged along with the necessary application of soft skills, practices contained within training and development of the People CMM would be reasonable to embrace.

The purpose of training and development is to ensure that all individuals have the skills required to perform their assignments. Training and development addresses both aspects of the short-term or tactical needs of a project and the long-term strategic needs of the organization. Individuals are made aware of the organizational competencies and potential strategic directions in order to help them pursue training/learning opportunities. Individual training needs are identified based on such informed decisions and aggregated at the unit level for timely administration of training and developmental activities. Periodic discussions on individual developmental needs are also used as basis for timely administration of competency development. In the process, the following specific goal and related specific practices are established:

SG1 Establish an Organizational Training Capability

SP1.1 Establish the Strategic Training Needs

SP1.2 Determine Which Training Needs Are the Responsibility of the Organization

SP1.3 Establish an Organizational Training Tactical Plan

SP1.4 Establish Training Capability

A summative evaluation such as the use of the Kirkpatrick model to measure effectiveness of the training program in accomplishing its stated goals is normally in place. Donald Kirkpatrick's model is a hierarchical model for evaluating training based on learning and results. These levels can be applied to technology-based training as well as to more traditional forms of delivery [Kirkpatrick 1998].

- Level One: Reactions—what did the learners think of the training?

- Level Two: Learning—what did learners learn during the learning experience?
- Level Three: Behavior—what learning and skills did learners apply on the job?
- Level Four: Results—what changes in results and productivity have been observed on the job? [Rothwell 1994, Brown 1992]

In doing so, the following specific goal and practices are enabled:

SG2 Provide Necessary Training[10]

SP2.1 **Deliver Training**

SP2.2 **Establish Training Records**

SP2.3 **Assess Training Effectiveness**

The practical sides to Organizational Training as experienced with some of the author's best professional associations are as follows:

Organizational Training

1. Establish a psychologically safe work environment that supports organizational learning from the highest level down.
2. Ensure that adequate time is made available to individuals to pursue competency-oriented learning.
3. Measure individual effectiveness based on training received before enrolling other organizational stakeholders into similar activities.
4. Establish learning centers or laboratories where opportunities to try out what was learnt are provided with a view to establish effectiveness of practices before large-scale changes can be rendered.
5. Institutionalize a mechanism of train-the-trainer in order to galvanize and create rapid specific learning opportunities within the organization.

Display 5.9 Interpreting Organizational Training

Source: Adapted from SITARA Process JewelBox™ © SITARA Technologies Pvt. Ltd. 2002 with permission

How does Organizational Training transform its capability when the transition to capability level 2 (or the managed level) is made?

Adequate funding is provided along with the support of a proactive training and administration staff to grow the individual learning orientation by actively sourcing training resources. A well-structured training and development administration team includes a balanced proportion of team leaders, project managers and divisional heads. Decision making around individual training needs within such a team is balanced and timely. Mentoring or some other rudimentary form of counseling is also employed so as to ensure that individuals feel psychologically safe and secure while pursuing a developmental program.

---

10 Goal title appears as "Provide Training" in version 1.3 across all three constellations. There is no noticeable/perceptible change to the informative content associated with this goal and therefore to its interpretation.

In mature development environments with strong competency orientation, individuals are perceived to be engaged in 'productive and billable activities' such as project activities, only for about 10 calendar months in a year. The other 2 months are allocated for personal competency development and personal renewal. Such a mechanism ensures that burnout is minimized and individuals are provided with an opportunity to foster a learning orientation. Role-based training is also provided in critical project skills that require specialized learning.

Those assigned training responsibilities within the organization are provided the necessary orientation and preparation necessary to be effective instructors. *Train-the-trainer* programs are normally provided to internalize capability and dissemination of information obtained from external sources using a train-the-trainer organizational policy.

Competency enhancements and individual demonstration of acquired knowledge as a result of training programs are objectively evaluated by the supervisor through an effective performance management and review system. Well-defined criteria that establish the individual's proficiency in the subject matter is used as basis for making waiver decisions on required training. And a well-executed training and development program ensures that a training database of individuals who have undergone specific training programs is maintained as a record of the knowledge and skills acquired by them.

Computer-based training (CBT) and other mechanisms such as virtual classrooms, which can be pursued by individuals without depending upon organizational professionals, are also employed. Most mature organizational processes establish collaborative agreements with established educational and research organizations to supplement and augment learning capacities available within the organization. Exposure to the latest techniques and industry best practices is also provided in such informal settings as organizational conclaves and conferences. Typically, such exposure is leveraged from institutionalizing a *train-the-trainer* program with necessary incentives.

In doing so, the generic goal 2 supporting a managed capability level with the associated generic practices of EPPAT MIMOR get institutionalized.

Author's Musing

The best cynical response I got for tool usage in low-maturity work cultures on the question *'how does a person learn how to use the tools?'* was "Press the F1 key!"

How does Organizational Training transform its capability when the transition to capability level 3 (or the defined level) is made?

Leaders in the organization demonstrate a passion for organizational transformation with training and development. Corporate socialization events such as staff meetings highlight to a good degree the extent of leadership involvement in the learning process. A recent Harvard Business Review interview by Diane L. Coutu [Coutu 2002] sums up the anxiety of learning to be of two types: learning anxiety and survival anxiety. Whereas learning anxiety is an organizational disability coming from the individual's fear of change that often threatens individual identity and self-esteem, survival anxiety is what truly contributes to learning due to the fundamental trait of coercive persuasion. Learning anxiety comes from the most difficult sentence to make public—*'I don't know enough!'* Often organizational goals established for learning are non-negotiable and cascade down from the highest level of authority. Leaders in the organization establish a psychologically safe environment for others by becoming true learners themselves.

The author has personally experienced that a high degree of individual commitment to learning comes with the creation of 'brain trusts'. As it is difficult to change the whole system, a brain trust works as a group of individuals who decide to do have well-meaning intentions for each other by openly sharing ideas and topics of common interest and just *lift off* the ground. Within a highly capable Organizational Training process area, a training database of individuals having critical skills and knowledge is maintained along with a defined expiration policy. Knowledge and skills are rendered obsolete if the specific skill has not been in use by an individual for an extended period of time. Such decisions are based on evaluating results from administering proficiency examinations or mandating individuals to go through periodic certifications awarded by standard certification bodies. As a result, generic goal 3 that establishes Organizational Training at a defined capability level is enabled, which is as follows:

GG3 Institutionalize a Defined Process

GP3.1 **Establish a Defined Process**

GP3.2 **Collect Improvement Information**

How does Organizational Training transform its capability when the transition to capability level 4 (or the quantitatively managed level) is made?

How does Organizational Training transform its capability when the transition to capability level 5 (or the optimizing level) is made? Or how does Organizational Training demonstrate a high maturity measurement and analysis capability?

It is difficult to justify and demonstrate Organizational Training at a capability beyond level 3. However, it is possible to identify quantitative goals for competency development and to realize them within the process infrastructure using causal analysis, so as to determine the special or common causes of process variation. Merits of such analysis may be worth noting: you can change the skill and knowledge profile of the organization by recognizing that variations to execution outcomes are due to common causes. However, this change has to be a planned strategic event and cannot happen overnight. The competency attitude currently bred within the organization is probably what the work culture or the organizational circumstances potentially have to offer at best. Such a fresh 'breeze of change' can be infused with proactive management of competencies with ownership right with the higher echelons. The author has witnessed organizations demonstrating radically different competency outlooks at short intervals of time by making changes at the highest levels in the organization through sourcing competent people using an engaged management leadership philosophy. From a theoretical perspective, the generic goal 4 and the related generic practices 4.1 and 4.2 need to be established for enabling Organizational Training at capability level 4.

GG4 Institutionalize a Quantitatively Managed Process

GP4.1 **Establish Quantitative Objectives for the Process**

GP4.2 **Stabilize Sub-Process Performance**

And to enable OT at capability level 5, the generic goal 5 and the associated generic practices 5.1 and 5.2 need to be institutionalized.

GG5 Institutionalize an Optimizing Process

GP5.1 Ensure Continuous Process Improvement

GP5.2 Correct Root Causes of Problem

It may be useful to point out that the specific practices of Organizational Training in general enable the realization of GP 2.5—'Train the People'—across the process areas of the three CMMI constellations.

INTEGRATED PROJECT MANAGEMENT (IPM)[11] CMMI-DEV (+IPPD), CMMI-ACQ AND CMMI-SVC

How does Integrated Project Management look when it operates at a capability level 1 (or the performed level)?

Integrated Project Management (IPM) belongs to the project management category of the continuous representation of the CMMI and is common to all three constellations. The purpose of IPM is to establish and manage the project and the involvement of the relevant stakeholders according to an integrated and defined process that is tailored from the organization's set of standard processes. For IPPD, IPM + IPPD also cover the establishment of a shared vision for the project and the establishment of integrated teams that will carry out objectives of the project. For those of us groomed in the Software CMM legacy, IPM is a combination of integrated software management and inter-group coordination. In these two key process areas of the Software CMM were included aspects of process tailoring and ensuring coordination of activities among collaborating groups or teams. IPM for IPPD also supports the establishment of team-based practices within a shared vision for the project. Wonder if there is any project that does not benefit from institutionalizing IPPD practices! Yet, IPPD is an addition in the CMMI-DEV. Within the context of implementing IPM practices, it is recommended that the People CMM process areas of work group development and empowered work groups are explored [Curtis 2002, Nandyal 2003].

Fundamentally, the specific practices of IPM support the following objectives:

- Project's tailored process is based on the organizational definition of the standard development process.
- Project is managed using the defined process with commitments from relevant stakeholders to ensure process adherence.
- Experiences and best practices resulting from the use of the tailored process are fed back to enrich the definitions of the organizational process assets.
- Individuals work in a collaborative nurturing environment with appropriate empowerment to ensure that work products are developed by leveraging complimentary skills.

Since the basic execution of the project's defined process is governed by engineering practices described in the engineering category process areas, they would not be repeated here. Project management practices align with the project management category process areas. Please refer to the appropriate engineering and

[11] In version 1.3, Integrated Project Management is renamed to Integrated Work Management only in the CMMI-SVC constellation.

project management practices for an in-depth interpretation. However, specific aspects of IPM that are noteworthy are described in what follows.

The project's defined process is tailored from the organizational standard process, when tailoring is required; no tailoring is also tailoring. Project plan is based on the tailored process and governs project activities related to the management and engineering practices employed on the project. Supporting process assets that can be used directly from the organizational process asset library such as forms, templates and guidelines are used by the project; else, they are tailored to meet the requirements of the tailored process.

An integrated plan refers to the master plan that synchronizes multiple plans for the development activities, quality audit activities and configuration management activities of the project. Consequently, the following specific goal and specific practices are rendered into the process infrastructure:

SG1 Use the Project's Defined Process

- SP1.1 **Establish the Project's Defined Process**
- SP1.2 **Use Organizational Process Assets for Planning Project Activities**
- SP1.3 **Establish the Project's Work Environment**
- SP1.4 **Integrate Plans**
- SP1.5 **Manage the Project Using the Integrated Plans**
- SP1.6 **Establish Teams[12] (CMMI-ACQ and CMMI-SVC only. Included in Version 1.3 of CMMI-DEV)**
- SP1.6 **Contribute to Organizational Process Assets (CMMI-DEV)**
- SP1.7 **Contribute to Organizational Process Assets (CMMI-ACQ and CMMI-SVC. Included in Version 1.3 of CMMI-DEV)**

In product development scenarios where participation of the end user or the customer is required, such engagements are scheduled within the master plan and are coordinated to include both internal and external stakeholder participation. This is more of a resource planning issue that is best addressed within the scope of Project Planning. In doing so, the following specific goal and specific practices are rendered into the process infrastructure:

SG2 Coordinate and Collaborate with Relevant Stakeholders

- SP2.1 **Manage Stakeholder Involvement**
- SP2.2 **Manage Dependencies**
- SP2.3 **Resolve Coordination Issues**

[12] By adding this specific practice, both the CMMI-ACQ and CMMI-SVC constellations have subsumed and therefore eliminated the need to carry a specific goal addressing IPPD aspects i.e., SG3 Apply IPPD Principles. CMMI-DEV v1.3 also adopts the same approach while eliminating the IPPD Addition.

Since multiple stakeholder involvement needs to be coordinated, establishing the project's shared vision is critical. Defining and establishing the project's shared vision implies that the master project plan is communicated to all relevant stakeholders using a *need-to-know* approach. Besides the schedule, the project's technical and functional requirements have to be communicated to those who will use them to develop the project. Establishment of the requirements specification and the governing project requirements while ensuring that those concerned understand them in the same sense ensures a partial realization of the specific goal for IPPD.

In order to fully institutionalize the IPPD practices, it is now possible to establish an integrated team of relevant stakeholders who work to common project objectives. Such a team is made up of individuals belonging into a home organization of subject matter experts (competency communities) who are enrolled into the project for the duration of the execution of the project (also known as project organization). By working on the project mandates to deliver upon established expectations, these empowered work groups of competency communities build the required core competencies for the organization. Upon completion of their assigned tasks within a project organization, they disband in an orderly fashion and return to the home organization to which they belong, thereby enabling the retention of competencies.

The purpose of integrated teams serve is to enable the development of work products by sustaining and continually improving levels of performance. To get best insights into how to engineer the required practices that govern integrated team operations, it would be extremely useful to integrate ideas contained within practices belonging to the process areas of competency-based practices, work group development and empowered work groups of the People CMM [Curtis 1995, 2002, Nandyal 2003].

Competency-based practices ensure that all workforce practices are based in part on developing the knowledge and skills of the staff. These practices involve recruiting against required knowledge and skills, using selection methods to assess knowledge and skills of candidates. Job performance is assessed against tasks and roles assigned to the position. Empowered work groups serve the purpose of equipping work groups with the responsibility and authority for determining how best to conduct their business activities. Themes from the relevant People CMM practices would be explored in what follows to gain an understanding of how to leverage value from the People CMM.

Work Group Development Being the process part of empowerment, a well-defined program is established to increase delegation of responsibility and to facilitate its envisioning through team charters. Individuals integrate lessons learnt into the project at every phase of project execution with Causal Analysis and Resolution meetings. Team decisions are normally driven by effective decision analysis processes with full team participation, thereby enabling shared vision. Multiple types of decision-making techniques for both technical and management decisions are advocated. Independent decisions are encouraged by the team for task-level decisions requiring minimal project leader involvement. Consensus decisions are used for resolving intra-group issues that require multiple internal stakeholder commitments. Coordinated decisions are used as a mechanism to ensure good inter-group visibility for decisions requiring external stakeholder commitments. Escalation of issues up to the senior management is a well-defined process and is resorted to after team reflection. Organizational policies support a host of decision-making techniques to maximize the use of empowerment and permit decisions to be taken at the most appropriate lowest level of authority.

Empowered Work Groups A high-trust environment is the hallmark of an empowered workforce. Individuals are seen to request management support while making decisions, only with a view to seek clarification. Management by exception renders the role of a manager to enable people working in the team to make appropriate decisions. If, after the manager provides the necessary clarification and information necessary for decision making to the individual, the individual decides to make another choice, then the management system is mature enough to realize that the individual did so after exercising professional judgment. Everyone in the organization actively supports the choice of the decision made by the individual, and the resulting outcomes. Use of partners in the learning process is highly encouraged within empowered work groups of a competency community.

Competency-Based Practices Assignment of individuals to projects is based on professed and demonstrated competencies. Periodic reviews and revisions to workforce practices are enabled by integrating the competency development activities into the process improvement framework. Performance feedback to individuals is also based on competency objectives established by units for individuals. Unit objectives for competency development are translated into staffing practices that improve and grow competencies by sourcing, developing and motivating the right talent. Compensation and reward structures are evolved to address competency-based adjustments. Competency-based practices could be multidisciplinary or single discipline specific. If multidisciplinary, then adequate practices that support integration of competencies are visible. A combination of a strong supplier management process using the practices of SAM, CMMI-ACQ and CMMI-SVC constellations, together with competencies that are business imperatives within the strategic framework and intent of the organization, is used to deliver upon commitments. Competency-based practices within such a high leverage system include the ability to evaluate supplier processes and supplier work products. As a consequence, the following specific goal and specific practices are enabled:

IPPD Addition (Relevant only to CMMI-DEV constellation)[13]

SG3 Apply IPPD Principles

- SP3.1 **Establish the Project's Shared Vision**
- SP3.2 **Establish the Integrated Team Structure**
- SP3.3 **Allocate Requirements to Integrated Teams**
- SP3.4 **Establish Integrated Teams**
- SP3.5 **Ensure Collaboration among Interfacing Teams**

The practical sides to IPM as experienced with some of the author's best professional associations are as follows:

[13] IPPD addition has been removed from the CMMI-DEV V1.3. A new specific practice SP1.6 with the title Establish Teams has been included instead.

Integrated Project Management

1. Understand the project constraints in terms of what the critical project drivers and the critical-to-quality characteristics are.
2. Based on the knowledge and skills required to execute the project, identify a project team along with resource ramp-up and ramp-down plans.
3. Compose a process to govern the project execution along with adequate visibility and controls.
4. Conduct a project kick-off meeting with the relevant stakeholders.
5. Initiate the project execution using the organizational engineering and management practices with adequate levels of empowerment.
6. Ensure timely resolution of issues with adequate escalation mechanisms.

Display 5.10 Interpreting Integrated Project Management

Source: Adapted from SITARA Process JewelBox™ © SITARA Technologies Pvt. Ltd. 2002 with permission

How does Integrated Project Management transform its capability when the transition to capability level 2 (or the managed level) is made?

The organizational policy supports a psychologically safe work environment that in turn supports and encourages learning at all levels. Projects are governed by a policy that empowers team members to take the right decisions for the right reasons. In order to ensure that these decisions are congruent, individuals are trained in both the technical and management aspects of the organizational process. Adequate support information on skills and competencies, metrics contained in historical databases and tools and technologies required along with decision support systems are made available for the project to enable decision making. Decisions are supported by the management in a spirit of collaboration and teamwork. In short, projects set individuals up to succeed.

Individuals actively participate in learning and pursue learning opportunities. Competencies and skills that are acquired as a result of executing projects are transferred into the organization in periodic project and process retrospectives. A profile of knowledge, skills and abilities of individuals is maintained in a competency database and updated periodically. Such a competency database is used to engage or enroll individuals into projects at the time of team selection.

An organizational policy that promotes the growth of competency communities is visible. While the units focus on improving workforce capabilities through training and development, the organization focuses on competency development. By creating an awareness of workforce competencies through a published competency dictionary and information about available development opportunities, individuals embark on nominating themselves for proficiency development programs. These competency development programs are sourced from both internal and external sources. Such development initiatives address individual need fulfilling skills, knowledge and process abilities. Graduated learning opportunities are provided for individuals who are at different proficiency levels—beginners, intermediates and those at advanced stages of learning. Setting goals which may be out of reach, also called stretched goals, help ignite the human spirit and permit individuals to take charge of their competency development activities.

The organization supports the growth of competencies by actively supporting and funding the creation of competency communities. Such communities in turn apply the necessary peer pressure to help individuals take the initiative to ensure competency development. A useful by-product of competency communities is the identification of internal mentors and coaches who facilitate and help catalyze the learning process by vocalizing individual learning experiences. Mentors share lessons learnt by them from first-hand experiences and offer learning aids to hasten the process of competency development. Creation of a community of practice is also fostered to enable learning in formal settings through sharing of war stories. A great degree of emphasis is placed on developing individual capability.

Competency communities publish their development activities and integrate their learning into the overall organizational competency framework by providing information on the latest advances in their competencies, best practices, competency profiles and lessons learnt through newsletters. The individual's performance objectives are linked to growing organizational workforce competencies. Key results are measured and tracked against specific accomplishments in competency development.

Individuals are seen to contribute to intellectual activities like paper publication, writing technical white papers and filing patent applications. Where applicable, they participate on standards committees such as the IEEE and define both technology and process standards. They take keen interest in becoming members of professional bodies and technical societies. The organization actively supports and sponsors individual affiliations to professional bodies. To understand the extent of self-limitation imposed by the work environment, if any, an assessment question could be '*what are the avenues open to individuals in the organization to express their capabilities?*' The author's belief stems from a long-held fact that unless individuals are geared to contribute to professional journals and technical forums, they are not likely to grow beyond their present competence levels. Intellectual curiosity is what kindles the flames of competency development. Organizational learning has to do with individual learning at all levels in the organization, beginning right at the top. A feeling that '*no one does it better than us*' begins to take root. If IPPD addition is included in scope, such a qualitative transformation is required.

Management reviews, team meetings and progress reviews ensure timely conflict resolution and nurture integrative behaviors among individuals. The organizational process repository containing the approved process descriptions is updated and revised based on experience reports on the tailored process from practitioners. The process repository itself is placed under configuration management to ensure that the most recent process is available for use. In order to attain capability level 2 for IPM, EPPAT MIMOR needs to be institutionalized.

How does Integrated Project Management transform its capability when the transition to capability level 3 (or the defined level) is made?

Competency profiles established for individuals belonging to the different competency communities, together with workforce practices of recruitment, performance management, promotions, compensation, and so on, are used to develop competency-based workforce practices. Assignment of individuals to projects is based on professed and demonstrated competencies. Periodic reviews and revisions to workforce practices are enabled by integrating the competency development activities into the process improvement framework. Performance feedback to individuals is also based on competency objectives established by units for individuals. Unit objectives for competency development are translated into staffing practices that improve and build competencies by sourcing, developing and motivating the right talent. Compensation and reward structures are evolved to address competency-based adjustments.

Competency-based practices could be multidisciplinary or single discipline specific. If multidisciplinary, then adequate practices that support integration of competencies are visible.

The OPD captures best practices resulting from project use, applicable standards and procedures with necessary execution work aids such as templates, forms, usage instructions and the like. The process definition also includes a tailoring guideline to ensure that the process is made fit for use. Improvements to the process based on the tailored practices are actively explored using process improvement proposals. These practices are institutionalized to achieve generic goal 3 with the following two generic practices:

GG3 Institutionalize a Defined Process

GP3.1 **Establish a Defined Process**

GP3.2 **Collect Improvement Information**

It is difficult to justify and demonstrate IPM at a capability beyond level 3. From a theoretical perspective, the generic goal 4 and the related generic practices 4.1 and 4.2 need to be established for enabling IPM + IPPD at capability level 4.

GG4 Institutionalize a Quantitatively Managed Process

GP4.1 **Establish Quantitative Objectives for the Process**

GP4.2 **Stabilize Sub-Process Performance**

And to enable IPM + IPPD at capability level 5, the generic goal 5 and the associated generic practices 5.1 and 5.2 need to be institutionalized:

GG5 Institutionalize an Optimizing Process

GP5.1 **Ensure Continuous Process Improvement**

GP5.2 **Correct Root Causes of Problem**

It may be useful to point out that the specific practices of IPM in general enable the realization of GP2.7—'Identify and Involve Relevant Stakeholders'—across the 22 process areas of the CMMI-DEV, 6 process areas of the CMMI-ACQ constellation and 7 process areas of the CMMI-SVC constellation.

RISK MANAGEMENT (RSKM) CMMI-DEV, CMMI-ACQ AND CMMI-SVC

How does Risk Management look when it operates at a capability level 1 (or the performed level)?

Risk Management (RSKM) belongs to the project management category of the continuous representation of the three CMMI constellations. The purpose of Risk Management is to identify potential problems before they occur so that risk-handling activities can be planned and invoked as needed across the life of the product or project to mitigate adverse impacts on achieving objectives. The process of identification of potential problems and planning appropriate remedial or abatement actions to mitigate their adverse impact on the achievement of project objectives constitutes Risk Management.

Author's Musing

Risks don't announce their arrival! This makes the process of planning and resolving problems more of a real-time response with very little reaction time. Such responses would not be considered as indicative of a lower capability planning or Risk Management process. That is exactly the way most untried initiatives involving the adoption of new technologies which have no history of prior use evolve.

However, a learning entity would make use of a Risk Management repository to document and log the risks with the organizational response that best addresses project issues. Should similar risks be encountered either within the same project or across the organization, the process is now capable of delivering an adequate response.

The challenge however is to enable a query-based Risk Management repository that is based on keywords. What is suggested is to have a Risk Management repository that is organized according to the constraint of operation. A specific project response to a risk has to consider the context of operation, which may or may not be the same. I have also come across situations where the risk is a reality that would never mellow.

Example 1: Where the communication standards and the supporting hardware have to keep in step while the standards themselves get revised every quarter after an international review. And if one has to render software solutions in such a dynamic environment, there is bound to be very little relevance to the reuse of risk abatement practices since every risk is a new risk that has to have a contextual response.

Example 2: Where the organizational process response has to accommodate a lower-maturity customer process with very little regard to structured development.

While the emphasis of Risk Management practices appears to be on project management, the same practices could be applied to handling and managing technical risks as well. However, in the CMMI, the practices related to Decision Analysis and Resolution lend themselves very well to the management of technical risks by exploring alternative solutions.

Risk Management begins with the identification of the potential sources of risk and the category to which the risk belongs (high, medium or low for instance, or a specific phase in the life cycle where it is most likely to occur). Understanding the risk in quantitative terms using dimensions such as likelihood of occurrence, impact and phase in which the risk occurs is useful for facilitating decisions and abatement of activities. For example, the following could be a decision process for Risk Management:

LIST OF ISSUES	LIKELIHOOD	IMPACT	PHASE	RPN = L × I × P

Each of these can have a number ranging from 1 to 10 as follows:

Likelihood: Low (1–3), Medium (4–6), High (7–10)

Impact: Low (1–3), Medium (4–6), High (7–10)

Phase: Early life cycle (1–3), Mid-life cycle (4–6), End life cycle (7–10)

Risk priority number (RPN) is the product of likelihood, impact and phase (L × I × P).

- If RPN < 30, then the individual assigned the issue will document the necessary abatement procedure and resolve the issue.
- If 35 < RPN < 215, the team will evolve the best abatement strategy using a brainstorming session and diffuse the issue.
- If 250 < RPN < 1000, the team along with senior management will diffuse the issue along with the other categories impacting decision making.

> **Author's Musing**
>
> Quantifying risks in the above manner is often subjective and not very easy. This is because it is easy to have 100 percent knowledge from hindsight! As is well said, the rearview mirror is often much clearer than the windshield.

Use of professional and management judgment coupled with team competencies that establish confidence in the selected solution is a prerequisite for ensuring a good Risk Management strategy. Just because the RPN is in the 250–1000 range, it does not mean that the risk cannot be handled. Team expertise and competencies have to be leveraged to ensure appropriateness of the project response—most technology-intensive endeavors, which have no prior history of trial, have high risk factors. Doing so leads to the following specific goals and related practices which get designed into the process:

SG1 Prepare for Risk Management

SP1.1 **Determine Risk Sources and Categories**

SP1.2 **Define Risk Parameters**

SP1.3 **Establish a Risk Management Strategy**

SG2 Identify and Analyze Risks

SP2.1 **Identify Risks**

SP2.2 **Evaluate, Categorize and Prioritize Risks**

The project develops appropriate risk mitigation plans, explores alternatives and implements the best option. A coordinated action plan by involving the relevant stakeholders and using the practices of Project Planning and Project Monitoring and Control could be used to track progress made in the resolution of the impact of risk.

SG3 Mitigate Risks

SP3.1 **Develop Risk Mitigation Plans**

SP3.2 **Implement Risk Mitigation Plans**

The practical sides to Risk Management as experienced with some of the author's best professional associations are as follows:

Risk Management

1. Ensure that the team meets periodically during project execution, especially in the initial stages of project definition, to explore and identify all possible technical and management risks.
2. Maintain an updated list of risks encountered and potential risks that could manifest themselves based on project execution using a collaborative team approach.
3. Explore timely remedial steps with the involvement of subject matter experts to correct issues that impact the successful execution of the project.
4. Maintain a risk repository of known risk abatement procedures and strategies that have worked well for the organization while serving the project context.
5. Maintain a list of both common and special causes of risks that are known to impact the process.

Display 5.11 Interpreting Risk Management

Source: Adapted from SITARA Process JewelBox™ © SITARA Technologies Pvt. Ltd. 2002 with permission

How does Risk Management transform its capability when the transition to capability level 2 (or the managed level) is made?

An organizational policy defines a general description for acceptable Risk Management procedures, strategies and methods based on constraints of operation. The organizational process asset library is suggestive of the techniques that could be adopted for establishing a plan of action to handle specific categories of risks. Resources to enable an organizational response to handle and mitigate risks in terms of additional funding, prototyping tools, simulators, procurement of target or end-user platforms and the like are provided for the projects after a thorough cost–benefit analysis.

Well-defined responsibilities are allocated to subject matter expert teams to advise and mentor projects which have known tendencies to get into trouble. Individuals on the project are mentored and coached on specific aspects of the project by more experienced individuals. Techniques such as wideband Delphi are used to understand and develop a shared vision for gaining collective ownership of the planned risk mitigation steps. Escalation of risks to the most appropriate level of management responsibility is used in cases where a specific level of responsibility is unable to make a decision using guidelines established in decision analysis and the resolution process.

Realization of the ten generic practices of EPPAT MIMOR institutionalizes a capability level 2 or the managed level of capability for Risk Management.

How does Risk Management transform its capability when the transition to capability level 3 (or the defined level) is made?

At the defined level of capability, Risk Management involves a defined process for handling and addressing both organizational risks (mostly, common causes of variation) and project-specific risks (mostly, special causes of variation). Such definitions of risk categories are typically identified in a risk repository maintained in the process asset library as special causes and common causes. Process improvement opportunities are explored to mitigate and minimize their impact. The risk repository also identifies successful abatement procedures employed to handle similar situations in the past.

In doing so, generic goal 3 and the two generic practices which define the level 3 capability are institutionalized. They are as follows:

GG3 Institutionalize a Defined Process

GP3.1 Establish a Defined Process

GP3.2 Collect Improvement Information

How does Risk Management transform its capability when the transition to capability level 4 (or the quantitatively managed level) is made? Or, how does Risk Management demonstrate a high maturity measurement and analysis capability?

Quantitative objectives are established for the RPN, for instance, and are tracked to stay within acceptable bounds. If the RPN exceeds a defined threshold, a management process for rendering the necessary abatements is automatically invoked.

Maintaining a list of both the special and common causes of risk sources that could potentially manifest in the project as risks, and making use of the process improvement framework to insulate, isolate and minimize the impact of such instances in the future, helps stabilize project performance. It would be useful to highlight the fact that practices contained in Quantitative Project Management enable a higher-capability Risk Management at level 4. The generic goal and associated practices that render a capability level 4 for Risk Management are as follows:

GG4 Institutionalize a Quantitatively Managed Process

GP4.1 Establish Quantitative Objectives for the Process

GP4.2 Stabilize Sub-Process Performance

How does Risk Management transform its capability when the transition to capability level 5 (or the optimizing level) is made? Or, how does Risk Management demonstrate a high maturity measurement and analysis capability?

Risk Management strongly complements Project Planning and Project Monitoring and Control practices. Together, they are ideal candidates to resolve common cause variations when they occur. It would be useful to stress that practices contained in Causal Analysis and Resolution should be explored to enable the realization of a capability level 5 for Risk Management. The generic goal and associated practices that render a capability level 5 for Risk Management are as follows:

GG5 Institutionalize an Optimizing Process

GP5.1 Ensure Continuous Process Improvement

GP5.2 Correct Root Causes of Problems

DECISION ANALYSIS AND RESOLUTION (DAR) CMMI-DEV, CMMI-ACQ AND CMMI-SVC

How does Decision Analysis and Resolution look when it operates at a capability level 1 (or the performed level)?

Decision Analysis and Resolution (DAR) belongs to the support category of the continuous representation of the CMMI constellations. The purpose of DAR is to analyze possible decisions using a formal evaluation process that evaluates identified alternatives against established criteria. DAR establishes an evaluation capability using which the most appropriate solution that is *fit for use* can be selected when several alternatives exist. The rigor and formalism of evaluation could vary depending upon the circumstances. Both numeric and non-numeric criteria can be used. The most common use of formal evaluation methods is for evaluating design alternatives, for evaluation of COTS solutions prior to integration into the final product and to decide upon the choice of development/integration platform. DAR guidelines can be established for a range of organizational processes covering the entire life cycle. While one could use the practices of Risk Management process area to evaluate technical issues and risks, evaluation capabilities within DAR establish a strong foundation of knowledge management in the organization.

First and foremost, one needs to decide whether the issue is non-trivial justifying formal evaluation. Such an assessment of the need to apply a formal evaluation technique ought to be the starting point. Technical issues could result as a consequence of a change to an existing constraint of operation (e.g., cost, time, quality, scope or performance). Or, such evaluations might be based on decision factors established to grow organizational capability in specific areas where the organization might want to improve. SITARA DAR guideline is an example of one such decision support system.

Other establishing evaluation criteria could include choices surrounding use of simulators, development of prototypes or proof of concepts, evaluating the merits and demerits of alternative supporting technologies (e.g., .NET or Java), use of COTS solutions and such. Since exercise of professional judgment is expected in all decisions, it would be very difficult to offer a canned solution on how this is to be done.

AUTHOR'S MUSING

On a different note, this process area would be slightly difficult to assess on an appraisal since a majority of such decisions are made by the customer and alternatives are explored in the requirements elicitation process during a project scoping activity by the sales and support personnel and firmed up much before one actually uses the development process to develop the solution. So, technically a site could justify that these practices are outside the scope of the development process.

Alternative solutions that best support the technical risk abatement strategy would be pursued in the solution. One or more of the evaluation options available among prototyping, simulations and use of decision trees could be explored before selecting the solution. An exercise such as this would result in clarifying the reasons leading to the selection of a particular solution. This is useful as an engineering record because when the design needs to be revisited later on by professionals who may not be the ones who developed the design, such engineering records could serve as an effective illustration of the thought process leading to convergence on the identified solution. Recording such design decisions in an engineering record is more of a good professional practice that helps fellow professionals along the way. In most organizations which are sensitive to patents and intellectual property, such an engineering record would serve the institution well in any defense leading to filing of innovations as patents/disclosures. These practices enable the realization of the following:

SG1 Evaluate Alternatives

- SP1.1 **Establish Guidelines for Decision Analysis**
- SP1.2 **Establish Evaluation Criteria**
- SP1.3 **Identify Alternative Solutions**
- SP1.4 **Select Evaluation Methods**
- SP1.5 **Evaluate Alternatives**[14]
- SP1.6 **Select Solutions**

The practical sides to DAR as experienced with some of the author's best professional associations are as follows:

Decision Analysis And Resolution

When to Apply DAR? The Decision Factors ...

1. When there are multiple issues that need to be balanced while arriving at the final solution [RISK MANAGEMENT]
2. When the underlying reasons for common and special causes of variation have to be understood before eliminating them from the process [PROCESS]
3. When multiple demands from stakeholders have to be accommodated requiring a trade-off [REQUIREMENTS MANAGEMENT]
4. In early stages of Project Planning when multiple options of realizing the solution can be considered [PROJECT PLANNING]
5. When an initiative is being explored for the first time with no organizational memory or experience [CORE COMPETENCY]
6. When multiple solutions can be rendered based on the possible domain choices [DOMAIN]
7. When postmortems or technical reviews offer untried or unexplored options with the potential to make the next release more efficient [LEARNING]
8. When a legacy application or a prototype can be studied before making choices on the final solution [EXPERIMENTS]
9. When considerable investments have to be made much before the realization of a product [MANAGEMENT]

Display 5.12 Interpreting Decision Analysis and Resolution

Source: Adapted from SITARA Process JewelBox™ © SITARA Technologies Pvt. Ltd. 2002 with permission

[14] Practice title appears as "Evaluate Alternative Solutions" in version 1.3 across all three constellations. There is no noticeable/perceptible change to the informative content associated with this practice and therefore to its interpretation.

As DAR has such diverse applications, one possible way to implement its intent is released from the SITARA Process JewelBox™ to get a head start.

Released from SITARA Process JewelBox™

How to apply the Decision Analysis and Resolution Guideline?

When the above decision factors are true, either singularly or in a combination:

- List the relevant decision factors in order of degree of importance.
- Explore the process assets for a relevant solution, otherwise use the SITARA DAR guidelines for each of the above as follows:

SITARA DAR Guidelines

RISK MANAGEMENT

LIST OF ISSUES	LIKELIHOOD	IMPACT	PHASE	RPN = L × I × P

1. Each of these can have a number ranging from 1 to 10, as follows:
   Likelihood: Low (1–3), Medium (4–6), High (7–10)
   Impact: Low (1–3), Medium (4–6), High (7–10)
   Phase: Early life cycle (1–3), Mid-life cycle (4–6), End life cycle (7–10)
2. Risk priority number (RPN) is the product of likelihood, impact and phase (L × I × P).
   If RPN < 30, then the individual assigned the issue will document the necessary abatement procedure and resolve the issue.
   If 35 < RPN < 215, the team will evolve the best abatement strategy using a brainstorming session and diffuse the issue.
   If 250 < RPN < 1000, the team, along with senior management, will diffuse the issue along with the other categories impacting decision making.

PROCESS

1. Conduct a brainstorming session with all stakeholders to list possible root causes of variation in execution outcomes.
2. Segregate the root causes to be either in process or outside the process.
3. For all the in-process root causes, classify them as either a common cause or a special cause of variation.

4. For special cause of variation determine the process fix that will insulate, isolate and eliminate such occurrences in the future.
5. For all common causes, conduct a Pareto analysis to identify the critical few from the trivial many.
6. Explore a time-bound implementation program to ensure a resolution of the critical few root causes with well-defined ownership.
7. If unique ownership cannot be identified, escalate it to the senior management.

REQUIREMENTS MANAGEMENT

1. List all the requirements from multiple stakeholders.
2. Prioritize the requirements using Joint Application Development sessions with the customer and the stakeholders.
3. Obtain team consensus on the feasibility of requirements.
4. Establish rough-order magnitude of work along with optimistic and pessimistic estimates.
5. Explore multitasking options and/or phased delivery and negotiate a solution.
6. If the negotiation does not result in ownership, escalate the matter to senior management.

PROJECT PLANNING

1. List the options available for consideration.
2. Determine the constraint of operation (cost, quality, schedule or scope).
3. For multiple constraints of operation, rank them in order of priority and significance.
4. Use brainstorming session with customer and stakeholders to decide if the available prioritized options result in ownership.
5. If ownership does not result, escalate the matter to senior management.

CORE COMPETENCY

1. Determine rough-order estimates for the solution schedule.
2. Determine if the available time to explore options is less than 10 percent of the solution schedule.
3. If the exploration time is more than 10 percent of the solution schedule then escalate the matter to senior management.
4. Use the build-buy decision-making process along with a knowledge-skill-ability assessment (KSA assessment).
5. Apply the SITARA 10W5D competency hierarchy and domain competency sandwich models, as applicable.
6. Determine candidate suppliers/vendors.
7. Apply the supplier selection process by evaluating supplier competencies and prior history of execution.

8. For COTS evaluation, use SITARA's package selection and integration process (http://www.SITARATECH.com/rsn_bp_html.htm).
9. If the solution does not have a defined ownership, then escalate the matter to senior management.

DOMAIN

1. List the domain options in which the solution can potentially be rendered, for example, in hardware, in software, in other systems (include reuse and COTS) or using custom software.
2. Explore if COTS solutions are applicable; use SITARA's package selection and integration process (http://www.SITARATECH.com/rsn_bp_html.htm).
3. Conduct a trade-off analysis based on a cost–benefit analysis to determine solution fitness.
4. Establish the interoperability of solution mix.
5. Explore if there are other decision factors that require to be balanced and apply the necessary decision steps.
6. Baseline and establish a requirements reconfirmation with the customer or stakeholder.
7. Assign unique ownership or ensure appropriate escalation to senior management.

LEARNING

1. List potential opportunities for improvement based on postmortems or technical reviews.
2. Identify the strengths in the current solution that could be leveraged.
3. Identify and archive the solutions into a reusable library (knowledge repository) based on team analysis.
4. Ensure use of knowledge repository in subsequent development.

EXPERIMENTS

1. Determine the rough-order estimates for the solution schedule.
2. Conduct a study of the legacy or prototype in parallel.
3. If this study is more than 10 percent of the solution schedule, then escalate the matter to senior management.
4. Identify and list the core and non-core features/functions of the legacy prototype.
5. Prioritize the core and non-core features along with technology and support choices that will drive the new solution.
6. Consider any other decision factors that require to be balanced and apply the necessary decision steps.

MANAGEMENT

1. When any of the decision options results in management escalation, determine if the escalation has a reasonable pros–cons analysis.
2. Check if a decision made earlier is effective to address the current requirements.
3. Study the impact of decisions on profitability, core competency, branding, image, organizational values and future potential.

4. Is the management willing to write off the money that will be spent? If no, then block the decision option with a no-go. Otherwise, consider the management imperatives before waving the green flag.

Additional Notes

Brief descriptions:

SITARA 10W5D Competency Hierarchy Model

The 10W5D is a structured competency hierarchy model that identifies organizational competencies as those that have a span of at least ten wide competencies (10W). Each competency is further organized into five-level-deep capabilities (5D). For example, Program Management, Software Engineering and Reliability Engineering, could be the ten wide or broad categories of competencies. And within each one of these competencies the organization needs to identify at least a minimum of five different capabilities to demonstrate that the competency is truly enabled. Within Program Management, for example: the potential candidates for 5D are the following:

- Product Specification
- Design Management
- Product Line Management
- Programming Languages
- Communication Strategies

Hence, it is only when the organizational competency description for program management demonstrates adequate capability within the identified 5D can its true potential as a competency be realized. In fact, this is a fan-out process wherein each one of the 5Ds themselves can be further broken up into mini-competencies. For example, Honda's competency with small engines is used to develop a product line of lawn movers, motorcycles, snow blowers, and so on.

While developing competencies is important, what is more important is to recognize and build efficiencies within the acquired competencies by becoming sensitive to the domains of operation. This leads to the following.

SITARA Domain Competency Sandwich Model

The 10W5D is based on yet another SITARA innovation: the Domain Competency Sandwich (Figure 5.11).

The reasoning behind the Domain Competency Sandwich model is as follows:

Competency development has a bearing upon the domains of expertise that the organization intends to build. And when a focused combination of knowledge, skills and talent is applied to the domains of specialization, competencies tend to grow. The enabler for acquiring knowledge is a learning mechanism that is supported by the organization. Learning mechanisms could include formal training programs, conferences, symposia, and so on. Skills are rendered meaningful if, and only if, they are supported by adequate tools and technology which the organization has to acquire. Individuals have a certain natural ability which is called talent which gets perfected by repeated practice through effective techniques and

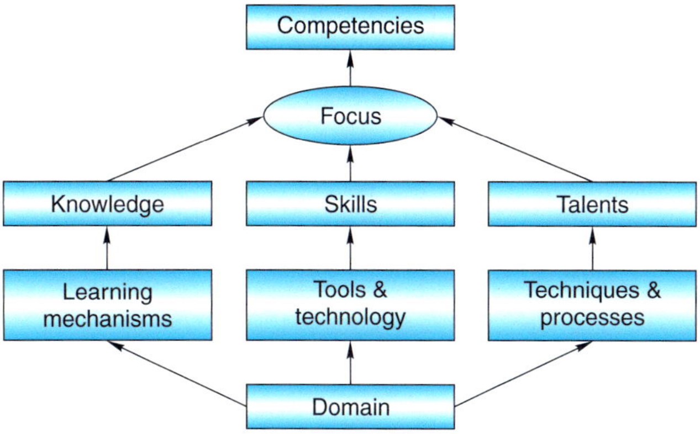

Fig. 5.11 SITARA Domain Competency Sandwich Model

Source: Adapted from SITARA Process JewelBox™ © SITARA Technologies Pvt. Ltd. 2002 with permission

processes. One of the most important factors that help to improve productivity is gaining familiarity with the types of problems encountered and solutions developed based on practice, and more practice. SITARA 10W5D can be applied after a deterministic and inferential evaluation of the specific knowledge, skills and talent is made.

Probing Questions

- Are guidelines for decision analysis provided within the process infrastructure effective to accommodate project constraints and risks?
- Does the evaluation criterion make use of potential opportunities for reusing decisions already made and that are known to work?
- Where necessary, are alternative solutions identified for the project's unique characteristics using brainstorming or similar group activities?
- Are evaluation methods selected based on the constraints of operation unique to the project (e.g., cost, quality, schedule, scope and performance)?
- Are alternatives evaluated on the basis of evaluation of circumstances and the context leading to identifying the most appropriate solution?
- Are solutions selected based on a documented rationale?

Author's Musing

"Why not have the specific goals of DAR as a Generic Practice instead of a PA?" This question was asked during one of the 'Introduction to CMMI' courses I taught and it set me thinking!

(Contd)

This would be my reasoning: 'Evaluate Alternatives', which is the only specific goal in DAR, has a 'greater' relevance while making 'engineering' decisions and for evaluating the choices available to make the following decisions:

1. Do we render the solution in software or hardware (system)?
2. Do we know the technical risks involved and what if any are the alternatives (Risk Management PA concerns itself to PP and PMC aspects . there must be an equivalent for engineering as well)?
3. For competency management: Do we build technical capability internally or use the buy option in the make-buy-reuse analysis?
4. For purposes of domain engineering: Do we outsource the solution development or grow a competency community?
5. How do we build the component interfaces? What should be the protocol or the message structure (more of a technical design issue)?

And so on .

Therefore, as the relevance of this specific goal on DAR—'Evaluate Alternatives'—is more for evaluating alternative 'technical decisions', keeping it as a generic practice is not an appropriate choice for a process design view of the fact that 'generic practices' must apply to every process area in the CMMI.

How does Decision Analysis and Resolution transform its capability when the transition to capability level 2 (or the managed level) is made?

Commitment to perform typically involves establishing organizational policies to set expectations in terms of how to use the practices contained in DAR guidelines, executive management sponsorship and assigned responsibilities for advising on and coordinating the implementation of DAR practices.

Well thought out plans for timely remedial steps to ensure the right response to handling the technical risk using appropriate resources and techniques (such as prototypes, simulators, technology platforms and tools) are offered within the institutionalized development environment.

Specific individuals who are quick to learn technologies and tools are also assigned the role of probing and scoping applicability of tools and technologies that the marketplace has to offer in what is termed software resource centers or SWAT (skilled with advanced technology) teams. Such individuals are provided the necessary orientation and training on the strategic intent of the organization and their job in the organization is to serve as antennae to play a leading role in articulating the technical architecture. Their skills are often deployed in the early stages of Project Planning and execution so that the right technical decisions on architecture and design are made upfront rather than as a technical risk abatement step.

Should technical priorities overrule earlier decisions made on the choice of technology or of the architecture or of the design, configuration management is used to enable an effective archival of knowledge base of decisions resulting for the exercise of professional judgment on the newer solution offering. Decisions leading to such changes and prioritization are documented for project use. Appropriate levels of escalation for decisions are enabled within a management oversight process. Being a level 3 process area, empowerment within the scope of other process areas which are described in this chapter takes note of the most appropriate level at which such decisions are best made in a nurturing, collaborative work environment. Within the CMMI, the ten generic practices of EPPAT MIMOR establish the minimum criteria for DAR to qualify as a managed process at capability level 2.

How does Decision Analysis and Resolution transform its capability when the transition to capability level 3 (or the defined level) is made?

At the level 3 capability, a formal DAR guideline is documented, as illustrated earlier in an example, within the OSSP. Practitioners' experience in using the DAR guidelines serves as a basis for improving its effectiveness. The two generic practices that support a level 3 capability while fulfilling the generic goal 3 are as follows:

GG3 Institutionalize a Defined Process

- GP3.1 **Establish a Defined Process**
- GP3.2 **Collect Improvement Information**

It is difficult to justify and demonstrate DAR at a capability beyond level 3. From a theoretical perspective, the generic goal 4 and the related generic practices 4.1 and 4.2 need to be established for enabling DAR at capability level 4.

GG4 Institutionalize a Quantitatively Managed Process

- GP4.1 **Establish Quantitative Objectives for the Process**
- GP4.2 **Stabilize Sub-Process Performance**

And to enable DAR at capability level 5, the generic goal 5 and the associated generic practices 5.1 and 5.2 need to be institutionalized:

GG5 Institutionalize an Optimizing Process

- GP5.1 **Ensure Continuous Process Improvement**
- GP5.2 **Correct Root Causes of Problem**

6

Quantitatively Managed Level—Interpreting the Level 4 CMMI Process Areas

AUTHOR'S MUSING

SITARA's surmise is that level 4 is about maintaining good control on Cost of Poor Quality (COPQ) and therefore minimizing the impact of variation arising out of special causes. So, if there is one metric that a level 4 must consciously collect and minimize, it should be the COPQ. High maturity is nothing more than a continuity of level 3 practices with quantitative and statistical management. The notion of process stability and process capability is enabled at level 3 by the relevant CMMI model practices. Noise in the system is minimized due to level 3 practices and these practices should serve as foundation on which high maturity is built as an extension

CHARACTERISTICS OF A LEVEL 4 PROCESS (QUANTITATIVELY MANAGED PROCESS)

We will review high-maturity concepts that are common to all three constellations of the CMMI in Chapters 6 and 7. In order to prove that the process has matured to a level 4 status as being quantitatively managed, one of the prerequisites is that the causes of process variation and their trend (pattern or behavior) within the actual use of the defined process established at a maturity level 3, must be known. For software, one of the most important pieces of information that organizations lack even when such quantitative analysis has been rendered is a *list of factors* that should exist as sufficiency conditions for a process to display a certain behavior. For example, when establishing schedule estimation accuracy or cost performance index of Project Planning under a control chart, it is not enough to show data points collected over a period of time lie within the control limits using adequate samples. It is also important to qualify these limits with a list of factors—actually, the facilitating factors—which help the project to perform within the control limits that have been established. Examples of such a list would include skill and competency levels of resources used on the project, customer's process maturity profile, correlation of special cause variations to requirements stability, adequacy of the project kickoff process for effective project orientation, project complexity based on a wideband Delphi or other brainstorming techniques.

Examples of contextual information which best qualify the control limits of a control chart include the following:

Project environment description

- Description of productivity enhancement tools institutionalized
- Description of development and testing tools used on projects
- Description of tools used to perform quantitative analysis of the process
- Description of the deployment of the process infrastructure for use by projects

Data collection

- Specific data collection process and templates used for raw data capture
- Tools integrated across project life cycle for data collection, analysis and reporting
- Training available for all relevant stakeholders to minimize errors in data collection, representation and analysis

Age of the metric

- Periodicity of data collection within and across life-cycle phases of projects in execution
- Controls for measuring and negotiating outlier and outdated data
- Periodicity of review of the development and management environment and revision of the process capability baselines

> **Author's Musing**
>
> It is my belief that software metrics that contribute to establishing current process performance baselines have to be periodically assessed for correctness and age of the metric (how old is the data?). Beware of relying entirely on past performance baselines while dealing with software metrics!

Without capturing the project context, knowing or establishing the control limits makes for little sense. Practically, most of the facilitating factors enabling process capability on software development initiatives tend to be qualitative, subjective and good-in-the-moment type of information; nevertheless, it very useful to take note of the facilitating factors. The facilitating factors generally tend to be the sufficient conditions and not the *necessary conditions* for a process to display a mature behavior. Necessary conditions must document the systems, tools and the defined process. Necessary conditions are like the needs—those which *must* be present. But the sufficiency conditions are more like the wants and should coexist with the needs for the realization of a high process capability. Typically, such facilitating process conditions must be verified in process audits using audit checklists. Even though such checklists use qualitative attributes of the process, they represent the most important process information, without which the control charts and the numbers contained in them are rendered meaningless.

A non-software example to highlight this point: if Ram is asked how long it takes him to get to work from home, Ram can be given a quantitative *forecast or estimate* based on *a trend* from past experience—say 10 minutes. Now, this estimate is actually based on several factors, the sufficiency conditions, such as what time of the day, horsepower of the car, the route taken *repeatedly*, number of signal lights encountered along the way, traffic density information, knowledge of any major road repairs and such. These sufficiency conditions must exist together with the necessary conditions: that the average speed of the car is 60 km/hr and that a defined process to drive the car is fulfilled. Importance of knowing the sufficiency conditions actually leads to a very important process attribute, namely *to be able to recognize common causes from the special causes of variation*. Also note that if the original estimates involved are small-value numbers, even a negligibly small difference in actual values (or outcomes) leads to a large enough deviation. For example: if it took 12 minutes instead of the estimated 10 minutes for this journey, then the deviation is 20 percent. Even though such deviations are statistically significant, in software terms, there is enough evidence to believe that such deviations are not often practically relevant.

When the effects of process changes have to be discerned, use of hypothesis tests and two-sample *t-tests* on process data resulting from before and after the process change proves useful. While describing how to scale up PPQA to capability level 4 and 5 in chapter 04, we have learned that hypothesis testing is a statistical technique to rule out randomness in an outcome based on data arising out of ambiguous circumstances. There has to be a well-reasoned basis for dealing with and negotiating outliers and out-of-date information. Knowing the natural process capability limits is obviously much better than taking a pure statistical view of variation for software because the causes of variation involving software development initiatives are mostly special causes from the classical SPC's point of view. Process stability is only as good as it can be on projects which have to deal with untried technology/domain, high rate of requirements churn due to multiple stakeholders, high risk of obsolescence of standards and infrastructure, research projects exploring solutions to ill-defined problems and situations where a high degree of collaboration on product development is required among differing process capabilities. Unfortunately, nothing significant can be done to remove their influences on variation involving such projects even if the best of processes can be defined.

As the causes of variation are primarily *special cause* in a level 4 process, software metrics such as effort estimation accuracy, size estimation accuracy, complexity, post-release defects, productivity, cycle time reduction and the myriad of other metrics that are often collected must be understood as operating within a known range of values or band of values. There is no single number such as the mean or average that can objectively define its identity. Sample mean is a point estimate or a single numerical estimate for the population mean. Standard deviation of the mean, also known as the standard error of mean (SE mean), is a good indicator for the reliability of using the sample mean as an estimate of the population mean. Lower the value of SE mean, the better it is. A level 4 process establishes and uses confidence intervals for the mean to account for the special cause variations besides being a better estimate.

A 95% confidence interval for the mean containing the natural process average is typically used to define the upper and lower specification limits for the process and for goal setting. Prediction models can then be established based on the factors or predictors (multiple regression) defining the dependent variable using regression equations, usually linear regression equations.

AUTHOR'S MUSING

Factors (predictors) in a regression model must be chosen such that they have negligible influence due to special cause variations. Variation, if any, ought to be mostly due to common cause whose effects are controlled with effective process management. If the predictors are themselves useless, then how can the predicted value be of any worth?

Unlike deterministic models encountered in natural sciences which describe the connection between independent variables and a dependent variable uniquely, for example $E = mc^2$, prediction models in software are probabilistic. A probabilistic model inherently suffers from random errors. Errors in measurement are due to residuals besides rounding-off errors. The regression equation establishes the relationship of the predicted variable and its predictor variables. The strength of a linear relationship between the predicted variable and the predictor variables is often understood using the coefficient of determination or R^2, which is nothing but the square of the sample Pearson correlation coefficient, r. *Why is correlation so important in software?* There is so much of a relationship between one set of process data and a derived measure that it impacts. An example is organizational COPQ and the different phase-wise rework costs. Another is that between one process measure such as review or inspection rate with another process measure such as phase containment effectiveness. Such relationships are useful to know if goal setting has to be meaningful and if reliable process prediction is to be rendered. Correlations also help us to know when adjusting and controlling a process should be considered and when it does not make sense. For example: When there is either a perfectly linear relationship or no relationship at all in scatter plots, then a correlation analysis summarizes the relationship. *Does the relationship show nonlinear or unequal variability in a scatter plot?* In such cases correlation can be misleading. When *bivariate* data need to be studied, two basic tools that are useful are *correlation analysis* to establish the strength of the relationship between the factors and *regression analysis* to predict or control one of the variables using the other one. Prior to engaging in either a correlation analysis or regression analysis, hypothesis testing must be conducted. Hypothesis testing looks for possible relationships that might exist in the data in order to decide if the relationship is significant or is due to randomness alone. More reasons for the importance of correlation of software measures are established with examples in Chapter 7 drawn from observations made by the author while appraising sites to high maturity.

AUTHOR'S MUSING

The mechanics of statistical analysis of software data is often delegated to a tool such as Minitab. While engineers involved in process management often learn the mechanics of using statistical packages in a Six Sigma tutorial, the logic behind the numbers is seldom comprehended. We shall devote a small section in what follows to understand the logic behind the numbers that statistical tools spew out using raw data.

R^2 is a quantitative measure defining the ratio of the explained variation to the total variation. The higher the R^2 value, the better is the model. When the coefficient of determination is greater than

70 percent, it is generally considered that the prediction model is adequately represented by its predictors. The adjusted coefficient of determination or R^2 (adjusted) is more accurate as it takes into account the sample size and the number of independent variables (predictors).

The usefulness of a multiple linear regression equation for prediction is also understood with the *F* value, which is the ratio of the mean square regression and mean square residual. Stated differently, *F* value is the ratio of the explained variation (regression variation) and the unexplained variation (residual variation) of the prediction model. So, the distinction between R^2 and *F* is that R^2 uses the total variation whereas *F* uses the unexplained variation alone in the ratio. Therefore, the higher the *F* value the better is the prediction model. Mean square residual is the sum of square deviations between the observed and predicted values divided by the degrees of freedom of the residuals. Sum of square deviations must obviously be 0, if the predicted and the observed values are the same. Mean square values of the regression and residual are therefore good indicators of the strength of the prediction model. If five factors are required to predict the value of a dependent variable, the degrees of freedom for the regression is 5.

While using regression models it is important to consider predictors that can be quantified. Even when a regression equation demonstrates a high R^2 adjusted value, note that in software such regression models still cannot explain the dependent variable fully. As an example, let us take the following regression equation for organizational cost of poor quality with an R^2 adjusted value of 100%, a very high value indeed:

$$\text{Org COPQ} = 0.147 + 1.04 \times (\text{Reqts. COPQ}) + 0.679 \times (\text{Design COPQ}) \\ + 0.998 \times (\text{CUT COPQ}) + 1.00 \times (\text{Test COPQ})$$

Yet, the prediction equation for Org COPQ is not fully resolved since it is logical to note that Org COPQ is affected by at least the following noise factors: elicitation techniques, requirements volatility, requirements complexity, requirements clarity, requirements to design traceability, design modularity, coupling of interfaces, cohesion of modules, coder experience, unit-testing efficiency and several others. To keep the example complete, the complete regression analysis from a high-maturity process is presented in Figure 6.1. Take particular note of the high R^2 adjusted value at 100% and the *F* value.

The *p*-values for the coefficients of Reqt. COPQ, Design COPQ, CUT COPQ and Test COPQ (the four predictors) are 0.000, indicating that they are significantly related to organization COPQ. The *P*-value (0.000) in Figure 6.1 shows that the model estimated by the regression procedure is significant at an alpha level of 0.05 (95% confidence level). While the regression equation modeling Org. COPQ fits the data well, as there are several unquantifiable parameters that influence the true value of Org. COPQ, it remains an approximation.

Prediction models in software are always going to be approximate since there are numerous noise factors which influence the predicted value that can never be quantitatively known. Prediction models based on a regression model are always conditional predictions, since the dependent variable depends on the range of values that the independent variable can take. Prediction of future values of Org COPQ can be made if and only if the future values of the regression or independent variables are known.

Admitting that the estimated or predicted value is not exact, we therefore use confidence intervals since approximate is not good enough.

Regression analysis: Org COPQ versus Reqt. COPQ, design COPQ, CUT COPQ, test COPQ

The regression equation is

Org COPQ = 0.147 + 1.04 Reqt. COPQ + 0.679 Design COPQ + 0.998 CUT COPQ + 1.00 Test COPQ

Predictor	Coef	SE Coef	T	F
Constant	0.1470	0.2227	0.66	0.538
Reqt. COPQ	1.03542	0.04228	24.49	0.000
Design COPQ	0.67922	0.03940	17.24	0.000
CUT COPQ	0.998249	0.009767	102.20	0.000
Test COPQ	1.00440	0.00756	132.00	0.000

S = 0.00679366 R-Sq = 100.0% R-Sq (adj.) = 100.0%

Analysis of variance

Source	DF	SS	MS	F	P
Regression	4	94.371	23.593	511176.82	0.000
Residual error	5	0.000	0.000		
Total	9	94.371			

Source	DF	Seq SS
Reqt. COPQ	1	43.804
Design COPQ	1	49.715
CUT COPQ	1	0.036
Test COPQ	1	0.815

Fig. 6.1 [MIMOS 2009]: Regression Analysis Used to Predict Organizational COPQ

Source: Q3 2009 Process Capability Analysis Report MIMOS Berhad, Malaysia, a site appraised by SITARA Technologies at CMMI-DEV V1.2 Level 5 (Continuous Representation) in October 2009. Reproduced with permission.

Author's Musing

Wrong use of prediction models would make one conclude that the current emphasis of prediction seems to be restricted to establish regression equation with which to predict the outcome variable. One might argue that it is quite possible that one variable could very well serve as basis to predict the outcome variable of a completely different metric even though its regression equation is not known! Example: PCE of 100% in CUT can predict a 100% first-pass yield in integration testing. 100% PCE in CUT is possible if unit test cases have been designed correctly. Regression equations become necessary and useful in situations where such ideal values can never be realized. They become even more desirable when prediction is to be based on more than one factor. Good prediction models must use multiple controlled and stable factors or predictors.

It is useful to draw the attention of the reader to the often misunderstood difference between confidence interval and prediction interval. Confidence interval is for the mean; prediction interval is for individual predictions that are made using the regression equation. Prediction interval must therefore contain the confidence interval. Confidence intervals specify a region around the sample average to reflect randomness of sampling. We do not need to survey the entire population if we use confidence intervals. The confidence interval suggests that the sample average could be in error in either directions because of variability and sample size chosen to estimate the population mean. The larger the sample size, the smaller is the confidence interval, as it would estimate the mean more closely. Using sample data to make probability-based statements about the population is called statistical inference. Confidence interval is an interval computed from the data in such a way that there is a known probability of including the unknown population parameter of interest. A normal variable will be within 2 standard deviations from the mean approximately 95% of the time. When samples are used, standard deviation of the sample average is less than the standard deviation of the population by $1/\sqrt{(n)}$, where n is the sample size.

Author's Musing

Sample sizes typically in excess of 30 are useful to make prediction more accurate. Software projects usually suffer the limitations that the number of baseline opportunities, which is the best time to draw measurements, is limited in number. Ingenuity of the process engineer is called for while designing the most realistic measurement baseline opportunity and I have found that the lowest practical level where measurements can be made meaningfully is at the component level. When measures are made at the component level instead at the function or program level, the number of measurement opportunities increases significantly—much beyond the desirable 30 sample points.

Recognition of the above facts and enabling a quantitative understanding of the process based on hard data is what level 4 process maturity is all about. We will now review the two process areas that make up the level 4 maturity. In a sense a 'culture of quantitative management' prevails.

Two process areas at level 4 are common to the three constellations and are contained in CMF:

- Organizational Process Performance (OPP) [CMMI-DEV, CMMI-ACQ, CMMI-SVC]
- Quantitative Project Management (QPM) [CMMI-DEV, CMMI-ACQ, CMMI-SVC]

ORGANIZATIONAL PROCESS PERFORMANCE (OPP) CMMI-DEV, CMMI-ACQ AND CMMI-SVC

How does Organizational Process Performance look when it operates at a capability level 1 (or the performed level)?

Organizational Process Performance (OPP) belongs to the high-maturity process management category of the continuous representation of the CMMI. The fundamental practices that enable a capability level 1 for OPP establish an ability to maintain a quantitative understanding of the performance of the process models in use. When the specific practices of OPP are enabled into the process infrastructure, process areas belonging to levels 2 and 3 are enabled to perform at a higher capability. Such enablement of growth in capability of the lower-level maturity process areas by merely enacting the level 4 process area practices is one of the most useful features of the CMMI that actually goes to suggest the philosophy behind its process design—*capability improves as organizational maturity improves.*

Needless to emphasize that such an understanding of process performance is possible only when projects are sensitive to collecting and providing valid execution data. Typical execution data or process parameters that are of interest to any development process are as follows:

- Effort (planned and actual) in time to provide effort variation
- Cost (budgeted and actual) across the different life-cycle phases to compute and collect the cost performance index which is a ratio of budgeted cost to the actual cost
- Schedule (planned and actual) across the different life-cycle phases to understand the extent of schedule variation
- Phase-wise error and defect data to enable insights into phase containment effectiveness, defect density and in-phase defect containment effectiveness
- Productivity across life-cycle phases (which can be understood in terms of extent of cycle time reduction instead of work product size produced per day)
- Post-release defect arrival rate
- Number of change or modification requests
- Effort to time ratio (ETR) by phase as a leading indicator to assess likelihood of on-time project completion based on effort expended and elapsed time

A qualitative inference of the CUPRIMDSO or FURPS (which were introduced earlier in the book while discussing Process and Product Quality Assurance practices) could also be collected.

Some of the other measures that might be of interest are as follows:

- Number of best practices resulting from the project
- Number of lessons learnt and the nature of risks encountered during the execution of the project
- Process tailoring resulting from an understanding of common cause variation in execution outcomes (primarily due to the *voice-of-process (VOP)*) and process definitions to address special cause variation (due to the *voice-of-customer (VOC)*)
- Number of instances referred from the reuse repository and number of instances committed to the reuse repository across the life cycle
- Updated lists of common and special causes of variation
- Defect density measures in terms of common cause and special cause

This list is limited to the imagination of the process owners and the objectives behind the measurement. The key point to note is that the measures collected and analyzed need to have an impact on establishing an understanding of the process performance.

The place to start is to identify the specific practices of the level 2 and level 3 process areas that lend themselves to measurement and statistical analysis. An indication of such a possibility can be had by examining the extent of variation of these practices and the influences, if any, of special and common causes. There could be a situation that the cause of variation has a team behavioral pattern or an individual's idiosyncrasies which cannot be addressed using a process. Such instances should be treated differently.

From the author's professional engagements, most level 4 and level 5 issues seem to suggest that a vast majority of the problems are management problems and not so much process problems—*otherwise, it is very difficult to believe that a defined process (level 3) was institutionalized in the first place!* Much worse, some of the issues or problems are self-inflicted or pseudo-problems. Meaning: there is no problem at all; it is just that projects want to appear complex to look different in the management's eye just to escape from the clutches of following a process! Such projects are most definitely not candidates for statistical analysis, but require process mentoring and some tough talk from senior management before data from their execution can be used.

Author's Musing

If you don't know what your problems are, then there is no way you can fix them!

After selecting the sub-process (specific practices or sub-practices of process areas that can be quantified) for statistical management, identify the primitives that define the project's performance characteristics. These primitives are, invariably, time, effort, complexity, errors or defects, clarity and cost. By knowing these primitives, a relationship can be established to understand the performance in terms of schedule performance or cost performance, effort overrun, schedule overrun, requirements volatility/stability, phase containment effectiveness, profitability, and so on.

Author's Musing

While the emphasis of process control seems to be placed by the CMMI at the sub-process level of a process area, it is very critical to understand that the sub-process instability or incapability in a process area could be due to a process level of a related process area. Modeling of the outcome variable can therefore be at the process level and need not always be at the sub-process level as is currently understood.

As it is very difficult to say the difference between a process and a sub-process in software, the emphasis that is being placed on 'sub-process' control is unrealistic. Example: do we treat peer reviews as a sub-process of Verification? Or, do we need to drill down peer reviews further to a level where activities such as 'preparation time, review meeting and such' become the sub-processes for Verification? My view is: identify quantifiable opportunities affecting stability and check their relevance for statistical analysis—such opportunities could be either at a process or sub-process level.

Project performance parameters can then be compared and measured against the quality or performance objectives established as goals. A set of stable measures which are not subjected to special cause variations can thereafter be used to establish a performance baseline. If there are any data points that are true outliers, they would be excluded from the baseline generation process.

One of the most important aspects of baseline generation is that the data aggregation has to happen considering the homogeneity of projects based on domain, technology and the process model used. Within the same organization, multiple types of process models could be in use. There may be multiple instances of COTS integration or package selection and integration, re-hosting projects, traditional development life-cycle projects, maintenance projects, research projects and such. Aggregation of process performance data for statistical analysis must consider the different categories of projects and constraints of operation common to them. Typical constraints of operation are cost, quality, time and scope. Alternatively, projects can be stratified by project type into application development, component development, maintenance and bug fixing. Project context information has to be considered before a baseline is established which serves as basis for goal setting using QPM practices. There could be other factors such as performance, adherence to SLAs, responsiveness to handle time-critical expectations of the customer and importance of the project. With the above measures in place, the following specific goal and associated specific practices are rendered into practice:

SG1 Establish Performance Baselines and Models

- SP1.1 **Select Processes**
- SP1.2 **Establish Process Performance Measures**
- SP1.3 **Establish Quality and Process-Performance Objectives**
- SP1.4 **Establish Process Performance Baselines**
- SP1.5 **Establish Process Performance Models**

Note the difference to the goal and practice titles across all three constellations of the CMMI in Version 1.3.

SG1 Establish Performance Baselines and Models

- SP1.1 Establish Quality and Process Performance Objectives
- SP1.2 Select Processes
- SP1.3 Establish Process Performance Measures
- SP1.4 Analyze Process Performance and Establish Process Performance Baselines
- SP1.5 Establish Process Performance Models

Author's Musing

While the emphasis of process control seems to be placed at the sub-process level of a process area, it is very critical to understand that the sub-process instability or incapability in a process area could be due to a process level of a related process area. Modeling of the outcome variable can therefore be at the process level and need not always be at the sub-process level as is currently understood.

The practical sides to OPP as experienced with some of the author's best professional associations are as follows:

Organizational Process Performance

1. Identify the project type by determining the 'constraint of operation' or stratify projects by type (application development, component development, maintenance and bug fixing).
2. Decide the most appropriate primitive data type that can be collected accurately without impeding project productivity to ensure integrity of the derived measure.
3. Sanitize the raw data by removing outliers which have causes that have no known process solutions within the process context (these can be known by using checklists).
4. Establish the derived measures and update the measurement repository to ensure accurate capture of project information for subsequent analysis.
5. Update any new 'special and common causes' identified within the project that has known tendencies for process variation and define new measures that adequately measure them.
6. Provide an organizational work environment that encourages and supports metrics collection which is perceived to be psychologically safe.

Display 6.1 Interpreting Organizational Process Performance

Source: Adapted from SITARA Process JewelBox™ © SITARA Technologies Pvt. Ltd. 2002 with permission

How does Organizational Process Performance transform its capability when the transition to capability level 2 (or the managed level) is made?

Data management policy defines the process performance measures that will be required in order to establish capability baselines. Typically these baselines are revised at periodic intervals using fresh data from projects. Capability baselines are typically expressed in terms of the actual limits within which expected values for the parameter of interest can lie, under known conditions and constraints of operation. Such data typically include, but are not restricted to, the following:

- **Project Management:** Effort deviation, schedule deviation, cost performance index, schedule performance index, estimation accuracy, effort distribution across the life cycle, customer satisfaction, tracking of the risk priority number across the project lifecycle
- **Engineering:** Productivity, cycle time reduction, inspection rate, preparation rate, review efficiency, requirements volatility, requirements clarity, post-release defects arrival rate, total number of system test cases planned, number of system test cases exercised, number of system test cases passed, number of system test cases blocked, number of system test cases rejected and number of defects uncovered, code complexity measures
- **Process Management:** Phase containment effectiveness, product quality in terms of escape defects, Cost of Quality, Cost of Poor Quality, number of process improvements suggested and number incorporated, target and achievement capability profiles for process areas, lists of common and special causes of process variation

Definitions for the above parameters are established and monitored using appropriate statistical analysis tools such as control charts, Pareto, fishbone and simple checklists. Individuals who perform statistical analysis of data are trained on techniques which have to be applied for data analysis of out-of-bound conditions, process of identifying outliers and eliminating them, generating the necessary analysis reports and communicating them to all relevant stakeholders. When new definitions of data are encountered, they are reviewed for effectiveness and the process improvement framework is used to render their definitions. Senior management oversight of process performance is enabled through specific management reviews of the operations.

In order to establish OPP at the level 2 rigor, EPPAT MIMOR has to be institutionalized for OPP in order to attain generic goal 2.

How does Organizational Process Performance transform its capability when the transition to capability level 3 (or the defined level) is made?

After the necessary consistency is established within the project practices at capability level 2, OPP can scale up to a capability level 3 by establishing common, usable definitions for the capability baseline measures of the sample data (both raw and derived) as identified earlier. One of the most useful level 3 practices is in the actual determination of applicability of the metrics and their definition. Should the organizational circumstances change (such as to be more inclusive of practices which were out of scope earlier, e.g., validation and end-user acceptance testing), then OPP has to recognize their definitions after running trials of their data collection and analysis from projects which are best capable of generating the numbers.

OPP also has to recognize a definition of capability baselines by domain, project type and the known constraint of operation. It would be wrong to establish baselines for projects without understanding their characteristics. Most first-time projects which are domain intensive suffer from lack of adequate historical data. For such projects, it is best to establish baselines using fresh data from actual results of execution without enforcing an inapplicable performance baseline.

A radical view the author carries today after extensive use of statistical process control techniques in several high-maturity processes is that knowing the natural process capability limits is obviously much better than taking a pure statistical view of variation for software as established within rules to interpret control charts. Most variation in a software process is always statistically significant, *but may not be practically significant*. If level 4 is all about establishing process stability by insulating the effects of special cause variations while isolating, correcting and eliminating the controllable causes of variation using process management, the nature of software development is such that it is impossible to *eliminate* the causes of variation.

It is the view of the author that process stability of a software process must be ascertained differently. A much better approach would be to draw two separate samples of process data and conduct a two-sample *t-test* while establishing the null hypothesis that two-sample means are equal. If the two-sample means are not equal, then the underlying process is not stable as illustrated in Figure 6.2 for the Cost of Poor Quality (COPQ)

Establishing a defined OPP process area renders a unique benefit. It naturally enables other lower-level process areas to scale up their capability levels to a level 4. This feature is a unique distinction of the CMMI where the growth of process capability is enabled by the framework itself.

Ho $p > 0.05$: Sample1 Mean COPQ% = Sample2 Mean COPQ%
Ha $p < 0.05$: Sample1 Mean COPQ% ≠ Sample2 Mean COPQ%

Two-sample t-test and CI: Sample1, Sample2

Two-sample T for Sample1 vs Sample2

	N	Mean	StDev	SE Mean
Sample1	7	1.231	0.121	0.046
Sample2	7	1.1943	0.0447	0.017

Difference = mu (Sample1) – mu (Sample2)

Estimate for difference: 0.0371

95% CI for difference: (–0.0690, 0.1433)

t-test of difference = 0 (vs not=): T-value = 0.76 P-value = 0.460 DF = 12

Both use Pooled StDev = 0.0911

Conclusion:

The above result displays a table of the sample size, sample means, standard deviation and standard errors for the two samples.

P-value greater than 0.05: Fail to reject null hypothesis. The stability analysis from two separate samples of data reveals that there is no difference in performance. Hence the process is stable and under control.

Fig. 6.2 [MIMOS 2009]: Two-sample t-test for Assessing Process Stability and Control

Source: Q3 2009 Process Capability Analysis Report MIMOS Berhad, Malaysia, a site appraised by SITARA Technologies at CMMI-DEV V1.2 Level 5 (Continuous Representation) in October 2009. Reproduced with permission

The necessary rigor for enabling OPP at level 3 capability is defined in generic goal 3 and the related generic practices which are as follows:

GG3 Institutionalize a Defined Process

GP3.1 Establish a Defined Process

GP3.2 Collect Improvement Information

It is very difficult to demonstrate and justify OPP at a capability beyond level 3. Being a process management process area common to all three CMMI constellations, it would also require enough business justifications and customer mandates to do so. However, purely from a theoretical perspective, the generic goal 4 and the related generic practices 4.1 and 4.2 need to be established for enabling OPP at capability level 4. And to enable OPP at capability level 5, the generic goal 5 and the associated generic practices 5.1 and 5.2 need to be institutionalized.

GG4 Institutionalize a Quantitatively Managed Process

GP4.1 Establish Quantitative Objectives for the Process

GP4.2 Stabilize Sub-Process Performance

GG5 Institutionalize an Optimizing Process

GP5.1 Ensure Continuous Process Improvement

GP5.2 Correct Root Causes of Problems

It may be useful to point out that the specific practices of OPP in general enable the realization of GP4.1—'Establish Quantitative Objectives for the Process'—and GP4.2—'Stabilize Sub-Process Performance'—across the 22 process areas of the CMMI-DEV, 6 process areas of the CMMI-ACQ constellation and 7 process areas of the CMMI-SVC constellation.

Author's Musing

What is process performance model in the context of CMMI and how is this to be established?

Process is a collection or a system of practices using which certain benefits can accrue in order to establish well-defined goals. This definition is not limited to just the development practices of analysis, design and coding but would be more inclusive of other subsidiary practices such as planning, reviews, documentation, configuration management and everything that CMMI classifies as acquisition, service establishment and delivery, project management and support process areas.

Performance is to know the effectiveness or the efficiency factors, which establishes the richness or rigor of the practices—in quantitative terms. The emphasis ison quantification. What are some of those critical quantitative terms? It depends on the critical-to-quality factors or the CTQs for the project. However, these are some of the generalized metrics that one is tempted to establish.

- Defect removal effectiveness for analysis, design, code* Static and/or dynamic testing effectiveness for containing post-release defects
- Post-release defects and associated root-cause analysis for understanding the injection pattern
- Effects of process improvement (such as tailoring) on overall cycle time reduction
- Reduction of Cost of Poor Quality
- Schedule and Cost Performance Index

Knowing the above for the delivered kLOC/function points as the size metric is suggested. Therefore if one is able to establish a defined process and is able to calibrate the effectiveness or the efficiencies behind the practices of engineering, project management, acquisition, service establishment and delivery and the support process areas, then it more than justifies that we know the process performance. The model for which these quantitative measures apply is the defined process or the tailored process.

How do we establish process performance?

- Knowing the effects of tailoring of the defined process quantitatively (as mentioned above) can serve as an affirmation to prove process performance is understood by practitioners to the necessary degree of detail.

(Contd)

- Establishing a target profile for some of the critical process areas beyond capability level 3 and tracking its achievement periodically would also prove that there is an organizational ability to understand process performance quantitatively.
- Establishing the CTQs for the project and tracking them quantitatively is yet another direct evidence that supports process performance modeling.

It is possible to demonstrate the above only when level 4 and level 5 aspectsof the CMMI are built into the organizational process infrastructure.

QUANTITATIVE PROJECT MANAGEMENT (QPM) CMMI-DEV, CMMI-ACQ AND CMMI-SVC

How does Quantitative Project Management look when it operates at a capability level 1 (or the performed level)?

Quantitative Project Management (QPM) belongs to the project management category of the continuous representation of the CMMI. Based on the established process and quality performance objectives for the project's defined process from the OPP process area, practices within QPM help to manage and achieve these goals. In fact, the actual targets that a project is able to attain would further refine the organizational baselines and serve as inputs to the next time around. Use of statistical management of data involves judicious use of seven popular statistical process control tools which will be described for completeness in what follows. However for a detailed and more thorough understanding of the statistical process control or ideas on random variables and probability theory one is referred to standard textbooks addressing these topics [Kan 1995].

Ishikawa's seven basic statistical process control tools are Pareto diagram, scatter plots, run chart, control chart, cause-and-effect diagram, checklists and histograms. We will review them here in their basic form and in their applicability to software while the reader can explore these topics in standard references [Florac 1997, Kan 1995, Wheeler 1992, 1993, 1995].

Pareto diagram is a bar chart depicted in descending order of the frequency count describing the types of problems (process or product). Joseph Juran applied the principles of Pareto, named after a nineteenth-century economist, Vilfredo Pareto, to understand the pattern of quality problems. It is typically known as the 80/20 distribution and identifies the critical-few from the trivial-many causes of a problem type. In other words, 80 percent of the problems are due to 20 percent of the causes or reasons, and eliminating the 20 percent is a high leverage solution—to go after the low-hanging fruits, as is recommended.

Scatter diagrams are particularly useful when there is a linear relationship between two variables (dependent and independent variables). These diagrams are useful as an aid to decision making by understanding how the independent variable affects the dependent variable. The scatter diagram is essentially a bivariate relationship between two specific variables in a linear relationship.

Run charts track the performance of interest over time. *X*-axis basically is represented as a time component and *Y*-axis describes the behavior of a system over time. Run charts are ideally suited to represent the uncovering of validation defects and number of system test cases run over a period of time.

A control chart is an extension of the run charts. After a certain sense of stability of data points is established over repeated trials (note that repetition is one of the best known mechanisms to minimize common cause variation), and a process capability can be defined, a pair of control limits (typically within $\pm 3\sigma$, where σ is the estimated standard deviation) can be established to bind the accepted range of values defining the natural tolerance around the average. The average has the highest probability of occurrence in a chance interval. We have explored these concepts earlier in this chapter while understanding the hallmarks of a level 4 process and with a non-software example in Chapter 1.

Cause–effect diagrams are known as fishbone diagrams since they depict a relationship between a quality parameter and factors that affect this parameter. This diagram actually represents all potential causal factors that affect the quality parameter.

Histograms are effective for representing a frequency count (more as a tallying mechanism) and for categorizing the distribution of a random variable to learn about the basic tendencies for the data. It is a graphic way to understand the central tendency (average value), skewness and modal value.

A checklist is the most fundamental type of verification mechanism to ensure adherence to product and process performance parameters. Several forms of checklists are in use in mature processes: review readiness checklists, product quality assurance checklists, process conformance checklists and such. Checklists are generally a yes/no type of questionnaire and the fundamental purpose of using such a tool would be to check special or assignable causes of variation. Checklists are a very useful way to bring in audit consistency to ensure process institutionalization. Knowing the questions on the checklists serves as a good aid to minimizing variation. It goes without saying that none of the tools described here can 'induce' quality. Quality must exist in the development process, more specifically in the design, as a capability to ensure product quality. Process quality is nothing but establishing a capability baseline for the system of practices.

The minimum expectations placed by the CMMI in order to achieve a capability level 1 for the QPM process area are to render a defined process based on the project's objectives knowing the constraints of operation. Appropriate specific practices under the scope of the development life cycle are selected for data collection, and statistical analysis and the project's performance are managed throughout the life cycle. In doing so, the following specific goal and related specific practices are enabled into the process infrastructure:

SG1 Quantitatively Manage the Project

SP1.1 **Establish the Project's Objectives**

SP1.2 **Compose the Defined Process**

SP1.3 **Select the Sub-Processes That Will Be Statistically Managed**

SP1.4 **Manage Project Performance**

Note the simplification and the difference to the goal and practice numbers and titles in all three constellations of the CMMI in version 1.3.

SG2 Quantitatively Manage the Project

SP2.1 **Monitor the Performance of Selected Subprocesses**

SP2.2 Manage Project Performance

SP2.3 Perform Root Cause Analysis

After the project objectives are established, it is important to select the measures that define the project's performance, more as sanity check. It is at this point that applying statistical methods to understand the underlying causes of variation would be helpful. The purpose of applying statistical methods to understand process dynamics could be to look for patterns of data and make informed judgments based on quantitative information. In order to make such analysis meaningful, the key questions to ask are as follows:

- How do we summarize the data?
- What should the sample size be? Should it be on individual terms, team terms or organizational terms?
- How does the execution outcome differ before and after introducing a process?
- How likely are the chances of getting similar results by fluke or by chance?
- Is there a close enough relationship between the process change and the improvement effect to justify that the improvement on the whole is due to the process change? (It might just be because of ingenuity of individuals.)

These sorts of questions give a purpose and direction to process improvement and breathe life and interest into pursuing the process program at the high maturity.

Practices that address the above help to enable the following specific goal and related specific practices:

SG2 Statistically Manage Sub-Process Performance

SP2.1 **Select Measures and Analytic Techniques**

SP2.2 **Apply Statistical Methods to Understand Variation**

SP2.3 **Monitor Performance of the Selected Sub-Processes**

SP2.4 **Record Statistical Management Data**

Note the difference to the goal and practice numbers and titles in all three constellations of the CMMI in version 1.3.

SG1 Prepare for Quantitative Management

SP1.1 Establish the Project's Objectives

SP1.2 Compose the Defined Process

SP1.3 Select Subprocesses and Attributes

SP1.4 Select Measures and Analytic Techniques

The practical sides to QPM as experienced with some of the author's best professional associations are as follows:

I would rehash the goal-question-metric paradigm introduced while describing Measurement and Analysis as follows:

Stages in Statistical Analysis ...	Drivers that facilitate thinking ...
Pose a Question	• Business goals and objectives • Process goals and objectives
Collect the necessary data	• Choose a group of projects in a sample which can offer data • Determine the most appropriate points or stages in the execution trail which offer 'stable-reliable-and-dependable' data • Conduct an experimental study of the data points to observe statistical significance (as opposed to being a result of chance variation)
Analyze the data	• Summarize the data into appropriate statistical representations by determining mean, mode and median • Represent them in a box plot, for example, to understand the spread
Interpret the results	• Test for cause and effect and make predictions using correlations, statistical tests of significance and theory of probability

Display 6.2 Interpreting Quantitative Project Management

Source: Adapted from SITARA Process JewelBox™ © SITARA Technologies Pvt. Ltd. 2002 with permission

How does Quantitative Project Management transform its capability when the transition to capability level 2 (or the managed level) is made?

After the level 1 specific practices are established as core practices, it is possible to build a layer of consistency on top of this core with the generic practices of EPPAT MIMOR. Within the scope of the organizational policy, projects define quantitative goals for process performance and attributes for product quality measures. Such goals are established in a metrics plan or within the process and product quality plan. The project plan identifies a tailored process that can be derived from the organizational best practices to address the constraints of operation and the critical-to-quality objectives. Data collection procedures defined in the organizational process database are employed to collect process and product measures.

Individuals who are vested with the responsibility to render project data into usable organizational information are trained with the application of statistical process control techniques and principles of quantitative management. Metrics champions are assigned to projects to enable the collection of right types of metrics at well-defined project milestones. Should the characteristics of the project's tailored process be different from the norm, newer process capability baselines are established. Data from project execution are analyzed and tracked in periodic project meetings and senior management reviews. Improvement information is gathered from such reviews and from the causal analysis of project postmortems and process retrospectives. Lessons learnt and best practices resulting from the use of tailored practices are fed back as organizational learning.

How does Quantitative Project Management transform its capability when the transition to capability level 3 (or the defined level) is made?

QPM practices, which are common to all projects, are defined in the organizational metrics guideline and metrics procedures for use across the organization. These practices define the process of metrics collection, analysis and communication of results for all relevant stakeholders. Improvements resulting from execution outcomes based on the use of tailored practices are studied for a generic organizational relevance and appropriate process performance models are redefined along with the establishment of capability baselines. The CMMI expects the following to be institutionalized to calibrate QPM at capability level 3:

GG3 Institutionalize a Defined Process

GP3.1 **Establish a Defined Process**

GP3.2 **Collect Improvement Information**

AUTHOR'S MUSING

I have been confronted with the question 'which comes first, the model or a baseline?' This is much along the same lines as 'was it the seed first or the tree?' Here is my interpretation. We always start with a model (be it the CMMI or Six Sigma). We try it out several times and each trial would offer some data. At this stage, it is impossible to say if the data are stable and, therefore, whether the process is capable. We conduct analysis of the data from each trial and establish the results into an easy-to-relate box plot. A box plot gives a graphic view as a five-figure summary of E_L, Q_L, MD, Q_U and E_U along with the sample size. Representing data in this way gives a much clearer sense of the overall information contained in the raw data values. Further, it offers good insights into predicting where a value might lie in the future if similar methods are applied by people who have similar competencies. One could use Q_U and E_U to define the likelihood of a random variable or event to lie in the upper or lower 25 percent of possible values. When such analysis is rendered for repeated trials, it becomes possible to make generalizations with respect to the capability of the process. At this stage, a process capability baseline can be established for the model that is used. An excellent recognition of this fact is in the continuous representation of the CMMI, where each process area can be understood in capability terms.

It is very difficult to demonstrate and justify QPM at a capability beyond level 3. Being a project management process area of all three CMMI constellations, it would also require enough business justifications and customer mandates to do so. However, purely from a theoretical perspective, the generic goal 4 and the related generic practices 4.1 and 4.2 need to be established for enabling QPM at capability level 4:

GG4 Institutionalize a Quantitatively Managed Process

GP4.1 **Establish Quantitative Objectives for the Process**

GP4.2 **Stabilize Sub-Process Performance**

And to enable QPM at capability level 5, the generic goal 5 and the associated generic practices 5.1 and 5.2 need to be institutionalized:

GG5 Institutionalize an Optimizing Process

GP5.1 **Ensure Continuous Process Improvement**

GP5.2 **Correct Root Causes of Problems**

It may be useful to point out that the specific practices of QPM in general enable the realization of GP4.1—'Establish Quantitative Pbjectives for the Process'—and GP4.2—'Stabilize Sub-Process Performance'—across the 22 process areas of the CMMI-DEV, 6 process areas of the CMMI-ACQ constellation and 7 process areas of the CMMI-SVC constellation.

Author's Musing

It might be useful to reinforce a few points made at the very beginning after gaining this understanding.

It is not possible to operate every project at a high capability because of the many influences, including the law of diminishing returns, that shape the destiny of a project

It is very natural for a high-maturity process, such as a level 5, to have projects which are being executed in a level 1 mode. However, such instances would be an exception rather than the rule, and the process improvement program would do *what is necessary* to put some controls on such projects and leave them alone as having a business reason for diktat. The obvious business reason is to stay in business long enough for it to be profitable! Besides, only a profitable company can afford to indulge in continuous process improvement and do it right.

It is possible and is to be expected that a process area which is operating at capability level 5 today may, at the worst, slip to a capability level 3 the moment the innovation becomes defined into the organizational process, or if the causes of a variation have a defined process response that is now part of the OSSP. This ping-pong effect which at SITARA we term as process harmonic, where a capability level 5 process area that once demonstrated the institutionalization of capability level 5 generic practices, having gained control over minimizing the impact of special and common causes of variation through a process definition, transforms itself to a capability level 3, is an excellent recognition of the framework of the fact that continuous process improvement is *continuous* and that the only purpose it serves is *to learn and know more about things we did not know earlier.* Again, one need not be perturbed or feel a sense of remorse because process area which operated at CL 5 *slipped back* to a CL 3. There is nothing like slipping back because, as a result of this, the OSSP has only become rich. Adding richness and rigour to a development process ought to be perceived in the same manner as one might think about other competency development initiatives.

The CMMI continuous representation recognizes the above implicitly.

7

Optimizing Level—Interpreting the Level 5 CMMI Process Areas

AUTHOR'S MUSING

SITARA's surmise is that level 5 is about maintaining a good control on Cost of Quality or, more appropriately, Cost of Assuring Quality (COAQ) and therefore minimizing impact of variation arising out of common causes. So, if there is one metric that a level 5 must consciously collect, it should be COAQ.

In several observations from sites having high-maturity practices, Cost of Quality is known as the sum of Cost of Poor Quality and Cost of Assuring Quality.

CHARACTERISTICS OF A LEVEL 5 PROCESS (OPTIMIZING PROCESS)

A true level 5 process establishes a culture of continuous process improvement and offers a psychologically safe organizational work environment where learning and reflection are promoted from the CEO down, to the people in the trenches. Not only are individuals seen to engage in an active dialogue with the process, they also relentlessly question status quo and pursue a path of continuous improvement by forcing a change while setting stretched goals using quantitative objectives when things get too comfortable. A level 5 process visibly demonstrates the use of a metrics program to shed light on both the effectiveness and the character of the system of practices. The richness and the power of the process are known in quantitative terms as a result of establishing quantitative objectives.

The focus of a level 5 process is to enable continuous process improvement through proactive learning from conducting process retrospectives and postmortems. In doing so, the objective is to understand the underlying causes of variation that can be attributed to the process itself (common causes of variation). It is impossible to eliminate the causes of variation, be they special causes or common causes, in a highly individual-dependent and customer-driven activity, such as software development. The true nature of variation is highly unpredictable even when the best of data are available for prediction. Does this mean that statistical analysis of data in software is not practical? The answer to this question depends upon what one is trying to measure, the accuracy with which the metric is known and the stability of the metric itself. Some metrics have a better appeal for statistical analysis, while others do not. It is useful to know which type of data are the most appropriate for a statistical rendering and interpretation using the seven most used statistical process control tools, and which are not.

Having been both a sponsor and an appraiser on different occasions in several high-maturity organizations, a lot of data arising from high-maturity processes have been scrutinized by the author from close quarters. Reviewing the merits of statistical analysis of process data, the conclusion that can be reached is that *product quality measures* established in terms of *review effectiveness* using in-process escape defect analysis (design review effectiveness, code review effectiveness, unit testing effectiveness, integration testing effectiveness and system testing effectiveness), validation errors and post-release defects are the best choices for statistical analysis and interpretation using statistical process control techniques. Useful *process quality measures* are *cost of poor quality, cost of quality* and *effort to elapsed time ratio*. These measures exhibit an influence because of both special and common cause variations and serve the purpose of quantitative analysis well. Whereas *process quality measures* such as cycle time reduction, productivity, effectiveness of postmortems, lessons learnt, customer satisfaction surveys, effectiveness of institutionalization of best practices, process conformance or adherence and, when the CMMI continuous representation is used, knowing the process area capability profile are best for obtaining a qualitative interpretation and understanding.

It would be both prudent and judicious to ask the following questions prior to collecting data for statistical analysis:

- What is it that we would like to know about the process that we do not know, already?
- Is this issue a process issue, an organizational issue or a behavioral characteristic of the people?

If it is a people or behavioral characteristic, it is better to address them using a humanistic or a management process, because not every problem is a process problem. A vast majority of the problems are actually management problems resulting from bad management decisions on business issues which should be addressed using a managerial process. As software measurement and analysis is still at a nascent stage, gross abuse and misuse of software metrics is possible, which will be related with a few examples.

Example 1: This example is with the use and interpretation of customer satisfaction survey results. First, every customer satisfaction survey is unique to that customer and to that project. One cannot generalize these results. What follows was witnessed in a highly obsessed-with-metrics style of management which wanted to establish a new metric called customer satisfaction index against which to benchmark every project. For the first two quarters, everybody was absolutely upbeat about getting the right numbers, and where they did not have one, the project leaders even concocted these numbers just to appear good in the eyes of the management. They even went on to establish a control chart by specifying an upper control and a lower control limit for this index. Before doing anything with SPC, first of all, one needs to understand whether the data are statistically significant and lend themselves to statistical analysis. In other words, it is important to answer: *does the theory of probability apply?* If it does not, then using SPC is like the statement 'he who wields a hammer well, sees everything as a nail'. Putting customer satisfaction survey results, in whatever form, into a control chart and then doing a root-cause analysis is the worst abuse of management information.

Example 2: The next example is misusing the productivity number to drive improvements. We will understand how ludicrous this number is with a self-explanatory non-software example. Let us suppose that since we know a good typing speed to be around 40 words per minute, we set a productivity target at say 40 words per minute. Being fairly proficient on the keyboard, 40 words per minute may not a very difficult goal. So, one would consistently demonstrate between 50 and 60 words per minute. Since the established limits were exceeded, the metrics manager establishes a *stretched goal* of 70 words per minute. In order to meet the new goal, it is imperative that a person should scale up his/her proficiency levels. Banging away at the keyboard and with a few exceptions (defects), the goal might still be achieved. On the whole, it is maybe possible to produce results made on the new demands for productivity at 70 words per minute with a little amount of rework. Seeing this pattern of compliance to the goals, the metrics manager establishes a new *stretched goal* of 120 words per minute. This time around, obviously due to ill-preparedness because the fundamental process of typing has not changed, meeting the new goal without committing lots of mistakes (increasing rework and therefore cost of poor quality), and actually having to revisit one's own work to ensure that everything is in order (cost of appraisal and therefore cost of quality would increase), is impossible. If one has reached one's natural limits of process capability, then the only solution is to change the typist or the process if results have to be any better. The same applies to using productivity improvement in software development—production of number of lines of debugged code or function points or whatever else is the basic unit of measurement for software size. Of course, the stretched goal of 120 words per minute would make sense if the typist is assisted with some form of speech recognition software into which one could potentially speak up, and the tool would render the speech-to-text translation. Unless the stretched goal is supported with such an organizational innovation, it would be highly impossible for an individual to meet the challenge. This example illustrates that goal setting for a metric has to take into account the associated and expected adverse or negative fan-out impact on other metrics.

Example 3: This example is on how cost of quality was being calculated wrongly and used wrongly. It is quite intuitive but fails to meet the eye if it is not correlated with a non-software example. Mathematically, when someone writes:

$$A = [B+C]/n$$

$$A = [B+C+D+E]/n$$

$$A = [B+C+Z]/n$$

One could easily say that A is not defined accurately. Now replace A with cost of quality, B with appraisal cost, C with prevention cost, D with training cost, E with rework cost, Z with penalty costs due to SLAs and n with total cost. Then what is evident is that cost of quality is being calculated inconsistently. Further, when the different rules of inconsistent calculations for cost of quality are averaged out and put under a *single* control chart for tracking, it does not require any additional insights into realizing that the metric itself is wrongly represented and the analysis so rendered for management information needs is based on a wrong premise. The only meaningful way to use cost of quality measure that has been computed in three different ways is to keep them separate without computing an average.

It is quite possible that all three forms of cost of quality representation are valid for a given organizational context. Think about it in this way: in the first equation, parameters D, E and Z are zero; in the second equation Z is zero; and, finally, in the third equation, D and E are zero. Even if this were true, it most definitely does not mean that in the organizational context where B, C, D, E and Z are all relevant and are used to compute cost of quality, one could use only those parameters which are relevant for a project and use an average value and track the average value. Such analysis would lead to wrong conclusions. A possible way of aggregating, but still using three different costs of quality values, would be to categorize projects as follows:

[Category 1] A = [B+C]/n

[Category 2] A = [B+C+D+E]/n

[Category 3] A = [B+C+Z]/n

All projects belonging into the three categories 1, 2 and 3 could have their respective average cost of quality values tracked independently, and that might not be incorrect.

Example 4: This example comes from a high-maturity practice which had the following way of calculating deviation for schedule and effort as a percentage of the estimated value:

Deviation = [Actual–Estimated]/[Estimated]

On face value, there is nothing wrong with this equation. The problem is with the way actual and estimated are calculated. In an onsite–offshore setting, the process handshake is mostly rough if the two collaborating processes differ in process maturity. There is a very good probability that a customer's development and management processes are far from being classified as high maturity. In such cases, it is not unreasonable for a significant turnaround time resulting from a delayed confirmation from the customer. Let us suppose that a task which had an estimated effort of 10 man-days for completion and the relevant stakeholder from the development site shot a question to the customer for clarification and the customer reacted only after 10 days have elapsed. The development site which patiently waited for 10 days for clarification now begins work and completes the assigned task within the assigned 10 days. Therefore, the total duration to complete the task is 20 days—or is it? Anyway we will know that soon. This process was computing the effort deviation religiously using the formula provided above and was getting an effort deviation value of 100 per cent. And this 100 per cent was being subjected to a causal analysis since it exceeded the trigger of 10 per cent and the attribution was to the customer's delay (and identified as a special cause). On an aside, as projects executed were on time and material basis, strictly speaking, an effort deviation so large is a welcome proposition, because the project gets paid even for waiting. But the project suffered from serious morale issues with engineers having to remain idle. The issue goes even deeper: since the metrics collection process was on autopilot using a tool which in turn updated the actual effort in the historical database, two things became wrong now. The next time over, the estimates were based on the wrongly updated measure from the historical database. *Why is the very calculation of 100 per cent effort deviation in the above manner considered wrong?* The reason is: metrics resulting from two different processes are being aggregated—one from the *voice-of-customer (VOC)* (10 days of turnaround time) and the other from the *voice-of-process (VOP)* (10 days of development effort). The 10 days of turnaround time because of a delay from the customer cannot be added up to the 10 days of development effort to arrive at the total effort. If this has to be right, the development time should be considered as 10 days and in which case the effort deviation is actually zero. It is my belief that if a metrics program cannot isolate metrics resulting from these two—voice of the development process and *voice-of-customer (VOC)*—then data from such metrics initiative yields absolutely worthless information. *Having wrong data is worse than having no data!*

> **AUTHOR'S MUSING**
>
> The examples I relate here prove that a value added or a high potential appraisal is one which cares to know the details by getting into the merits of the process. It is my belief that a qualitative assessment or appraisal of the system of practices in vogue applying professional judgment is the only known bulletproof mechanism that ensures transfer of responsibility back into the organization with value addition. Anything else makes for a textbook style of conducting an appraisal with little or no value addition.

Numerous such examples get highlighted when an appraisal cares to know the merits of the practices. When the right metrics exist, it should be possible to weave a story using them.

For example: There must be an inferential mechanism which is suggestive of the following. 'For a level 3 development process with a 100 per cent adherence to the established coding standards if code walkthrough is conducted at a walkthrough rate of 50 LOC per hour on a fully debugged code module then the inspection must be able to detect zero severity level 1 escape defects, at most two severity level 2 escape defects and no more than four severity level 3 escape defects for a 2000 line code module after the unit-testing phase is completed with 100 per cent code walkthrough effectiveness. If the walkthrough rate were to be increased to 100 LOC per hour, then the inspection must have noticeably higher values for escape defects and the code walkthrough effectiveness comes down by about 85 per cent based on faults detected in system testing.'

Or, for example: 'If the phase containment effectiveness across the life cycle (also termed as in-process fault distribution in some work cultures) is known resulting from stabilizing several iterations of capability baselines of postmortem reports as follows: 70 per cent of all in-process faults are captured in requirements phase, 80 per cent of all in-process faults are captured in design, 80 per cent of all in-process faults are captured in unit-testing phase, 90 per cent of all in-process faults are captured in system-testing phase and 80 per cent of all in-process faults are captured in validation phase; and if there have been 20 post-release defects reported, then the distribution of these 20 defects is as follows: at least 6 must be attributed to the requirements phase, 4 to the design phase, 4 to the unit-testing phase, 2 to the system-testing phase and 4 to the validation phase based on defect distribution.'

The focus of a level 5 process is to understand the root causes of *common cause* variation (due to the *voice-of-process (VOP)*) and minimize the impact using innovations such as tools, or process definitions with the use of standards, templates and checklists that have a significant role to play in minimizing common cause variation. It is also expected that return on investment for such improvements and innovations ought to be showcased. Return on investment could be realized not just in dollar terms but also in terms of cycle time reduction, extent of reduction to cost of rework, extent of monotony reduced and productivity gains with the deployment of tools such as code beautifiers, regression test suites, and so on. In a sense, a 'culture of informed learning' prevails.

Two process areas at level 5 are common to the three constellations and are contained in CMF:

- Causal Analysis and Resolution (CAR) [CMMI-DEV, CMMI-ACQ, CMMI-SVC]
- Organizational Innovation and Deployment (OID) [CMMI-DEV, CMMI-ACQ, CMMI-SVC]

CAUSAL ANALYSIS AND RESOLUTION (CAR) CMMI-DEV, CMMI-ACQ AND CMMI-SVC

How does Causal Analysis and Resolution look when it operates at a capability level 1 (or the performed level)?

Common to all three constellations of the CMMI, Causal Analysis and Resolution (CAR) belongs to the support category of the continuous representation of the CMMI. Being a support category process area, its applicability is to the rest of the process areas. The purpose of CAR is to identify causes of defects and other problems and take action to prevent them from occurring in the future. One of the prerequisite process areas that should exist before CAR can be established firmly is a solid Measurement and Analysis orientation at maturity level 2 and Quantitative Project Management at maturity level 4. A metrics program offers the necessary raw data—be they defects or unrelated to defects, which could be understood using quantitative analysis methods such as the Pareto analysis—and would form a very critical input to the effective application of CAR. The necessary condition for quantitative analysis is to establish a stable process. Practices of CAR can help to improve the capability of such stable processes.

Enabling CAR within the process infrastructure must necessarily grow the capability of other process areas in the CMMI to a capability level 5. For instance: it is easy to comprehend the use of CAR on Verification process area (of the engineering category). As a consequence, when the specific practices of CAR are applied to make Verification effective, its intrinsic capability must necessarily improve to a level 5.

Author's Musing

The most useful feature of the CMMI framework is that the process areas contained in the framework itself enable the growing of capability profiles of other related process areas. For example: enabling Causal Analysis and Resolution on Verification process area, helps to grow the capability of Verification. In a sense, this feature is a useful attribute for what a Design for Six Sigma (DFSS) process ought to have.

A high-leverage option for making Verification effective and efficient is to enable a CAR process on data that are collected from conducting the Verification process. The peer review data or verification data are rich and contain valuable information that lends itself well to such analysis. Application of the causal analysis to the process is limited by the imagination of its user. The principles of CAR can be applied to analyze product attributes using the defect metric, and to understand common cause variations that affect process attributes such as cycle time reduction, cost of poor quality, cost of quality and productivity or even for conducting effective management reviews of business issues.

A question that often comes up is '*Should CAR practices be applied at the project level or, at the organizational level?*' CAR can be applied to both project issues at the project level and at the organizational level to address organizational or management issues. In fact, going one step further, CAR can be applied by an individual to measure one's own contributions to the causes of variation (failure or discontinuity). What is extremely important to bear in mind is to assess the generalization of the cause–effect relationship to a larger whole, before large-scale process changes are recommended or made. In most cases, due diligence has to be exercised to understand whether the issue is a real issue or was it just a false alarm.

Explore the process discontinuity that lends itself to a formal causal analysis using the relevant data. Using a structured technique such as the five-whys approach, get to the root cause of the issue.

> **AUTHOR'S MUSING**
>
> The five-whys approach is a structured approach to determine the most likely cause of the issue that has surfaced. In this process, a group of experts along with the relevant stakeholders facilitate the session. Each issue is considered after identifying several common themes or patterns that could probably cause the issue.
>
> Techniques such as the five-whys are used to ensure that linear simplification of a single cause–effect relationship does not lead to wrong analysis. The five-whys technique is to ask 'why did this happen' and iteratively probe 'what else could be the reason', all the while ensuring that no individual is assigned a blame. When a process discontinuity or deficiency is identified, the reasons for the effects manifested as a defect or process discontinuity can be identified [Nandyal 2003].

Many times, the effects could be because of multiple causes. It is quite possible that the multiple causes could be of both due to special causes (due to the *voice-of-customer (VOC)*) and common causes (due to the *voice-of-process (VOP)*). When there is more than one cause, and when it is equally important to study the impact of all possible causes and their interactions on the effect, one-way ANOVA (analysis of variance) can be used on the Pareto data to test for differences, if any, among equally likely causes of variance. The *P* value (area of the upper tail distribution beyond the ratio of explained causes of variation and unexplained causes of variation) offers quantitative justification and rationale into whether there is a difference or otherwise because of all possible causes considered as illustrated in Figure 7.1.

It is needless to emphasize that it is easier to correct and rectify the *voice-of-process (VOP)* as it is under the control of the process assurance practices of the development process. The above set of practices enables the realization of

SG1 Determine Causes of Defects[1]

SP1.1 Select Defect Data for Analysis[2]

SP1.2 Analyze Causes

[1] Goal title appears as "Determine Causes of Selected Outcomes" in version 1.3 across all three constellations. There is no noticeable/perceptible change to the informative content associated with this goal and therefore to its interpretation.

[2] Practice title appears as "Select Outcomes for Analysis" in version 1.3 across all three constellations. There is no noticeable/perceptible change to the informative content associated with this practice and therefore to its interpretation.

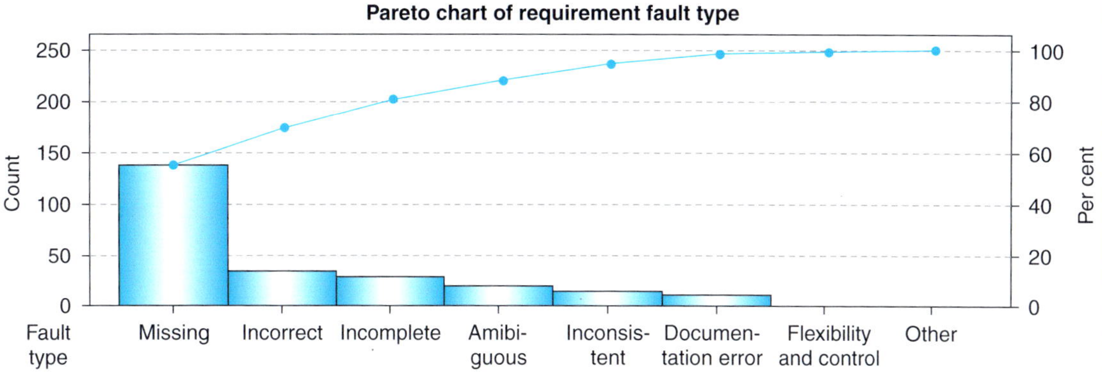

Count	142	36	30	22	14	12	2	2
Per cent	54.6	13.8	11.5	8.5	5.4	4.6	0.8	0.8
Cum %	54.6	68.5	80.0	88.5	93.8	98.5	99.2	100.0

- Ho $p>0.05$: Mean fault density by category is '='
- Ha $p<0.05$: At least 1 mean fault density by category is '≠'

One way ANOVA: Missing requirement, incomplete requirement incorrect Requirement, documentation error, ambiguous requirement, inconsistent requirement

Source	DF	SS	MS	F	P
Factor	5	57.31	11.46	2.94	0.28
Error	31	120.76	3.90		
Total	36	78.08			

S = 1.974 R-Sq = 32.18% R-Sq (adj) = 21.25%

Level	N	Mean	StDev
Missing requirement	7	3.420	3.763
Incomplete requirement	10	0.063	0.117
Incorrect requirement	6	0.050	0.067
Documentation error	4	1.532	2.316
Ambiguous requirement	5	0.877	0.826
Inconsistent requirement	5	1.645	2.051

Pooled StDev = 1.974

Conclusion:

P value is more than 0.05%: fail to reject the null hypothesis. The fault data do not provide sufficient evidence to conclude that the mean fault density is significantly different across categories.

Considerable overlap among the distribution of the six factors causing requirement faults is evident. This implies that it is difficult to tell the difference in the six types of distributions.

While prioritizing the fault categories using the Pareto chart for requirements phase, 'all' fault types have to be considered and prioritized equally for an adequate resolution.

Fig. 7.1 [MIMOS 2009]: One-way ANOVA for Statistical Analysis of Requirements Fault Type

Source: Q3 2009 Process Capability Analysis Report MIMOS Berhad, Malaysia, a site appraised by SITARA Technologies at CMMI-DEV V1.2 Level 5 (Continuous Representation) in October 2009. Reproduced with permission.

Based on determining the cause, record the data from causal analysis and apply the principles of Pareto to identify the critical few from the trivial many. Use the process improvement framework to enable a process fix to make sure that the problem does not surface again. If a problem appears more than once after a fix has been rendered, then the only assignable cause is to the very process improvement program itself.

Study the applicability of the process solution to the organizational context as a whole with the use of pilots and deploy those solutions which have a perceived use for the larger process audience in the organization. These practices realize the following:

SG2 Address Causes of Defects

SP2.1 **Implement the Action Proposals**

SP2.2 **Evaluate the Effect of Changes**

SP2.3 **Record Data**

Note the difference to the goal and practice titles across all three constellations of the CMMI in version 1.3.

SG2 Address Causes of Selected Outcomes

SP2.1 Implement Action Proposals

SP2.2 Evaluate the Effect of Implemented Actions

SP2.3 Record Causal Analysis Data

The above set of five specific practices helps to render a capability level 1 process for CAR.

The practical sides to CAR as experienced with some of the author's best professional associations are as follows:

Causal Analysis and Resolution

1. List the prioritized issues resulting from a formal peer review or verification from all the necessary stakeholder perspectives.
2. Differentiate the issues as either a process issue, business issue or a people characteristic. Note: There is very little you could do if it is people characteristic.
3. For all process issues, explore the possibilities of establishing a common theme or a common pattern of events from prior experience records or historical database.
4. Render the causes into a Pareto to identify the critical few from the trivial many.
5. Go after the low-hanging fruits or those which seem to be the cause for a majority of the issues through a process improvement or a tool innovation after exploring the results from pilots.
6. If the issue is a business issue (due to commercial arrangements for example), then treat it with appropriate senior management escalation and exception-handling process.

Display 7.1 Interpreting Causal Analysis and Resolution

Source: Adapted from SITARA Process JewelBox™ © SITARA Technologies Pvt. Ltd. 2002 with permission

How does Causal Analysis and Resolution transform its capability when the transition to capability level 2 (or the managed level) is made?

At capability level 2, CAR entails the creation of organizational mandates (or policies) that lay down a set of expectations for performance based on executive management sponsorship. Well-defined roles and responsibilities are assigned to individuals for advising and coordinating the implementation of systematic identification of defects in work products and other process discontinuities. Within the CMMI, an explicit generic practice requiring a documented policy for CAR activities implies management commitment to building organizational capability for all the four CMMI constellation-specific categories of engineering/acquisition/service establishment and delivery, process management, project management and support. When management commitment takes such a broad view, it means perfecting a system of practices (the process) to render customer benefits and, not just commitment to a specific process or product opportunities. Being a support category process area, CAR can be applied to analyze both process-related and product-related issues.

Activities for conducting CAR are best planned into the verification schedule of the overall project plan. It is best advised to use the data from verification or peer reviews upon which to conduct a formal CAR session. CAR can be conducted before a baseline is established to internalize the learning resulting from uncovering errors in a work product. CAR can also be conducted at the time of reopening a baseline to fix a change or modification request to understand the root cause of rework. Such use of a CAR process helps to quickly build and grow an organizational understanding of what is *voice-of-process (VOP)* and what constitutes *voice-of-customer (VOC)*.

CAR being a crucial learning process, the best stakeholders of its practices are either the project manager or a designated process champion who could also be playing the role a quality specialist at the organizational level. Stakeholders of the CAR process should be provided with the necessary training on statistical process control, failure modes and effects analysis (FMEA) techniques, and rendering of Ishikawa diagrams to understand cause–effect patterns both within a project and across the organization. Outcomes from such CAR activities could include process improvement proposals or action plans to minimize impact due to common cause variation, suggestions for tool development using the OID process by tool specialists, management records of specific strategic directions which are useful as a measure to insulate the organizational process from causes of variation and the like, placed under a configuration management system.

CAR records could also result from PPQA or postmortem activities. Such logs could be maintained as an organizational learning record (please refer the PPQA process area for a suggested template for logging PPQA activities). In doing so, the ten CMMI generic practices at capability level 2 must be institutionalized.

How does Causal Analysis and Resolution transform its capability when the transition to capability level 3 (or the defined level) is made?

When CAR operates at the defined level of capability, use of formal methods such as cause–effect diagrams, process mapping and FMEA could be defined in the process. FMEA is a disciplined procedure that is used to determine high-risk process activities, or product features based on impact of failure and the likelihood that a failure could occur without detection. The concept behind FMEA is *identify ways the product or process can fail and then plan to prevent those failures*. Benefits of FMEA are as follows:

- Improve the quality, reliability and safety of products
- Increase customer satisfaction
- Reduce product development timing and cost
- Document and track actions taken to reduce risks

When each of the key output variables (or customer deliverables) is not correct, that represents a potential *effect*. And when each process step or key input variable (or customer requirement) is not correct, that represents a *failure mode*. This is illustrated in Figure 7.2.

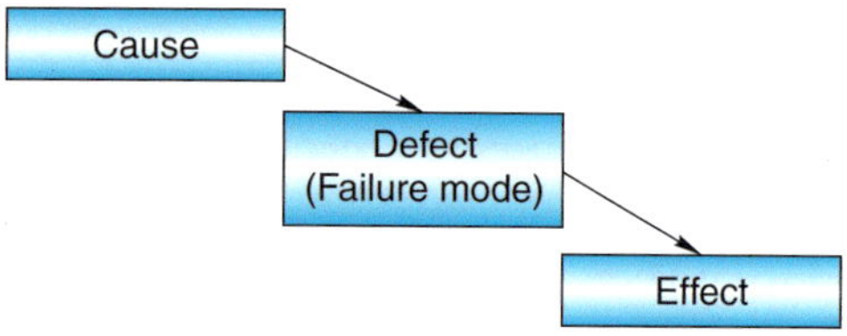

Fig. 7.2 Interpreting FMEA in the Context of Causal Analysis and Resolution

Source: Adapted from SITARA Process JewelBox™ © SITARA Technologies Pvt. Ltd. 2002 with permission

Institutionalization of CAR is a necessary condition for using a structured mechanism such as conducting a process FMEA or system FMEA or design FMEA. Any new process change has a potential to create side effects which are either desirable or undesirable. Process FMEA studies the effects resulting from possible failure modes with the introduction of a process change. In a systems engineering process, FMEA could be used to assess and analyze the manufacturing and assembly process. System FMEA is used to analyze systems and subsystems in early concept and design stages, and focuses on potential failure modes associated with the functions of the system caused by design. Design FMEA is used to analyze product components before they are released to product integration.

A failure mode is linked to cause and effect. The manner in which a process or work product could fail to meet its intended use or specification usually results in either a process non-conformance or a product failure. Failure mode visibly manifests itself as a failure effect. By knowing the failure mode, one could go after identifying the causes or sources of variability associated with key process input, and appropriate control steps could be initiated to prevent or detect the failure mode. The CMMI expects the following to be institutionalized to calibrate CAR at capability level 3:

GG3 Institutionalize a Defined Process

GP3.1 Establish a Defined Process

GP3.2 Collect Improvement Information

It is very difficult to demonstrate and justify CAR at a capability beyond level 3. Being a support process area common to all three CMMI constellations, it would also require enough business justifications and customer mandates to do so. However, purely from a theoretical perspective, the generic goal 4 and the related generic practices 4.1 and 4.2 need to be established for enabling CAR at capability level 4.

GG4 Institutionalize a Quantitatively Managed Process

GP4.1 Establish Quantitative Objectives for the Process

GP4.2 Stabilize Sub-Process Performance

And to enable CAR at capability level 5, the generic goal 5 and the associated generic practices 5.1 and 5.2 need to be institutionalized.

GG5 Institutionalize an Optimizing Process

GP5.1 Ensure Continuous Process Improvement

GP5.2 Correct Root Causes of Problems

It may be useful to point out that the specific practices of CAR in general enable the realization of GP5.2—'Correct Root Causes of Problems'—across the 22 process areas of the CMMI-DEV, 6 process areas of the CMMI-ACQ constellation and 7 process areas of the CMMI-SVC constellation.

Author's Musing

From a study of the rigor of Causal Analysis and Resolution activities in most high-maturity sites, I find that the causes that impact the development process fall into three major categories. 'Oversight' as a common cause tops the list. 'Lack of domain training' as a common cause comes at a close second, and the third, a special cause, is 'changes to customer requirements'.

A broad classification of causes into 'common and special' offers very little insights into the true nature of the process discontinuity. At the very least, it is suggestive of an unstable development process. Root-cause analysis makes sense only when the development process is stable. An insight which I would like to reduce to a rule of thumb would be the following:

The number of root causes must be 7±2, to qualify the effect or the discontinuity observed as a 'real issue' which is worthy of causal analysis. Otherwise, the complexity of the issue is trivial enough for it to have shown up in the first place.

ORGANIZATIONAL INNOVATION AND DEPLOYMENT (OID)[3] CMMI-DEV, CMMI-ACQ AND CMMI-SVC

How does Organizational Innovation and Deployment look when it operates at a capability level 1 (or the performed level)?

Organizational Innovation and Deployment (OID) belongs to the process management category of the continuous representation of the CMMI. The purpose of OID is to explore both innovative and

[3] All three constellations of the CMMI have renamed this process area to "Organizational Performance Management (OPM)". Though the goal and practice titles have been modified, the material content or the informative material and therefore its interpretation has not changed significantly.

incremental opportunities to improve the process, tools and technologies in use. Incremental improvements usually are those which have a specific objective with a tactical focus on a process, whereas innovative improvements usually impact the whole system and might require additional reinforcements with respect to making changes to tools, technology or the process itself. In the context of CMMI-SVC, innovative improvements also impact changes required to be made to the infrastructure. Change authorization for the new system configurations after a problem resolution along with an effective release management process, wherein such configuration changes are rolled out to impact the system as a whole, must also be considered within the scope of OID. One of the measurable impact of having good OID practices can be assessed from examining the tendencies of cost of quality and cost of poor quality metrics, overall cycle time reduction, improvement of customer satisfaction, empowerment of individuals to make the day-to-day changes necessary for optimal execution and, as a result, improved employee satisfaction. The purpose of OID is to align the innovations to the overall business objectives and goals.

OID can invoke the practices belonging to the Organizational Process Focus and Organizational Process Definition process areas to collect and analyze improvement proposals in what is known as *best practice review* (BPR) sessions. Innovations are those which have a significant measurable impact on the above-identified factors. Such innovation proposals are examined for larger organizational relevance using a team of experts along with the process engineering group and process champions. Pilot improvements are studied and selected for deployment. These practices enable the realization of the following:

SG1 Select Improvements

SP1.1 **Collect and Analyze Improvement Proposals**

SP1.2 **Identify and Analyze Innovations**

SP1.3 **Pilot Improvements**

SP1.4 **Select Improvements for Deployment**

After innovative improvements are selected based on their relevance and successful demonstration of results on pilots, the deployment across the organization is planned keeping considerations such as training the people, implications resulting from such a change to the overall productivity, cost of deployment, allowances for learning curve, and so on. In doing so, the following specific goal is rendered into the process design:

SG2 Deploy Improvements

SP2.1 **Plan the Deployment**

SP2.2 **Manage the Deployment**

SP2.3 **Measure Improvement Effects**

Note the similarities and differences to the goal and practice titles across all three CMMI constellations of Organizational Performance Management in version 1.3.

The significant change in OPM is due to the very first specific goal and the associated practices which expect business objectives to serve as basis to drive process measurement and analysis. All of

the interpretations of the CMMI process areas described in this book, especially so for those process areas which were identified to demonstrate a high maturity measurement and analysis capability, must first establish a business performance need prior to embarking on quantification.

SG2 and SG3 in OPM and the associated practices resemble the equivalent of OID specific goals and practices.

SG1 Manage Business Performance

- **SP1.1 Maintain Business Objectives**
- **SP1.2 Analyze Process Performance Data**
- **SP1.3 Identify Potential Areas for Improvement**

SG2 Select Improvements

- **SP2.1 Elicit Suggested Improvements**
- **SP2.2 Analyze Suggested Improvements**
- **SP2.3 Validate Improvements**
- **SP2.4 Select and Implement Improvements for Deployment**

SG3 Deploy Improvements

- **SP3.1 Plan the Deployment**
- **SP3.2 Manage the Deployment**
- **SP3.3 Evaluate Improvement Effects**

The above seven specific practices enable OID within the process infrastructure operating at a capability level 1 or the performed level of capability.

The practical sides to OID as experienced with some of the author's best professional associations would relentless answer the following questions by all constituencies of the high-maturity work culture. Called the SITARA Ten Question Indicator for Total Quality Assurance^{SM} (TQI for TQA^{SM}), as they were designed to serve as a high-maturity probe to gauge implementation rigor in the high-maturity process appraisals/audits by SITARA, they are shown in Display 7.2.

How does Organizational Innovation and Deployment transform its capability when the transition to capability level 2 (or the managed level) is made?

Management is committed to improving the capability of practices on the engineering, acquisition, services and project management methods. It ensures the use of formal techniques for improving product quality, decreasing cost of poor quality and cost of quality and reducing cycle time with a view to improve customer confidence and therefore customer satisfaction. Assurances of quality of services and products takes on a new meaning when OID practices are enhanced from a capability level 1 to a capability level 2.

A well-staffed function such as a software research center or a software tools division is created to serve the organizational workforce as a think tank to improve the overall development capability. Having

Organizational Innvoation and Deployment

1. What was a new idea/improvement we tried this month on our project?
2. Can we offer instances of how this improvement has led to demonstrate quantitative benefits on the process/product measures used within the organization?
3. What new measures do I need, that are not already available, for me to conduct my project better, faster, cheaper?
4. Can we demonstrate using 'test of hypothesis' or other statistical techniques how the project's measures are in alignment with the organization-level process capability baseline with respect to central tendency and variance?
5. What are the types of innovations we can adopt and institutionalize in our projects to demonstrate cycle time reduction or defect reduction?
6. What effects does DAR have on effective deployment of CAR practices?
7. What has been the effect of Risk Management on cycle time reduction, defect prevention and customer satisfaction?
8. What steps do I have in place for my project to identify and take corrective actions even before the customer notices it?
9. What are some of my project-specific practices with which I can 'delight my customer'? Are they part of the standard operating practices?
10. What aspects of my project have been quantified and stabilized with which I can demonstrate prediction of process capability?

Display 7.2 Interpreting Organizational Innovation and Deployment

Source: Adapted from SITARA Process JewelBox™ © SITARA Technologies Pvt. Ltd. 2008 with permission

such a group of experts helps in many ways, as the development staff is generally preoccupied in getting the product out the door and would have little or no bandwidth to explore better ways of doing things. Simple examples of what could increase productivity are as follows:

- Use of scripts to remove the monotony of tasks which are necessary to bring code into coding standards
- Use of regression test scripts and test cases to test code that is modified to ensure that a fix does not break something else
- Enabling effective measurement of code documentation by establishing the comment-to-non-comment ratio without much human effort, to flag the readiness of code for code walkthrough
- Using tools such as lint to clean up the code modules prior to unit testing
- Using static and dynamic test tools to study the structure and functionality of code modules before system testing is attempted
- Developing scripts to link documentation tools and development tools in order to import and export information without manual intervention

- Creation of documentation management system with a round-robin or parallel-style document review mechanism with workflow management
- Tools that can support and augment the capacities of the measurement process and build the intent of the CMMI practices in an automated way

And so on. The above list is limited to the ingenuity and imagination of the engineers and practitioners.

Such an expert team of individuals would have to receive the necessary process orientation and training on the process discontinuities before they can become contributing members. When dealing with level 5 maturity practices, it is very important to have a couple of individuals (or more) who are Six Sigma black belts having a good understanding of process mapping, FMEA methods and the discipline of statistics and the science of measurement. It would also be helpful if such individuals have also burnt their fingers as development team members. An appreciation of the harsh realities in the trenches is extremely important; otherwise, innovations could at worst become costly experiments. While every innovation appears useful, process data, before and after an innovation is tried, must be analyzed using a two-sample *t-test* and graphically analyzed using simple box plots and control charts. This is illustrated in Figures 7.3–7.5.

Author's Musing

One of the key challenges that would remain while making OID effective is to explore the integration of the multiple tools that a project would use. Oftentimes, the choice of the software tool for development or for project management has a dependency upon the customer's process. And in a software services environment where multiple customers are serviced under one roof, establishing a common suite of tools is impossible. I would scale this observation up to suggest that having one common development process is also not possible. Some practices (as required and mandated by the customer) would be mature, while others might not be mature. In such cases, it is not impossible to imagine a suite of process responses emerging from a single business. The only impact from such an imbalance of practices is on the identification of the appraisal scope. The greatest challenge in such cases where a potpourri of both mature and not so mature practices co-exist having little or no connection to the organizational standards and the organizational goals is that it makes the dynamics of both the process appraisal and process improvement extremely difficult.

An effective organizational policy which addresses OID must consider both the implementation and institutionalization practices. Policy should emphasize conducting a cost–benefit analysis of process innovation proposals besides the statistical verification of process performance information; those innovations having a high cost–benefit ratio are candidates for rejection. Proposals which highlight a potential barrier to implementation and have high risk factors are also candidates which could be rejected.

The ten generic practices at capability level 2 address the institutionalization aspects of OID into the organizational process infrastructure.

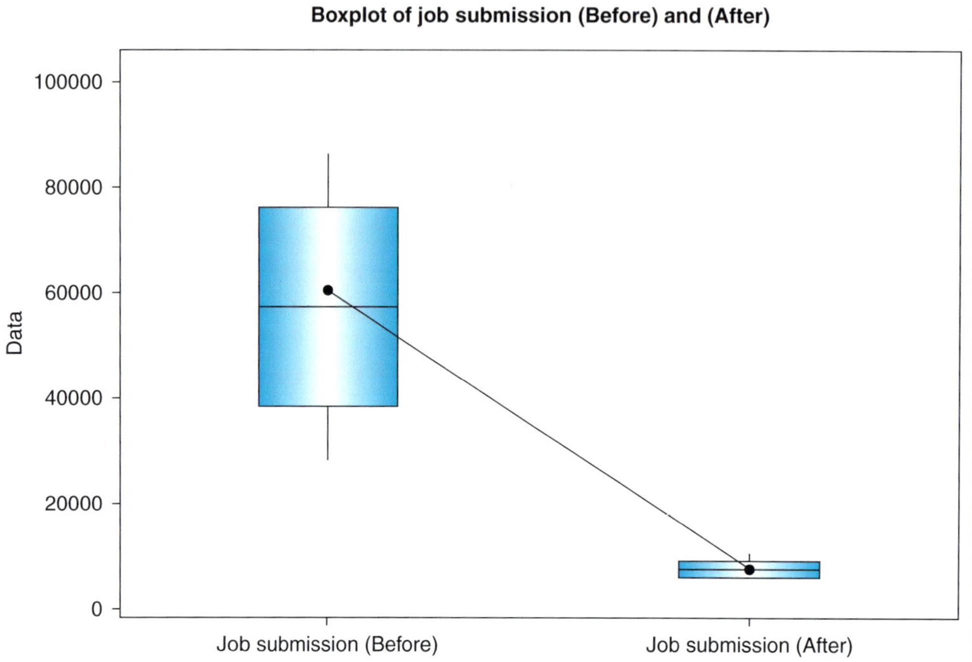

Two-sample T:
Ho: Job management mean BEFORE improvement <= Job management mean AFTER improvement
Ho: Job management mean BEFORE improvement > Job management mean AFTER improvement

Two-sample T-test and CI: Job Management (Before). Job Management (After)

```
Two-sample T for Job Management (Before) vs Job Management (After)

                          N    Mean    StDev    SE Mean
Job Management (Before)  10    3732      512        162
Job Management (After)   10    2241      752        238

Difference = mu (Job Management (Before)) - mu (Job Management (After))
Estimate for difference: 1491
95% lower bound for difference: 986
T-test of difference = 0 (vs >): T-value = 5.18 P-value = 0.000 DF = 15
```

P-value = 0.000	Reject null hypothesis
Conclusion	• This is to conclude that Job Management cycle time mean after improvement is significantly lesser than before improvement.

Fig. 7.3 [MIMOS 2009]: Box Plot and Two-sample *t-test* on Samples of Process Data Chosen for Analysis of Improvement Effect

Source: Q3 2009 Process Capability Analysis Report MIMOS Berhad, Malaysia, a site appraised by SITARA Technologies at CMMI-DEV V1.2 Level 5 (Continuous Representation) in October 2009. Reproduced with permission.

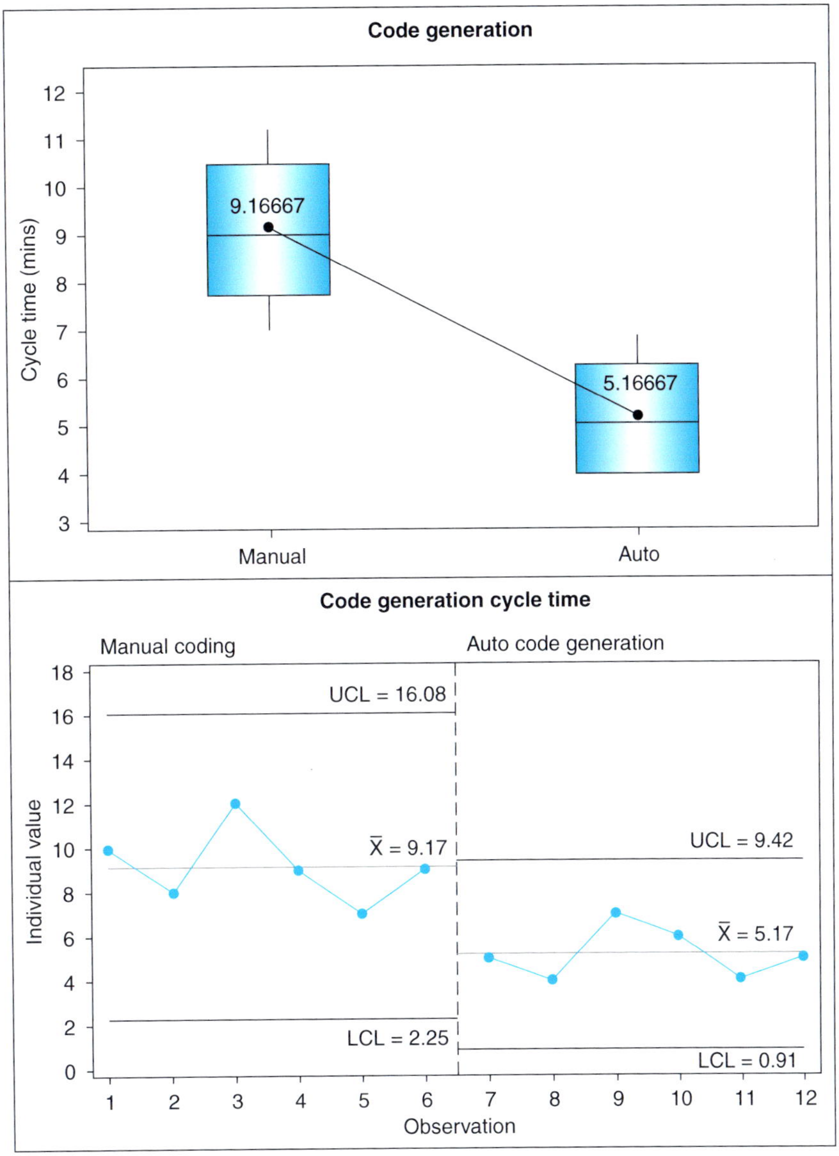

Fig. 7.4 [MIMOS 2009]: Box Plot and Control Chart Proving Effectiveness of the Innovation to Minimize Common Cause Variation While Demonstrating Improvement of the Average Performance Using Process Data

Source: Q3 2009 Process Capability Analysis Report MIMOS Berhad, Malaysia, a site appraised by SITARA Technologies at CMMI-DEV V1.2 Level 5 (Continuous Representation) in October 2009. Reproduced with permission.

Paired T-Test: Ho $p > 0.05$: Manual coding cycle time = Auto code generation cycle time Ha $p < 0.05$: Manual coding cycle time ≠ Auto code generation cycle time	
P-value = 0.000	Reject null hypothesis
Conclusion	Based on the P-value, manual and auto do not perform equally.

```
Paired T for Manual - Auto
              N     Mean     StDev
Manual        6     9.167    1.722
Auto          6     5.167    1.169
Difference    6     4.000    0.894
95% CI for mean difference: (3.061, 4.939) P-Value = 0.000
```

Fig. 7.5 [MIMOS 2009]: Hypothesis Testing Using Paired *t-test* for Statistically Inferring the Performance Results of the Innovation

Source: Q3 2009 Process Capability Analysis Report MIMOS Berhad, Malaysia, a site appraised by SITARA Technologies at CMMI-DEV V1.2 Level 5 (Continuous Representation) in October 2009. Reproduced with permission.

How does Organizational Innovation and Deployment transform its capability when the transition to capability level 3 (or the defined level) is made?

With a defined OID process area capability, business goals cascade down from the CEO down to the last individual in the organization either using a balanced score-card method or through a commitment building process for every innovation or improvement having a breakthrough effect. The balanced score-card uses four distinct perspectives to measure performance. The *strategic perspective* directs attention to the organization's people and infrastructure. The *operational perspective* aids in the creation of a true learning organization. The operational perspective focuses attention on the performance of the key internal processes that drive the business objectives. These internal processes need to be seen through the customer's eye—the *customer perspective*. It is only then that process improvements will have a lasting sponsorship and financial success. *Financial perspective* measures the ultimate results that the business provides to its shareholders. Together, these four perspectives provide a balanced view of the present and future performance of the business. SITARA has successfully piloted the balanced score-card method in what was called the *tear-down reengineering teams* using one more perspective with useful results to report—the *employee perspective* [PR Newswire 2000]. One of the most useful results is the high degree of employee commitment to the capability/competency development program. This perspective is needed to insulate and isolate erosion to the *knowledge base*. Competency identification and development is possible only with the creation of appropriate mechanisms to identify, retain and grow knowledge, skills, process abilities and talent. It has also been observed that building a sense of internal ownership through the employee perspective is the only lasting way to increase dividends and return on investment. Besides, it requires a patient study and organizational contribution (through employee perspective) to get the right balance. SITARA's current attempts with the balanced score-card method suggest establishing the following three main criteria as prerequisites:

Internal Handoffs

Every measure selected for a balanced score-card should be part of a chain of cause-and-effect relationships that represent the strategy.

Enablers and Performance Drivers

Measures common to most companies within an industry are known as *lag indicators*. Examples for a lag indicator include improved market share or customer retention. The drivers of performance or *lead indicators* tend to be unique because they reflect what is different about the strategy addressing the unique business objectives and goals of the organization. A good balanced score-card should have a mix of both lead and lag indicators.

Linked to Financials

With the proliferation of change programs underway in most organizations today, it is easy to become preoccupied with generic goals such as quality, customer satisfaction or innovation. While these goals are frequently strategic, they also must translate into measures that are ultimately linked to financial indicators.

The CMMI expects the following generic practices to be institutionalized to calibrate OID at capability level 3:

GG3 Institutionalize a Defined Process

GP3.1 **Establish a Defined Process**

GP3.2 **Collect Improvement Information**

It is very difficult to demonstrate and justify OID at a capability beyond level 3. Being a high-maturity process management process area common to all three constellations of the CMMI, it would also require enough business justifications and customer mandates to do so. When OID is institutionalized addressing the underlying causes of variation due to a process area, GP5.1 for that process area gets addressed. However, purely from a theoretical perspective, the generic goal 4 and the related generic practices 4.1 and 4.2 need to be established for enabling OID at capability level 4:

GG4 Institutionalize a Quantitatively Managed Process

GP4.1 **Establish Quantitative Objectives for the Process**

GP4.2 **Stabilize Sub-Process Performance**

And to enable OID at capability level 5, the generic goal 5 and the associated generic practices 5.1 and 5.2 need to be institutionalized:

GG5 Institutionalize an Optimizing Process

GP5.1 **Ensure Continuous Process Improvement**

GP5.2 **Correct Root Causes of Problems**

It may be useful to point out that the specific practices of OID in general enable the realization of GP 5.1—'Ensure Continuous Process Improvement'—across the 22 process areas of the CMMI-DEV, 6 process areas of the CMMI-ACQ constellation and 7 process areas of the CMMI-SVC constellation.

Author's Musing

The typical use of control limits for estimation accuracy that I have seen is as follows: for effort it should be ±*X* percent, and for schedule it must be ±*Y* per cent; this is monitored to be within these limits across the development life cycle. The trouble with this approach is that effort estimation in the early stages of a project which has no prior history of execution is bound to be over the +*X* per cent limit and so would schedule the estimation accuracy, as clarity levels are the lowest in say the requirements capture and needs analysis phase.

Also, in my opinion, spending more time in the early stages of development (even though there would be an overrun), to understand the project better, is a desirable project management practice. I would not be unduly concerned if there has been an effort and schedule overrun in the initial stages of the project. Naturally, more clarity in the initial stages would mean better control as the project begins its execution cycle.

To this effect, I would suggest the use of 'distributed' control limits across the life-cycle phases. For example: effort estimation accuracy of ±30 per cent in requirements capture and needs analysis phase, ±20 per cent in high-level design, ±15 per cent in detailed design and ±5 per cent in construction or coding phase. The same would apply for schedule estimation accuracy. Establishing tighter control limits as the life-cycle phases of the project get executed is both a realistic phenomenon and therefore a practical thing to do.

Epilogue

Author's Musing

"If you always put limits on what you can do, physical or anything else, it will spread over into the rest of your life. It will spread into your work, into your morality, into your entire being. There are no limits. There are plateaus, but you must not stay there, you must go beyond them. A man must constantly exceed his level."–Bruce Lee—(John Little, *Bruce Lee: The art of expressing The Human Body*, 1998)

Systemic failures are a result of a lack of process orientation. Commonplace incidents such as what we read in newspapers and magazines suggest that applying a process to day-to-day management and the process of decision making are no longer *a nice thing to have*; they must become a core competency if an organization has to differentiate itself from the rest of the breed. We reviewed the major CMMI concepts in this book in its *triumvirate avatar*—of CMMI-DEV (addressing the development aspects), CMMI-ACQ (addressing the acquisition aspects) and CMMI-SVC (addressing the services aspects)—and established a clear distinction between process capability and process maturity while exploring the two CMMI frameworks of the staged and the continuous representations. Establishing process maturity happens as a result of growing process capability. One way to enable growth in capability is by adopting the specific practices (and therefore, the attainment of specific goals) of the higher-maturity process areas. We have come to appreciate the process design of the CMMI, wherein process improvement is facilitated by the framework itself. The process frameworks of the CMMI (staged and continuous) by themselves enable minimizing the causes of variation (both special and common causes). Therefore, we concluded that CMMI serves as an example of what a Design for Six Sigma framework would be for software and systems development.

If true leverage from having a process program has to be realized, we have seen the importance of ensuring that circumstances that best promote a process culture must be ingrained. The integrated product and process development or IPPD aspects of the CMMI specifically address these humanistic and people issues in building a progressive process culture. With the attainment of each maturity level, we have seen that a whole new culture is grown and the foundation for seeding the next is established. We saw that a level 2 process maturity establishes a *culture of professionalism*. With a set of mature project management practices a sense of process management is established and forms the foundation upon which to seed practices of the level 3 process maturity in the creation of a *culture of best practices*. Attaining the level 3 maturity using practitioners' insights into knowing *what works and what does not*, a foundation for the next level of organizational maturity at level 4, a *culture of quantitative management*, is established. This is known in objective terms by consciously minimizing the cost of poor quality metric. Using the program of metrics collection and analysis, continuous exploration of practices that minimize cost of quality and therefore the institutionalization of level 5 maturity is rendered, wherein a *culture of continuous process improvement* or a *culture of informed learning* is established.

Since the release of CMMI version 1.1 in March 2002 and the development constellation version in August 2006, considerable progress has been made, with understanding and interpretation of the practices of high-process-maturity work environments operating at level 4 and level 5 maturity, mainly for the better. This book captures my current understanding resulting after implementing high-maturity practices, primarily with the development constellation in work cultures pursuing Six Sigma strategies in a multi-model context.

We saw that quality in products and service offerings is a very good differentiator and that this cannot happen by chance; it has to be designed into the process. We have seen that the main benefits of having a program of process improvement are

- To learn more and know more about the circumstances which surround the current context of execution and
- To ensure a structured mechanism to minimize the impact of variation.

Irrespective of the level of process maturity, if the essence behind the improvement program does not translate into the above two fundamental philosophies, the process improvement program will soon become an add-on activity which is done for its own sake.

Practicing the discipline advocated by the CMMI framework can be both enjoyable and rewarding. One thing is for sure: there is nothing like you have arrived. After attaining a level 5 process maturity, there is in fact more work to do. We have understood this concept with what we term at SITARA as the *process harmonic*, wherein a process area that once demonstrated the institutionalization of capability level 5 generic practices, having gained control over minimizing the impact of special and common causes of variation through a process definition, transforms itself to a capability level 3; this is an excellent recognition of the framework of the fact that continuous process improvement is *continuous* and the only purpose it serves is *to learn and know more about things we did not know earlier.*

To me, Bruce Lee personifies the spirit behind the limitless dynamism required to institutionalize and sustain high process maturity. He personifies the importance of gaining mastery of not just the process but also of the complete system of competencies that are essential and required to execute the process of Gung-fu effectively. Anyone who merely knows and understands what Gung-fu is all about, is only aware of the process. While that may be necessary, it is not sufficient. What makes such awareness sufficient is for one to gain an in-depth mastery of the associated network of competencies that are required to perfect the process which make-up the whole system. *"There are no limits. There are plateaus, but you must not stay there, you must go beyond them".* The same idea holds true of the CMMI constellations!

Most high maturity work cultures which have the capability to sustain such Bruce Lee like potential relentlessly pursue excellence. Having appraised close to twenty large level 5 organizational units in the last decade and having worked all of my professional engagements in high maturity work environment settings, I can confidently state that, true high maturity organizations exhibit a very unique and a distinct behavior–*they are passionate about ensuring quality in every aspect of their work*. You notice they innovate constantly and do things which–*exceed their levels* of mastery. They enact high maturity practices with pride, as if it were their second nature. Sponsors in such organizations ensure adequate investments with the realization that, returns or gains are directly proportional to the investments!

Consider this: in societies we live in, we see both functional and dysfunctional families. It is very evident observing the behavior of functional families that they have become so because of the *enormous investments* they make in building family values, a strong sense of ethics, understanding what is right and what is more right, commitment to bringing out the best in each other while bringing to bear a strong sense of belonging to one another. Such families do not consider these investments a waste. Individuals in such families lead extraordinary lives since development of an individual in such family settings is a fundamental core value viewed from a larger holistic perspective! They don't merely look at family members as either money making or money draining machines. Dysfunctional families are the exact opposite.

Much the same way, we see organizations that are both functional and dysfunctional. Functional organizations are so because of the investments they make in building individual competencies, establishing strong systems and processes, understand the right ways from the wrong ways, and ensure a shared vision among all constituencies of the organization in order to build a sense of organizational belonging. Such organizations do not consider these investments a waste as well! Functional organizations invariably belong to the high process maturity work cultures! They consider making investments in building competencies in their people as a necessary prerequisite to reap rich dividends and profits. Most definitely, functional families and functional organizations don't become that way by a stroke of luck. It is a lot of hard work and a lot of tenacious pursuit of excellence with strong ground rules with every single member involved. Dysfunctional organizations are the exact opposite!

One of the constant sponsorship concerns while embracing the CMMI constellations is–"*these frameworks are implementation intensive, cost much and involve making huge investments without the promise of anything tangible!*" Or, so it seems. But not true at all. Such investments almost definitely guarantee many 'intangibles' one of which being–*a predictable process performance leading to a quality outcome!* The importance and the need for institutionalizing robust processes only become evident when things go wrong and very badly at that! Unfortunately, it is such situations that teach the importance of having a process orientation best, but painfully so. When situations are handled with a 'business as normal' face instead of a crisis staring the organization in its face, one must commend the investments and effort of the process designers that have put a working process in place. In summary, the three constellations of the CMMI offer ready to use best practices for the process designers to put such a working process in place.

CMMI-DEV V1.2

Version 1.2 of the CMMI development constellation retains only 22 process areas of version 1.1. Since it also includes IPPD aspects as an addition, it is more appropriately called CMMI-DEV+IPPD. If one chooses to ignore the IPPD aspects of the constellation, then the CMMI-DEV results. For a quick look at what has changed, the major changes can be summarized into ten points and can be summarized as follows. The purpose of these changes has been to reduce complexity and size of the model, expand model coverage and increase confidence and usefulness of the appraisal results. At a high level, the ten major changes between versions 1.1 and 1.2 are as follows:

1. CMMI version 1.1 had the notion of advanced practices that were exclusive to the engineering process areas and it was quite a challenge to understand the rationale justifying their presence. The institutionalization aspects of the process areas bore reference to the term *common features* and the institutionalization practices related to ensuring a *Commitment to Perform, Ability to Perform, Directing Implementation and Verifying Implementation.* While retaining the intent to these types of practices, specific references to either the advanced engineering practices or to the common features have been eliminated in version 1.2.
2. Integrated Supplier Management has been removed and its intent is now part of maturity level 2 and not a separate component of the model under Supplier Sourcing, just as Supplier Agreement Management is part of the core model itself at level 2. Two Specific Practices were added to SG2 in SAM:
   - **SP2.2 (NEW)**: Monitor Selected Supplier Processes
   - **SP2.3 (NEW)**: Evaluate Selected Supplier Work Products
   - SG2 of SAM now has five specific practices instead of four:
     - SP2.1 Execute the Supplier Agreement
     - SP2.2 and SP2.3 stated above
     - SP2.4 Accept the Acquired Product
     - SP2.5 Transition Products
3. Practice removed from SAM:
   - **SAM**: SP2.1: Review COTS Products has been deleted from SG2. This practice is now a sub-practice under Technical Solutions Process Area: SP1.1 'Develop Alternative Solutions and Selection Criteria'.
4. With hardware additions, CMMI for development constellation will now take a single-book approach as CMMI-DEVELOPMENT+IPPD, where DEVELOPMENT could include Software Engineering, Systems Engineering and Hardware Engineering; *six hardware amplifications were added.*
   - Users can choose 'representation-specific content', 'addition-specific content' and the appropriate amplifications for hardware, software and systems.
   - Two other constellations of the CMMI address are CMMI for Acquisition and CMMI for Services.
5. The number of 'Not Applicable' process areas in the CMMI-DEV is significantly constrained to only Supplier Agreement Management and such decisions must be recorded in the appraisal disclosure statement during SCAMPI appraisals.

6. **Added emphasis on project start-up**: Two 'work environment' practices were added: one each into OPD (for an organizational look) and IPM (for project specifics), as follows:
   - **OPD**: SP1.6 (NEW): Establish Work Environment Standards
   - **IPM**: SP 1.1 *(Statement Modified): Establish and maintain the project's defined process from project start-up through the life of the project*
   - **IPM**: SP1.3 (NEW): Establish the Project's Work Environment
   - **OPF**: SP1.2 *(Statement Modified)*: Appraise the 'organization's process' (instead of processes of the organization) periodically and as needed to maintain an understanding of their strengths and weaknesses
   - **OPF**: SG2 *(Statement redefined)*: Plan and Implement Process Improvements
   - **OPF**: SG3 (NEW): Deploy Organizational Process Assets and Incorporate Lessons Learned; contains four specific practices. Two new and two old from SG2 were reshuffled.
     - ***(RESHUFFLED SP2.3)* SP3.1**: Deploy Organizational Process Assets
     - **(NEW) SP3.2**: Deploy Standard Processes
     - **(NEW) SP3.3**: Monitor Implementation
     - ***(RESHUFFLED SP2.4)* SP3.4**: Incorporate Process-Related Experiences into the Organizational Process Assets
7. IPPD process areas of OEI and IT have been incorporated into OPD and IPM *respectively* by adding a new goal in OPD and consolidating the goal statements in IPM as follows:
   - **OPD+IPPD has SG2 (NEW)**: Enable IPPD Management
     - **SP2.1**: Establish Empowerment Mechanisms
     - **SP2.2**: Establish Rules and Guidelines for Integrated Teams
     - **SP2.3**: Balance Team and Home Organization Responsibilities
   - **IPM+IPPD: SG3 (NEW, Consolidation of SG3 and SG4 with Integrated Teaming)**: Apply IPPD Principles
     - **SP3.1**: Establish the Project's Shared Vision
     - **SP3.2**: Establish Integrated Team Structure for the Project
     - **SP3.3**: Allocate Requirements to Integrated Teams
     - **SP3.4**: Establish Integrated Teams
     - **SP3.5**: Establish Coordination among Interfacing Teams
8. All six engineering process areas of CMMI-DEV have changed as follows:
   - **REQM**: SP 1.4: Bidirectional traceability in Requirements Management is now re-worded as "Maintain Bidirectional traceability among the requirements and work products." No longer mentions project plan and the capability level (*also note the dropping out of high capability attribute–2*).
   - **RM**: SP1.2: Obtain Commitment to Requirements (*also note the dropping out of–2*).

- **RD**: All references to lower-level specific practices have been eliminated in the engineering category; so, SP1.1–1 of RD—Collect Stakeholder Needs has been subsumed into SP1.1 of RD and reads as SP1.1–Elicit Needs (*Also note the dropping out of –1*).
- **RD**: SP3.4–3: Dropped attribute –3 for Analyze Requirements to Achieve Balance.
- **RD**: SP3.5: Validate requirements has been combined with Validate Requirements using Comprehensive Methods and now reads "Validate Requirements."
- **PI**: SP1.2–2: Establish Product Integration environment, and SP1.3–3—Establish Product Integration Procedures and Criteria (*higher-level capability attributes have been dropped*).
- **TS**: SP1.1: Develop Alternative Solutions and Selection Criteria has been combined with Develop Detailed Alternative Solutions and Selection Criteria and now reads as "Develop Alternative Solutions and Selection Criteria."
- **TS**: SP2.3: Establish Interface Descriptions has been combined with Design Interfaces Using Criteria and now reads as "Design Interfaces Using Criteria."
- **TS**: SP2.4–3: Dropped–3 attribute for 'Perform Make Buy or Reuse Analysis'.
- **TS**: (DELETED SP1.2: Evolve Operational Concepts and Scenarios) and incorporated into RD: SP3.1—Establish Operational Concepts and Scenarios. Resulting in renumbering of SP1.3 as SP1.2—Select Product Component Solutions.
- **VER**: SP1.2–2—Establish Verification Environment, and SP1.3–3—Establish Verification Procedures and Criteria, SP2.3–2—Analyze Peer Review Data, SP3.2–2—Analyze Verification Results ~~and Identify Corrective Action~~ (*higher-level capability attributes have been dropped; words with a strikethrough have been deleted*).
- **VER**: SP3.2 (Statement Title Modified): Analyze Verification Results ~~and Identify Correction Actions~~ (Note: Corrective Actions is handled in PMC SG2—Manage Corrective Actions to Closure. Words with a strikethrough have been deleted.)
- **VAL**: SP1.2–2—Establish Validation Environment, and SP1.3–3—Establish Validation Procedures and Criteria (*higher-level attributes dropped*).
- **VAL**: SP2.2 (*Statement Modified*): Analyze the results of validation activities ~~and identify issues~~. (*Words with a strikethrough have been deleted.*)

9. Practices in OID and OPP have been revised as follows:
    - **OID**: SP1.4: Select Improvements for Deployment

      Select process and technology improvements ~~proposals~~ for deployment across the organization. (Words with a strikethrough have been deleted.)
    - **OPP**: SP1.1: Select the processes and sub-processes (*not process elements*) in the organization's set of standard processes that are to be included in the organization's process performance analysis.
10. Changes to generic practices and PA overlap

    GP1.1: Perform 'specific' practices and not base practices

GP2.2: Plan the Process (informative material was condensed), GP2.3: Provide Resources, **GP2.4**: Assign Responsibilities (includes 'authority' in the informative component), GP2.7: Identify and Involve Relevant Stakeholders ⟷ PP

GP2.5—Train People ⟷ OT, PP SP2.5

GP2.6: reads as Manage Configurations: Place designated work products of <PA NAME> under appropriate levels of control (not, configuration management). ⟷ CM

GP2.8: Monitor and Control the Process ⟷ PMC, MA

GP2.9: Objectively Evaluate Adherence—informative material emphasizes work products ⟷ PPQA

GP2.10: Review Status with Higher-Level Management ⟷ PMC

GP3.1: Establish a Defined Process ⟷ IPM SP 1.1, OPD

GP3.2: Collect Improvement Information ⟷ IPM SP 1.6, OPF

GP4.1: Establish Quantitative Objectives for the Process ⟷ OPP, QPM

GP4.2: Stabilize Sub-Process Performance ⟷ QPM, OPP

GP5.1: Ensure Continuous Process Improvement ⟷ OID

GP5.2: Correct Root Causes of Problems—added notes that the focus is on a quantitatively managed process ⟷ CAR

CMMI-ACQ V1.2

CMMI-ACQ version 1.2, released by the SEI in November 2007, addressed the requirements for an acquisition environment. CMMI-ACQ integrates bodies of knowledge essential for an acquirer. Practices in the CMMI-ACQ constellation are contained in six process areas which are designed to enable a network of competencies, wherein the acquiring organization leverages the capabilities of supplier organizations by striking healthy relationships. Building the necessary communication processes that help to establish good teamwork between the acquiring organization and the supplying organization holds the key to the successful implementation of the CMMI-ACQ constellation. The six acquisition category process areas define practices for the acquirer process while dealing with suppliers. Such practices include mechanisms for sourcing suppliers, development and award of supplier agreements and managing the acquisition of capabilities. Supplier agreements govern the acquirer–supplier relationship. A predictable performance of the solution or product that is being developed for the end customer becomes possible by understanding the dependencies between the acquiring and supplying organization.

CMMI-SVC V1.2

CMMI-SVC version 1.2, released in February 2009, was designed to meet the requirements of services industry. The services constellation is a collection of best practices to provide guidance on developing and improving mature service practices. Like all CMMI constellations, the CMMI-SVC also allows for either an incremental improvement of a process area (with continuous representation) or improvement of an entire group of process areas required to be institutionalized at a maturity level (with staged representation). Since both representations essentially provide the same content, either representation can be chosen while ensuring achievement of business objectives. The CMMI-SVC constellation provides best practices with which to promote a quality approach to *delivery services* and *achieving business effectiveness and efficiency*. Such delivery capability should also consider minimizing process overheads while juggling between development of solutions and delivery of services based on such solutions. CMMI-SVC embodies the best practices required of a service provider in 24 process areas, 16 of which are common to all CMMI constellations, 7 are service-specific process areas and 1 of the process areas is an addition. Service agreements establish the contractual terms that bind the service provider and those affected by the service into a relationship of mutual understanding, good faith and positive disposition.

What to Expect in the Version 1.3 of the Three Constellations?

Design of the three CMMI constellations is such that they will continue to complement each other. Sixteen process areas (the core) remain common to all three constellations. CMMI-DEV provides guidance for measuring, monitoring and managing the development process; CMMI-SVC provides guidance for those providing services within organizations and to external customers and the CMMI-ACQ provides guidance to enable informed and decisive acquisition leadership. A new process area called Organizational Performance Management (OPM) has been carved out of Organizational Innovation and Deployment at the Level 5. The number of process areas in CMMI-DEV will still remain 22 with the following break up, the 16 core process areas with 1 shared process area of Supplier Agreement Management and the 5 engineering category process areas of Requirements Development, Technical Solution, Product Integration, Verification and Validation. Requirements Management, originally an Engineering category process area is moved into the project management category in the continuous representation. IPPD addition of the CMMI-DEV, optional in version 1.2 is mandatory and included as an integrated teaming specific practice in Organizational Process Definition and Integrated Project Management. CMMI-ACQ will still have 22 process areas with the following breakup: OPM at level 5, 16 core process areas, the 6 Acquisition category (renamed Acquisition Engineering in version 1.3) process areas of Solicitation and Supplier Agreement Development (SSAD), Acquisition Requirements Development, Acquisition Technical Management, Agreement Management (AM), Acquisition Validation, Acquisition Verification. SSAD and AM is moved to Project Management category in the continuous representation. So, in the continuous representation, the Acquisition Engineering category will only contain 4 process areas. We know the reasons why Supplier Agreement Management does not apply in the CMMI-ACQ (it is redundant). CMMI-SVC maintains 16 core process areas with 1 shared process of the Supplier Agreement Management, OPM at level 5 along with the following 7 process areas, Service Delivery, Capacity and Availability Management, Service System Transition, Strategic Service Management, Service Continuity, Incident Resolution and Prevention and Service System Development as an Addition. To clarify the importance of achieving performance improvement in high maturity implementation, a new process area called Organizational Performance Management has been carved out of OID in the Optimizing maturity level or the level 5 maturity. That would make the CMMI-SVC contain 24 process areas in all. Project management category of the continuous representation is renamed project and work management. Project planning and project monitoring and control is renamed work planning and work monitoring and control. This renaming will impact the practice titles of these process areas. While these are the major changes some of the other notable process area specific changes which have been made in version 1.3 are briefly summarized below with a probable justification.

Generic Goals 4 and 5 of the continuous representation have been rendered redundant since their intent is well established within the scope of the specific practices of the higher maturity process areas. All process areas can at most achieve a capability level 3; not beyond. The quantitative and optimizing tendencies of a process area described under—*'how a process area would demonstrate a high maturity measurement and analysis capability'* are extremely useful and important to enable the transition to high maturity.

The level 4 process area of Organizational Process Performance has brought business needs to focus while establishing process performance objectives. A significant improvement is with respect to the clarification it now offers with respect to selection of either the process and/or the sub-process for performance analysis, definition of measures in such analysis and establishment of the process performance models (PPM) and process capability baselines (PCB). Further, stratification of data, analysis and the establishment of PCB and PPM can occur at multiple levels of relevance–at the organizational level, the project level or at the level of a cluster of related projects (wherever data homogeneity can be assured).

The level 4 process area of Quantitative Project Management has removed the significant emphasis it once placed on using 'statistical methods to understand variation'; alternative methods besides using control charts are acceptable.

The level 5 process area of Causal Analysis and Resolution is focused on 'outcomes' that improve process performance rather than merely on defects and problems that impact process performance. This reorientation from a problems and defects only study to a more general study of process outcomes is bound to improve the efficacy of CAR practices to spur performance improvement to a higher gear.

The level 5 process area of Organizational Innovation and Deployment will be renamed Organizational Performance Management (OPM). It builds on top of the version 1.2 practices besides including practices in the new process area that will be carved out as OPM. The process engagement of the organization is rendered proactive by bringing the focus of improvement on business performance. Such a focus on business performance typically cascades down as quantitative objectives for quality and process performance.

Practices contained in the new level 5 process area of Organizational Performance Management, ensure management of process performance objectives of the organization to address business needs of the organization.

Fortunately, the intent of these changes with the creation of version 1.3 have been more than adequately addressed in this book. If anything would require to be revisited, it would be limited to the new practice statements of the high maturity process areas contained in levels 4 and 5. However, since the author was invited to review early drafts of the proposed changes in version 1.3, it is believed that interpretations offered in this book for the level 4 and 5 process areas will still have a significant relevance in the context of the expected changes.

CONCLUDING REMARKS

Observations in this book are based on long personal experience with change management initiatives in world-class organizations. This experience has taught me that truly world-class software development organizations implement methods and practices advocated within the CMMI as a *necessary* discipline in order to succeed. However, having the right system of practices is only half the requirement! They are only the necessary conditions in such organizations, but not sufficient conditions to operate at high process maturity. Beyond sound methods, there must be a passion to excel which forms the bedrock of what could be termed the sufficient conditions. What are some of those sufficiency conditions necessary for building a world-class software organization? I will relate to them from in the trenches of what some of my best professional associations have taught me.

Sufficiency Criterion 1

Establish a strong visionary leadership council for evaluating core competencies:

The single most important characteristic that distinguishes visionary leadership from the other styles is when such a leadership council is used as a sounding board for ideas, the input comes back value-added manifold. The process of building trust is often based on frank and open communication which is always firm. Members of this council know the intrinsic talents available in their organizations and keep an eye on the more promising individuals in the organization. Truly visionary leaders make a big difference to individual lives. They facilitate the so very crucial internal learning process that eventually plays out as the single most determining factor to be a highly capable organization.

Sufficiency Criterion 2

Establish highly talented and empowered leadership at all levels:

When you have a strong visionary leadership council at the top, leadership across all levels is a natural extension within the rest of the organization. Capability of a world-class organization is actually the collective capability of this chain of leadership. They are flexible in adopting best practices, adapting to changes that are necessary and modifying their behavior to newer circumstances. The finesse with which they team up, organize and reorganize is demonstrated by their ability to draw out the best performance in each other. They are also sensitive and recognize the fact that their performance operates in a broad band, ranging from poor to exceptional. There is no single value that determines their performance measure. A combination of factors determines the individual performance capability and they ensure that they draw out their best performance from leveraging upon their intrinsic talents.

Sufficiency Criterion 3

Build teams of people who live by a can-do attitude and are all Quality Champions:

In the present-day IT setup which requires extremely technical people who understand technology, the days of a traditional Quality Manager is over! A technocrat who can define the boundaries for the core competencies of an organization is the best choice for today's Quality Manager. Having such a person within an organization and to mentor the professional teams is a definite advantage. It takes a whole lot of can-do attitude among people who are inspired to live out the dreams of their leaders. For people to be effective followers, they must have high self-esteem and be highly geared to accepting responsibilities. The spirit often is: the job is not done until we accomplish what we set out to accomplish! Such unstoppable teams just happen out of good chemistry and sheer good luck.

There is a strong sense of sharing of lessons learnt and they often rewrite the rules of engagement and the underlying process if they feel they no longer serve the purpose. When each individual assumes the role of a Quality Champion, Quality does not happen by chance but gets designed into the probability of success. It is under such conditions alone that *Quality Is Free*. In such an orientation, not only does everybody think about *what* they do, but they also reflect upon *how* they do such work. They make the day-to-day changes that are necessary for optimal performance. It is taboo to schedule a work product peer review, if the author of the work product feels it is not up to the mark. Extreme care is exercised while creating the intermediate work products that become inputs to phases later in the life cycle, to ensure that the handoff is clean. The means employed are as important as the end objectives. They are naturally oriented to continuous exploration of best practices and force a change when things get too comfortable. The exhibited characteristic of such teams of individuals is that they take ideas from inception to closure by brainstorming and rapid prototyping. They normally visualize through the customer's eye by keeping a customer perspective in all of their peer reviews. Their sense of pride in their work accomplishments and their organizational affiliations to which they belong is extremely high and one can say it by looking at the manner in which they hand out their business cards!

Sufficiency Criterion 4

An organizational sponsor who is supportive of proactive growth:

Ideas that have business value are often actively sought out by the organization and rewarded suitably. Sponsorship is in touch with everything that is happening in the organization. Sponsors are found communicating their dreams with clear deadlines, share their vision for the company, coordinate action and facilitate collective understanding. The sponsor makes sure that process improvement is everybody's job—a community affair. There is a clear focus on developing competencies and the will to do whatever it takes to support their growth.

Sufficiency Criterion 5

Establish gymnasiums for continuous personal competency development:

Setting up gymnasiums and learning laboratories to exercise the brains of individuals where leadership and management lessons are taught by recognized gurus and internal mentors is an organizational culture. Personal competency development is oriented toward building organizational core competencies. Personal competency development plans are laid out with a *stick-to-your-knitting* approach. With the pace at which technology changes, one is often tempted to keep moving to newer and newer horizons. That has been the single most important contributor for mediocrity and dilution of competencies. The only meaningful way to overcome the impact from this shifting terrain is to make sure that organizational core competencies have a long-term focus. Most individuals at all levels pursue personal learning as an obsession.

A well-articulated process improvement plan must ensure that both the necessary and sufficiency conditions are addressed to make sure that the process maturity really sticks long enough to make a positive behavioral transformation. Organizations realize that they need world-class development methods to survive and thrive in this business. In order to achieve this, they will need to deploy world-class tools, hire highly energetic, talented individuals and have in place a system of coordinated action for continuous renewal.

Practicing the discipline advocated by the CMMI framework can be both enjoyable and rewarding. I hope that the information presented to readers here has broadened their perspective and has offered them a range of choices to make.

In order to establish a collaborative mind share with the growing experience of practitioners in the CMMI community, we have created a knowledge laboratory called AskSITARA. AskSITARA is a learning group to establish a brain trust among professionals who would like to collaborate while establishing an understanding of process improvement and the different issues concerning IT management. We would be pleased to have you amidst our learning group and learn from your experience. I welcome you to join this group from http://www.SITARATECH.com.

Appendix

Approved for Public Release from SITARA Process Jewelbox™

From years of experience working with strategic management consulting and assessments, SITARA Technologies has a very surprising finding to report:

"Organizations often underestimate the quantum of work involved in change management initiatives and as a consequence are often underprepared to face up to the challenges that are often encountered."

In order to facilitate organizations to think through the software process improvement scenario, the following questions from SITARA Process JewelBox™ are approved for public release, to give a feel for the extent of work that might be required to leverage full potential and value from change management initiatives (either a software or a people process improvement program).

It is advised that the senior management along with the process management group such as the Software Engineering Process Group address these questions in unambiguous terms to de-risk the change management program and protect investments.

1.	Is the site primarily looking for a CMMI or the People CMM implementation? Or both?
2.	Is the site looking for consultancy, assessment or both?
3.	What is the primary focus of software activity (development, maintenance, services, acquisition or a combination) of the site that wants an assessment?
4.	What is the main domain (telecom, web applications, product development, etc.) around which the software activity (development, maintenance, services, acquisition or a combination) is being carried out?
5.	What is the scope of the assessment (only the development process, or only the maintenance process, or only the services process, or only the acquisition process or a combination)?

(Contd)

6.	Is the assessment restricted to a single site or is the process (development, maintenance, services, acquisition or a combination) distributed across multiple sites?
7.	Would you require a People CMM implementation along with CMMI?
8.	What internal organizational abilities (such as process owners who can drive the initiative) exist at this time?
9.	When was the most recent SCAMPI appraisal done?
10.	What were the appraisal recommendations?
11.	Can we have a copy of the action plan since the last appraisal?
12.	Has the site been formally assessed in the recent 1 year? If Yes: 1. What was the process capability? 2. What is the primary nature of software activity for the assessed site? Development, maintenance, services, acquisition or a combination? 3. How many projects does the appraised site execute on an average, typically in a year? 4. What is the total strength of the appraised site? 5. Who was the lead appraiser on the appraisal? 6. How closely did the appraisal results map to your business needs? 7. Did the appraisal give you enough insight into a follow-on action program? 8. How many people are involved in the follow-on action program? 9. What are your present business needs that fall short from being met with the process improvement initiative? 10. Have you identified the process areas you want to improve? 11. What is the process improvement road map?
13.	Is the site working currently on a process improvement initiative? If Yes: 1. What has worked well? 2. What has not worked well?
14.	Can we have the organization structure for the division/unit that was appraised and what is the current structure?
15.	What was the size of the organization/division/unit that was appraised?
16.	What is the current size of the organization that is proposed to get appraised?
17.	What is the size of the team engaged in the different process improvement activities?
18.	What percentage of the organization participates in the different process improvement programs?

(Contd)

19.	What is the size of the Software Engineering Process Group?
20.	What is the role of Software Quality Assurance (SQA) in the software process improvement initiative?
21.	What is the size of the SQA in the organization?
22.	Do you have a separate group such as the testing group which conducts activities independent of the development teams?
23.	What are the different process groups that have been identified for the process improvement activities and what is the reporting structure?
24.	What is the commitment of the senior management to software process improvement initiatives?
25.	What is the primary reason for the software process improvement? What are the business goals/objectives that the senior management wants to address with the software process improvement program?
26.	How does the organization come to know of better development/testing/QA processes and strategies that are not yet part of the organization?
27.	What action, if any, is taken by the senior management to internalize these newer techniques into the organization?
28.	Does the organization have any impact with either changes to technology/tools or process innovations?
29.	What is the proposed Return on Investment (RoI) with the software process improvement initiative and what was the deviation from the actual RoI and estimated RoI from building the infrastructure?
30.	Since when did the organization start the different software process improvement initiatives?
31.	How difficult is it for the organization to come to grips with the demands made while addressing change initiatives?
32.	How acceptable is the team that is driving the change initiative within the organization?
33.	What are the different types of development processes/testing processes that are in use and documented to be the organizational standards?
34.	How were they established as the organizational standards?
35.	Do all project execution efforts in the organization use these standards either "as is" or "derive" what is reasonable for use on projects?
36.	What is the role of the SEPG/QA in such tailoring activities?

(Contd)

37.	How many projects have been able to deliver on time, on budget with acceptable levels of quality in the recent 6 months?
38.	How many projects are in execution since the past 6 months?
39.	What are the different project-specific and organization-wide tools in practice?
40.	What formal mechanisms are established in projects to ensure that the software developed is correct, complete and consistent with the stated and implied requirements?
41.	What is the testing procedure and testing strategy?
42.	How critical is the software developed to end-user concerns? In other words, how critical is it for the organization to develop deliverables with zero known defects?
43.	What are the quality goals for the organization?
44.	How often is the project tracked against milestones and who participates in these tracking mechanisms?
45.	How often are risks identified and how adequately are the abatement procedures addressing the risks?
46.	How frequently does a role in the organization review the configuration management activities?
47.	What is the role, if any, of subcontractors on development initiatives?
48.	What is the mechanism, if any, for selecting and using subcontractors?
49.	How easy is it for the organization to obtain the enrollment of the better-qualified and better-skilled individuals into SQA functions?
50.	Does the organization have long-term imperatives with their CMMI initiatives after getting to level 3?
51.	Is the organization going in for the SCAMPI appraisal for any specific business reasons?
52.	What are the proposed annual budgets for software process improvement activities?

Note: A level on the CMMI is *only* an abbreviation to the detailed process infrastructure that is institutionalized, used and continuously improved upon. So, asking the question '*what level of process maturity should we target?*' requires resolutions and answers to the above set of questions.

Glossary of Terms

CAR	Causal Analysis and Resolution
CCB	Change Control Board
CFD	Control Flow Diagram
CL	Capability Level
CM	Configuration Management
CMMI	Capability Maturity Model Integration
CMMI-ACQ	CMMI for Acquisition
CMMI-DEV+IPPD	CMMI for Development+IPPD
CMMI-SVC	CMMI for Services
CMP	Configuration Management Plan
COAQ	Cost of Assuring Quality
COPQ	Cost of Poor Quality
COQ	Cost of Quality
COTS	Commercial Off-the-Shelf Software
CPI	Cost Performance Index
DAR	Decision Analysis and Resolution
DDE	Data Dictionary Entry
DFD	Data Flow Diagram
DFSS	Design For Six Sigma
EIA	Electronic Industries Alliance
ETVX	Entry-Task-Verification-eXit

FBRS	Functional and Business Requirements Specification
FCA	Functional Configuration Audit
FRS	Functional Requirements Specification
GG	Generic Goal
GP	Generic Practice
GQM	Goal, Question, Metric
IDEAL	Initiating-Diagnosing-Establishing-Acting-Leverage
IEEE	Institute of Electrical and Electronics Engineers
IPD-CMM	Integrated Product Development Capability Maturity Model
IPM	Integrated Project Management
IPPD	Integrated Product and Process Development
ISO/IEC	International Organization for Standardization/International Electrotechnical Commission
HLDD	High Level Design Document
JAD	Joint Application Development
MA	Measurement and Analysis
ML	Maturity Level
MSpec	Module Specification
OPD	Organizational Process Definition
OPF	Organizational Process Focus
OPP	Organizational Process Performance
OID	Organizational Innovation and Deployment
OT	Organizational Training
PA	Process Area
P-CMM, People-CMM	People Capability Maturity Model
PCA	Physical Configuration Audit
PDCA	Plan, Do, Check, Act (Shewart-Deming Cycle)
PDRO	Product Development and Roll-Out
PI	Product Integration
PIID	Practice Implementation Indicator Document
PM	Project Manager or Program Manager
PMC	Project Monitoring and Control
PP	Project Planning
PPQA	Process and Product Quality Assurance
PPSS	Project Planning and Support Service

PMC	Project Monitoring and Control
PSpec	Process Specification
PSEE	Process Support and Solution Enablers
PS*IP*	Package Selection and Integration Process
PSIP	Package Selection and Integration Plan
PSMS	Product Survey and Market Screening
QAP	Quality Assurance Plan
QFD	Quality Function Deployment
QPM	Quantitative Project Management
RCPI	Requirements Confirmation and Product Interoperability
RD	Requirements Development
REQB	Requirements Book
REQM	Requirements Management
RMF	Review Meeting From
RMNF	Review Meeting Notice Form
RSKM	Risk Management
RF	Reviewer's Form
RoI	Return on Investment
RDQAF	Review Disposition and Quality Assurance Form
RDRA	Requirements Definition and Requirements Analysis
SAS	Systems Acceptance Specifications
SAM	Supplier Agreement Management
SASR	Solution Alternatives and Solution Recommendation
SCAMPI	Standard CMMI Appraisal Method for Process Improvement
SEPG	Software Engineering Process Group
SG	Specific Goal
SME	Subject Matter Experts
SP	Specific Practice
SPI	Software Process Improvement
SQA	Software Quality Assurance
SSE	Software Systems Engineer
SSTE	Software System Test Engineer
SSTP	Software System Test Plan
SW-CMM	Software Capability Maturity Model
TCO	Total Cost of Ownership

TQM	Total Quality Management
TS	Technical Solution
UTE	Unit Test Engineer
UTP	Unit Test Plan
VAL	Validation
VER	Verification
VDPR	Vendor Demonstration and Product Ranking

References

[Basili 1984] Basili, V.R., and D.M. Weiss, "A Methodology for Collecting Valid Software Engineering Data", *IEEE Transactions on Software Engineering*, Vol. SE-10, 1984, pp. 728–738.

[Beizer 1990] Beizer, Boris, *Software Testing Techniques*, Coriolis Group, 1990.

[Beizer 1995] Beizer, Boris, *Black Box Testing*, John Wiley, 1995.

[Boehm 1981] Boehm, Barry, *Software Engineering Economics*, Prentice-Hall, 1981.

[Brown 1992] Brown, Mark Graham, "Baldrige Award Winning Quality, How to Interpret the Malcolm Baldrige Award Criteria", ASQC Quality Press, 1992.

[Coutu 2002] Coutu, L. Diane, "The Anxiety of Learning", *Harvard Business Review*, 80(3):100-6, 134, March 2002.

[Creech 1994] Creech, Bill, *The Five Pillars of TQM*, Truman Talley Books/Plume, 1994.

[Curtis 1995] Curtis, Bill et al., "People Capability Maturity Model", CMU/SEI-95-MM-02, Overview of the People Capability Maturity Model® Version 1.0, CMU/SEI 95-MM-01, Software Engineering Institute, Carnegie Mellon University, September 1995.

[Curtis 2002] Curtis, Bill et al., *The People Capability Maturity Model*, Addison-Wesley, Pearson Education, Inc., 2002.

[DeMarco 1995] Demarco, T., *Why Does Software Cost so Much?* Dorset House Publishing, 1995.

[Gale 2002] Cengage Learning, "Found: 13-inch retractor was left inside a patient", http://www.thefreelibrary.com/Found:+13-inch+retractor+was+left+inside+a+patient.-a083143221

[Florac 1997] Florac, William A., Robert E. Park, Anita D. Carleton, "Practical Software Measurement: Measuring for Process Management and Improvement" CMU/SEI-97-HB-003, 1997.

[Hatley 1998] Hatley, Derek J., and Imtiaz A. Pirbhai, *Strategies for Real-Time System Specification*, Dorset House Publishing, 1988.

[Kan 1995] Kan, Stephen H., *Metrics and Models in Software Quality Engineering*, Addison-Wesley Publishing Company, 1995.

[Kaplan 1996] Kaplan, R.S., and D.P. Norton. *The Balanced Scorecard—Translating Strategy into Action*, Harvard Business School Press, 1996.

[Kirkpatrick 1998] Kirkpatrick, D.L., *Evaluating Training Programs* (2nd Edn), Berrett-Koehler, 1998.

[McMenamin and Palmer 1984] McMenamin, Stephen, and John Palmer, *Essential System Analysis*, Yourdon, 1984.

[MIMOS 2009] Q3 2009 Process Capability Analysis Report MIMOS Berhad, Malaysia, a site appraised by SITARA Technologies at CMMI-DEV V1.2 Level 5 (Continuous Representation) in October 2009.

[Moseman 2009] Moseman, A., "Study: Like Earthquakes & Financial Markets, Terrorist Attacks Follow Laws of Math", Discover Magazine, December 17, 2009, http://blogs.discovermagazine.com/80beats/2009/12/17/study-like-earthquakes-financial-markets-terrorist-attacks-follow-laws-of-math/

[Nandyal 1993] Nandyal, R.S., "Function Analysis Tool: FAT", Software Engineering Symposium, Motorola, Phoenix, AZ, 1993.

[Nandyal 1994] Nandyal, R.S., "Integrated Software Engineering Tool", Motorola Software Engineering Symposium and Tools Fair, Schaumburg, IL, 1994.

[Nandyal 1997] Nandyal, R.S., *Making the Use of Structured Methods More Effective*, Tata McGraw-Hill, Computer Society of India, Bangalore, 1997.

[Nandyal 2003] Nandyal, R.S., *People CMM*, Tata McGraw-Hill, 2003.

[Nandyal 2007] Nandyal, R.S., *Making Sense of Software Quality Assurance*, Tata McGraw-Hill, 2007.

[PR Newswire 2000] P.R. Newswire, "Intelligroup Global Development Center Achieves SEI Certification for Continuous Improvement of Software and People Development", October 2000.

[Rothwell 94] Rothwell, W.J. & Kazanas, H.C. (1994). *Human Resource Development: A Strategic Approach*, Amherset, MA: HRD Press, Inc., pp. 484–486.

[SITARA 2000b] SITARA Process JewelBox™, 2000b.

[SITARA SE/JUNE 2001b] http://www.SITARATECH.com/innovations.htm [SITARA Technical Report], SITARA Technologies Pvt. Ltd, 2001b.

[SITARA Tutorials 2001c] 'CMMI as a Second Language' course Version 2.0 SITARA Technologies Pvt. Ltd, 2001c.

[Wheeler 1992] Wheeler, Donald J., and David S. Chambers, *Understanding Statistical Process Control*, SPC Press, 1992.

[Wheeler 1993] Wheeler, Donald J., *Understanding Variation: The Key to Managing Chaos*, Knoxville, Tenn.: SPC Press, 1993.

[Wheeler 1995] Wheeler, Donald J., *Advanced Topics in Statistical Process Control*, Knoxville, Tenn.: SPC Press, 1995.

Recommended Readings

[Albrecht 1992] Albrecht, K., *The Only Thing That Matters*, Harper Business, 1992.

[CMU 1995] Carnegie Mellon University, Software Engineering Institute, M. Paulk, et al., *Capability Maturity Model: Guidelines for Improving the Software Process*, Addison-Wesley, 1995.

[Constantine 1993] Constantine, L., "Work Organization: Paradigms for Project Management and Organization", Communications of the ACM, Vol. 36(10), October 1993, pp. 35–43.

[DeMarco and Lister 1985] DeMarco, T., and T. Lister, "Programmer Performance and the Effects of the Workplace", Proceedings of the 8th International Conference on Software Engineering, London, 1985, pp. 269–272.

[Gibson 1997] Gibson, R., *Rethinking the Future*, Nicholas Brealey Publishing, 1997.

[Humphrey 1997] Humphrey, W., *Managing Technical People*, Addison-Wesley Longman, Inc., 1997.

[Humphrey 1997] Humphrey, W.S., *Introduction to the Personal Software Process*SM, Addison-Wesley, 1997.

[Humphrey 2000] Humphrey, W.S., *Introduction to the Team Software Process*SM, Addison-Wesley, 2000.

[Kaplan 1992] Kaplan, R.S., and D.P. Norton, "The Balanced Scorecard—Measures That Drive Performance", *Harvard Business Review*, Vol. 70(1), 1992, pp. 71–79.

[Kelley 2001] Kelley, T., *The Art of Innovation*, Doubleday, 2001.

[Nandyal 2002] Nandyal, R.S., "Do You Really Have a Software Development Strategy?", Accepted for presentation at the 7th Annual European SEPG Conference, 2002.

[Pande 2000] Pande, P.S., et al., *The Six Sigma Way: How GE, Motorola, and Other Top Companies Are Honing Their Performance*, New York: McGraw-Hill, 2000.

[Satir 1991] Satir, Virginia, *The Satir Model*, Science & Behavior Books, 1991.

[Scholtes 1998] Scholtes, P, *The Team Handbook*, Joiner Associates, Inc., 1988.

[Schulmeyer 1990] Schulmeyer, Gordon G., *Zero Defect Software*, McGraw-Hill, 1990.

[SITARA 2000a] SITARA's People CMM Assessment Survey Questionnaire (People CASQ) released from SITARA Process JewelBox™ with permission from SITARA Technologies Pvt. Ltd, 2000a.

[SITARA 2001a] SITARA 10W5D Competency Hierarchy Model and SITARA Domain Competency Sandwich Model released from SITARA Process JewelBox™ with permission from SITARA Technologies Pvt. Ltd, 2001a.

Index

Adjusted PSIP, 93
An example target profile which the units must meet, 26
Architecture Context Diagram, 58

Capability Profile
Target profile, 26, 40, 228, 271
Carnegie Mellon University, 27
Software Engineering Institute, 8, 139, 201, 305
Characteristics of a Level 3 Process (Defined Process), 164
Characteristics of a Level 4 Process (Quantitatively Managed Process), 258
Characteristics of a Level 5 Process (Optimizing Process), 278
CMMI, 1, 2, 3, 6, 8, 9, 10, 11, 12, 13, 14, 15, 16, 18, 19, 24, 26, 27, 28, 30, 32, 34, 35, 37, 38, 39, 40, 41, 42, 44, 45, 47, 48, 50, 54, 56, 100, 102, 103, 104, 105, 107, 108, 111, 114, 115, 120, 128, 129, 131, 133, 134, 136, 137, 142, 143, 145, 149, 151, 154, 157, 159, 163, 164, 167, 172, 178, 185, 186, 187, 191, 192, 198, 200, 207, 225, 226, 230, 234, 238, 244, 245, 249, 256, 257, 258, 264, 269, 271, 272, 273, 276, 277, 278, 279, 283, 287, 288, 289, 293, 297, 298, 299, 307, 310
Acquisition Constellation, 3, 4, 6, 7, 8, 17, 18, 19, 20, 22, 23, 25, 28, 43, 44, 45, 46, 47, 77, 78, 102, 103, 115, 119, 129, 133, 136, 142, 143, 149, 150, 152, 154, 155, 156, 157, 160, 166, 167, 204, 207, 208, 225, 230, 231, 234, 238, 239, 241, 244, 248, 264, 271, 272, 277, 283, 289, 298, 299, 305, 306
Acquisition Requirements Development (ARD), 17, 103, 157, 159
Acquisition Technical Management (ATM), 19, 167, 204
Acquisition Validation (AVAL), 19, 167, 208
Acquisition Verification (AVER), 19, 43, 44, 167, 207, 306
Agreement Management (AM), 17, 103, 152, 153, 154, 306
AM, 17, 18, 44, 103, 149, 150, 151, 152, 153, 154, 155, 156, 204, 206, 302, 306
ARD, 17, 44, 103, 155, 157, 159, 208, 306
Appraisal types-Class B, 11, 227
Appraisal types-Class C, 11
AVAL, 19, 43, 44, 167, 208, 306
CAM, 20, 167, 212, 213, 214, 215, 306
Capacity and Availability Management (CAM), 20, 167, 212
CAR, 23, 43, 77, 114, 122, 187, 240, 248, 283, 287, 288, 289, 292, 307
CM, 17, 18, 24, 43, 44, 54, 81, 85, 103, 133, 134, 135, 136
Configuration Management (CM), 17, 18, 103, 133

Continuous Representation, 6, 13, 37, 41, 45, 47, 147, 148, 174, 175, 199, 200, 263, 270, 285, 294, 295
  Categories, 6, 7, 45, 142
  Project Management Category, 7, 45, 142
Continuous Process Improvement, 1, 4, 15, 25, 29, 33, 277, 278, 300
Decision Analysis and Resolution (DAR), 19, 20, 43, 110, 142, 167, 184, 185, 205, 245, 248, 249, 250, 251, 256, 257
Defined, 4, 13, 14, 15, 18, 19, 20, 21, 22, 25, 26, 29, 30, 33, 35, 36, 41, 45, 48, 103, 107, 108, 109, 120, 121, 132, 136, 140, 141, 146, 151, 152, 154, 157, 159, 162, 163, 164, 165, 166, 172, 173, 180, 185, 186, 190, 192, 197, 198, 203, 206, 211, 214, 215, 217,219, 220, 221, 224, 225, 228, 229, 230, 233, 236, 237, 243, 244, 247, 248, 256, 257, 258, 265, 266, 269, 270, 271, 276, 277, 282, 287, 288, 296, 297, 300, 307
Development Constellation, 3, 4, 6, 7, 8, 17, 18, 19, 20, 22, 23, 25, 28, 33, 38, 40, 41, 42, 43, 46, 47, 77, 78, 102, 103, 115, 119, 129, 133, 136, 142, 143, 147, 148, 149, 150, 153, 154, 156, 157, 158, 166, 167, 168, 171, 174, 175, 178, 187, 189, 191, 196, 199, 200, 204, 206, 207, 208, 215, 216, 217, 225, 230, 231, 232, 234, 238, 239, 241, 244, 248, 263, 264, 270, 271, 272, 277, 283, 285, 289, 294, 295, 298, 299, 301, 302, 303, 306
Directing Implementation, 302
Generic
  Ability to perform, 302
Generic Goal 1, 14
Generic Goal 2, 15, 35, 36, 132, 185, 233
Generic Goal 3, 15, 35, 121, 132, 136, 141, 146, 151, 154, 157, 159, 163, 172, 186, 190, 198, 203, 206, 211, 215, 217, 220, 221, 224, 229, 233, 237, 244, 248, 257, 270, 276, 288, 297
Generic Goal 4, 15, 136, 141, 152, 154, 157, 159, 163, 190, 198, 204, 230, 233, 237, 244, 248, 257, 270, 276, 289, 297
Generic Goal 5, 14, 15, 136, 142, 152, 155, 157, 160, 163, 187, 191, 199, 204, 230, 234, 238, 244, 248, 257, 271, 277, 289, 297
Generic Goals, 12, 35, 38, 111, 204, 226, 233, 297
Generic Practice, 14, 16, 19, 21, 23, 27, 106, 107, 108, 111, 114, 119, 121, 128, 129, 132, 133, 135, 136, 141, 142, 145, 146, 149, 151, 152, 154, 155, 157, 159, 160, 162, 163, 172, 173, 177, 178, 185, 186, 187, 190, 191, 198, 199, 203, 204, 206, 211, 215, 217, 220, 221, 224, 229, 230, 233, 234, 237, 238, 244, 248, 257, 270, 271, 276, 277, 288, 289, 297, 298
  Commitment, 302
GP2.1, 16, 106, 119, 151, 154, 162, 185, 233
GP2.10, 16, 107, 119, 151, 154, 157, 162, 185, 233
GP2.2, 16, 106, 119, 129, 151, 154, 162, 185, 233, 305
GP2.3, 16, 106, 119, 129, 151, 154, 162, 185, 233, 305
GP2.4, 16, 106, 119, 151, 154, 162, 185, 233
GP2.5, 16, 106, 119, 151, 154, 162, 185, 233, 305
GP2.6, 16, 106, 119, 135, 136, 151, 154, 162, 185, 233, 305
GP2.7, 16, 106, 119, 129, 151, 154, 162, 185, 233, 244, 305
GP2.8, 16, 106, 119, 132, 133, 142, 151, 154, 162, 185, 233, 305
GP2.9, 16, 107, 119, 145, 149, 151, 154, 162, 185, 233, 305
GP3.1, 19, 108, 121, 132, 136, 141, 146, 151, 154, 157, 159, 163, 172, 186, 190, 198, 203, 206, 211, 215, 217, 220, 221, 224, 229, 233, 234, 237, 244, 248, 257, 270, 276, 288, 297, 305
GP3.2, 19, 108, 121, 132, 136, 141, 146, 151, 154, 157, 159, 163, 172, 186, 190, 198, 203, 206, 211, 215, 217, 220, 221, 224, 230, 233, 237, 244, 248, 257, 270, 276, 288, 297, 305
GP4.1, 21, 111, 128, 133, 136, 141, 149, 152, 154, 157, 159, 163, 173, 190, 198, 204, 230, 233, 237, 244, 248, 257, 270, 271, 276, 289, 297, 305
GP4.2, 21, 136, 141, 152, 154, 157, 159, 163, 173, 190, 198, 204, 230, 233, 237, 244, 248, 257, 270, 276, 289, 297
GP5.1, 23, 114, 129, 133, 136, 142, 149, 152, 155, 157, 160, 163, 177, 187, 191, 199, 204, 230, 234, 238, 244, 248, 257, 271, 277, 289, 297, 298, 305
GP5.2, 23, 114, 129, 133, 136, 142, 149, 178, 187, 191, 199, 204, 248, 257, 271, 277, 289, 297, 305
Incident Resolution and Prevention (IRP), 20, 167, 222
Initial, 2, 3, 13, 14, 15, 16, 27, 29, 32, 35, 41, 45, 48, 100, 101, 102, 103, 104, 105, 106, 115, 118, 129,

131, 133, 134, 136, 138, 143, 149, 152, 155, 157, 160, 167, 178, 180, 184, 187, 188, 191, 200, 201, 204, 205, 207, 208, 209, 212, 213, 215, 216, 218, 220, 221, 222, 225, 230, 234, 238, 244, 248, 264, 272, 273, 275, 277, 282, 283, 286, 289, 291, 292
Institutionalization, 36, 38, 217, 224, 288
Institutionalization at Capability Level 2, 107, 119, 132, 135, 140, 145, 151, 154, 157, 159, 162, 172, 185, 190, 197, 202, 206, 211, 214, 217, 219, 221, 224, 229, 236, 243, 247, 257, 269, 275
Integrated Teaming, 303
IPM, 19, 20, 25, 43, 167, 233, 238, 242, 243, 306
IRP, 20, 163, 167, 215, 222, 223, 224, 306
ISM, 302
IT, 303
Level 2, 100, 258
Level 3, 164
Level 4, 41, 45, 48, 136, 141, 152, 154, 157, 159, 163, 190, 198, 204, 230, 233, 237, 244, 248, 257, 258, 270, 276, 289, 297
Level 5, 4, 21, 41, 45, 48, 136, 142, 152, 155, 157, 160, 163, 187, 191, 199, 204, 230, 234, 238, 244, 248, 257, 271, 277, 278, 289, 297, 306
MA, 17, 18, 43, 75, 103, 136, 137, 138, 139, 140, 141, 142, 155, 275, 283
Managed, 3, 12, 13, 14, 15, 16, 17, 18, 19, 20, 22, 24, 25, 26, 29, 33, 35, 36, 41, 45, 48, 100, 102, 103, 105, 106, 107, 108, 119, 120, 131, 132, 135, 140, 145, 151, 153, 154, 157, 159, 162, 164, 171, 172, 176, 184, 185, 186, 190, 197, 202, 206, 209, 211, 214, 216, 217, 219, 221, 223, 224, 228, 229, 232, 235, 242, 243, 247, 256, 257, 265, 268, 269, 275, 282, 283, 287, 292, 295, 300, 302
Maturity Level, 3, 4, 9, 12, 13, 15, 17, 18, 19, 20, 22, 24, 26, 27, 34, 35, 41, 45, 47, 48, 166, 258, 283, 299, 302, 305, 306
Measurement and Analysis (MA), 17, 18, 103, 136
OID, 23, 43, 77, 128, 217, 231, 283, 289, 292, 296, 306, 307
OPD, 19, 20, 25, 43, 77, 167, 186, 220, 229, 230, 232, 233, 290, 306
OPF, 19, 20, 43, 76, 77, 167, 186, 220, 225, 228, 229, 290
OPP, 22, 25, 43, 77, 167, 220, 264, 268, 269, 307
Optimizing, 2, 4, 9, 12, 13, 20, 22, 23, 29, 30, 33, 36, 37, 41, 45, 48, 102, 103, 110, 112, 113, 114, 128, 129, 133, 136, 141, 146, 147, 148, 149, 152, 154, 157, 159, 163, 174, 175, 177, 178, 187, 191, 199, 200, 203, 204, 206, 211, 215, 217, 220, 221, 224, 230, 234, 237, 244, 248, 257, 263, 266, 270, 272, 277, 278, 282, 283, 285, 289, 293, 294, 295, 297, 300, 301, 306, 307
OT, 19, 20, 25, 43, 167, 234, 235, 236, 237, 238
PI, 19, 166, 187, 189, 190, 304, 306
PMC, 17, 18, 36, 43, 103, 129, 131, 132, 133, 149, 246, 248
PP, 14, 17, 18, 24, 25, 34, 36, 38, 43, 44, 103, 109, 110, 115, 118, 119, 120, 121, 128, 129, 130, 132, 133, 149, 239, 246, 248, 250, 256, 258
PPQA, 17, 18, 37, 43, 103, 143, 145, 146, 149, 265
Process and Product Quality Assurance (PPQA), 17, 18, 103, 143, 145, 146
Process Area, 6, 16, 24, 25, 38
Process Capability Level, 9, 13, 14, 15, 16, 17, 18, 19, 20, 21, 22, 23, 25, 26, 27, 29, 30, 35, 36, 37, 38, 103, 104, 105, 106, 107, 108, 109, 110, 111, 112, 113, 114, 115, 118, 119, 120, 121, 128, 129, 131, 132, 133, 134, 135, 136, 138, 140, 141, 143, 145, 146, 147, 149, 151, 152, 153, 154, 155, 157, 159, 160, 162, 163, 167, 171, 172, 173, 174, 177, 178, 184, 185, 186, 187, 188, 190, 191, 197, 198, 199, 200, 201, 202, 203, 204, 205, 206, 207, 208, 209, 211, 212, 213, 214, 215, 216, 217, 218, 219, 220, 221, 222, 223, 224, 225, 228, 229, 230, 232, 233, 234, 235, 236, 237, 238, 242, 243, 244, 247, 248, 256, 257, 260, 264, 268, 269, 270, 271, 272, 273, 275, 276, 277, 283, 286, 287, 288, 289, 291, 292, 295, 296, 297, 300, 303, 307
Project Monitoring and Control (PMC), 17, 18, 129, 131, 132, 133
Project Planning (PP), 17, 18, 115
QPM, 22, 25, 43, 77, 138, 248, 264, 272, 275, 276, 283, 307
Quantitatively Managed, 4, 9, 12, 13, 15, 20, 21, 22, 29, 33, 36, 41, 45, 48, 103, 109, 110, 111, 121, 122, 128, 132, 133, 136, 138, 141, 146, 147, 149, 152, 154, 157, 159, 163, 172, 173, 174, 175, 177, 178, 186, 187, 190, 198, 200, 203, 204, 206, 211, 215, 217, 220, 221, 224, 230, 233, 237, 244, 248, 257, 258, 260, 264, 266, 269, 270, 272, 273, 276, 283, 288, 297, 300, 307

RD, 17, 19, 36, 44, 70, 103, 155, 157, 158, 159, 166, 167, 171, 172, 177, 208, 264, 283, 306
Requirements Development, 17, 19, 36, 44, 70, 103, 155, 157, 158, 159, 166, 167, 171, 172, 177, 208, 306
RM, 7, 17, 18, 34, 36, 38, 43, 44, 47, 102, 103, 105, 106, 107, 108, 109, 110, 111, 112, 113, 114, 119, 158, 175, 204, 303, 306
RSKM, 19, 20, 43, 44, 118, 141, 163, 167, 204, 224, 244, 245, 246, 247, 248, 249, 256, 292
SAM, 17, 18, 103, 149, 151, 152, 153, 155, 156, 157, 159, 160, 302, 306
SCON, 20, 167, 208, 209, 210, 211, 306
SD, 18, 46, 103, 160, 161, 162, 212, 213, 214, 215, 216, 217, 218, 222, 224, 306
Service Continuity (SCON), 167, 208
Service Delivery (SD), 18, 103, 160, 162
Service System Development (SSD), 167, 215
Service System Transition (SST), 20, 167, 218
Services Constellation, 3, 4, 6, 7, 8, 18, 19, 20, 22, 23, 25, 28, 43, 46, 47, 48, 77, 102, 103, 104, 115, 116, 117, 118, 119, 129, 130, 131, 133, 135, 136, 142, 143, 149, 150, 154, 160, 162, 166, 167, 208, 212, 215, 216, 218, 220, 221, 222, 223, 225, 230, 231, 234, 238, 239, 241, 244, 248, 264, 271, 272, 277, 283, 289, 290, 298, 299, 305, 306
Solicitation and Supplier Agreement Development (SSAD), 17, 103, 155, 157, 306
Specific Goals, 12, 13, 14, 15, 27, 34, 35, 38, 105, 111, 118, 134, 156, 158, 184, 188, 198, 201, 205, 207, 208, 209, 213, 216, 218, 221, 222, 231, 246, 255, 291, 299
Specific Practice, 105, 116, 117, 118, 130, 131, 150, 168, 170, 171, 184, 186, 189, 192, 196, 201, 202, 207, 208, 223, 231, 232, 239, 241, 267, 273, 274, 286, 290, 291, 303, 305
SSAD, 17, 103, 155, 157, 306
SSD, 20, 167, 215, 216, 217, 306
SST, 20, 167, 218, 219, 220, 306
Staged Representation, 3, 13, 35, 42, 45, 48, 285, 295
Strategic Service Management (STSM), 20, 167, 213, 220
Structure of the CMMI Continuous Representation, 37
Structure of the CMMI Staged Representation, 35
STSM, 20, 167, 213, 220, 221, 306
Supplier Agreement Management (SAM), 17, 18, 103, 149, 151, 153, 156
Target Profile, 26, 40, 228, 271
Transition management, 219
TS, 19, 37, 74, 75, 76, 78, 166, 171, 178, 184, 186, 187, 205, 206, 264, 283, 302, 306
VAL, 19, 25, 37, 43, 44, 57, 60, 63, 71, 76, 133, 149, 166, 167, 200, 201, 202, 203, 204, 206, 207, 208, 209, 212, 215, 216, 218, 220, 222, 304, 306
VER, 19, 25, 37, 43, 44, 75, 76, 78, 83, 88, 93, 95, 96, 98, 132, 133, 149, 166, 167, 191, 192, 196, 197, 198, 199, 200, 204, 205, 206, 207, 209, 216, 266, 283, 304, 306
Verification, 207
Verifying Implementation, 302
CMMI Continuous Representation, 37
CMMI Staged Representation, 35
CMMI-Continuous Representation, 6, 8, 9, 12, 13, 14, 15, 16, 17, 18, 20, 21, 22, 25, 26, 30, 34, 38, 40, 44, 47, 48, 103, 105, 115, 129, 134, 137, 143, 149, 167, 174, 178, 187, 191, 200, 207, 212, 225, 226, 230, 234, 238, 244, 249, 264, 272, 276, 277, 279, 283, 289, 299, 305, 306, 307
CMP
Configuration Management Plan, 85
COAQ A level 5 metric, 4, 278
Combine the three models, 72, 73
Concurrency control, 72
Context Diagram, 58, 59
Continuous Representation, 207
Contract, 96, 97
COPQ
A level 4 metric, 4, 258, 269
COQ
A level 5 metric, 4, 268, 278
Creech, 107
CTQ, 7, 23, 242, 271, 275
culture of best practices, 120, 164, 166, 300
culture of continuous process improvement or a culture of informed learning, 300
culture of informed learning, 282, 300
culture of professionalism, 102, 300
Current System Analysis Report, 81, 85
Cycle Time Reduction
SITARA ISET, 123

Data Flow Diagram for Time Display System, 60
Definition, 18, 38, 86, 192, 232
Design for Six Sigma, 9, 37, 107, 283, 299

EIA IS 731, 8
Essay on Personal Software Process for Testing, 179, 205
Event trace for scenario 2, 66
Event trace for scenario 3, 66
Event trace for scenario 4, 67
Example structure chart of the application code, 183
Example structure chart of the user interface, 183

FBRS
  Functional & Business Requirements Specification, 85
Final product, 91, 98
Final Solution Recommendation Report, 95
First level data flow diagram for update time after validation, 70
First level dataflow diagram for display time, 69

Goal-Question-Metric paradigm, 226

IDEAL, 9, 10, 11
  Acting, 11
  Diagnosing, 11
  Establishing, 11
  Initiating, 10
  Learning, 11
IDEALSM Model, 10, 12
  Acting Phase, 10
  Diagnosing Phase, 10
  Establishing Phase, 9, 10, 33, 57, 77, 93, 100, 113, 121, 137, 228, 229, 249, 269, 271, 298, 299
  Initiating Phase, 10
Initial object model with inheritance, 64
Integration Test Report, 96, 97
Internal Standards Alignment Report, 90, 91
Interpreting FMEA in the context of Causal Analysis and Resolution, 288
Introduction to CMMI V1.1, 188, 201, 255
IPD CMM, 8

Mentoring, 235
Motorola, 100, 102, 123, 179, 188

Object model with inheritance and attributes, 65
Organization Chart, 83

P-CMM, 28, 54, 101, 234, 238, 240
Peer Reviews, 196, 198
People CMM, 137, 226, 287
  Assessment types-Class B, 11, 227
  Change Management, 4, 11, 25, 28, 29, 33, 225, 226, 227, 307
  Compensation, 241, 243
  Competency development, 255
  Competency Development, 255
  Competency Framework, 243
  Competency-based practices, 240, 241, 244
  Empowered Workgroups, 240
  Framework for growing workforce competencies, 28, 54, 101, 234, 238, 240
  Level 1, 3, 14, 35, 41, 45, 48, 100, 101
  Maturity, 4, 8, 27, 41, 45, 48, 226
  Measurement and Analysis, 17, 18, 136, 139
  Mentoring, 235
  Optimizing, 2, 4, 9, 12, 13, 20, 22, 23, 29, 33, 35, 36, 37, 41, 45, 48, 103, 110, 112, 113, 114, 128, 129, 133, 136, 141, 146, 149, 152, 154, 157, 159, 163, 177, 178, 187, 191, 199, 203, 206, 211, 215, 217, 220, 221, 224, 230, 234, 237, 244, 248, 257, 266, 270, 272, 277, 278, 282, 283, 289, 293, 297, 300
  Organizational transformation, 236
  Process Area, 6, 16, 25
  Team Building, 11
  Threads, 243
  Training and development, 234
  Workgroup Development, 240
People CMM Assessment
  Preparing Phase, 14, 38
Process, 26, 55, 101, 226, 227, 236, 237, 240, 241, 296, 308, 309
  Improvement, 241, 296, 309
  Maturity, 1, 2, 3, 4, 5, 6, 9, 12, 13, 14, 15, 16, 17, 18, 19, 20, 21, 22, 23, 24, 25, 26, 27, 29, 32, 33, 34, 35, 41, 45, 47, 48, 50, 75, 76, 77, 101, 103, 109, 113, 114, 121, 129, 132, 133, 140, 146, 164, 165, 166, 172, 176, 177, 186, 187, 197, 198, 199, 203, 206, 207, 211, 215, 217, 220, 221, 222, 224, 225, 227, 228, 229, 236, 237, 245, 248, 258, 259, 261, 262,

264, 265, 269, 274, 277, 278, 279, 281, 283, 289, 291, 293, 297, 299, 300, 301, 302, 305, 306, 307, 308, 309
Process Improvement
  Sufficiency Criteria, 308, 309
Process Measurement, 137, 140, 163, 291
Process Tailoring, 238
Product Development & Roll-Out, 78, 97, 98
Product Survey & Market Screening, 78, 85, 88, 89, 90
Project organization in SITARA Synergy Approach, 56
PSIP
  Package Selection & Integration Plan, 85

QAP
  Quality Assurance Plan, 85
QFD, 107, 109, 168, 169, 170, 171
Quality Champion, 308

Requirements Confirmation & Product Interoperability, 78, 82, 95, 96, 97
Requirements Definition & Requirements Analysis, 78, 80, 82, 83, 84, 85, 86, 89, 91, 158

SCAMPI, 11, 145, 227, 302
SEI
  IDEAL Model, 10, 12
Selection Criteria and Coverage Report, 95
SITARA, 26, 55, 56, 58, 59, 60, 62, 63, 64, 65, 66, 67, 68, 69, 70, 71, 72, 73, 86, 87, 105, 118, 123, 131, 135, 139, 142, 144, 145, 147, 148, 151, 153, 156, 159, 171, 174, 175, 176, 183, 184, 189, 197, 199, 200, 202, 205, 228, 232, 235, 242, 247, 250, 255, 263, 268, 270, 275, 285, 287, 288, 292, 294, 295
  10W5D Competency Hierarchy Model, 252, 254, 255
  Domain-Competency Sandwich Model, 254, 255
  Implementation idea—core process area practice, 36
  Interpreting Acquisition Requirements Development, 159
  Interpreting Acquisition Technical Management, 205
  Interpreting Agreement Management, 153
  Interpreting Causal Analysis and Resolution, 287
  Interpreting Configuration Management, 135
  Interpreting Decision Analysis and Resolution, 250
  Interpreting Integrated Project Management, 242
  Interpreting Measurement and Analysis, 139
  Interpreting Organizational Process Definition, 232
  Interpreting Organizational Process Focus, 228
  Interpreting Organizational Process Performance, 268
  Interpreting Organizational Training, 235
  Interpreting Process and Product Quality Assurance, 145
  Interpreting Product Integration, 189
  Interpreting Project Monitoring and Control, 131
  Interpreting Project Planning, 118
  Interpreting Quantitative Project Management, 275
  Interpreting Requirements Development, 171
  Interpreting Requirements Management, 105
  Interpreting Risk Management, 247
  Interpreting Solicitation and Supplier Agreement, 156
  Interpreting Supplier Agreement Management, 151
  Interpreting Technical Solution, 184
  Interpreting Validation, 202
  Interpreting Verification, 197
  process harmonic, 29, 35, 277, 300
  PSIP, 81, 82, 83, 98, 99, 158, 170, 253
SITARA SET Version 2.0, 123, 124
SITARA Synergy Approach lifecycle description, 55
Smith, George, 100
Software CMM
  Framework for establishing a capable development process, 2, 24, 25, 31, 32, 33, 102, 238
Solution Alternatives & Solution Recommendation, 78, 94, 95
State diagram for time display, 67
State diagram for update time after validation, 68
Structure Chart for Time Display System, 71
SW-CMM, 2, 24, 25, 31, 32, 33, 102, 238

The Basics of QFD, 169
Time display system classes identified from the knowledge of problem domain, 62

Updated RDRA deliverables, 91

Vendor Demonstration & Product Ranking, 78, 91, 93, 204
VER, 207
Verification, 207
Victor Basili, 137
VoC, 23, 109, 110, 111, 122, 130, 133, 168, 170, 173, 199, 265, 281, 284, 287

Made in the USA
Las Vegas, NV
03 November 2026

57424106R00219